# LANGUAGE ARTS INSTRUCTION AND THE BEGINNING TEACHER: A PRACTICAL GUIDE

*Edited by*

**Carl R. Personke**

*University of Wisconsin—Madison*

**Dale D. Johnson**

*Education Research and Development Institute*
*—West Newbury, Massachusetts*

PRENTICE-HALL, INC., *Englewood Cliffs, New Jersey 07632*

*Library of Congress Cataloging-in Publication Data*

Language arts instruction and the beginning teacher.

Bibliography: p.
Includes index.
1. Language arts (elementary)—United States.
2. English language—Study and teaching (Elementary)—United States. I. Personke, Carl R. II. Johnson, Dale D.
LB1576.L295 1987 372.6 86-22681
ISBN 0-13-521675-3

Editorial/production supervision: **Susan E. Rowan and Dee Josephson**
Cover design: **Wanda Lubelska**
Manufacturing buyer: **John B.Hall**



Printed in the United States of America
10 9 8 7 6 5 4 3 2 1

ISBN 0-13-521675-3 01

PRENTICE-HALL INTERNATIONAL (UK) LIMITED, *London*
PRENTICE-HALL OF AUSTRALIA PTY. LIMITED, *Sydney*
PRENTICE-HALL CANADA INC., *Toronto*
PRENTICE-HALL HISPANOAMERICANA, S.A., *Mexico*
PRENTICE-HALL OF INDIA PRIVATE LIMITED, *New Delhi*
PRENTICE-HALL OF JAPAN, INC., *Tokyo*
PRENTICE-HALL OF SOUTHEAST ASIA PTE. LTD., *Singapore*
EDITORA PRENTICE-HALL DO BRASIL, LTDA., *Rio de Janeiro*

# CONTENTS

## *SECTION III*
## *USING MEDIA AND COMPUTERS IN THE LANGUAGE ARTS*



## *SECTION IV*
## *ORGANIZING AND MANAGING LANGUAGE ARTS PROGRAMS: SOME PLANS THAT WORK*

# PREFACE

In our combined 40-plus years of involvement in teacher preparation programs we have discovered that students leave methods courses with an almost overwhelming, and often disorganized, store of knowledge in research, curriculum, theory, and methods designed to make them ready to plunge into a full-time teaching career. And, although this background is excellent preparation for long-term growth as a classroom teacher, students often complain that they are not really ready for "the plunge." The things they seem to need the most are activities—not just random "things-to-do," which they have usually sampled in abundance, and not just basic guidelines in classroom management and lesson planning—but real programs with shape and structure that they can put to immediate use while they become "their own teacher." The purpose of this book is to fill that need.

The area we call *language arts* is a very encompassing and almost limitless field. It can be, and often is, broken down into various component parts, which can be treated handily in textbook chapters and college lectures. We have done this to some extent in this book. However, because almost all school learning is involved with verbal learning, we find that we can keep on expanding the boundaries of the language arts. We also find that the boundary lines are not as distinct as we may have thought, and that the mere addition of new chapters to describe new "subjects" is not adequate to the task. Thus, either because of limitations we have placed on our own mentalities or limitations from outside factors such as text size or course length, we put on arbitrary stops and say, "These are the language arts."

The student teacher-to-be is thus left with this potpourri of methods that are to be used in an integrated fashion throughout the school day, but without the programs to do so. Like Topsy, perhaps, these will just grow.

Another poser faced by some students is the textbook or college instructor directed totally to the concept of "integrated language arts," a concept we wholeheartedly adopt in this book. Several potential problems confront this student. In many cases the concept is painstakingly and repetitiously developed, explained, validated, and so forth, but the methods course itself is taught according to discrete topics, and any process of integration in a classroom situation is left hopelessly vague. On the other hand, the student from another section of the course may feel well equipped to embark on an integrated, student-centered program only to walk into a school system where discrete subjects—reading, spelling, handwriting, grammar—are designated in a curriculum guide and weekly time-allotment plans. In either situation the student is left to "make the plunge" with feelings of inadequacy to the task.

In this text we have attempted to examine all possible topics in the language arts, from mundane and traditional subjects like spelling to the rapidly expanding fields of nonprint media and personal computers. We have provided chapters specifically devoted to the evaluation of and the problems encountered by the below-average reader. We have examined many aspects of children's literature *and* we have provided some programs that have been tried and tested—and which work.

Probably no language arts text can be considered "comprehensive," because each author would hold a different definition of "comprehensive" and have a personal bias or favorite approach. The advantage of the multiauthor scheme we have used is that no author was assigned to write on a particular topic. Instead, we invited persons we knew were actively involved with some aspect of the language arts at the teacher-preparation level and, most importantly, in elementary classrooms. We asked authors to volunteer to write on those topics of greatest interest to them *right now.* In this manner we obtained a language arts text at least as comprehensive as other language arts books and written with the zest and purpose one brings to a current, favorite interest.

We also asked authors to write to teachers, just as we selected those we know have been talking with, and working with, teachers. This is not intended as an intellectual exercise written to impress the reader. Although the reader will find that all programs and activities suggested are based on the latest educational theory and research, and the content is both scholarly and current, the style leans toward informal "teacher talk," that is, teachers talking to teachers.

Joanne Yatvin, Principal of Crestwood School, Madison, Wisconsin, has been most successful in helping her teachers to develop an integrated language arts program. She has written and lectured about this program extensively; we begin with her statement on integrated language arts as a philosophical basis for the chapters that follow. We hope that the recourse to discrete topics in the format will always be approached by the textbook user bearing in mind the concepts developed by Ms. Yatvin.

In Section I, many discrete subject-heading chapters, each related to a specific skill, are presented. We have done this to assure that no skill has been left untouched, but also with no intent of compartmentalizing skill learning in the language arts.

Chapters in Section II are devoted to literature, which must take a prominent position in any language arts program. In Section III we examine uses of nonprint media and personal computers, a visible acceptance on our part of the role these play in today's world of communication. Finally, Section IV offers some "programs that work" structures in which the activities of previous chapters may be used. No teacher will be able to use all of these, and you will find commonalities among them, but we wanted to offer you more than one choice for your program.

We intended a book that could be read and used not only by teachers in the classroom, but also by those who soon intend to be classroom teachers. We feel that we have achieved that goal. We hope you will agree with us.

*Carl R. Personke*
*Dale D. Johnson*

# INTRODUCTION INTEGRATING THE LANGUAGE ARTS

Once upon a time a mother and her child sat down to write to Grandma. While the mother swiftly penned the events of family life that had occurred since she had written last, the little girl struggled to form letters and get her thoughts down on paper. She found it necessary to interrupt her mother frequently for help: "How do you spell 'broccoli'? Is this how you make a 'k'? My pencil's broken!" For a while the two wrote together in silence, but soon the child tired. "I'm done," she announced.

"Well, let me see what you wrote," said the mother. The sentences were few, marked by ill-formed letters and lack of punctuation. But the mother had little interest in correction. "Here," she said, printing a single word on a scrap of paper, "this is how you write 'Tuesday.' " She decided to let the rest go. Her own mother would no doubt be less critical of errors, letting the message of love fly straight to her heart.

As anachronistic as this little vignette may seem in the age of the telephone, it in fact represents a common reality: integrated use of language. Language is integrated when people use the four language modes—reading, writing, speaking, and listening—interchangeably and in varying proportions to serve purposes that grow out of the circumstances of their daily lives.

As an educational theory, *integrated language arts* asserts that schools can teach language in much the same way that children learn it and use it outside of school. This theory is based on scientific knowledge, everyday observations, and common sense that can be summarized in four generalizations about the nature of language learning.

1. Children are experienced and capable language learners by the time they come to school.
2. In the world outside school, language is used in meaningful contexts that help people understand the world.
3. In the world outside school, language is largely instrumental.
4. Language learning is a broad, flexible process not amenable to narrow curriculum structuring.

The major portion of this chapter is devoted to explaining these generalizations, but it also describes the type of classroom program that will preserve and carry forward language learning in a manner compatible with children's accomplishments and strategies and the demands of living in the world.

## CHILDREN ARE EXPERIENCED AND CAPABLE LANGUAGE LEARNERS BY THE TIME THEY COME TO SCHOOL

Children begin learning language at birth. Although babies and toddlers make difficult subjects for language studies, scientists have been able to establish that even the youngest can discriminate among language stimuli. According to Britton (1970), a baby only a few days old recognizes its mother's voice; at one month, babies can distinguish some speech sounds. Starting at about three months of age, babies play with sounds they make themselves, repeating and varying them in patterns that certainly seem deliberate. Even before they can speak real words, infants show by their actions that they understand—at least in a general way—many of the things that are said to them, such as "Do you want some juice?" or "Go get your doggy" (Britton, 1970, pp. 33–39).

McNeill (1970) asserts that most children begin formal, grammatical speech between the ages of 18 and 28 months. Even though early productions may consist of only one word, with respect to meaning those single words are sentences. Depending on the physical situation, the word "baby" uttered along with gestures and body movement may mean, "Look at that baby just like me" or "Give me the doll you're holding." Usually, the adult involved can figure out what is meant without too much difficulty. One-word sentences soon grow to two-word sentences, and a grammar emerges that, while far simpler than adult grammar, is nonetheless rule governed and consistent (McNeill, 1970, pp. 16–36).

As they develop grammar, children add vocabulary. Templin (1957, pp. 105–114) estimates that a child's vocabulary grows at the rate of 15 to 20 new words a day between the ages of six and eight. All those new words are drawn from experience. Of course, children hear thousands of words in adult conversation and on television, but according to Cazden (1972, pp. 2–3) only those that are significant in their experience are learned.

All early language learning takes place without the aid of curriculum, textbook, or teacher. Although adults do play a critical role in helping children learn, they do not teach in the usual sense of the word. Rather, they act as intermediaries between children and the world of words, ideas, and things. At the most basic level, adults supply children with names of objects, definitions of words, and patterns for sentences, not in a didactic way but as illustrations and explanations that are part of the flow of talk occurring naturally between them. At the same time, adults interpret experience, demonstrating to children how one should respond to different situations: what to laugh at and what to be afraid of; how to treat animals, objects, and people; what is important to attend to and what should be ignored. Adults also demonstrate social rituals that give children the words and actions for getting along in the world: "please," "thank you," "I have to go to the bathroom."

Most important, however, adults foster language development by responding to and expanding upon children's speech. That is, they listen to the partially formed sentences of young children, such as "Billy go bye-bye," and say, "Yes, Billy is going 'bye-bye.' Billy and Mommy are going to the park." In this brief exchange, the adult has not only expanded the child's grammatical construction to an acceptable adult form but has also offered more precise words for who is going and where. Cazden (1972, pp. 105–122) says that parents do this sort of thing often, not with any conscious intention to improve their child's speech, but to make sure they and the child understand each other.

It is important to emphasize that clarifying meaning, not improving grammar, is the central thrust of most of the correcting that parents do. If, for example, a child holds up her teddy bear and says, "My dolly breaked her leg," the father is much more likely to answer, "That's your *teddy*" rather than, "No, she *broke* her leg." And the daughter would be much more likely to get the point of the first type of correction than the second. McNeill (1970, pp. 106–107) quotes an exchange between a parent and a child that illustrates these points very nicely:

Child: Nobody don't like me.
Mother: No, say "nobody likes me."
Child: Nobody don't like me.

(eight repetitions of this dialogue)

Mother: No, now listen carefully: say "nobody likes me."
Child: Oh! Nobody don't likes me.

## IN THE WORLD OUTSIDE SCHOOL, LANGUAGE IS USED IN MEANINGFUL CONTEXTS THAT HELP PEOPLE UNDERSTAND THE WORLD

Not even educated adults communicate by words alone. In any physical situation, what we see and hear and know from experience goes a long way toward making the language involved intelligible. In books, authors provide us with similar assistance by describing characters, action, and settings.

Nonlanguage clues to meaning are varied and plentiful. We see facial expressions, body language, movement, objects, backgrounds, and the weather. The sentence "That's where she hid the surprise" explains little unless there is a visual image to go with it. Aural clues can be voice inflections, the sounds of movement, or background noise. Past experience helps us to know what to expect or how words are to be interpreted. Most of us recognize, for example, the language patterns that signal a criticism from the boss, a quarrel with our spouse, or wheedling from our children. We recognize, too, that some people mean just the opposite when they say, "I hate to tell you this," and that simple rituals such as "Can I help you?" have far different meanings in different situations.

In the world outside school there is no such thing as an isolated word. Even though words may stand alone, they are always related to other words and events. "Fire!" shouted in a theater, "Women" printed on a door, "Mommy" wailed in the night—all have unspoken texts. And there are no "generic" words except in dictionaries. For example, although the word "back" may mean a part of the anatomy, or to move in reverse, or to return, or many other things in a dictionary sense, it means only one of those in a particular spoken or written discourse.

If these observations about context in everyday life seem too obvious to mention, remember that language in school often does not have context. Textbooks, tests, workbooks, and exercises are deliberately designed to delete context on the premise that background information might distract children from the specific material to be learned and that real learning means figuring things out without any help. Thus, in the classroom, words often appear in lists or in isolation; sentences are often vapid and unconnected to other sentences. In one sense children are being asked to learn within a framework that is much less demanding than the outside world because it has no distractions; in another sense, this framework is much more difficult because it offers no clues and bars children from using other knowledge and skills. In either case, practice material lacking context is unrealistic and unfair to children, who will soon have to apply their school learning in situations rich with context in the outside world.

## IN THE WORLD OUTSIDE SCHOOL, LANGUAGE IS LARGELY INSTRUMENTAL

People use language not for its own sake but to serve purposes in their lives. It is toward those purposes that we direct our attention and from them that we choose our means. For most purposes, language is only part of a complex process that also includes thinking, movement, interaction with other people, and creative effort.

A purpose can be doing one's job or enjoying recreational activities. It can also be self-assertion, social service, moral and intellectual growth, or even getting along with others. While we are working at achieving a purpose, our language, physical skills, and social skills are at best secondary concerns. Often we do not think about them at all. But if we do, it is because we are making choices about the best way to do something, the way that will be most effective and efficient in accomplishing our purpose.

In this respect children are like adults. Before the end of their first year, they are using their minds, bodies, and voices purposefully. They search a group of faces for the one they trust, reach out to grasp a toy, ask for a favorite food. By the time they come to school, children are quite adept at using their abilities to serve the purposes of their own small world (Britton, 1970, pp. 190–193; Smith, 1975, pp. 170–171).

Yet, to a great extent, school runs counter to this successful pattern. Traditional instructional practices provide long periods—often years—of "learning how" before children are allowed to use their skills to serve purposes. The customary basal reading book has no purpose other than teaching children "how to read." Its content, sentence structure, and vocabulary are manipulated in the service of teaching an arbitrary and contrived sequence of reading skills, not to provide useful information, facilitate work in other subjects, or even give pleasure. If those things do occur, they are incidental to the "how-to" goal. Handwriting programs teach children "how to write," using letters, words, and sentences unconnected to any other purpose. Spelling programs teach them "how to spell," no matter that the words taught have no relation to what children might want or need to write about. Even after children have mastered the essentials of letter formation, punctuation, and spelling, they are often not allowed to write to accomplish a purpose but only to practice the forms that the teacher designates: the haiku, the business letter, the three-paragraph essay. Speaking is taught "so you can give a speech"; listening, "so you will know how to listen." Sad to say, many students go all through high school and even college without ever having used language in the classroom to serve their own purposes. Sadder still, in many classrooms language learning is not even connected to any purpose of the teacher. That is, children speak, read, write, and listen only in exercises.

## LANGUAGE LEARNING IS A BROAD, FLEXIBLE PROCESS NOT AMENABLE TO NARROW CURRICULUM STRUCTURING

The notions of scope and sequence in the school curriculum are so pervasive that it is hard for people to recognize that at least one school subject, Language Arts, does not fit the usual pattern. Better descriptors for Language Arts would be "expanse" and "progression," because language learning operates on many indeterminate fronts at once and moves in many directions at uneven rates. Along its diverse pathways, learning may sometimes run, make huge leaps, meander, pause to admire the scenery, stroll, or come to a dead end. The trip from baby talk to mature control of language—shaped by cognitive, physical, and social development, economic and ethnic background, and the particular experiences of the individual—is not the same for any two children.

Neither does Language Arts lend itself to the curriculum concepts of "discrete skills" and "mastery." Work on most language skills begins long before the child comes to school and continues well into adulthood. In a precise sense, few skills are ever mastered: One can always write better sentences, hear more subtle nuances, make more powerful speeches, read with deeper understanding.

One might argue that reading and writing, the two language modes that school is most concerned with, do lend themselves to traditional curriculum structuring. Children begin learning both modes at school, or at least around the time when they first come to school. Both reading and writing are narrower, more easily defined areas than the larger field of language, and within them learning patterns are more predictable, evenly paced, and controlled. Both include mechanical skills that are discrete and can be mastered. What, then, is wrong with devising a scope and sequence for each area and expecting children to move through it in systematic fashion? The problem is that, although these observations about writing and reading are true, it is also true that those modes have many aspects that are not so easily "scoped" and "sequenced." Growing as they do out of the larger field of language, writing and reading depend on general language skills, developed diversely and unevenly. And children bring habits and strategies from early language learning to these new areas that worked well for them and are not readily abandoned.

Let us examine the facts. Children learning to write do not progress from letter to word, to sentence, to paragraph, to essay. Most children try to write words before they know how to form any letters, drawing pictures and squiggles that they "read" back in imitation of adults reading letters or books. Once they gain enough control over letter forms to really write, they go for whole stories, not just sentences. Children do not wait for forms or conventions either. They write as they speak, adding as many literary and social conventions as they have picked up from listening to adults. Although, in general, young children prefer to write narrative, which is what the textbooks prescribe for them, they may also experiment with description, exposition, and argumentation, all mixed together. Or they may cling stubbornly to one type of writing for years without the slightest desire to try any other.

Smith (1975) explains that the situation is much the same for reading. Children beginning to read can command much more than letter sounds and one-syllable words. They want whole meanings so much that they are willing to memorize stories and make up words they can't yet read. Their ability to learn a word depends more on how important it is to them than on its length or regularity of spelling. The number of new words a child can learn at one time appears to be at least somewhat elastic, depending on prior knowledge, support from context, and interest (Smith, 1975, pp. 64–82).

When it comes to decoding new words, children use both sentence structure and meaning as well as letter sounds. And they work on learning many different sounds at once, not waiting to master short vowels before they go on to long ones and silent letters. Initial sounds seem always to be the focus of attention, no matter how much instruction has been given on medials and finals. Children (and probably adults, too) hardly look at final letters at all, letting what they know of syntax and meaning decide how a word ought to end.

The material children can read best is the material they want to read. Then it is possible for comprehension of context to bolster weak decoding skills and enthusiasm to compensate for unrecognized words. According to Smith (1971, pp. 179–182), the language most easily read is the language of experience: what children have heard and used in conversation and listened to in stories. Cazden (1972, pp. 158–159) says that children often unconsciously convert words and sentences on a printed page to the forms they are most familiar with from speech.

Acting on the generalizations we have just explored, we need to look for a school approach to language arts that will preserve all the achievements and successful strategies of early language learning. We must try to prepare children for future schooling and future careers while still serving the lives they are living outside of school today. The result is integrated language arts.

The starting point is a disclaimer. Schools cannot reproduce life in the outside world. Aside from the fact that the school is "closed," literally and figuratively walled-off from the diversity and profusion of the world, it is by definition a controlled environment. The school's central aims are to select knowledge from all that exists, organize it so that patterns and meanings become apparent, and accelerate the pace of learning so that it won't take children a whole lifetime to rediscover the knowledge society already possesses.

Nevertheless, much can be done to make classroom learning more like natural learning by careful selection of curriculum, materials, and teaching techniques. Primarily, language in the classroom should be authentic: real, whole, varied, and purposeful. The best way to ensure authenticity is to bring materials from the real world into the classroom and to allow children to respond to them and use them as models for their own language production. Although textbooks can still be used to do what they do best, namely, introduce, organize, and summarize information, the examples used to represent speaking, listening, reading, and writing should be authentic. If textbooks include such examples, fine, use them by all means; but once and for all, let us get rid of "the fat cat" who "sat on the flat mat."

Authentic school materials can be books, newspapers, handbills, instruction manuals, television programs, songs, cereal boxes, personal messages, and so forth—all the print and sound that surround people in their work and everyday lives. Naturally, schools will use books more than music videos or comic strips because of the school aims previously mentioned, but teachers should not act as if the forms of popular culture did not exist or as if students did not need to deal with them.

Authenticity also implies that language examples will not be truncated. Although people may sometimes put aside a book unfinished or, more often, choose to read only certain sections of the newspaper, they do not read isolated paragraphs or sentences from a text. If they do not like racy scenes and strong language, they avoid the likely sources rather than cut up library books or cover their eyes in a movie theater. If the words in a language example are considered too difficult or too frank for children of a certain age, then the whole piece should be omitted and another substituted. Such a course of action is almost always preferable to piecemeal censorship. If children speak or write unacceptable words, teachers can say the same thing parents say at home: "You may hear those words in the street, but we don't use them here."

Most important, authentic language has a purpose behind it. Writing is used to reach an audience to be informed, persuaded, or entertained. Speaking is for immediate, practical kinds of communication. Reading, when it is not primarily for pleasure, serves to further research, inform a discussion, or prepare for a performance. Listening enables people to understand other points of view. Within the classroom enough opportunities exist for purposeful activities—book making, construction, puppet shows, mini-museums, surveys of opinion, computer programs, greeting cards, thank-you notes, bulletin board displays, invitations, videotaped commercials, journals, observation records—so that teachers should not be reduced to saying, "Read the next chapter, then write a sample letter of complaint."

Combining language modes is another way to make classroom learning more like natural learning. Let writing grow out of reading, speaking out of listening, and more reading out of what children have heard and said and written. Let spelling, punctuation, usage, grammar, and handwriting be a part of learning and practicing all written forms. It may seem neat and logical to adults to divide instruction into a spelling period, a writing period, and a reading period; to keep social studies, science, and math isolated from all taint of language arts; but those separations do not make sense to children. And they do not help them to learn the things we want them ultimately to be able to do: spell correctly in their public writing, read history with ease, use standard grammar and usage when they stand up to address an audience.

A third way to approximate natural language learning is to let form follow function. Instead of being bound to a curriculum that specifies the study of "the ballad," "the topic sentence," or "the index," children should be able to choose the language modes, structures, and strategies that best fit their purposes. That does not mean that teachers must sit around waiting for "outlining" to happen. They can engineer happenings by designing topical units that call up certain forms, then teach a form so children can use it.

School language learning can be made more like natural learning if the year-by-year curriculum grows out of the lives of children rather than adult logic. Decisions about the types of language activities to be taught should be based on children's development, the academic knowledge they already have, their out-of-school experiences, and their interests, not adult notions of "the structure of the discipline." With an emphasis on child appropriateness, there are bound to be differences in what is taught from year to year and from class to class, but is that bad? Omissions and repetitions are common phenomena in language learning in the outside world; if we do not comprehend something the first time it will come around again when the conditions for learning may be more favorable. A spiral curriculum organized around language purposes works the same way, enabling children to meet all the modes, all the forms, the processes, and the strategies many times in their school careers. Yet each time is different, not only in the activities offered but also in the ways that age and experience shape children's responses.

Until now we have focused on the curriculum and materials that help to make school language learning more natural and integrated. We need to look also at teaching techniques. Teachers can change their teaching in many small, subtle ways that foster a more spontaneous and interactive flow of language in the classroom. Without surrendering order or structure, they can create a place where language is integrated and skills improve.

One way is to encourage the imitation of spoken and written models. Where do children get the conventions and styles of mature language if not from observing adults and imitating them? That's how they find out what a story or a poem is, how to ask for help and give it, how to persuade and please others, how to lead, cooperate, dissent, and follow in a group. That's how they experience literary styles, journalistic styles, technical styles, elegance, and plain talk. When they imitate, using variations to fit their own purposes, they are learning language naturally. But because much of the imitative language children produce, especially in the early grades, verges on plagiarism, teachers are uncomfortable with it and try to steer their students toward more original expression; hence the widespread emphasis on "creative writing." They forget that when it comes to language forms and conventions, there is no such thing as originality. All language is a social invention that must follow established patterns or be unintelligible. Adult writers and speakers use the standard patterns; only the content is original. As beginners, children need to rely more heavily on established forms until they gain sufficient control over them. With control comes freedom, freedom to adapt, expand, and deepen, and ultimately to raise one's own true voice about the conventional framework.

Another way to alter teaching techniques is to provide opportunities for oral communication that is not just conversation but a purposeful exchange of ideas. The communication can be between two classmates, between an older child and a younger child, between teacher and child, and it can have collaboration, criticism, or tutoring as its purpose. The student-teacher conference, a key feature of the new *process approach* to teaching writing, advocated by Graves (1983), is one type of such communication aimed at helping children to understand their own composing processes. On a larger scale, *oral interaction* is a means for small groups of children to make decisions, solve problems, organize joint activities, and share information. As a learning device, it works far better than just answering the teacher's questions.

A third technique is *project teaching,* mentioned earlier in connection with purpose and authenticity. When children learn through integrated, sustained work that produces tangible results, they are coming very close to what adults do in the outside world. Not only do projects help them to use language to get things done, they also provide built-in self-correction devices that exert pressure for clearness, coherence, and economy in language. Children find out quickly that, when language is sloppy, projects fail. Projects also offer a background for expansion of vocabulary and grammatical structures as children try new things and talk about what they think will happen. Although not all classroom work can be projects, many discrete skills and much miscellaneous information can either be worked into projects or taught as preliminaries to them. Far less rote learning is necessary in school than most of us have always believed.

Although it is rarely used in typical classrooms, one final technique bears mentioning: encouraging children to use language to explore ideas. *Exploratory language,* as described by Barnes (1975, pp. 108–138) in his book *From Communication to Curriculum,* is thinking out loud, alone, or with others. Unlike the techniques just described, exploratory language does not aim at production or even communication. It is tentative, hypothetical, and imaginative; it is language that ruminates, builds on itself, backtracks, and may stop short without arriving anywhere. Yet it is still purposeful language, helping users make sense of their world, put flesh on shadowy notions, hold on to ideas, and force their words to express more precisely what they are thinking.

It might be argued that this particular way of using language will not help children to learn the information they need to become competent adults; it only enhances that pearl of dubious price in a practical world, namely, imagination. Actually, considerable evidence abounds to show that it does both, but that is not the point. Exploratory language helps children to own knowledge, control language, and develop thinking strategies, all important educational accomplishments.

All that has been discussed here forms the theoretical foundation upon which an integrated language arts curriculum and an integrated teaching style are built. We have looked at natural language learning in the outside world and attempted to hypothesize what its counterpart would look like in the classroom. But for the most part we have stopped short of dealing with specific areas of the curriculum, methods, or activities. Throughout the rest of this book various authors get down to those specifics, describing in detail what an integrated language arts program can be at its best.

## *REFERENCES*

BARNES, D. (1975). *From communication to curriculum.* New York: Penguin.

BRITTON, J. (1970). *Language and learning.* London: Allen Lane, The Penguin Press.

CAZDEN, C. (1972). *Child language and education.* New York: Holt, Rinehart & Winston.

GRAVES, D. (1983). Teacher intervention in children's writing: A response to Myra Barrs. *Language Arts 60,* 841–846.

MCNEILL, D. (1970). *The acquisition of language: The study of developmental psycholinguistics.* New York: Harper & Row.

SMITH, F. (1971). *Understanding reading: A psycholinguistic analysis of reading and learning to read.* New York: Holt, Rinehart & Winston.

———. (1975). *Comprehension and learning: A conceptual framework for teachers.* New York: Holt, Rinehart & Winston.

TEMPLIN, M. C. (1957). *Certain language skills in children: Their development and interrelationships.* Westport, CT: Greenwood Press.

## SUGGESTED READINGS

ASHTON-WARNER, S. (1964). *Teacher.* New Bantam.

BARNES, D. (1976). *From communication to curriculum.* Harmondsworth, UK: Penguin.

MARTIN, B., JR., & BROGAN, P. (1974). *Sounds of language readers, Teacher's edition.* New York: Holt, Rinehart & Winston.

MOFFETT, J. (1968). *A child-centered language arts curriculum, grades K–13: A handbook for teachers.* Boston: Houghton Mifflin.

# ONE SPEAKING AS A LANGUAGE ART

## INTRODUCTION

Speaking is a skill that is important throughout life, not just a skill used for success at school. As a beginning teacher you should be informed about techniques and ideas that will prove successful in helping your pupils learn to speak with fluency. There are many activities that will allow youngsters to practice speaking in various formats. It is important that the teacher practice the art of having something worthwhile to say. The word "worthwhile" is the key. When the teacher speaks to the pupils, it is necessary to say something that will prove its value to the pupils. This is a model to aid pupils in knowing they too should speak clearly and fluently. Teachers may be inclined to talk too much and say too little to pupils. Begin your teaching career by practicing the art of saying a great deal but talking very little.

Read a story, read the directions from the textbook, read a paragraph from a newspaper, read the words from a piece of music, or read the math problems, giving the answers. Each of these activities provides a pupil with a reason for listening to a speaker and indicates the value a teacher places upon speaking clearly and fluently.

Speaking clearly and effectively can be taught. When teachers plan lessons in speaking, they indicate that they recognize the importance of speaking as part of communication skills.

## CHORAL READING

*Choral reading* is one of the best ways to provide practice in speaking and reading for all pupils within a classroom. As a new teacher initiating a speaking program within a classroom, it is necessary to plan practice exercises that will allow all pupils to participate. It is difficult for a teacher to provide individual speaking experiences for all pupils. When choral reading is included in the weekly lesson plan as an integral part of the speaking program, all students have an opportunity to speak. By using a given choral reading repeatedly, even pupils who have weak reading skills can begin to join the speaking process.

To introduce a new choral reading the teacher needs to read the material aloud for the pupils. Initially, pupils should see the choral reading as a transparency on the overhead projector or have their own copy at their desks. The second step is encouraging pupils to read it aloud as a group. The third step is moving to small-group or individual speaking parts.

There are many ways to divide speaking parts in a choral reading. In the teacher's initial planning for using a selection for choral reading, the teacher can decide the various grouping patterns that will prove most effective for the pupils in speaking.

***The Pirate***

In a tree house high in the air,
Lived a pirate strong and brave.
He sailed the seven seas,
Taming the strongest wave.

At his side was his trusty sword,
His right eye wore a patch.
He was the handsome pirate king,
In a duel he had no match.

The pirate set sail at dawn,
To search for jewels and gold.
He didn't return for days, and days til,
''Dinner'' called mother's voice bold.

Groupings for the above poem could include:

1. total group reading
2. narrator and small groups
3. one group for each verse
4. pairs of readers.

Many effective speaking habits can be introduced, such as varying the sound of the voice for emphasis. Voice control and modulation can often be carried over to classroom management techniques. In choral verse another important outcome can be the contrasting and blending of various voices and the effect they have upon the reading. Ask children: "Do deep voices and high voices blend for a pleasant experience?" Help children to regroup for blending different voices to achieve different sound groupings.

A choral reading of conversation provides an opportunity for pupils to try many voices, expressing anger, fear, happiness, or calmness. Favorite choral readings should include many types of poems, narrative passages, and conversations. Repeat the favorite ones at least once a month for increased fluency in speaking.

## CONVERSATION: A SPEAKING TECHNIQUE

Activities in *conversation* should be as progressive in sequence as possible. The first-grade teacher begins the teaching of how to speak in a conversation. Two toy telephones allow pupils to converse. The teacher asks one pupil to telephone a second pupil for a given reason. For example, "Find out what program John watched on television last night. Did he like the program? Why or why not?"

In second grade, conversation continues as a way of learning to speak to others. Puppets are an ideal way for children to learn to express themselves and also practice the art of speaking. At first the teacher encourages free verbal expression using the puppets. Later conversation may be guided by giving the pupils a problem to discuss and solve. The problem may center around problems within the school; for example, what can be done about shoving in the lunchroom? Follow-up questions point out the value of sharing a conversation, which allows a pupil to learn about someone else's point of view.

Third grade expands conversation to introducing oneself to a new friend. Pupils begin the practice of asking questions that draw information from another person. Each pupil thinks of important information he or she wishes to share at the introductory meeting. This type of activity may be planned as a semester activity with pupils practicing once a week. It may be expanded by introducing one friend to another friend and relating some detailed type of information about the friend. For example, "This is my friend John. John, this is my friend, Mary. Mary lives in the Village Apartments. Her favorite game is Scrabble. Do you play Scrabble, John?"

The make-believe radio or television using a tape recorder is an exciting way for fourth graders to communicate. Social studies projects can become part of this speaking experience. While studying the United States or the state in which the pupils live, prepare interviews or questions to ask another pupil about the state. The interview is a higher level of conversation in that it calls for one pupil to be prepared with questions and the other student must respond extemporaneously.

At fifth grade the book review can become a technique to increase conversation. Two or more pupils can discuss characters within a book. The pupil who has just read the book begins by describing one or more of the characters. The other pupil(s) ask questions about the character to form an opinion about the type of person the character is. Questions should aid the pupil in determining whether the character is friendly, outgoing, helpful to others, physically attractive, has a sense of humor, or other important characteristics. Both pupils can then converse about why or why not this is a character they like.

Mealtimes are an excellent place for exchanging ideas and information. Sixth graders need to practice conversation in which recent events are the subject of discussion. A simulated experience for conversing not only with their own age group but also with adults can be an excellent way to learn advanced speaking or conversation skills. Problems relevant to this age group can be used in the simulation exercises. For example: Should middle-grade pupils be allowed to select the subjects they wish to study at school? Are 15-year-olds too young to drive? Should middle graders be allowed to get a job and work?

Building children's speaking vocabularies should become an integral portion of a teacher's instructional program. As a new teacher, plan to read to your pupils daily. Reading for at least 10 minutes a day provides an opportunity to introduce new words to the pupils. Include the pupils in the reading of the story whenever possible. For example, while reading a sentence, stop and let the pupils supply the next words (context clues). When more than one word is suggested, have the class pick the best one. Compare with the word the author used.

Participation with stories or books can follow a sequence of difficulty in the level of participation. First-grade pupils may interact with the story and reader by providing words to complete a sentence. In a book about the zoo, the pupils provide the name of the animal each time the teacher describes the section of the zoo or an animal in it.

Second-grade pupils can be provided with a specific word for which they must give a synonym. Each time the word *beautiful* is read, everyone in the class has an opportunity to say *pretty, gorgeous,* or another synonym. If the teacher is following a plan that teaches new vocabulary the pupils are to use in speaking, he or she may contribute *attractive, handsome,* or *lovely.* Then pupils are responsible for using the new word(s) in an oral sentence.

The task for third graders should be more sophisticated and practice a new interaction. When the teacher reads a word in the story to practice a certain characteristic, the pupils practice saying or repeating the word with different voice qualities. For example, words beginning with the initial *h* sound receive a medium voice sound when repeated by the class, or words ending with *ing* get a high voice sound when the pupils say the word, or words containing the long *u* sound should receive a whistle.

By fourth grade, pupils should be serving as speakers for characters within a book. A designated sound can also be applied to three or four characters. If the character is Mother, pupils speak softly. Another character is the heroine; she gets an *ah* sound and high voice. Father gets an *ahem* or clearing of the throat with a deep voice. The villain gets a sneering sound added to his voice.

Fifth graders can use the feelings described or exhibited by the characters within the book to decide how to modulate their voices to reflect the feeling or mood. For example, the lady in gray, who looked very *sad,* should get a soft, sad voice. When pupils read characters, the voice should indicate the type of characters they are.

A more sophisticated but fun interaction for sixth graders is speaking as the good person with a soft, dulcet tone and speaking with a sneer to represent the villain. So when the good person speaks, everyone says "Yeah!" softly. When the villain or suspected villain appears, students give a soft hiss.

Interaction with the selection being read aids pupils in learning. The teacher allows interaction for specific selections, not for every book or story presented orally. Do not allow interaction to become a common occurrence. Keep interaction as a special reward for supporting certain speaking or reading activities.

## STORYTELLING

*Storytelling* is an excellent means of achieving good speakers. Show children how to initiate storytelling with an attention-getter. The pupil may begin the storytelling session by singing an appropriate song or saying a rhyme that may include a finger play. Storytelling is an art. It provides the speaker with an opportunity to try many voices. Pupils learn the value of changing voice inflections to gain the attention of their group.

Storytelling should include unusual ways for pupils to maintain the interest of other pupils. A student can prepare finger puppets to identify story characters. A pupil may use objects that will call attention to happenings within the story. For example, a miniature spinning wheel would add to the story *Rumpelstiltskin,* a broom could enhance *Hansel and Gretel,* or a toy flute could bring the *Pied Piper of Hamelin* to life.

Flannel boards are an effective way for a pupil to gain a positive attitude toward speaking while showing the story characters. The illustrations from a book may be cut out and a flannel strip glued to the back so the figures will adhere to the board.

## GIVING VERBAL DIRECTIONS

*Directions* are difficult to present in sequential order. Pupils need to learn how to present a string of verbal directions so that a listener can follow them. A brief discussion on the importance of correct sequencing in directions should provide pupils with the goal of making a complete set of oral directions. Use a humorous example that shows how strange directions can become if given out of order. For example: "Get the milk out of the refrigerator. Pour the milk into the glass. Open the carton. Get the glass out of the closet." Verbal directions with multiple steps are difficult to present if pupils do not have a system for remembering them in order. Pupils can be taught to repeat each step of a verbal direction, thus allowing the listener to repeat the direction for clarity. As a pupil's second part of the direction is presented, the first part of the directions is repeated, adding the new direction to it each time.

First graders can learn to give two-step oral directions. A pupil should give the complete direction first. Next, the first step of the direction is repeated. Then the pupils should say it softly to themselves. Then the teacher says step two of the direction and the pupils repeat it softly to themselves. This procedure should make pupils more independent in carrying out the directions because they are applying a technique to the process of listening.

At the second-grade level, pupils need to present an increased number of verbal directions. Many fun activities can be used to increase speaking opportunities. For example, a pupil leader gives the following direction to other pupils. "Listen and then do the following five things. Go to the door, stand on one foot and hop, touch your ears, hum the song 'Ten Little Indians' while hopping, and stop at the end of the sixth Indian."

Pair pupils in a peer-teaching experience. Have the lead pupil present oral, multiple directions for completing a worksheet. For example, color the crayon blue; color the wagon red; color the doll's dress yellow; color her socks green.

Another example of giving pupils multiple directions for reading is to present verbally a series of follow-up activities to complete after reading a chapter or story.

1. Read Chapter 3 of the library book (pick one popular with your own children).
2. Write two questions about something that happened in this chapter. We will ask our classmates to answer the questions tomorrow.
3. Draw a picture showing two things you might like to do at a (picnic, rodeo, parade—event from the book).
4. Put your name on your two papers and put them in your desk. When everyone is ready, we will share our questions and pictures.

Pupils in fourth grade are ready to present verbal directions for locating a place. Begin by having a pupil give a two-step direction to locate something within the classroom that is already familiar to the other pupils. Mary says, "John, walk to the large closet in the back of the room. Look at the things on the second shelf. You will see a small box. Behind the box is a book. Please bring the book."

Move to locations outside the classroom. When pupils are ready, have them give directions for locating a place. Bill says, "Sarah, walk down the hall to the back entrance. When you reach the outside, turn to the right and walk to the big oak tree. At the big oak tree turn left and walk to the large cardboard box. You will find an activity for everyone in the box." Sarah follows the directions and her classmates follow Sarah.

Sets of verbal directions should become more complex when presented by fifth graders. The pupils can be presented with outline maps or they can draw their own maps following verbal directions. If pupils use a street map, another student may present the following set of directions orally. Bill will say, "We wish to locate the place where we are going to build the new firehouse. Using your blue crayon, draw a line that begins at the *X* on Garden Street and move along the streets I say until you locate the place where the new firehouse will be built. Draw a box to represent the firehouse. Here are the directions:

1. Begin at the *X* on Garden Street and draw a line going north until you reach Main Street.
2. Turn right onto Main Street and draw your line to Brown Street.
3. On Brown Street, turn left and go halfway down the second block of Brown Street.

This is where the new fire station will be built." Pupils should practice giving directions to the school gymnasium, library, or even the principal's office.

*Origami* is a simple to complex paper-folding exercise. After sixth graders have practiced the basic steps of origami using a picture and written directions, they should be ready to give other pupils oral direction for folding a shape by presenting two verbal steps at a time. All the steps may be presented verbally two at a time until one pupil has helped other pupils complete an origami shape. Assure pupils that it may take several attempts for the direction-giver to provide the directions that will achieve the correct result.

Sixth graders often become involved with activities like salt maps, papier-mâché animals, or building a volcano. After simple activities have been attempted from verbal directions provided by the teacher, students should select partners and give the directions for creating one of these more complex forms from verbal directions. Students could place the directions on an audio tape so other pupils can use them to complete a project.

## GIVING DETAILS ORALLY

Children at the first-grade level can begin good reading behaviors that involve their classmates. When the first story is read to pupils by the teacher, they are shown how to set a purpose for listening. The teacher gives the pupils something specific for which they should listen. "Find out why Betty spilled the milk." After the selection has been read, the pupils are guided in asking and answering questions that help determine if they were able to listen for details. Second graders continue this experience but are expected to ask more oral questions about the paragraph or story than the teachers ask them.

By third grade, verbal information can present the pupils with a task to perform. The pupils should be able verbally to feed back the details of the information needed to carry out the task. For example: "These materials need to be arranged on the Science table. This is the way they need to be grouped. All items that are living plant life should be placed on the left side of the table.

The books about plants may be arranged neatly in the middle of the table. The objects that are dried plant life need to be placed on the right side of the table." Before the pupil undertakes this task, the directions for arrangements on the table should be repeated orally by the pupil. In later arrangements a pupil or group of pupils should give the directions to other pupils for arrangement of an exhibit.

Pupils in the fourth grade may increase their ability to speak by preparing an audio tape that presents information about a subject. Factual information presented as a selection in the reading textbook is an excellent source for this audio tape. An example is a biography of a famous airplane pilot, like Charles Lindbergh or Amelia Earhart. The pupil includes statements and questions that will motivate other pupils to read the biography.

Noting details is an important skill. Fifth graders may listen to information read orally from an encyclopedia and make simple notes that can be used to write a descriptive paragraph. Subjects like spiders, dinosaurs, and horses are usually of interest to this age group. Next, the teacher encourages the pupils to read a selection from the encyclopedia themselves, making notes from which they will present information orally to other pupils. Oral reports on factual information, or oral book reports, provide an opportunity for pupils to learn to say a "lot" in a limited time frame.

Sixth graders know the telephone is an instrument that is in constant use in our busy world. We telephone the doctor, the dentist, businesses, family, and friends. We answer the phone for other people. Taking messages for different types of telephone conversations has become a must. A variety of simulated telephone conversations can be placed on an audio tape. Pupils listen to the conversation and respond orally, giving information, providing addresses and telephone numbers, and answering questions. This is a practical speaking experience that is beneficial in providing better communication.

## SUMMARY

We have suggested here many opportunities for developing speaking skills among childen. Most often these have been related to other classroom activities, such as science, social studies, or reading. Often the verbal interactions that accompany these learning situations are only incidental, whereas accompanying written activities are planned in advance. The implication here is that speaking activities also deserve advanced planning and structure in order to be maximally effective.

### *REFERENCES*

AULLS, M. W. (1978). *Developmental and remedial reading in the middle grades.* Boston: Allyn & Bacon. This book contains practical ideas and language activities that would help new teachers in preparing interesting experiences for pupils.

BAUER, C. F. (1977). *Handbook for storytellers.* Chicago: American Library Association. A rich resource of language communication activities, this book contains sections on storytelling, puppetry, poetry, and reading aloud.

Boothroy, B., and Donham, J. (1981, April). Listening to literature: An all-school program. *The Reading Teacher, 34,* 772–774.

Gamby, G. (1983, January). Talking books and taped books: Materials for instruction. *The Reading Teacher, 36,* 366–369.

Nessel, D. D. (1985, January). Storytelling in the reading program. *The Reading Teacher,* 378–381.

Wixson, K. K. (1983, December). Questions about a text: What you ask about is what children learn. *The Reading Teacher, 37,* 287–293.

## *SUGGESTED READINGS*

Smith, J. A. (1973). *Creative teaching of the language arts in the elementary school.* Boston: Allyn & Bacon. (Chapter 4.) This book has many creative ideas that will aid beginning teachers in making their classroom an interesting place to learn.

Van Allen, R. (1976). *Language experiences in communication.* Boston: Houghton Mifflin. Topics of value for new teachers that are discussed in this book include: discussing and conversing, writing individual books, dramatizing experiences, and sharing of ideas orally.

# TWO
# DRAMA AS A LANGUAGE ART

This chapter describes ways in which drama may be used to encourage children's language development through the exploration of themes and issues occurring in children's literature. Historically, children's literature has served as a rich resource for teachers of educational drama. However, too much stress is often placed on plot—what happens next?—so that both teacher and children become overconcerned with slavishly "acting out" the story rather than attempting to create their own dramas.

The literal performance of a story inhibits the sort of experimentation with language and ideas that can be observed in young children's spontaneous play. Children's early language development often occurs in their social play with care-givers, siblings, and peers. By the time they reach school age, many children have a fluent command of language and have become increasingly proficient in adapting their speech patterns to meet the linguistic demands of differing social contexts. Typical examples of this kind of language behavior occur when children are engaged in playing "school" or "hospital" with each other.

Improvised classroom drama can afford children the same sort of protection from failure that they experience in their spontaneous play. As a teacher, you have a crucial role to play in the establishment of a positive learning environment where every child is guaranteed some measure of success. In

*The author wishes to acknowledge the contribution of Carole Tarlington, Vancouver School Board, in the formulation of some of the ideas expressed in this chapter.

creating a climate of trust and cooperation, you will be able to offer your students the opportunity to express their thoughts, feelings, and attitudes openly and frankly. The most challenging task that all teachers of drama face is in finding ways of translating this "open climate" of discussion and self-expression into a valuable learning experience for both teacher and students.

## PLANNING THE DRAMA

Creating opportunities for children to gain the understanding and insights that can occur in drama and helping them to find the language to express their thoughts require considerable preplanning for you, the teacher. At the same time, no amount of planning can help if the drama suddenly takes an unexpected change of direction. Therefore, your planning should be sufficiently flexible to accommodate alternative suggestions from the children so that they recognize that you value their contributions.

On the other hand, some children may seem inhibited and reluctant to join in both the drama and the discussion that arises out of the work. This does not necessarily imply that they are uncommitted to the drama, but it does place extra responsibility on you to find ways of helping students to have more confidence in themselves.

## GENERAL CLASS MANAGEMENT

Effective class control in drama is dependent on a range of factors, including the relationship that exists between you and your students, and the sorts of attitudes toward the work that you signal to the children. At the same time, less obvious reasons can also affect class control. For instance, the physical space in which the drama takes place can influence the quality of work. You would be well-advised to use the regular classroom rather than moving to an unfamiliar environment.

The sort of improvisational drama described here can be conducted in a normal size classroom with the chairs, tables, or desks moved back. Provision should also be made for a small area in which students and teachers can sit down together for periods of discussion and reflection away from the drama area but still in the classroom.

Costumes and props can often be a great hindrance to the flow of a drama particularly if too much time is spent deciding on what each character should wear and in dressing up. Costumes can also inhibit the sort of imaginary work that you wish to encourage. As long as you and the students have agreed to believe in the imaginary world of the drama then everyone is prepared to accept each other in different roles. The physical space of the classroom can then become any make-believe situation you wish to create.

At times, props and costumes are vital to the children's belief in the work, and on these occasions they should be included. However, these should be limited to those few items that are absolutely necessary, such as a king's crown to symbolize power or a cross to symbolize the early Christian church.

Most teachers agree that classroom management and control in drama pose few problems if a class is completely absorbed in the work. This entails careful preplanning while remaining sensitive to the needs and interests of the class throughout the drama lesson.

## THE TEACHER'S ROLE

The role that the teacher plays in the drama is of crucial importance to the success of the work. Rather than merely initiating the drama process and then directing from outside the drama, many teachers now choose to assume a fictional role in the drama itself. In this way teachers can work alongside their students, lending support to their work and, whenever necessary, challenging them to think more deeply about a problem. More importantly, the teacher-in-role can guide the direction of the drama, slowing down the action if it appears to be moving too quickly to the superficial resolution of a problem.

Taking a role in the drama does not require a great deal of acting experience, but you should be totally committed to the part you have chosen to play. When explaining to the class that you will have a role in the drama, you might say that you will be establishing a place in the classroom where you will meet with them out of role for discussion purposes. Having an area like this helps the class to recognize when you are in or out of role.

In deciding what sort of role you will assume, you should be guided both by the needs of the children and the theme of the drama. Taking an authority role such as king, president, or boss enables you to control the action more directly in such a way that the children are extended and challenged in their thinking. On the other hand, by taking an intermediary role such as a president's delegate or a general's messenger you do not have the final authority to take decisions, thus placing more responsibility on the shoulders of the students. Examples of these two types of roles are given in the drama of *The Pied Piper* presented later in this chapter.

## SELECTING SUITABLE SOURCES

In using children's literature as a source for drama you can draw on your favorite stories to select those situations you think would form the basis of an improvised drama. For example, the many rich layers of meaning to be found in myth, folktale, and legend are well suited to drama because they deal with people's deep concern about themselves in relation to the world in which they live.

On most occasions you may wish either to read or tell the story to the students before starting the drama. This is an excellent way of engaging the children's interest in helping them identify with the characters and their problems. Sometimes you may only need to read or tell part of the story so that one situation alone acts as a stimulus for the drama created by you and your class.

Oral storytelling is probably the best method of introducing a story as this allows you to maintain eye contact with the children and you can quickly gauge their interest in the story. Sometimes the author's language and the illustrations are crucial to the children's appreciation and understanding of the story; thus, you may wish to read to them.

Whatever method you choose to introduce the story, select literature that is rich in dramatic possibilities because of its many levels of meaning. Avoid books in which the authors tend to moralize or are overly didactic. Books that respect a child's intelligence will challenge children to make up their own minds about a moral issue.

Above all, select stories that you enjoy reading yourself and that you think will appeal to your students.

## DEVELOPING THE DRAMA

### Deciding on a Source

*The Pied Piper of Hamelin* is an excellent example of a story rich in themes for story drama. At different stages of the tale, problems arise that could form the basis of a story drama. For example, before the Piper arrives to save Hamelin from its plague of rats, you as teacher-in-role as the mayor of Hamelin can say:

> The council and I have explored every possibility for ridding the town of rats. Does anyone else have any suggestions?

This might lead into a competition for the design of a revolutionary new rat trap with the inventors explaining to other citizens the finer points of their inventions. The mayor and town council (teacher and students in role) might act as judges on a panel to decide which trap has the best prospect of ridding the town of rats. This is a useful preparatory stage in the drama, particularly for younger children.

### Identifying the Issues

The central theme of the story is the breaking of the contract that the mayor and the council have made with the Pied Piper. This theme involves a number of important universal concepts involving community and individual rights and responsibilities.

These concepts can be used by the teacher to explore the central theme of the broken contract. However, you should always keep the central theme clearly in focus. This is the issue that lends tension to the drama and maintains the children's involvement in the work. There is always a danger that if you use the drama as an opportunity for directly teaching the concepts, the children will lose interest in the drama. At the same time, many problems related to these concepts may arise as the drama proceeds.

For instance, when you are planning a way to start the drama so that all the children have a role, you may wish the class to have a clear image in its mind of the community of Hamelin. Here the initial focus will be on the concept of community characteristics. This will inevitably lead into a discussion considering how the life of the community has been affected by events in the story—the central theme of the drama.

### Introducing the Drama

For the purposes of the story drama described here, the action of the drama starts after the Piper has disappeared into the mountainside with the children of Hamelin. After you have either recited or read the class parts of Robert Browning's poem "The Pied Piper of Hamelin" to give students the main details of the story, ask the class to consider which townspeople would be most affected by the loss of the children. Lists I have compiled with the assistance of children (ages 7 to 14) usually include some or all of the following:

parents
teachers
candy store owners
pet store owners
recreation leaders
doctors
dentists
toy store owners
clothing store owners
farmers

As the children make their suggestions, write them on the chalkboard; accept every idea and give the children time to think about the problem. When students appear to have exhausted all their opinions, ask the children to select one occupation from the list that they would like to depict in role. They must choose a job or occupation, although they can also be a parent or relative to one of the lost children. Permit the children to choose any occupation they wish from the list even if four or five make the same choice. There is no need to ask them what they have chosen to be; this will be revealed in the next activity.

In order to give the children time to reflect on their roles, take a roll of white paper long enough for each child in the class to draw a picture of the place where he or she works in Hamelin. The paper can be spread across the classroom floor to form one continuous line of pictures. You may need to cut the paper in half so that each child has sufficient space to draw. If the children use felt markers to draw their pictures you will have a colorful frieze, which may later be hung on the classroom wall as a backdrop to the drama.

Give the children time to draw their pictures so that they become absorbed in the task. While they are drawing, ask them to consider ways in which the loss of the children has affected their lives. You might say,

> What are the little things that you remember about the children? Perhaps it was one special child who always came to your store after school. Perhaps there was a child who used to help you.

### Building Belief

When you are satisfied that the children have completed their drawings, you now have an opportunity to enter the drama as teacher-in-role. Explain that you are going to play the role of a representative of the town council inquiring how citizens feel about the disappearance of the children and how this tragic event has affected their lives. Ask the children to remain by their pictures and then move down the line asking questions about them and their places of work

For example, you might ask:

> Just how large is your store?
> How has the loss of the children affected your business?
> What suggestion do you have for finding the children?

As you proceed down the line of children, some of them may be very angry at the way in which the mayor and town council have handled the affair. In your role, you might want to appear bland and offhand, saying you are merely a representative of the town hall and taking an intermediary position. You might also assume a more aggressive or defensive role. These attitude alterations reflect the teacher-in-role positions as either directive or nondirective.

### Writing in Role

When all the children have had an opportunity to speak in role, suggest that they could write letters to the mayor outlining their concerns. Younger children could write short notes, whereas older children should be encouraged to write more formal business letters. Many children will need help with this style of writing and, out of role, you should give them an example of a business letter on which they can model their own letters.

The writing of the letters will conclude the first part of the drama, which may have taken more than one lesson to complete. When concluding a section of the drama, try to leave the class with a sense of anticipation about what will happen in the next lesson. For example, at this point, you might say casually:

> I wonder what will happen at the next council meeting when they have received these letters?

### Finding a Focus in the Drama

To start the next episode in the drama, invite the children to share in the planning of the work by saying:

I thought it might be interesting to find out what happens at the next town council meeting. If you will agree to play the roles of councillors I could play the role of mayor. How do the councillors feel about the mayor? What do they think about all the letters that have been sent to the town hall?

Confiding in the children in this manner gives them a small but important element of power in this stage of the drama. Asking them to assume different roles to those they took in the previous lesson means that the children now have to take a different point of view about the problem as people with community responsibilities. From the language perspective, the council meeting also provides opportunities for the children to engage in discussion and debate.

At this point the teacher has a number of choices. You may feel that your students need time to build their roles as councillors or you may feel that they are ready to debate the real issue—the recovery of the lost children. Whatever you choose to do you should not lose sight of this focus in the drama.

The following suggestions are intended to help you maintain both direction and focus. You do not have to include all of them in your work. Select those activities that you feel will best suit the needs and interests of your class.

Each child creates a personal history of the councillor he or she is portraying.

Ask the children to think back to the time when they were first elected councillors. What were their feelings and hopes at that time? Have they remained faithful to the promises they made to the voters who elected them?

Write broadsheets to be distributed throughout neighboring villages outlining Hamelin's problems since the disappearance of the Piper with the children. The broadsheet should contain an appeal from the parents of the children beseeching the Piper to return the children.

At this stage in the drama, you should discuss with your class the return of the Piper. You might suggest that you are willing to play the role of the Piper if everyone is in agreement. On occasion I have invited a teaching colleague to play the Piper as second adult-in-role. Whoever plays this part must clearly understand that the town has to convince him or her that its citizens are now worthy to have the children returned to them. This involves pressing the students to reflect on what has happened and to offer genuine solutions rather than simplistic ones involving large sums of money.

### Deepening the Drama

At this moment, you are again faced with a number of choices concerning the conduct of the meeting with the Piper. These choices include:

Asking the children when they wish to start the meeting; before the Piper arrives or as he enters the room.

Finding out their reactions about the Piper as he enters the room for the first time, the councillors are asked to speak their thoughts.

Teacher-in-role as reporter interviews each councillor about his or her past history and personal record on the council.

What are the councillors' attitudes to the present crisis in Hamelin?

Teacher-in-role as mayor (authority figure) summons council to debate the problem of finding the children.

The mayor says he or she is not prepared to accept complete responsibility for what has happened in spite of the letters from the business sector.

In role as mayor, ask the children, in role as councillors, for advice to help recover the lost children.

Whatever decision the council reaches, you should ask the children to consider the implications of their decisions. On each occasion when I have used this drama with either children or adults participating, the councillors have decided to recall the Piper. The means used to find him have been varied and they open up a wide variety of language experiences for the students involved, including:

Sending a town crier to local villages to announce that the Hamelin Town Council is seeking the Pied Piper to reopen negotiations.

Councillors compose the town cry.

Writing WANTED notices to be placed in prominent positions throughout the countryside, offering a reward for any news of the Piper.

Asking the councillors what they think their prospects of success are now that they have seen the Piper. You can "stop time" to allow them to speak their thoughts.

The success of the final stages of the drama will largely depend on the Piper, who has to sustain the momentum of the council meeting possibly by casting doubts on the town's honor in view of the shabby treatment the Piper has already received. The Piper may inform the councillors that the children are perfectly happy in their present circumstances and have lost all memory of their former lives. Indeed, there may be no resolution to the problem as the students, in their roles as councillors, use their full powers of persuasion to convince the Piper that the children should be returned. On the many occasions that I have used this drama I have merely agreed, as Piper, to meet with the council again at some future date.

A useful activity to conclude the drama involves the writing of a diary entry by each of the students in their role as councillor. Here the students are given the opportunity to reflect on their meeting with the Piper and to consider the discussion that took place. This activity often produces some very sincere and thoughtful writing.

One final cautionary note: The students should always be aware in drama that this is a make-believe situation. As teacher, you have the responsibility to provide the distance that is required for children to understand they are engaged in an imaginary rather than a real-life situation.

In this chapter I have demonstrated that drama in the classroom can be a cognitive process that requires children to make choices, to reach decisions, and to consider the implications and consequences of their actions. At the same time I have also shown that the drama context is a language context that is created from the contributions of the students and provides them with the opportunity to express their ideas, feelings, and attitudes in a secure and supportive atmosphere.

## *SUGGESTED READINGS*

TARLINGTON, C., and VERRIOUR, P. (1983). *Offstage elementary education through drama.* Toronto: Oxford University Press. This book offers a sequential program of drama games and activities, story dramas, and suggestions for classroom performances. It is written for the teacher who has little or no experience in drama. Suitable for teachers of kindergarten through grade seven.

WAGNER, B. J. (1976). *Dorothy Heathcote, Drama as a learning medium.* Washington, DC: National Education Association. This is a detailed and thoughtful description of the teaching practice by an outstanding contemporary drama educator.

# THREE
# LISTENING STRATEGIES FOR THE LANGUAGE ARTS

We are a society of listeners, and listening has an impact on all aspects of life (Wolvin & Coakley, 1979). Listening is the first language skill that children develop, and it provides the basis for the other language arts (Lundsteen, 1979). Devine (1982, p. 1) describes listening as "the most used and perhaps the most important of the language (and learning) arts." Despite its importance, listening is the "neglected" language art. Researchers report that little time has been devoted to listening instruction in schools, and they suggest that teachers do not receive enough instruction in how to teach listening (Devine, 1982; Friedman, 1978; Landry, 1969; Wolvin & Coakley, 1979). Too often listening instruction has been equated with activities such as listening to stories read aloud, completing following-directions worksheets, and practicing behaviors such as sitting still and folding one's hands.

The purpose of this chapter is to describe a strategies approach for teaching listening skills to students. First, we will explain what is meant by a strategies approach. Second, we will describe a variety of strategies children need to develop and use while they are listening and activities through which to teach them. In the final section of this chapter, we will suggest some ways to help students choose strategies appropriate for particular listening tasks.

## A STRATEGIES APPROACH TO LISTENING INSTRUCTION

If you think about what you do when you teach a skill, you probably envision a series of steps in which you first explain the skill and then give students an opportunity to practice it. That process is a *strategies approach*. Unfortunately, we seldom use that approach in listening instruction. Most of what has traditionally been called *teaching listening* has only been the practice part of instruction. For example, if you ask your students to listen to a story in a listening center and answer questions about the story, you are assuming that the students know what to do when listening so that they will be able to answer the questions. Such a listening center is a practice activity, but it does not teach listening skills.

In a strategies approach to listening instruction, students are taught approaches they can use while they are listening so that the message they receive is clearer and more easily remembered and recalled. For example, a teacher might begin a listening lesson by instructing students to create a picture in their minds of what she or he describes aloud. At first, a simple, brief description (for instance, a dripping ice cream cone) would be given. In later lessons, complex images would be used (possibly a scene with several characters and a variety of actions). Class discussions would focus on what to include in the mental picture, and only after students were comfortable making such pictures would comprehension questions be introduced. What we have just described is one listening strategy: *imagery.*

Although there are many listening strategies you could teach to students, the following are the ones described in this chapter: (1) Making a Picture in your Mind (imagery), (2) Putting Information in Groups (categorization), (3) Asking Questions (seeking more information and self-questioning), (4) Discovering the Plan (organization), (5) Getting Down Important Information (note-taking), and (6) Getting Cues from the Speaker (attention-directing).

## LISTENING STRATEGY 1: MAKING A PICTURE IN YOUR MIND

Students can use imagery or draw a mental picture to help them remember while listening. This strategy is especially useful when the information being presented has many visual images, details, or descriptive words. Two activities are suggested:

### 1. Building with Lego Blocks

Divide a set of Lego blocks in half and put them into two containers. Label one container *A* and the second *B.* Give the containers to two students and ask them to sit with a screen between them. The student with container *A* begins by constructing an object using some or all of the blocks. Then student A explains the construction to student B, and student B listens, trying to visualize the object as it is being described. Then student B tries to construct a replica of student A's object. After finishing, the students compare their objects.

### 2. Picture Series

Have one student select a picture from a collection to describe to classmates. Next, the student describes the picture as vividly and in as much detail as possible. The students who are listening to the description should try to visualize or make a mental picture as it is being described. Then students are shown several pictures from the collection including the picture that was described, and they try to identify the correct picture.

## LISTENING STRATEGY 2: PUTTING INFORMATION IN GROUPS

Students can use the categorization strategy to group or to cluster information when the material they are listening to contains many pieces of information, comparisons, or contrasts. Two activities are suggested:

### 1. Remembering Lists of Words

Read the following list of *unrelated* words to students and ask them to try to remember them. Next, read the list of *related* words to students. Ask them which list was easier to remember and why.

| UNRELATED WORDS | | RELATED WORDS | |
|---|---|---|---|
| clock | spoon | lion | cat |
| tree | telephone | turtle | kangaroo |
| bicycle | sun | dog | elephant |

### 2. Clustering

Select an informational book about an animal to read to the class. Before starting to read, draw a cluster on the chalkboard (see Figure 3–1). Explain that the book will provide information about the categories in the cluster (for example, what the animal looks like, what it eats, where it lives) and that they should remember the important information about each of these categories. Next, read the book aloud to the class. Then ask the children to recall important information about each category and complete the cluster by adding information on rays drawn out from each category. Finally, have students listen in small groups to tape-recorded informational books about other animals and then complete a similar cluster.

## LISTENING STRATEGY 3: ASKING QUESTIONS

Many students need to learn how to use questions to increase their understanding of a speaker's message. There are two parts to the questioning process: (1) asking the speaker questions to aid in comprehension, and (2) asking oneself questions to monitor understanding. Questioning strategies are especially important in school because so much information is presented in a lecture format and so much responsibility for comprehension monitoring is placed on the students. Two activities are suggested:

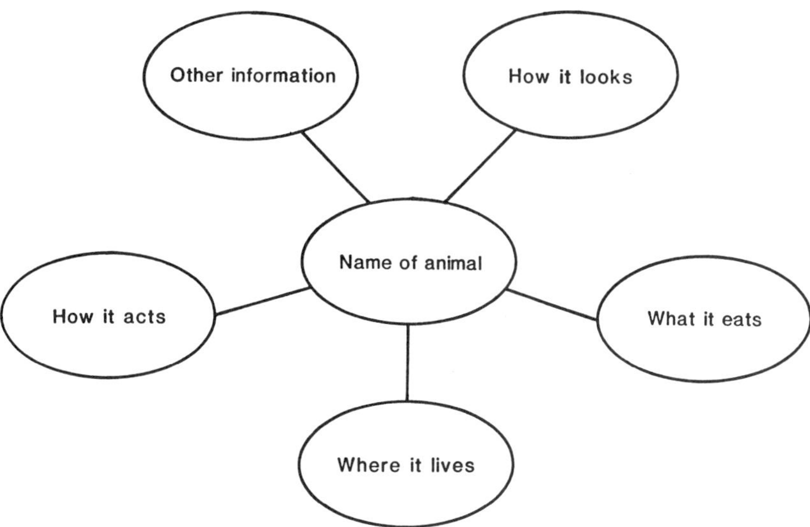


**FIGURE 3-1** Information on Animals Web

### 1. Telephone Game

Students can practice using questions to clarify a message they are listening to by playing a variation of the traditional telephone game. Prepare a message of three or four sentences. Explain to the students that they will play "Telephone," but that because the message is rather lengthy, listeners should ask questions to be certain they understand it. Read the message to the first student, encouraging questions to be asked. Students continue to relay the message (each listener becomes the next speaker), and the final listener repeats the message aloud for the group.

### 2. Modeling Self-Questioning

Select a passage containing fairly difficult material, perhaps a science or social studies passage introducing new terms or concepts. Read the passage to the class. Ask for questions students have about the content and write these on the chalkboard. After the list of questions has been generated, repeat each one and ask how many children need to know the answer to each question to understand the passage. This part of the activity helps children realize that they do not necessarily understand every message.

Next, ask pupils how they know when to ask a question. Have them generate a list of questions, such as the ones listed below, that they can ask themselves in order to determine whether they comprehend a message:

Do I know what the word ____________ means?
Do all the parts of this follow in order?
Does this idea make sense to me?

Could I explain this to someone else?
Can I picture exactly what I'm supposed to do?

Using another passage, perhaps one which involves following directions, model the use of the self-questions. Read aloud until a new word is introduced, and then pause and ask aloud whether the students know the word's meaning. Continue through the passage using this approach. Gradually transfer the modeling to students by having a student state aloud the self-questions while listening to a passage. The self-questions can also be written on sentence strips, and students can hold up or point to an appropriate self-question. Further practice can involve students whispering the appropriate self-questions to themselves and eventually asking the self-questions silently with follow-up later by the teacher.

## LISTENING STRATEGY 4: DISCOVERING THE PLAN

Good speakers use a clear and familiar organization around which they structure the main ideas and details of their message. Some common organizational patterns used in expository (that is, informational) speech are *comparison-contrast, problem-solution, cause-effect, description,* and *time-order.* Students can learn to recognize these patterns and to use them in order to understand and remember oral presentations. Two activities are suggested:

### 1. Playing Detective

Introduce two or more of the common expository structures using graphic representations to help students visualize the structures. Graphic representations of the common expository structures are shown in Figure 3–2. After describing the structures, read short passages that exemplify each of the structures. Ask students to be detectives and search for clues in the passage in order to identify the structure illustrated in each passage. Have them list clues they found and the reasons why they chose a particular structure.

### 2. Word Clues

Speakers often use words to signal the organizational structure that they are following. These signals may vary from words that signal the portions of a presentation (such as the phase "in summary") to words that signal the main points of a presentation (for example, "Today I will talk about the four P's of a righteous life") to words that signal the particular organizational pattern of the presentation (for example, "in contrast"). Before reading a passage with clear organizational signals to students, tell them the number of such "clues" that they will hear. Ask students to write down the clues as they hear them.

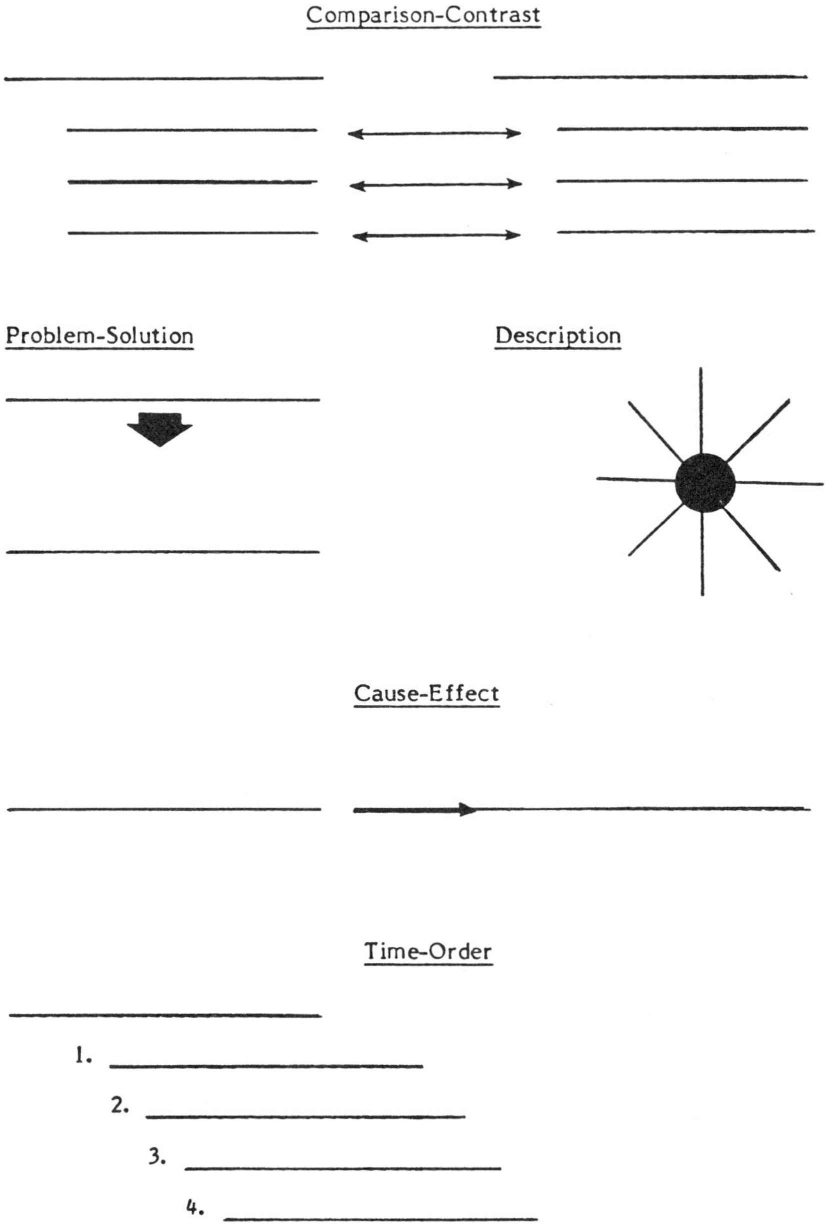

Comparison-Contrast

Problem-Solution

Description

Cause-Effect

Time-Order

1.

2.

3.

4.

**FIGURE 3-2** Graphic Representations of Expository Structures

## LISTENING STRATEGY 5: GETTING DOWN IMPORTANT INFORMATION

*Note-taking* is a strategy that helps us think about what we are hearing as we hear it and remember what we have heard. Central to skill in note-taking is an ability to match the purpose of listening with the type of notes taken. The activities listed below not only provide practice in taking notes but also illustrate the purpose of note-taking. Two activities are suggested:

### 1. Telephone Messages

Have students play the roles of message-giver, message-taker, and message-receiver in a telephone-message activity. Have the student who is playing the message-receiver role leave the room. The student who is playing message-giver begins by reading the message aloud to the message-taker at a normal rate of speech. Then the message-taker takes notes of the pertinent information. Remind the message-taker to keep the message-receiver and the purpose of the message in mind when selecting those facts worth noting. Once the message-taker has the message, the message-receiver may return to the room. The message-taker can refer to the notes as he or she recounts the message. Classmates who have observed the activity should determine whether or not the message has been adequately conveyed.

### 2. Class Notes

Select a short expository passage, and have a student read the passage while you model note-taking procedures on the chalkboard. Think aloud to clarify your purpose for listening to the passage. Then, as the student reads the passage, make notes relevant to your purpose for listening. You might also vocalize why you are noting some points and not noting others. Use indenting and skipping spaces to indicate the relationships and subordination of ideas. Next, ask a student to go to the chalkboard and take notes. The student should be asked to take notes over the same passage, but with a different purpose for listening. Ask the student to explain as he or she takes notes why he or she is noting particular facts and not others. A sample passage is presented in Figure 3–3, and examples of notes about the passage that vary according to the listener's purpose are presented in Figure 3–4.

## LISTENING STRATEGY 6: GETTING CUES FROM THE SPEAKER

Speakers employ many cues to convey their messages, including gestures, facial expressions, and writing information on a chalkboard. Students who recognize these cues can use them to increase their comprehension of the message and to discern the most critical aspects of the message. Two activities are suggested:

Lots of people think that building and programming computers is really men's work. It is true that many men have been involved in the history of computers. But did you know that one of the first people to think about how to program a computer was a woman? Ada Lovelace lived during the 1800s. She was very, very good in math. She was also the daughter of a famous English poet named Lord Byron.

Lady Lovelace became interested in a machine called Babbage's Analytic Engine, the great-grandparent of today's computers. Because electric power was not used during Babbage's day, Mr. Babbage planned to use steam power to run his machine. Ada Lovelace spent several years studying the machine, and to show how it might work she wrote the first computer program. This program told what steps the analytic machine would have to go through in order to calculate with a group of numbers. Babbage's machine was never really finished because the manufacturing equipment of his day could not build the parts needed for such a machine. So Lady Lovelace's program was never used.

Ada Lovelace also predicted some of the questions that people ask today about computers. For instance, she wrote about the question of whether computers can really "think."

Lady Lovelace has not been forgotten. The United States Department of Defense chose to name their own special computer programming language in her memory. It is called Ada.

**FIGURE 3-3** Sample Passage for the Class Notes Activity-Augusta Ada Lovelace, the First Computer Programmer

### 1. Visual Cues

Locate or produce a videotape or film of a teacher presenting information to a group of students. Play the tape for the class with the volume turned off. Have students raise their hands each time they think the speaker is relaying especially important information. Stop the tape and discuss the nonverbal cue that suggested a critical point in the message. After the tape has been played, replay it with volume turned up to verify student responses.

Cues to incorporate into the videotape and teach to students include these:

gestures (for example, pointing finger, hand hitting desk or lectern)

written information (items printed on the chalkboard, items circled or underlined on a transparency)

facial expressions (exaggerated expressions, raised eyebrows, nodding)

pauses (prolonged stops during a speaker's message)

An alternative to the above activity is to play an adaptation of the game Charades with students. Have one student attempt to convey a simple message without speaking while the rest of the group guesses the message. Discuss the role of nonverbal cues in conveying information. Teachers may also want to

PURPOSE: DETAILS ABOUT WHO ADA LOVELACE WAS

Augusta Ada Lovelace
—First computer programmer
—mathematician
—lived in 1800s
—daughter of Lord Byron
—wrote about Babbage's Analytic Engine
—wrote a program to run on Babbage's machine
—wrote about questions people ask about computers
—has computer programming language, Ada, named for her

PURPOSE: DETAILS ABOUT WHAT AN ANALYTIC MACHINE WAS

Babbage's Analytic Engine
—invented in 1800s
—great-grandparent of today's computers
—not electric, supposed to be steam-powered
—never completed because parts could not be made
—supposed to calculate with a group of numbers
—written about by Ada Lovelace

PURPOSE: WHAT ADA MEANS

Ada
—name of Lady Lovelace, the first computer programmer
—a computer programming language used by the Department of Defense that is named for Lady Lovelace

PURPOSE: THE MAIN IDEA OF THE PASSAGE

Women and Computers
—women involved with computers for a long time
—first computer programmer was a woman, Ada Lovelace

**FIGURE 3-4** Variations in Notes According to Purpose

share John Stewig's *Sending Messages* (Houghton Mifflin, 1978) with children. This book illustrates a myriad of possible ways to send nonverbal messages.

### 2. Cues You Can Hear

Tape-record a passage from a social studies textbook. Use these techniques to emphasize the important information: *pitch* (voice noticeably higher or lower), *speed* (slow down to stress key points), and *repetition* (say key information at least twice, with repetition being either immediate or slightly delayed). Then have students listen to the audio tape and write down only information they believe is very important. Score two points for each piece of information correctly noted; subtract one point for each piece of information omitted or incorrectly included. This activity could be set up in a learning center. Students could listen to the tape using headphones and in a self-checking format select the key points from a list of information.

## CHOOSING THE APPROPRIATE STRATEGY

The first step in the strategies approach to listening instruction is to introduce students to a variety of strategies in order to help them build a repertoire of possible strategies to use when listening. The second step is to teach students to make conscious choices in selecting an appropriate strategy to use for specific listening situations. To make a decision, students should consider both their own purpose for listening as well as the speaker's purpose. Then, based on the type of information presented and the type of information students need to remember, they should choose an appropriate strategy. Students may want to generate a list of questions similar to those presented below to ask themselves as they select a strategy and monitor the effectiveness of their choice:

### BEFORE LISTENING

What is the speaker's purpose?
What is my purpose for listening?
What am I going to do with what I listen to?
Will I need to take notes?
Which strategies could I use?
Which one will I select?

### DURING LISTENING

Is my strategy still working?
Am I putting information into groups?
Is the speaker giving me clues about the organization of the message?
Is the speaker giving me nonverbal cues such as gestures and varied facial expressions?
Is the speaker's voice—pitch, speed, pauses, and repetitions—giving me other clues?

### AFTER LISTENING

Do I have questions for the speaker?
Was any part of the message unclear?
Are my notes complete?
Did I make a good strategy choice? Why or why not?

To teach this concept, use a list of questions your students generate for choosing a strategy and monitoring its effectiveness. Prepare a listening activity and model the procedure by thinking aloud and asking yourself questions from the list of questions. Proceed through the activity, stopping to ask yourself some questions during listening and other questions after listening. Discuss the procedure with students and continue with another listening activity in which a student models the procedure. Then students can work in small groups to practice the procedure and, finally, to use the strategy selection procedure individually.

Learning to choose an appropriate listening strategy is a critical step in improving listening skills. Using the wrong strategy is probably as valueless as not using any strategy at all! Conversely, more than one strategy may be appropriate to a specific listening task. To illustrate, students might find either imagery or the structuring strategy equally useful in remembering the steps in making folded-paper or origami animals.

## SUMMARY

The traditional way to teach listening has been an activities approach that focuses on practicing supposedly learned listening skills. An alternative approach to listening instruction, a strategies approach, was presented in this chapter. Six listening strategies that elementary students can learn and use to improve their listening were described, and activities to practice these strategies were suggested. Introducing students to a variety of strategies is the first step in this approach. A second and equally critical step is teaching students how to select the appropriate strategy for a particular listening situation.

### *REFERENCES*

Devine, T.G. (1982). *Listening skills schoolwide: Activities and programs.* Urbana, Il: ERIC Clearinghouse on Reading and Communication Skills.

Friedman, G. (1978). *Listening processes: Attention, understanding, evaluation.* Washington, DC: National Education Association.

Landry, D.L. (1969). The neglect of listening. *Elementary English, 46,* 599–605.

Lundsteen, S.W. (1979). *Listening: Its impact on reading and the other language arts.* Urbana, Il: National Council of Teachers of English.

Wolvin, A.D., & Coakley, C.G. (1979). *Listening instruction.* Urbana, Il: ERIC Clearinghouse on Reading and Communication Skills.

### *SUGGESTED READINGS*

Patterson, C.J., & Kister, M.C. (1981). The development of listener skills for referential communication. In W. P. Dickson (Ed.), *Children's oral communication skills.* New York: Academic Press.

PRESSLEY, M., & LEVIN, J.R. (Eds.). (1983). *Cognitive strategy research: Educational applications.* New York: Springer-Verlag.

RUSSELL, D.H., & RUSSELL, E.F. (1979). *Listening aids through the grades.* New York: Teachers College Press.

WEAVER, C.H. (1972). *Human listening: Processes and behavior.* Indianapolis: Bobbs-Merrill Educational Publishing Co.

# FOUR
# LISTENING ACTIVITIES FOR THE LANGUAGE ARTS

Most educators agree that children need formal instruction in developing and refining the skills essential for good listening. However, as was suggested in the previous chapter, listening instruction is one of the "most neglected areas" of the language arts. This chapter presents teachers with a set of activities that will help them teach children how to become better listeners. The tips and ideas that follow are organized into two categories: The first section presents some general suggestions teachers may employ to develop a classroom climate conducive to good listening. The second section describes specific activities that will help children establish and strengthen listening skills.

## DEVELOPING THE LISTENING ENVIRONMENT

Developing a listening environment is no easy task, but the following suggestions may help:

### The Teacher as a Listening Model

What can a teacher do to model good listening behavior? Affirmative answers to the following questions indicate a good listening model: Do I give students my full attention when they speak to me? Do I have eye contact with them when they talk to me? Do I indicate I am listening and thinking about what they are saying by making comments or asking questions to clarify what they say? Is my listening etiquette the same one that I expect of children; that is, do I wait until children stop speaking before speaking myself? Do I show enjoyment and appreciation when children share humorous or especially appealing language? In essence, teachers must demonstrate good listening behaviors themselves if they expect their students to listen well.

### Conditions for Good Listening

The environment must be conducive to good listening. This means that speakers must talk clearly and distinctly, and the surrounding noise level must not be so high that it interferes with communication. Teachers, therefore, must promote clear articulation and demand that listening/speaking communications be conducted in such a way that children respect each other's right to talk and be heard. This means that if a teaching activity involves many independent conversations, such conversations must be quiet enough so others are not distracted; if the teaching activity involves the entire class, students must learn to talk loud enough to be heard by all, and the listeners must be respectful of the speaker.

### Opportunities to Listen

Children need practice to become good listeners. Consequently, ample opportunities must be provided. Probably the most powerful means to reinforce good listening is by reading regularly to children. To get the most listening practice during oral reading, it is reasonable to expect your students to only sit and listen, rather than allow them to draw, color, read a book, or do something else. This may be difficult for some children to do initially, for we seldom expect children to sit and listen without some form of visual stimulation, but it will make the listening experience more effective. Initiating a traditional "Show and Tell" time in which children stand in front of the room and share something orally with the rest of the class is also helpful in promoting good listening.

### Develop a Listening Consciousness

Let children know that you, the teacher, value good listening. Although actions are more powerful than words, telling and reminding children to practice good listening habits will do no harm.

## TEACHING SPECIFIC LISTENING SKILLS

The following activities can be used to develop in students specific listening abilities. The listening subskill that each activity reinforces is stated parenthetically after the name of the activity.

*1. Close your eyes and listen* (auditory awareness). Have students close their eyes and listen to the sounds around them. Have them concentrate on sounds outside the classroom and also those within the room. Bring in objects that make sounds (for example, a bell), or make sounds yourself (drop an eraser, jingle some coins, move a desk, etc.) and have the students try to identify the objects.

*2. Listen for sounds* (auditory awareness). Use recordings of sound effects and animal sounds. Have children listen and try to identify the sounds they hear.

*3. Riddles* (auditory discrimination). Have students guess answers to riddles in which clues require auditory-discrimination skills. For example:

"The word I am thinking rhymes with like. It also rhymes with hike. I love to ride it up and down the street. Who knows what it is?" (bike)

*4. Name game* (auditory discrimination). Have students say a word that begins with the same sound the previous word ended with: for example, cap—paw—wig—gun—number—rat—turtle—lamp—etc.

*5. Build a story* (auditory memory). Begin a story, and then ask each successive student to add one additional word. Each student, however, must repeat the entire story in the process: for example, The dog ran . . . into . . . the . . . fence . . . and . . . broke . . . its . . . neck. . . . The . . . cat . . .

*6. I'm going on a trip* (auditory memory). Provide students a stem such as, "I'm going on a trip, and in my suitcase I'm going to put a . . . . " Then ask each student to think of something to include in the suitcase. Each student must repeat the entire list and add their word: for example, "I'm going on a trip, and in my suitcase I'm going to put a toothbrush . . . a camera . . . a sweater . . . a blow dryer . . . etc."

*7. Cumulative songs* (auditory memory). Sing songs that require children to remember prior verses. Two traditional songs that are especially effective are "I Know an Old Lady Who Swallowed a Fly" and "There's a Hole in the Bottom of the Sea."

*8. Details from a poem* (details). Have children listen to a poem or short story, and ask them to cue-on the details.

Captain Hook must remember
Not to scratch his toes.
Captain Hook must watch out
And never pick his nose.
Captain Hook must be gentle

When he shakes your hand.
Captain Hook must be careful
Openin' sardine cans
And playing tag and pouring tea
And turnin' pages of his book.
Lots of folks I'm glad I ain't—
But mostly Captain Hook.

—Shel Silverstein (1974)

Then ask questions such as: (1) What must Captain Hook remember not to do? (2) When must Captain Hook be gentle? (3) When must Captain Hook be careful?

*9. What's missing?* (details). Describe a picture to the class. Ask your students to listen very carefully, especially to the details, for you are going to fail to mention some part of the picture. When you finish describing the picture, show it to them, and see if they can detect what you left out. Pictures from children's literature work especially well; for example, describe one of Garth Williams' exquisite illustrations from *Charlotte's Web* (White, 1952).

*10. Little ideas* (details). Read a short selection to students and ask them to concentrate on details (the little ideas). Afterward, ask them questions to test their comprehension of details. Short, descriptive selections from children's literature are especially effective for this listening activity. For example:

> Andrew Marcus wanted freckles. Nicky Lane had freckles. He had about a million of them. They covered his face, his ears and the back of his neck. Andrew didn't have any freckles. He had two warts on his finger. But they didn't do him any good at all. If he had freckles like Nicky, his mother would never know if his neck was dirty. So he wouldn't have to wash. And then he'd never be late for school.
>
> —from *Freckle Juice* (Blume, 1971, p. 11)

1. Who had freckles?
2. Who didn't have freckles?
3. How many warts did Andrew have?
4. Where does Nicky have freckles?
5. If Andrew had freckles on his neck, what wouldn't his mother be able to tell?

*11. Peer reports* (details). Have students pair off and interview each other about their likes and dislikes, about their families, hobbies, etc. Then without being able to write this information down, have each student tell the class what she or he can remember about the student that was interviewed.

*12. Choose a sentence* (main idea). The easiest way to begin listening for main ideas is to have children choose one sentence that states the main idea of a paragraph (assuming there is a topic sentence). For example (topic sentence underlined):

> *Nancy loves ice cream.* She likes vanilla ice cream. She enjoys eating strawberry ice cream, and she eats chocolate ripple every week. But her all-time favorite ice cream is banana with peanuts.

*13. Say it in a sentence* (main idea: inferred). Not all paragraphs have explicitly stated main ideas. In this case, students must infer the theme. To do this, have them listen to paragraphs and then construct a sentence that captures the essence of the paragraph.

> Robins build nests in trees. Pheasants build nests in bushes. Eagles build nests in rocks. Meadowlarks build nests in pastures. And flamingoes build nests in marshes.
>
> *Main idea:* Birds build nests in a variety of places.

*14. The informer* (main idea/summarizing). Have students be responsible for summarizing a prior day's events and assignments for students who were absent the preceding day.

*15. Headliners* (main idea). Read a newspaper article and require the students to construct an appropriate headline.

> Johnny Miller, a fourth grader at Oaklawn Elementary School, won first prize in the state competition for the National Spelling Bee. Johnny will now go on to Washington to compete with other children of his age in the national finals. When asked how he felt about winning, Johnny responded by saying: W-O-N-D-E-R-F-U-L.
>
> *Possible headline:* "Local Boy Wins State Spelling Bee."

*16. Bong story* (context). Tell children that you will read a story and every so often you will say the nonsense word *bong*. Tell them they should try to listen so they can guess what word you could say in place of *bong*.

> Martha and I went for a *bong* in the woods. We saw many tall trees, and lots of wild *bongs*. We saw a squirrel gathering *bongs* off the forest floor. We saw a bumblebee hopping from *bong* to *bong*. And we saw a bluejay repairing his *bong* in the oak tree. Because it was autumn, many of the leaves were *bonging* down from the trees. It was a beautiful *bong* for a walk.

*17. Guess the word meaning* (context). Read a passage with a word you are reasonably sure most children do not know. Then, after reading the selection, have them guess what the definition of the word is. For example:

> Some animals are carnivores; that is, they eat meat only. For example a lion or tiger is a carnivore. Some animals are herbivores; that is, they eat plants. For

example, a cow is a herbivore. Some animals are omnivores, however. For example, a bear is an omnivore; bears are known to munch on wild berries in the morning and then have lunch by eating a fish caught from a stream. What do you think the meaning of *omnivore* is?

*18. Finger plays* (following directions). Have children follow directions by acting out various movements with their hands and bodies. Poems like "Eensy Weensy Spider" and "I'm a Little Teapot" work well.

For Shel Silverstein's poem "Boa Constrictor," have the students pretend that their hands are the boa's mouth, and have them place the "mouth" around the body parts as they are mentioned in the poem.

***Boa Constrictor***[1]

Oh, I'm being eaten
By a boa constrictor,
A boa constrictor,
A boa constrictor,
I'm being eaten by a boa constrictor,
And I don't like it—one bit.
Well, what do you know?
It's nibbling my toe.
Oh, gee,
It's up to my knee.
Oh, my,
It's up to my thigh.
Oh fiddle,
It's up to my middle
Oh heck,
It's up to my neck.
Oh, dread,
It's upmmmmmmmmmffffffffff . . .

*19. Trust me* (following directions). Blindfold a student and have another volunteer student try to direct the first student about the room by giving oral directions only. For example, a student could be directed to go from her desk to the pencil sharpener: "Stand up, walk three steps forward. Then turn left, walk four steps forward. Reach out and touch the pencil sharpener."

*20. Draw me* (following directions). Have children follow oral directions by drawing a picture you describe. Tell the students to complete each direction before going on to the next. For example, have the students draw a person according to the following directions:

[1]From WHERE THE SIDEWALK ENDS: The Poems and Drawings of Shel Silverstein: "Boa Constrictor." Copyright ©1974 by Snake Eye Music, Inc. Reprinted by permission of Harper & Row, Publishers.

1. I have a round head.
2. I have a real skinny neck.
3. I'm wearing a striped shirt.
4. I'm wearing a pair of tweed pants.
5. I have a round buckle on my belt.
6. My left arm is longer than my right arm.
7. I have no thumb on my right hand.
8. I'm smiling.
9. I have a little nose.
10. I'm wearing glasses.
11. My ears are big.
12. My shoes have floppy laces.

When finished, have students compare each other's pictures.

*21. Simon says* (following directions). The traditional game Simon Says works well with all ages of children in developing concentration and following direction skills.

*22. Clap, clap* (sequence). Have students listen for rhythmic sequences and cadences in a series of hand claps you model. Have them repeat these sequences as a group after you.

*23. Listen and act* (sequence and auditory memory). Read to a student a short list of directions that describe some simple actions. Then have the student act out the directions. Ask the rest of the class to judge whether or not the directions were followed correctly and in the proper order. For example: "Go over to the chalkboard and write your name. Go to the pencil sharpener and sharpen your pencil. Walk over to John and shake his hand. Go back to your desk and sit down."

*24. Listen and put in order* (sequence). Read a story to the class and then have students number a series of events from the story in the appropriate order. Short, descriptive selections from children's literature work well for this activity. For example:

> Ribsy uncurled himself from the foot of the steps and got up to examine the golf ball. He picked it up in his teeth and trotted to the top of the driveway, where he dropped it and watched it roll down the slope to the sidewalk. Just before it rolled on into the street, he raced down and caught the ball in his mouth. Then he trotted back up the driveway and dropped the ball again.
>
> —from *Henry and the Paper Route* (Cleary, 1957, p. 4)

____The ball rolls down the slope to the sidewalk.

____Ribsy uncurled himself from the foot of the steps.

____Ribsy picked up the golf ball in his teeth and trotted to the top of the driveway.

____Just before the ball rolled in the street, Ribsy raced down and caught the ball in his mouth.

*25. Scrambled sentences* (sequence). Read aloud several sentences that have a single logical order. Ask the students to listen carefully and then retell the story in the proper order. For example, "Sam ate breakfast. Sam took his books off the table. Sam got out of bed. Sam left the house for school."

*Variation:* Use sentences that could have several logical orders; have the students sequence them and then explain why they ordered them that way. For example: "Julie watched TV. Julie went to bed. Julie read her little sister a story. Julie washed the dinner dishes."

*26. Who said it?* (inferring roles). Read phrases like the following and see if children can guess who might say these things: "All aboard." "Strike three; you're out!" "It's time to go to bed." "I'll take your order now." "You got a 100 on your spelling test."

*27. Behind the lines* (infer the topic). Read some dialogue among several persons and have students infer what the discussion is about. For example:

John: Oh yea, you missed it; you didn't even come close.
Mary: You're wrong; I ticked it.
John: You're crazy; you missed it by a mile.
Mary: I think you better get both your ears and your eyes checked, John Miller.
John: Mary, you better get your head examined.
Mary: Here, John, you take this and this and that; I don't want to be a part of your dumb game.

*Answer:* Argument over whether Mary struck out playing baseball.

*28. Guess the moral* (infer the theme). Read the children an Aesop fable or other selection that has a moral, and see if they can guess what it is.

*29. Unnamed biographies* (infer specific personality). Read a description of some well-known person and have students guess whom you are describing. For example: "I am a famous American. I lived back in the 1700s. I was a pretty good horseback rider, if I don't say so myself. My real fame, however, came on an evening in 1775 when I helped warn the American colonists of a British attack. My words were, 'The British are coming!'"

*30. Tell me why* (infer causal relations). Read short groups of sentences containing causal relations. Probe with questions to determine if the cause-effect relationship was comprehended.

"John was driving along the highway. He heard a flop, flop, flop outside and stopped the car." (Why did John stop the car?)

"Mary loves to eat green apples. She had four dozen all in one afternoon. Later that evening, she developed a stomachache." (Why did Mary's stomach hurt?)

*31. Finish the story* (inference: drawing conclusions). Read a short, narrative selection to children, but leave off the conclusion of the story. Have the students either orally state a possible ending or have them write conclusions. Ask the students to share their endings with one another as well as "the real ending."

*32. Three questions* (infer specific personality). Place the names of famous persons on the backs of a group of students without letting them know their identity. Then allow everyone to ask everyone else only three questions. Any questions are fair except "Who am I?" See how quickly they can guess who they are.

*33. Real or make-believe* (reality vs. fantasy). After discussing what kinds of things are real and can possibly happen and those that are fantasy, read statements or describe situations, and have students assess their level of reality.

> Little green men landed in the parking lot of the supermarket.
> Mary Morgan got all "A's" on her report card.
> Mickey Mouse moved next door to Ralph.
> Tom Murphy has learned how to fly like Superman.

*Variation:* Have the children make up their own statements and require their classmates to decide whether they are real or make-believe.

*34. Super detective* (listen for clues). Read a mystery or detective story and have the children try to guess the solution before you read "the answer." For example:

> Tommy bought a birthday present for his sister Sandy. Sandy tried to guess what the present was. Tommy said, all right, but he would only answer yes or no. Here are the questions Sandy asked and Tommy's answers. See if you can guess what the present was.
>
> Is the present something alive? (No.) Is the present a doll or toy? (No.) Is the present something I can wear? (Yes.) Can I wear it on my head? (No.) Is it a blouse or coat? (No.) Is it pants or a skirt? (No.) Is the present something I can wear on my feet? (Yes.) Is it shoes? (No.) Is it slippers or boots? (No.) Is it some kind of athletic footwear? (Yes.) Is it swimming flippers? (No, silly.) Is it ice skates? (No.) Do they have moving parts? (Yes.)

*Answer:* roller skates.

(*Note:* Encyclopedia Brown stories by Donald Sobel work well for Super Detective.)

*35. Back it up* (verify truth and falsity). Read a short selection to the students and then make some statements that are either true or false when compared to what you read. Then have the students indicate whether the statements are true or false, and have them verify their responses by "telling you why." For example:

> Rocks can be grouped into three categories: igneous, sedimentary, and metamorphic. Igneous rocks are made from molten materials, as when a volcano erupts. Sedimentary rocks are made when little bits of other rocks or dead animals collect on the ocean bottom and are pressed together. Metamorphic rocks are rocks that change into new ones because of tremendous heat and pressure.

1. There are two categories of rocks.
2. A good title for this paragraph would be "How People Use Rocks."
3. You might find igneous rocks in Hawaii.
4. Limestone when placed under pressure and heat becomes marble. Limestone, therefore, is a metamorphic rock.

*36. What's that say?* (ambiguous statements). Have children identify several possible meanings for ambiguous statements such as the following:

> Flying planes can be dangerous.
> The turkey was ready to eat.
> The drawing of the lad made people stop and stare.
> Henry took the pills.
> Everyone was pleased that Mr. Jones was cooking.

*37. Fact or opinion* (fact or opinion). After discussing what facts and opinions are, read statements that are either *facts, nonfacts,* or *opinions,* and have students identify them. For example:

> Texas is the second largest state in the U.S. (fact)
> California is the most beautiful state in the U.S. (opinion)
> South Dakota is farther south than Nebraska. (nonfact)

*38. Propaganda techniques* (detecting bias in speaking). Discuss various devices speakers use to persuade people to purchase something or support a particular issue or position (for example, testimonial, name-calling, transfer, glittering generalities). Then have students listen to statements that use some of these devices and see if they can identify the various propaganda techniques used. For example:

Eddie Powerhouse, famous NFL fullback, says, "Hot Foot football shoes have gotten me to the end zone many times." (testimonial)

Presidential candidate Wordsmith has stated, "My opponent is inaccurate, irresponsible, insensitive, and perhaps insane." (name-calling)

The American Doggie Council recommends Fido-Burger dog food for all pet owners. (transfer)

Candidate I.M. Proud recently stated that, "I favor law and order, freedom of speech, and equal opportunity." (glittering generalities)

*39. Pick a word* (connotative word meanings). To sensitize students to how meaning is affected by word selection, present pairs of sentences that contain words that denote the same thing but possess different connotations. Then have the students comment on how the sentences differ in meaning.

John was a *large* boy. *vs.* John was a *fat* boy.

That *policeman* gave me a ticket. *vs.* That *cop* gave me a ticket

The Cowboys *beat* the Cardinals. *vs.* The Cowboys *annihilated* the Cardinals.

Your dinner was *palatable. vs.* Your dinner was *delicious.*

*40. How do they feel?* (emotional involvement). Read several short narrative selections, and then ask students to speculate how various characters felt. For example:

"John tried his hardest to win the 100-yard dash. He came in second, but his best friend, Martin, came in first. How do you think John felt? How do you think Martin felt?"

*41. Fairy tale heroes* (character identification). Describe a fairy tale character without using the character's name. Tell the students to listen and try to identify the character.

"When I was a child, my mother told me to sell our old cow. I bought some beans from a man. He said the beans were magic. I brought them home and showed them to my mother who. . . . " (Jack and the Beanstalk)

*Variation:* Use real historical characters. For example, "I grew up in Boston. I ran a print shop and later published a newspaper. I liked to tinker, and hence made many inventions. Later. . . . " (Benjamin Franklin)

*42. Poems with feelings* (emotional involvement). Read various poems to children, and have them describe the kinds of feelings and emotions such poems evoke. For example:

***Buffalo Dusk***[1]

The buffaloes are gone.
And those who saw the buffaloes are gone.

[1]From SMOKE AND STEEL by Carl Sandburg, copyright 1920 by Harcourt Brace Jovanovich Inc.; renewed 1948 by Carl Sandburg. Reprinted by permission of the publisher.

Those who saw the buffaloes by thousands and
  how they pawed the prairie sod into dust
  with their hoofs, their great heads down
  pawing on in a great pageant of dusk.
Those who saw the buffaloes are gone.

—Carl Sandburg (1920)

*43. Visualizing poetry* (visualizing). Have children close their eyes and listen to a poem and try to visualize what is happening. Afterward, discuss what was "seen."

***Mud***[2]

Mud is very nice to feel
All squishy-squash between the toes!
I'd rather wade in wiggly mud
Than smell a yellow rose.

Nobody else but the rosebush knows
How nice mud feels
Between the toes.

—Polly Chase Boyden (1930)

*44. What's wrong with the picture?* (visualizing). Select an interesting picture with lots of details and describe it to the class. However, make an error either mislabeling something or adding or deleting something from the picture. Then show the picture to the class and see who can identify "what's wrong." Again, illustrations from children's books are very effective.

## *REFERENCES*

BLUME, J. (1971). *Freckle juice.* New York. Four Winds Press.
BOYDEN, P. C. (1930, April). Mud. *Child Life.*
CLEARY, B. (1957). *Henry and the paper route.* New York: Scholastic.
SANDBURG, C. (1920). *Smoke and steel.* New York: Harcourt Brace Jovanovich.
SILVERSTEIN, S. (1974). *Where the sidewalk ends.* New York: Harper & Row.
WHITE, E.B. (1952). *Charlotte's web.* New York: Harper & Row.

## *SUGGESTED READINGS*

DEVINE, T.G. (1982). *Listening skills schoolwide: Activities and programs.* Urbana, IL: National Council of Teachers of English. Devine's text focuses on activities for teaching listening skills at the middle and secondary school levels.

[2]"Mud" by Polly Chase Boyden originally published in *Child Life,* April 1930. Reprinted by permission of the estate of Polly Chase Boyden and Rand McNally.

LUNDSTEEN, S.W. (1979). *Listening: Its impact on reading and the other language arts.* Urbana, IL: National Council of Teachers of English. This volume discusses both the theoretical and practical aspects of developing a listening program in public schools.

TOUGH, J. (1977). *Talking and learning: A guide to fostering communication skills in nursery and infant schools.* Exeter, NH: Heinemann. Tough's *Talking and Learning* presents instructional strategies for young children in fostering speaking and listening abilities.

# FIVE
# CHILDREN'S WRITING AS A LANGUAGE ART

Have you ever watched young children with crayons, pens, and markers? A one-year-old knocks over his sister's box of 65 Crayolas, sticks the red-orange one in his mouth, and later makes a mark on the table. A three-year-old writes a few lines of circular and angular scribbles on a page. These marks signify "I love you, Daddy," or the "directions to repairing the child's chair." A five-year-old draws a picture of herself at the doctor's office, writes the letter "D" for *doctor,* the letter "K" for *cry,* and "H" for *happy,* then scribbles a line under the picture signifying, "I am at the doctor"; or scribbles a story about the Care Bears, while asking Mommy to spell the words. Later in school, she will learn to transcribe the thoughts in her mind into conventional letters, spellings, and sentences. In addition, she will develop these in the greater context of learning the process of composing.

Most of you will be guiding children's growth in writing. This guidance must go far beyond teaching letters, spellings, and sentence structures; it will involve motivating creativity in composition. For you to teach writing well, you must know children's writing. To *know* the process of writing involves both knowing the children you are teaching and making decisions about methods and techniques that help children become independent writers (Graves, 1983). The purpose of this chapter is to interpret recent findings on the writing process and children's development of the writing process so as to guide beginning teachers in making decisions about classroom instruction in writing.

This chapter is divided into three parts. We first review the cognitive aspect of the writing process; secondly, we note some of the developmental differences in children's acquisition and development of writing; and third, we outline guiding principles to help beginning teachers in motivating and facilitating children's growth in writing.

Before we proceed we must understand writing as part of general language/communicative competence. Thus, the first part of this chapter emphasizes what competencies a fluent writer possesses in producing a text for real audiences. First we will examine the concept of *communicative competence* as it relates to writing and learning to write. According to Roger Shuy (1981), communicative competence in speaking, listening, writing, and reading consists of two broad categories: *linguistic competence* and *sociolinguistic competence.* Linguistic competence consists of mastery of basic language elements (for example, sounds, sentence structure, vocabulary, as well as—in written language—spelling and punctuation). Sociolinguistic competence refers generally to the use of language to get things done in various social situations such as using language to persuade a merchant to reduce the price of an appliance that has a scratch on it, requesting help at the airport, or shifting language styles from formal to informal settings. The distinction between linguistic competence and sociolinguistic competence is important for teachers to recognize because it helps provide a balanced perspective on language arts curricula. Beginning teachers should be aware that much of the published materials and curriculum guides based on the "basic skills" movement emphasize (and overemphasize) linguistic competence, when the real emphasis should be placed on sociolinguistic competence with linguistic competence placed in its context. In language learning, form follows function. Children learn oral and written language by using it for functional purposes and in using it frequently (with help from the teacher) to gradually refine the conventions of written language.

## THE WRITING PROCESS

### Writing as a Functional Process

With this brief sketch of communicative competence, let us examine more closely competencies involved in writing. It is this area where great advances in theory and practice have occurred in recent years. Various theorists contribute to our understanding of writing competence. According to Odell (1981, p. 103), writing competence is "the ability to discover what one wishes to say and to convey one's message through language, syntax and content that are appropriate for one's audience and purpose." According to Staton (1981, p. vii), writing is "communicative interaction . . . " including "the writer's intentions and purpose, which lead to the decision to write; interactions with others in order to gather information, and the relationship to an audience, including potential responses from the audience."

In essence, writing is a communicative event with a primary emphasis on purposeful, functional language use (Staton, 1981, p. vii). According to Britton (1978), there are three major functions of discourse: expressive, transactional, and poetic. In expressive writing, the writer writes about his or her own feelings or perceptions as a means of displaying oneself. This writing tends to be more egocentric. In transactional writing, the writer writes to get things done (for example, to persuade or to relay information). In poetic writing, the writer produces language and content as an art form such as in writing stories or poems. Most children begin composing with the expressive voice and tend to remain in the expressive voice for some time. This writing reads "a lot like talk" (Temple, Nathan, & Burris, 1982) and sometimes even contains dialogue. Children's initial attempts to move out of the expressive voice are not often completely successful. These attempts are called "transitional" and should be considered positive signs of growth.

In research by Shuy (1982), it was found that sixth graders use written language in dialogue journals for many functions, such as reporting opinions; reporting personal facts; reporting general facts; responding to questions; predicting future events; complaining; giving directives; apologizing; thanking; evaluating; offering; promising; asking information questions; asking procedure questions; and asking opinion questions. This list clearly shows the functional uses of writing that middle-grade children use.

Also important to understanding writing competence is the role of the writer–reader (audience) relationship. Good writers also have good audience awareness because a close interrelationship exists between authors and readers. Writers must establish an interaction with the reader(s) by being sincere, informative, relevant, clear, and by establishing points of contact between the developing text and the reader's experience (Tierney & LaZansky, 1980). Readers tend to "negotiate meaning" in terms of who the author is and what the author is trying to do. Reading and writing involve transactions between readers and writers (Tierney, LaZansky, Raphael & Cohen, 1983; Shanklin, 1982). Thus, writing can control readers, and readers can control their own interpretation of a writer's message. Authors and readers bring their own intentions to a text (Smith, 1982).

### Demands on the Writer

In addition to being functional and purposeful and reader-directed, writing involves overcoming the many cognitive demands on the writer. According to Bartlett (1981, p.3), writers must "juggle" two kinds of tasks: (1) using a "consistent overall plan for a discourse, which guides the selection and arrangement of potential content;" and (2) "turning that potential content into coherent, unambiguous text." Frank Smith (1982) presents two sides of writing that are in competition with each other: *composition,* or putting ideas together, and *transcription,* or representing the ideas into a conventional form. These two aspects of writing compete for the writer's attention much like decoding competes with the construction of meaning during reading. Smith states his suggestion for resolving this conflict:

> The rule is simple: Composition and transcription must be separated, and transcription must come later. It is asking too much of anyone, and especially of students trying to improve all aspects of their writing ability, to expect that they can concern themselves with polished transcription at the same time that they are trying to compose. (Smith, 1982, p. 24)

This view challenges what happens in many classrooms where teachers focus on precise sentence structure, spelling, and punctuation as opposed to the creation of meaningful text.

Bartlett's juggling metaphor is also used by Flower and Hayes (1980), because the act of writing involves juggling the demands on the writer. These include: (1) the demand for integrated knowledge, (2) the linguistic conventions of the written texts, and (3) the rhetorical aspects of the text (purposes, audience awareness, etc.).

In their theory of writing, Flower and Hayes (1980) discuss several strategies for "juggling" the constraints on the writing. One strategy is to "throw a constraint away" by ignoring specific elements of writing while working on a draft; for example, not worrying about transitions between paragraphs or syntactic complexity until a later draft. Another strategy is to "partition the problem" into smaller subproblems; for example, to plan to write and revise. A third strategy is to "set priorities." For example, in a letter to Grandma, a writer may decide to put less emphasis on polished syntax and more emphasis on expression of thoughts and feelings; or a writer can decide on the specific length of the paper in relation to specific purposes. In addition, a writer can choose the first *acceptable* way of stating a low-priority idea, rather than the *best* way, then move on to placing energy on the more important element of the discourse. Experienced writers also rely on "routine or well-learned procedures." These are, in a sense, learned formulas for a particular genre or type of letter. For instance, a letter of recommendation usually contains positive comments about the candidate, a description of personality strengths, and evidence of past accomplishments that will lead to a prediction that the candidate will be successful in the new position. The major way for reducing the cognitive demands on writing is to *plan,* or sketch out, the process and product of the composition. These can be (1) plans to *do* something with written language; essentially language functions; (2) plans to *say* something; decisions about content; and (3) plans for composing; in essence, decisions that guide the writing process. These strategies are helpful in relieving the cognitive strain on the writer (Flower and Hayes, 1980). Frank Smith (1982, p. 129) classified writing blocks into three categories—procedural (getting started), psychological (nothing to say; anxiety) and physical.

Smith recommends two ways for overcoming writing blocks:

1. Do not expect the writing to come out right the first time.
2. Accept the block (this is normal).

Now that we understand the demands on writers and the functions of writing competence, what does research tell us about how a composition evolves?

### Aspects of Composing

Many researchers have described the composition process. We will present two similar views of the components of writing. According to Flower and Hayes (1980), the writer's world has three main components: the task environment, the writer's long-term memory, and the writing process itself. The first two components provide a context for the writing process itself, which consists of three main processes: *planning, translating,* and *reviewing*. In *planning* the text, ideas are *generated* from long-term memory. From these ideas, some are selected, some discarded, but generally they are *organized* into a writing plan. In addition, goal-setting processes identify and store criteria for judging the text in editing, especially related to the overall purposes for writing.

The *translating* process involves the production of language matching the ideas generated. The *reviewing* process improves the quality of the text as it relates to the goals of the writer and the conventions of written language. Involved in reviewing are *reading* and *editing;* however, editing (and the generating process) may interrupt other processes in brief episodes but writing proceeds.

Whereas Flower and Hayes (1980) codify the composition process in terms of planning, translating, and reviewing, other writing experts describe the writing process as *rehearsing, drafting,* and *revising* (Murray, 1980). In *rehearsing,* the writer discovers ideas and plans for the writing. This may include such activities as jotting down ideas, reading material on a given topic, and making decisions about the organization of the discourse. The *drafting* stage implies that both the experienced and the novice writer develop drafts that will be molded and revised into more refined drafts. *Revising* is the ongoing stage, and it involves reading the text as a reader, surveying the text for appropriateness of content and style, and editing the manuscript for final presentation. Note that these stages are not independent of each other; rather, they are intertwined. For example, revising can lead to more rehearsing and drafting; and revising can also occur simultaneously with drafting.

With this brief sketch of the writing process in mind, let us examine aspects of children's development of writing.

## LEARNING TO WRITE

Thus far in this chapter we have tried to explain the current thinking about the writing process in general. Because you will be working with writers, we think it is important to look at how children learn to write. In this way you will derive some notion of the development of the writing process.

### Early Stages of the Writing Process

*Awareness of print.* Much of what is seen in the "writing" of very young children (ages 3, 4, 5) is termed *perceptual learning.* These youngsters seem to be responding to an urge to express something to someone through print. Harste, Woodward, and Burke (1984) examined the language encounters that children have long before school-related experiences. Such encounters (for example, identifying that a road sign such as WEST I-10 says "This is the way to the zoo" or that the Wendy's Hamburgers logo on the side of their cup says "Wendy's Cup") demonstrate that very young children expect written language to make sense. Assuming that children have been surrounded by language in all its forms (talking, writing, reading, listening), somewhere around the age of three they will begin to demonstrate an understanding that some scribbles on a piece of paper are different from others. Lavine (1972), as cited in Temple, Nathan, and Burris (1982), identifies this understanding as the learning of distinctive features that children use to separate writing from other graphic displays. These features are: (1) *nonpictoriality*—knowing that pictures are not writing; (2) *linearity*—knowing that writing consists of figures arrayed horizontally in a straight line; (3) *variety*—knowing that to be writing, figures in a display should vary from one another; and (4) *multiplicity*—knowing that writing consists of more than one figure.

*Early writing.* The next major developmental step in learning to write involves discovering and manipulating principles of writing. Marie Clay's (1975) work offers us insight into this area. She discusses several principles that can be demonstrated in children's early writing. Some of the more important ones are: (1) the *recurring principle*—writing consists of the same moves repeated over and over again; (2) the *generating principle*—writing consists of a limited number of signs (characters) that can be repeated in different combinations; (3) the *directional principle*—writing begins at a top-left position and proceeds left to right; (4) the *flexibility principle*—there is a limited number of written signs (for example, both lower- and upper-case alphabet letters), and a limit to the number of ways they can be made (that is, children will make letters and also some signs that are *not* letters. This principle also relates to the problem of directionality that some children experience with *p, d, b, q,* etc. Clay found that children continue to have directional difficulty in *writing* long after this issue is resolved in reading); (5) the *inventory principle*—the child records an exhaustive list of known letters and/or words for which a copy is not needed in order to reproduce; (6) the *contrastive principle*—two symbols that are similar yet different are compared; and (7) *page-arrangement principle*—which refers to the way print is arranged on the page (for example, fitting everything in, space between words, running past the margin).

*Invented spellings.* Young writers also show much creativity and an understanding of the phonetic principles of the language in their early spellings. Although these early spellings, often called *invented spellings,* may not appear at first glance to be very insightful, further examination demonstrates children's knowledge of the phonological and phonemic aspects of language.

As summarized by Temple, Nathan, and Burris (1982), children pass through several stages. An initial strategy used is what is called the *letter-name strategy.* There is only one rule—each letter used represents a sound. There are no such things as silent letters. Thus, for each letter that a child has written, a sound is intended.

Eventually letter-name spelling develops into what is called *transitional spelling.* In transitional spelling, more speech sounds are represented. For example, letter-name: I L N GLEAD TXS (I live in Goliad, Texas); transitional: A MAN ROB SOS THE PLES FID HEM. (A man robbed shoes. The police found him.) (Temple, Nathan, & Burris, 1982). From transitional spelling, the writer proceeds to standard spelling. (See also Chapter 7 in this text for further discussion of spelling.)

*Composition.* Although it may seem at this point of the discussion that children first learn surface features of writing (that is, letters, spelling, principles), children demonstrate strong awareness of the functional, meaningful, and composing aspects of written language at a very young age. Children do not learn basic skills prior to composing for meaning; rather, children develop writing skills in the context of producing meaningful texts (Harste, Woodward, & Burke, 1984).

Figure 5–1 demonstrates Peter's (age 3) use of writing to record information. In this writing sample, Peter is writing a list, dictated by his father, of the names of players on the Chicago Cubs (Ryne Sandberg, Rich Sutcliffe. . .). Peter is also writing the letter *A,* which he knows, but writes the ball players' names in his version of cursive writing following the page-arrangement principle: left to right, top to bottom. Peter at this stage knows that writing is *functional* in recording and presenting information. Peter has also produced similar writing samples to function as directions for fixing or assembling something. Thus, a preschool child in a literate environment learns naturally the writer–reader connections.

Finally, Rachel (prior to entering kindergarten—age 5) produced the text in Figure 5–2. She drew a picture of Mommy and Daddy, and she used what she knew about written language to create an expressive composition. When asked to interpret (read) the various elements of the text, she related that D = Doctor, K = Cry, H = Happy. (Note the initial attempts at spelling.) The scribble at the bottom of the text is the topic sentence (a complete sentence, "I am at the doctor"), illustrating the awareness of written syntax. When asked why she wrote two *K*'s, she responded that she didn't like the first one, so she wrote the second one. At an early age, this child naturally has an awareness of the role of *revision* in the writing process. In addition, drawing a picture is a common rehearsing strategy of young children.

**FIGURE 5-1** Text Produced by Peter (Age 3)

For the most part, children can accomplish this much composition development on their own. However, at this point young writers need to be exposed to a classroom environment that will allow them to progress as writers, who use language to get things done. The remainder of this chapter provides some guidelines for providing such an environment.

## FACILITATING WRITING IN THE CLASSROOM

The guidelines that follow were compiled after reviewing several of the current major works on children's writing. Thus, these guidelines reflect the thinking of Graves (1983), Murray (1980), Temple, Nathan, and Burris (1982), Harste, Woodward, and Burke (1984), and Calkins (1983).

### GUIDELINES FOR FACILITATING WRITING IN THE CLASSROOM

1. Encourage young writers to write about what they know or something they want to know more about.
2. Honor what a child already knows about writing.
3. Provide *many* meaningful encounters with print.

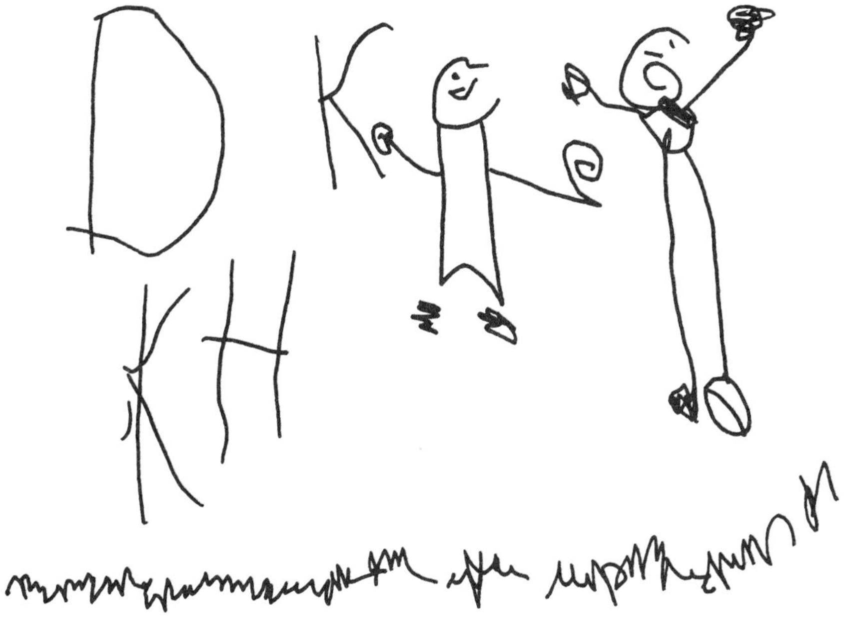

**FIGURE 5-2** Text Produced by Rachel (Age 5)

4. Allow children free access to a wide selection of writing materials, writing instruments, and good literature to provide models.
5. Allow time for and give attention to all three stages of writing: rehearsing, drafting, and revising (Murray, 1980).
6. Become a good listener. You must know your students in order to help them. Also, "The presence of a listener encourages writers to become readers of their emerging texts" (Calkins, 1983, p. 60).
7. Allow for the sharing of writing.
8. Basic writing skills need to be taught in the context of the composition process.

These guidelines should be helpful toward developing the kind of low-risk classroom atmosphere necessary for writing growth. In the following chapters instructional practices that facilitate writing in the classroom are presented in detail.

## CONCLUDING REMARKS

Much research has been conducted on the writing process and on children's development of writing. Learning to write involves more than mere rote learning of letters, spellings, punctuations, and sentence structures. Rather, learning to write involves learning the functional, complex dynamics of composing, which involves much support from teachers and parents. Writing is best learned not as a formal subject but in the process of learning and doing other things. Frank Smith (1982, p. 211), summarizes this best:

> My own recommendation for how writing and reading should be taught is perhaps radical; they should not be taught at all. Not in any formal sense, as subjects. All the busywork, the meaningless drills and exercises, the rote memorization, the irrelevant tests, and the distracting grades should go (to the extent that the teacher can get rid of them). And in their place teachers and children together should use writing (and reading, spoken language, art, and drama) to learn other things. Writing should be used to tell stories and to produce artifacts—books to be published, poems to be recited, songs to be sung, plays to be acted, letters to be delivered, programs to be consulted, newspapers to be distributed, advertisements to be displayed, complaints to be aired, ideas to be shared, worlds to be constructed and explored. Children should learn to write in the same manner that they learn to talk, without being aware that they are doing so, in the course of doing other things.

## *REFERENCES*


BARTLETT, E.J. (1981). *Learning to write: Some cognitive and linguistic components* (Linguistics and Literacy Series: 2). Washington, DC: Center for Applied Linguistics.

BRITTON, J. (1978). The composing processes and the functions of writing. In C. R. Cooper & L. Odell (Eds.), *Research on composing*. Urbana, IL: National Council of Teachers of English.

CALKINS, L.M. (1983). *Lessons from a child: On the teaching and learning of writing*. Exeter, NH: Heinemann.

CLAY, M. M. (1975). *What did I write: Beginning writing behaviour*. Exeter, NH: Heinemann.

FLOWER, L. & HAYES, J.R. (1980). Plans that guide the composing process. In C. H. Frederiksen & J. F. DOMINIC (Eds.), *Writing: Process, development and communication: Vol. 2. Writing: The nature, development, and teaching of written communication*. Hillsdale, NJ: Erlbaum.

GRAVES, D.H. (1983). *Writing: Teachers and children at work*. Exeter, NH: Heinemann.

HARSTE, J.C., WOODWARD, V.A., & BURKE, C.L. (1984). *Language stories and literacy lessons*. Portsmouth, NH: Heinemann.

LAVINE, L. (1972). *The development of perception of writing in prereading children: A cross-cultural study*. Unpublished doctoral dissertation, Cornell University, Ithaca, NY.

MURRAY, D. (1980). Writing as process: How writing finds its own meaning. In T. R. Donovan & B. W. McClelland (Eds.), *Eight approaches to teaching composition*. Urbana, IL: National Council of Teachers of English.

ODELL, L. (1981). Defining and assessing competence in writing. In C. W. Cooper (Ed.), *The nature and measurement of competency in English*. Urbana, IL: National Council of Teachers of English.

SHANKLIN, N.K. (1982). *Relating reading and writing: Developing a transitional model of the writing process*. Bloomington, IN: Monographs in Teaching and Learning, School of Education, Indiana University.

SHUY, R.W. (1981). A holistic view of language. *Research in the Teaching of English, 15,* 101–111.

SHUY, R.W. (1982). Analysis of language functions in dialogue journal writing. In J. Staton, R. Shuy and J. Kreeft (Eds.), *Analysis of dialogue journal writing as a communicative event: Vol. 2.* Washington, DC: Center for Applied Linguistics.

SMITH, F. (1982). *Writing and the writer*. New York: Holt, Rinehart & Winston.

STATON, J. (1981). In E. J. Bartlett (Ed), *Introduction to learning to write: Some cognitive and linguistic components* (Linguistics and Literacy Series: 2). Washington, DC: Center for Applied Linguistics.

TEMPLE, C.A., NATHAN, R.G., & BURRIS, N.A. (1982). *The beginning of writing*. Boston: Allyn & Bacon.

TIERNEY, R.J., & LAZANSKY, J. (1980). *The rights and responsibilities of readers and writers: A contractual agreement* (Reading Education Report No. 15). Center for the Study of Reading, University of Illinois at Urbana.

TIERNEY, R.J., LAZANSKY, J., RAPHAEL, T., & COHEN, P.R. (1983). *Authors' intentions and readers' interpretations* (Tech. Rep. No. 276). Center for the Study of Reading, University of Illinois.

## SUGGESTED READINGS

CALKINS, L.M. (1983). *Lessons from a child: On the teaching and learning of writing*. Exeter, NH: Heinemann. This book documents how a child's writing growth is enhanced in a "writing workshop" classroom. One child's growth in composition is traced, and guidelines for successful writing instruction are provided.

CLAY, M.M. (1975). *What did I write: Beginning writing behaviour*. Exeter, NH: Heinemann. Clay provides many examples of young children's writing and the various strategies that children use in early literacy.

GRAVES, D.H. (1983). *Writing: Teachers and children at work*. Exeter, NH: Heinemann. This book presents practical guidelines for starting to teach writing, making the writing conference work, helping children learn the skills they need, understanding how children develop as writers, and documenting children's writing development.

HARSTE, J.C., WOODWARD, V.A., & BURKE, C.L. (1984). *Language stories and literacy lessons*. Portsmouth, NH: Heinemann. This text provides a comprehensive discussion of sociolinguistic and psycholinguistic phenomena in young children's writings, based on children's oral and written language. Implications for changing literacy instruction are presented.

SMITH, F. (1982). *Writing and the writer*. New York: Holt, Rinehart & Winston. Frank Smith presents a readable discussion of the writing process, useful in developing a theoretical framework for teaching writing.

TEMPLE, C.A., NATHAN, R.G., & BURRIS, N.A. (1982). *The beginnings of writing*. Boston: Allyn & Bacon. This text is a highly readable and practical presentation of young children's writing, which demonstrates how young children discover writing through the stages of scribbling, spelling, and composition.

# SIX
# WRITING AS PROCESS IN THE LANGUAGE ARTS

The purpose of this chapter is to describe the writing process and provide a framework for developing instructional plans for your classroom. Because one of your goals as a teacher is to help students become communicators via the written language, this chapter will include ideas and strategies that emphasize the premise that writing is meaningful communication and that basic developmental skills are necessary for children to become skillful writers. Therefore, an important question to consider when planning your writing curriculum will be: What writing skills are important to my students not only now but in their future? From the answer to that question you can create meaningful assignments that have a definite, understood sense of purpose and give your students opportunities to receive feedback from real and varied audiences.

Seven guiding principles are suggested as you plan your program:

1. Know your students' *skill levels* and their *writing needs* both in and out of the classroom.
2. Create writing activities that *develop the skills, provide application* across the content areas, and reflect the interrelated nature of writing, thus giving credibility and purpose to your writing class.
3. Take into account the *appropriateness* of the activity. Does it reflect the students' interests, age, maturity, ability, and experience? Does it relate to ideas and materials being used?
4. *Stimulate* the writer to engage in controversy, a quest for answers, or an observation that gives choices and offers options.

5. *Provide instruction* that draws upon or furnishes adequate data; that offers a controlling idea which the writer is to explain or support; that specifies limits and conditions of expected performance; that focuses on one writing skill that has been previously taught; that encourages experimentation and original thinking.
6. Help the writer use or find appropriate, *purposeful* audiences. Enable students to discover a way to use what has been learned, and to learn what can be used.
7. Set expectations within the reach of students and provide a *measure* for evaluation.

The following section describes the stages of the writing process, giving a brief description of each stage and suggesting responsibilities of the teacher.

*Process* is the series of stages one may use in order to arrive at a specific end product. These stages, and the steps within each stage, are not necessarily sequential nor are they dependent on another step or stage for a successful end product. Because writing is a unique, creative process, the steps described in each stage are only suggested ways to proceed through the process. The degree of their use is dependent on the writer, the audience, the purpose, and the form of the writing. The more you as a teacher know about how a writer composes, the better prepared you will be to plan instruction that can enhance and guide this process. The same is true for a student. The more the student knows about how a writer structures text, the better the chance for success in writing.

The stages described below are those generally used by teachers and researchers in the field. You will find them in many of the programs described in Section IV of this book. Sometimes the stages and steps are outlined in somewhat different form; however, whatever the "system" used, the "process" is the same.

## THE WRITING PROCESS

### Prewriting Stage:

*Prewriting* is a crucial stage in the composition process and often comprises about *80 percent* of your writing period. As you prepare lessons keep in mind the process by reflecting on your long-range goals (usually the product) and your short-range objectives (usually the process). A long-range project goal may be to learn how to write a term paper, whereas the daily objective may deal with one step in that process; for example, how to write footnotes.

A good understanding of what the students already know is important so that instruction can be geared to their level. Diagnosis of individual and group needs comes from ongoing evaluation of their compositions.

Skills may be taught in isolation and then applied, or may be taught directly in the context of the process. They are not discrete and do not necessarily reflect a developmental sequence, nor are they dependent on one another for a successful end product. However, they should always be reflected in an end product.

Writing is an individualized, personal, creative, and interactive process that every writer approaches differently. Ideas do not always come automatically just because at 1:13 P.M. it is time for writing class. An important part of the prewriting period is to motivate children to want to write and to give them time and help in developing ideas. The steps listed below are often found in the *prewriting stage.*

#### WRITING ENVIRONMENT

Providing a place or an attitude that reflects an atmosphere where writing is considered an important and effective means of communication.

*Teacher Responsibilities:* Plan an environment that is complementary and stimulating to the specific writing experience or goal. Encourage exploration, manipulation, and creative expression in a nonthreatening, open situation. Place a high value on *any* efforts a student makes to express thoughts in writing. Activities that allow for student input, problem solving, and constructive feedback help develop a positive attitude toward the writing experience.

#### EXPERIENCING

Actively involving students in learning that expands on prior knowledge and introduces new experiences;

Providing instruction and activities that motivate the children to *want* to communicate in a written form.

*Teacher Responsibilities:* Plan for students to have many opportunities to explore various forms of writing and continuously provide new experiences that spur them to want to express themselves in writing. Topics and audiences should be interesting, varied, and relevant to the student. When teaching a new skill, eliminate undue anxiety by allowing flexibility regarding the subject matter. It is always easier to write about something we know lots about or for which we have an intense interest.

#### DISCOVERING

Deciding what is already known and planning for or discovering what it is that one still needs to know in order to successfully communicate the message;

Discovering a need and purpose for communicating in writing. A writer's general purpose might be to persuade, inform, or entertain the proposed audience;

Determining the audience for whom the message is proposed. The audience may be self, personal you, or unknown you. Determining purpose and audience is necessary for consideration of questions of style.

*Teacher Responsibilities:* Instruct students in how to recognize and use forms appropriate for conveying the intended meaning. Show students ways to gather and organize information and techniques for retrieving from memory information that has been previously stored. Activities that jog one's memory usually begin by getting students to reflect on everything they know about the topic. By starting with the whole of the topic, which is often chaotic, the student is able to look at all possible ideas, see relationships, and begin to consider ways in which the topic can be narrowed and focused to meet the needs of both the author and the reader. A few techniques to get students to write include brainstorming, wordmaps, note taking, or finding resources and models that define or exemplify skillful writing.

### MANIPULATING

Manipulating and playing with language to encourage flow of imagination;

Examining the many options available for choosing words that best convey the desired message.

This stage involves exercises in dissecting, expanding, ordering, rearranging, and changing words in sentences, and sentences in paragraphs. There should also be instruction in the avoidance of overused or trite words (good, nice, cute), pejorative words (dumb, stupid), and excessive word repetition.

*Teacher Responsibilities:* Give students many opportunities to play with words, sentences, and ideas by allowing them to make choices in their writing. Encourage them to make changes and to experiment with words and sentences. One way to demonstrate to students that there are many correct options to choose from is to write a sentence on the board and have them write the sentence in as many ways as they can while still keeping the same approximate meaning. Then discuss the subtle differences created because of word or structure changes, and why one might choose one way over another depending on purpose and audience. In Chapter 10 you will find many other suggested activities.

### MAKING FORMAL CHOICES

Basing choices on audience, purpose, and form of the composition.

In order to make these choices, the following questions may be considered: How will the information or message be organized? Should the writer use chronological order, comparison and contrast, or some other technique? Will the problem be defined and solutions given or will the text be constructed to include examples or illustrations to clarify meaning? What language and structure choices are needed? Will style be formal, informal, or casual?

*Teacher Responsibilities:* For students to become independent and skillful writers they must receive instruction regarding the conventions of our language. For each composition you must encourage them to consider matters of purpose, form, audience, and style as they plan for writing. Activities during prewriting may range from discussion to formal outlining, before the actual composing begins. Many activities of this type are described in the programs in Section IV of this book.

### Writing or Composing Stage

It is important during the writing or composing stage that all of the actual writing be conducted in the classroom, where you can provide the guidance and support that some students may need.

Because writing is a thinking process, ideas often flow faster than the pen is able to write; consequently, first drafts may be messy and have errors. Don't expect or even encourage perfection on the first draft; this is a time to create and let ideas flow. Have dictionaries and thesauri available for students to explore words, meanings, and relationships, but do not require their use at this time.

Students should realize that after they do their initial writing they may want to rearrange or rewrite parts of their compositions. They should understand that first drafts are just first drafts and that most of the improving of composition comes during the final stages.

Because the composing stage is a very fluid condition, it is not always possible to specify certain steps during this period. Each child, with or without the teacher, may be involved in something different from the others at any given time. However, the following "steps" may occur.

#### FORMING IDEAS

The jotting down of ideas in a first draft, prose form: These ideas have been formed, and perhaps even outlined, in the prewriting stage. Now they are written out in sentence and paragraph form.

*Teacher Responsibilities:* Circulate among the students to lend support, guidance, and direction to individual students; be sure they have necessary resources available while writing. At times, the teacher may write with the children, as an example that we all want to write.

#### MAKING LANGUAGE CHOICES

Making decisions about what is to be said and how to say it based on previous planning regarding audience, purpose, form, and content.

*Teacher Responsibilities:* Your task is to be available, answer questions, and provide help to those who need it. Individual conferences should be conducted during the writing stage. These may arise from student questions or from your observations as you observe them writing.

### Revision Stage

When the first drafts are completed it is time to revise and rewrite, perhaps once, even several times. Revising and rewriting are very difficult for students and adults alike. It is difficult to change something you have created, even if the intent is to improve on that creation. Therefore, approach this stage positively by working *with* students to explore and expand their learning capabilities. Use positive reinforcement regarding the good points of the student's writing and discuss how improvement in other areas could help make the message clearer to the audience. Stress that improving one's writing is a natural part of the process of becoming a skilled writer.

Revision, like composing, is a very fluid situation. Some students may need only one revision; others may need or want several. Revision goes on until student, peers, and teacher are satisfied that our goals *for this activity* have been attained.

#### CRITICAL ANALYSIS

Comparing what was written in relation to audience expectations and the purpose established earlier.

*Teacher Responsibilities:* Expectations for the writing assignment should be clear. Students should have available to them written copies of the guidelines and/or models used to compare against their own work. These guidelines should include written statements of student-selected audience, purpose, and form.

A number of methods may be used in the revision process. Self-editing is always important in growth toward independence in writing. Groups of peers, or a peer-pal, can help the student in the revision process. The teacher–pupil conference is highly desirable but may not be possible for each student in every writing situation.

#### MAKING REVISIONS

Making changes and modifications necessary to conform to either the writer's or the audience's expectations, and the choices made earlier.

At this point the writer makes changes before submitting the composition for editing and evaluation.

*Teacher Responsibilities:* At this time reteaching may occur by focusing instruction either on an individual's, a group's, or a class's needs. This feedback should be done in a positive, helpful manner.

### Editing and Evaluating Stage

Only after the composition has been revised and rewritten to the point of final draft should editing and evaluation take place. Again, these may be done by student, peer(s), or teacher (it is not necessary that the teacher evaluate every paper).

Emphasis in evaluation should be on individual growth and meeting the expectations of a given writing assignment. A number of evaluation methods are suggested in Section IV of this book. Others can be found in the Suggested

Readings at the end of this chapter. The important point to remember is that the evaluation should provide specific suggestions to aid the student's growth in writing.

#### PROOFREADING

Preparing the composition in final form for publication.

*Teacher Responsibilities:* Consistent practice will help students to recognize, correct, and evaluate not only one's own writing but also the writings of others. Careful instruction is important to assure a positive attitude and an acceptance of a peer's critical remarks. Create a helping atmosphere by capitalizing on individual strengths and giving each student a responsibility in which he or she can succeed. For example, one student might be in charge of correcting capital letters at the beginning of a sentence while another could be responsible for checking for punctuation at the end of a sentence. These jobs could be rotated weekly. Begin with simple tasks that have been fully explained and focus on only a few points at a time. Later, expand your evaluation measure to cover areas previously taught. Be sure to include in your measure at least one or more areas for students to make positive comments.

#### FORMAL AND INFORMAL EDITING AND EVALUATION

Submitting of the writer's best effort for correction, evaluation, and feedback.

Judgment is usually based on how well the expectations were met and the effectiveness of the message. *Formal editing* may take on the form of a corrected or edited composition, feedback that reflects acceptance or rejection by the audience, or grades that reflect the writer's ability to meet the evaluator's expectations on specified criteria.

*Informal editing* may take on the form of a response from the audience indicating that the message was understood or appreciated, or by the audience following through with a set of directions as stated in the message.

*Teacher Responsibilities:* Teach the skills necessary and provide clear expectations so the student has a fair chance at being successful in the writing task. Provide a clear and specific evaluation of each of the expected outcomes and explain how the student met or failed to meet these criteria.

This is also a time for you to evaluate your teaching in light of your students' abilities to complete the assignment. Check to see if there are areas that require reteaching either for individuals or the group. Use this diagnosis as you plan the next writing experience for your class.

### Publication Stage

Only after each composition has been finally proofread and evaluated is it time for publication. Because compositions have been written for a variety of purposes and audiences, a variety of publication forms are also needed. Publication is *not* just making a book or writing a paper!

**PUBLISHING**

Sharing the written product with the audience for whom it was intended.

*Teacher Responsibilities:* The teacher should be aware of the many ways in which publication can be achieved. These could be as local as the school newspaper or as commercial as a children's magazine. It could be putting together a book for the class to enjoy, making a card for parents at Easter, or submitting a composition to a commercial publisher for consideration. The more resources you have at your fingertips and the more ideas you can think of for stimulating students to write using real audiences the more success you will have with your writing program. A few possible audiences and activities are listed below. Many others are suggested elsewhere in this and other books. Still others remain for you to invent.

**AUDIENCES**

1. Local contests
2. Friends and relatives
3. Retirement, convalescent homes
4. Hospitals
5. Tourist information centers
6. Other teachers
7. Day-care centers
8. Other classrooms
9. Other schools
10. Sports heros, authors, etc.
11. School personnel
12. Pen pals
13. Restaurants, historical societies, museums, etc.
14. Newspapers

**ACTIVITIES**

1. Books: These may be collections of poems or stories, individual books, or books modeled after other books (pattern books, ABC books, and so forth). The type of book will depend upon the audience and the purpose.
2. Class or school newsletters or newspapers: Audiences could be parents, classmates, or the community, and the purpose could be to provide information that students or parents may need, or to give students an opportunity to write articles and publish their best writing efforts.
3. Note-passing: Set times and criteria in which note-passing is "OK."
4. Issues that affect students can be expressed through a variety of writing activities, such as letters to the editor or to the principal.

5. Placemats for local restaurants or a Chamber of Commerce brochure.
6. Letters sent to get information on a topic of interest to the individual or used as part of a project such as a research paper in class.
7. Writing job résumés for summer employment.
8. Writing plays for puppets or for classmates to perform live or on video or audio tape.
9. An oral reading of poetry on local public television or radio.
10. A 2-by-2 slide presentation putting poems to pictures and music.

## SUMMARY

The *process approach* in writing is more than a methodology, although it offers a method to use. With this approach, the emphasis is on the *process* of writing; the objectives of the teacher and the learner are toward growth in the various stages of the process. Evaluation is based on growth in each stage of the process. To be sure, a product is the final outcome, and our pride in sharing that product is a mighty motivator. However, it is to how we reached the product that process approach directs itself.

### *SUGGESTED READINGS*

*Teaching the writing process,* and other booklets available through the Wisconsin Writing Project, 225 North Mills Street, Madison, WI 53706.

BRITTON, J. (1978). The composing processes and the functions of writing. In C.R. Cooper, & L. Odell, (Eds.), *Research on composing.* Urbana, IL: National Council of Teachers of English.

*Composition in the language arts, Grades 1–8: An instructional framework.* Madison, WI: Wisconsin Department of Public Instruction.

MOFFETT, J. & WAGNER, B. (1983). *Student-centered language arts and reading, K–13.* Boston: Houghton Mifflin.

TWAY, E. (1976). Writing: An interpersonal process. *Language Arts,* 53, (5), 594–596.

# SEVEN
# SPELLING AS A LANGUAGE ART

It is not the purpose of this chapter to engage in the debate on the importance of spelling in the curriculum, or in life. It may, indeed, be true that our modern technological age will soon make the need to spell extinct. However, the fact is that in most American schools today spelling is a specified subject of the curriculum with specified weekly time allotments devoted to its teaching through grade six or even grade eight. In almost as many schools a specific spelling series has been adopted for use. In other words, it is an odds-on chance that you will be teaching spelling in a formal manner in *your* elementary classroom. The purpose of this chapter, then, is to assist you in doing it.

The suggestions here may be used with whatever spelling series you may encounter, or with no spelling series at all. They are consistent with linguistic knowledge of the language and with the bulk of the research on teaching spelling. Because we have in this book emphasized integration of the language arts—and of the language arts with other areas of the curriculum—approaches are suggested that will help children to transfer knowledge learned in formal spelling lessons to real writing situations.

## THE PERSONKE-YEE MODEL

In 1966, Carl Personke and Albert Yee proposed a theoretical model for spelling based on the behaviors that spellers actually use in spelling situations. This model suggested the need for instruction to develop a large store of known words, the use of spelling generalization, and techniques of proofreading. We will not attempt here to discuss all aspects of that model, but the interested reader will find detailed descriptions in Personke and Yee (1966) and Kean and Personke (1976). For our purposes we will select certain aspects of the model that seem of most concern to the practicing teacher.

## INTERNAL INPUTS

*Internal inputs* were suggested as those ideas, attitudes, and knowledge available to the speller for use in a given situation. For the teacher, the development and expansion of these inputs should be the goal of the spelling program. We shall examine each of these and suggest ways to include them in your program.

### Learned Words

*Learned words* are a necessary part of any speller's stock of "spelling aids." Indeed, the more words I *know* how to spell, without any recourse to memory devices or external help, the more fluent I will be as a speller and, to some extent at least, as a writer. These become a major final outcome of any spelling program and were, in fact, for years the only expected outcome of most commercial spelling series.

As might be expected, the methods suggested in your spelling series are generally adequate to the task and also correlate with the Personke/Yee suggestion that we use audio, visual, and kinesthetic cues in spelling. Five steps are usually suggested for introduction of the weekly spelling list.

1. Look at the word.
2. Say the word.
3. Write the word.
4. Check what you have written.
5. Rewrite the word if incorrect.

This is generally an acceptable and sound approach for whole-word learning. However, some special considerations are needed if you want to assure this soundness.

Often teachers do not insist upon the child completing all five of these steps, but simply "assign the page." If you want each child to do this with each word, it is best to do this as a group experience, having different children say each word as others write it. This also gives opportunity for the teacher to be certain that correct pronunciations are given.

Because this method is usually part of a 5-day program with study exercises on the 1st, 2nd, and 4th days and testing on the 3rd and 5th days, it is usually referred to as the *study–test–study method.* Much research has indicated that the test–study method is preferable because it permits children to use their time more efficiently by studying only those words they do not know.

Because the children probably make this choice anyway, especially if the first day's lesson is done individually, the entire debate may be moot.

Another consideration with this method is, how many times must a word be written before it is learned? Unfortunately, there is no simple answer to this question because three factors are involved that may individually, or in conjunction with each other, affect the learning process. These factors are: (1) the nature of the word, (2) the learner, and (3) the situation in which the word is introduced. One try may be sufficient for learning, and a hundred may not be enough.

Finally, scant attention is paid to word meaning when using this method. The assumption generally is that the children will know the meanings of these words. This is a dangerous assumption. Because we view a good spelling program as a good vocabulary program, we will discuss this aspect again later in the chapter.

Two further aspects of the Personke/Yee model, which enter in here and elsewhere in the program, are the importance of motivation and of immediate, positive feedback to learning. Because these aspects are so important, they too will be discussed at length later.

### Generalizations

*Generalizations* to assist in spelling an unknown word are also important to the learner because no program, or learner, can possibly learn to spell all the words that will be needed in a lifetime of writing.

Most of today's spellers include instruction in generalization as a part of the weekly format. This usually is apparent by the grouping of words in the weekly list (to teach particular generalizations), in a unit title that states the generalization(s) involved, and in a workbook format generally conducted on day 2 of each week. Unfortunately, we can again find major problems occurring if you simply "assign the page." Fortunately, we can also suggest better and more effective approaches. Among the chief problems with the "assign the page" route are lack of motivation and lack of direction, compounded by inattention to transfer in learning and to vocabulary development. Try some of the following approaches instead.

*Discovery method.* Instead of introducing the word list, examine it yourself to see what generalizations are being introduced. These may be of two kinds: phonetic or structural.

*1. Phonetic generalizations.* These involve sound-to-letter correspondencies and are generally best taught by use of common phonograms ( -an, -ight, -ay) rather than one-to-one correspondencies. Lists of common phonograms and one-to-one correspondencies are available in many spelling and reading books; excellent lists are contained in Chapter 9 of Kean and Personke (1976). If the phonogram to be learned is " -ook," you can begin by putting a word from the spelling list (say, "look") on the chalkboard or overhead projector (children's spelling books are closed at this time). Now ask the children to provide another word that sounds like look (book, cook, etc.) and add these to the list.

When the list reaches five or six words, ask them what is the same about all of our " -ook" words; draw a line down to demonstrate that they all have " -ook" in them. Now ask them to spell a word that sounds like " -ook" but which is not on our list (perhaps "crook" or "book"). Only after we have completed this discovery process do we turn to our spellers in order to check on our discovery. You might, by the way, use a word from the list to discover a phonogram not intended in the speller itself.

Be aware that although this is a phonetic generalization, word meaning is always important. If "rook" is used, for example, be sure the students know that rook is a crowlike bird, or even a castle in chess.

*2. Structural generalizations.* These involve attaching meaningful units (*affixes*) to known words in order to make new words. These affixes are called "inflectional" (grammatical) morphemes, and "derivational" (lexical) morphemes. Because there are only eight inflections in English (plural, possessive, past tense, third person present tense, present participle, past participle, comparative, and superlative), the major concern with structural generalization involves the use of derivational morphemes (prefixes and suffixes). These will often be indicated as the subject of attention in your speller, or in your reading books. An extensive list is available in Kean and Personke (1976). Because these are meaning units, it is with those exercises that we can turn our spelling program into a vocabulary program.

Again, a *discovery process* is used as described above except that now we are discovering *morphophonemic* rules of the written language (*morpho,* words or meaning; *phono,* sounds). Each morphophonemic rule includes a given, or condition, and three interdependent outcomes. These are:

When adding ( -xxx) to a word ending (or beginning) with (xxx), the following changes take place:

1. Pronunciation: Something will be added and changes may be made in the root word.
2. Spelling: Something may be added and changes may be made in the root word.
3. Meaning: A new meaning will be attached or *form class* (part of speech) will be changed.

Let's see how this works in a real situation.

List these words on the chalkboard:

| | |
|---|---|
| illegal | imply |
| illuminate | imbibe |
| irresponsible | indent |
| irrigate | indecent |
| impossible | include |
| immobile | inconclusive |
| immaculate | |

Lead the children to discover that all the words begin either with "il- ," "im- ," "ir- ," or "in- ," and that in some of these the prefix has the meaning of "not." Sort these out and make new words like them in which the prefixes also mean *not*. See if they can discover when to use "il- , ir- , im- , or in- ." They are all different forms of the same prefix, "in- " and add the meaning of "not." (The only one that may cause trouble is "im- ," which precedes words beginning with "m, b, or p," all *bilabials,* or sounds made with the lips.)

Our morphophonemic rule would now look like this:
When adding the prefix "in- " to a word, we:

1. Add the sound /il-/, /im-/, /ir-/ or /in-/.
2. Add the spelling il- , im- , ir- , or in- . (In 1 and 2 above, the choice of form is determined by the first letter in the root word.)
3. The meaning is changed to "not."

We may go back from here and look at the words we initially discarded. We could find, with the help of a dictionary, that these words came from a combination with another Latin prefix, in- , probably no longer used in English but still often apparent in word meanings and spellings, and can forward our vocabulary and spelling development. This prefix meant "in," "into," or "toward."

Another affix, this time a *suffix,* which is fun to work with, is " -tion." By discovery, we can learn that it can be [-shən] and is spelled " -tion" or " -ssion," or [-zhən] and spelled " -sion." We can also learn that it is used to change a verb to a noun (subscribe, subscription; decide, decision) and has many variations such as those above. We can even learn that it sometimes occurs with another combiner ("a" or "i") to give us "simulation" and "admonition," for example.

From all of the lore about what makes for a good speller and what makes for a poor speller, one factor that stands out is that "good spellers are those who attend to words." The discovery methods suggested here involve children attending to words in an exciting and fun way. This objective alone would be worth the effort, not to say all of the new words we learn to spell and understand in the process.

The important aspects of motivation and direction, and immediate, positive feedback were mentioned earlier. Let's look at these again. Teacher-guided discovery is active and meaningful, and can be lots of fun. By being highly motivational and offering many examples, discovery promotes transfer of learning. Moreover, two additional teaching techniques can extend these positive attributes and improve on the type of feedback received.

*Corrected test method.* This was first proposed and studied by Thomas Horn (1947). Since then it has been reexamined many times and remains the single best method for learning to spell words. The reason for its success is simple: it provides immediate, positive feedback.

Using this method, students correct their own test papers as soon as they have completed the test. This may be done individually (using their spelling books) or in a group with the teacher. In the group method, the teacher asks different children to spell the words and write them on the chalkboard. The children make appropriate changes (rewrites) on their own papers immediately. They may later practice writing words they missed an appropriate number of times.

Children will not cheat, especially if emphasis is placed on growth rather than grades. They may make an occasional perceptual error, especially when using the individual-correcting method. You can spot-check for this type of error.

The corrected test method is so well proven that it should also be used in correcting the *challenge test* described below.

*Challenge test.* I began using the *challenge test* while teaching sixth grade in the 1950s. Since then hundreds of teachers and student-teachers have used it successfully.

We have mentioned *direction* before. Even in spelling books where children perform exercises relating to spelling generalizations, they know that they are tested on word lists. Therefore, the direction of their studies is aimed at learning by rote the word list for the week. The exercises on generalization become mere diversions.

The challenge test is based on, but not necessarily tied to, the usual 5-day lesson plan, which involves a pretest on Wednesday and a final test on Friday. Instead of this format, you establish a set cutting limit, say a score of 22 out of 25 correct, on the pretest. Students who achieve this get to take the challenge test on Friday. This test consists of words we have *not* studied this week, but which can be spelled from the words and generalizations we have learned. Thus, we may have learned *marry, married,* and *marrying* during the week, but the challenge test will include *tarry, tarried,* and *tarrying*. Or if we learned to make *division* from *divide,* the challenge test may ask *decision*.

This type of test is highly competitive and, as the name suggests, challenging. However, the competition is not among children but between the children and you, which can be kept light and fun, or for each child's own growth. I have also discovered an additional plus for the challenge test; children will use their dictionaries avidly to try to find all the words you might use on the test. (I usually try to throw in a few "stinkers," like *signature* from *sign*.)

Here are a final few words for you to consider when you think about teaching spelling generalizations to children:

1. Generalizations are not rules. They do not have to be verbalized, nor do they have to hold true in all situations. They are simply things that are true enough in English orthography to be worth attending to.
2. Generalizations are not used simply because they are "learned." Research on generalization tells us that we must learn to use generalizations, that is, have a

tendency to try them out, before they will be used. This tendency does not appear overnight, but will develop with the use of the discovery process, the challenge test, and the proofreading methods that follow.

## Proofreading

*Proofreading* is emphasized in the Personke/Yee model as a major way of learning to spell new words and as a key approach to spelling unknown words in written compositions. You will also find repeated reference to the importance of proofreading in the chapters of this book devoted to written composition.

In these chapters you will discover that the authors generally emphasize that spelling should *not* be a concern in first drafts because it might inhibit word choice and flow of thought. You will also discover that the various authors of these chapters often recommend peer-editing and that there must be direction provided for such editing.

These suggestions are consistent with the findings of a series of research studies on proofreading for spelling conducted by graduate students under my direction both at the University of Texas and the University of Wisconsin—Madison.[1]

These studies were based on the proposition that, although we often admonish students to proofread for spelling, we seldom provide any instruction in how to do so. With this assumption in mind, Knight developed a 3-week program to provide such instruction. Knight's program was used with certain modifications by the three researchers who followed him.

Knight's findings, supported by continuing studies at other sites and grade levels, were that (1) students made fewer spelling errors in compositions; (2) students used a larger number of different words (a wider variety of word choice), and (3) students wrote a greater number of words after completing the instructional program.

Space does not permit replication in this chapter of all of the lessons contained in the program. However, a brief description, emphasizing the most pertinent factors, follows:

1. *Motivation* to want to proofread for spelling was developed by each researcher using devices that suited the situation. These were either films or actual letters that were examined and discussed. In addition, each student was instructed to write "Proofread for Spelling" and sign each paper before it was turned in.
2. *Proofreading technique* was taught by instructing children to underline any word they wanted to use but were uncertain of the spelling. This made it easier for children to check with a dictionary later; however, they were told not to limit

[1]Descriptions of these programs can be found in Personke and Knight, Proofreading and Spelling: A Report and a Program, *Elementary English,* 1967, *44,* 768–784; Personke and Yee, *Comprehensive Spelling Instruction: Theory, Research, and Application.* Scranton, PA: INTEXT, 1971; and Kean and Personke, *The Language Arts: Teaching and Learning in the Elementary School.* New York: St. Martins Press, 1976.

their proofreading to only the underlined words. For experimental reasons, this checking was conducted as self-editing. We would suggest that you include peer-editing as part of your instructional plan.

3. *The Best Alternate Choice* was taught as a specific dictionary technique children could use for checking spelling. With this method, children are provided with a copy of the "Common Spellings of English Chart" (Figure 7-1), which is also posted on a bulletin board or chart rack in poster size. You should note that it is important that each child have a dictionary during all instructional periods.

   Using this chart, the child first looks for the most likely way that the word in question might begin, and then looks for it in the dictionary. If this search does not provide the word, an alternate choice is taken from the chart and looked up in the dictionary. The child makes successive alternate choices until the desired word is discovered (usually this takes only one or two attempts).

Instruction during the 3-week period progresses from students checking words on lists distributed by the teacher, to checking words on short paragraphs distributed or dictated by the teacher, to checking for misspellings on their own compositions. These three modes are used in list, paragraph, and composition order three different times at increasing levels of difficulty during the instructional period.

In each study, the researchers suggested that this instruction be conducted during the regularly assigned spelling period, in lieu of the "normal" spelling instruction. They also suggested that the teacher remind students of these techniques, usually by referring to a chart that lists the steps in proofreading, during each written composition period subsequent to the instruction.

You can devise your own set of instructional plans, suitable to the age of your children, by following these descriptions. They have been proven effective in transferring accurate spelling from the formal spelling period to the written composition, which is the only place where spelling matters!

Remember, the reasons for this success are based on some very sound principles clearly stated in the Personke/Yee Model:

1. Motivation or attitudes toward spelling accuracy are developed.
2. A step-by-step method to follow is provided.
3. A specific technique for dictionary use is learned.
4. "Spelling conscience" is maintained at a high level by the signing of papers and provision of time and materials (chart and dictionaries) to conduct the actual proofreading.

## SUMMARY

Although it may be true, and is certainly argued, that we put undue emphasis on good spelling in our culture, the fact is that formal spelling instruction remains as a discrete subject in the elementary schools in most districts. Your problem as a teacher is to take this usually remote, often frustrating, and generally bland topic and make it fun, interesting, and exciting. You must

**FIGURE 7-1 Common Spellings of English Chart**

| SYMBOL | SPELLINGS | EXAMPLES |
|---|---|---|
| a | a, ai, al, au | at, plaid, half, laugh |
| a | a, ai, ao, au, ay | age, aid, gaol, gauge, say |
| | e, ea, eigh, et | suede, break, eight, bouquet |
| | ei, ey | vein, they |
| a | a, ae, ai, ay | care, aerial, air, prayer |
| | e, ea, ei, hei | where, pear, their, heir |
| a | a, ah, al, e | father, ah, calm, sergeant |
| | ea | heart |
| b | b, bb | bad, rabbit |
| ch | ch, che, t, tch | child, niche, future, watch |
| | te, ti | righteous, question |
| d | d, dd, ed | did, add, filled |
| e | a, ai, ay, e, ea | any, said, says, end, bread |
| | ei, eo, ie, u | heifer, leopard, friend, bury |
| e | ay, e, ea, ee, ei | quay, equal, eat, eel, receive |
| | eo, ey, i, ie | people, key, machine, believe |
| | is, oe, y | debris, phoebe, city |
| er | ea, er, err, ir | earth, stern, err, first |
| | irr, olo, our | whirr, colonel, journey |
| | or, ur, urr, yr | word, urge, purr, myrtle |
| f | f, ff, gh, ph | fat, effort, laugh, phrase |
| g | g, gg, gh, gu | go, egg, ghost, guest |
| | gue | catalogue |
| h | h, wh | he, who |
| hw | wh | wheat |
| i | e, ea, ee, ei | England, near, been, weird |
| | i, ie, o, u | it, sieve, women, busy |
| | ui, y | build, myth |
| i | ai, ais, ay, ei | Hawaii, aisle, bayou, eider |
| | eigh, eye, i, ie, | height, eye, ice, lie, high |
| | igh, is, uy, y, ye | island, buy, sky, rye |
| j | d, dg, dge | gradual, judgment, bridge |
| | di, g, gg | soldier, gem, exaggerate |
| | gi, j, ge | allegiance, jam, large |
| k | c, cc, ch | coat, account, chemistry |
| | che, ck, cq, cu | ache, back, acquire, biscuit |
| | k, q, qu, que | kind, quit, liquor, pique |
| l | l, ll | land, tell |
| m | gm, m, mb, mm | diaphragm, me, climb, common |
| | mn | solemn |
| n | gn, kn, n | gnaw, knife, no |
| | nn, pn | manner, pneumonia |
| ng | n, nd, ng, ngue | ink, handerkerchief, long, tongue |
| o | a, ach, ho, o | watch, yacht, honest, odd |
| o | au, eau, eo, ew | chauffeur, beau, yeoman, sew |

*(continued)*

**FIGURE 7-1 *Continued***

| SYMBOL | SPELLINGS | EXAMPLES |
|---|---|---|
| | o, oa, oe, oh, ol | open, oak, toe, oh, folk |
| | oo, ou, ough, ow | brooch, soul, though, own |
| o | a, ah, al, au | all, Utah, walk, author |
| o | augh, aw, o, oa | taught, awful, order, broad |
| | ou, ough | cough, bought |
| oi | oi, oy | oil, boy |
| ou | hou, ou, ough, ow | hour, out, bough, owl |
| p | p, pp | pay, happy |
| r | r, rh, rr, wr | run, rhyme, carry, wrong |
| s | c, ce, ps | cent, nice, psalm |
| | s, sc, ss | say, scent, miss |
| sh | ce, ch, che | ocean, machine, cache |
| | ci, psh, s, ch | special, pshaw, sure, schwa |
| | sci, se, sh | conscience, nausea, she |
| | si, ss, ssi, ti | tension, issue, mission, nation |
| t | bt, ed, pt | doubt, stopped, ptomaine |
| | t, th, tt | tell, Thomas, button |
| th | th | thin |
| th | the, th | breathe, then |
| u | eau, eu, eue | beauty, feud, queue |
| | ew, iew, u, ue | few, view, use, cue |
| | yew, you, yu | yew, you, yule |
| u | o, oo, oul, u | wolf, good, should, full |
| u | eu, ew, ieu | maneuver, threw, lieutenant |
| | o, oe, oo, ou | move, shoe, food, soup |
| | ough, u, ue | through, rule, blue |
| | ui, wo | fruit, two |
| v | f, ph, v, ve | of, Stephen, very, have |
| u | o, oe, oo | son, does, flood |
| | ou, u | trouble, up |
| w | o, u, w | choir, quick, will |
| y | i, j, y | opinion, hallelujah, yes |
| z | cz, s, sc, ss | czar, has, discern, scissors |
| | x, z, zz | xylophone, zero, buzz |
| zh | ge, s, si | garage, measure, division |
| | z | azure |
| | a, ah, ai | alone, rajah, bargain |
| | e, ea, eo | moment, pageant, dungeon |
| | i, o, oi | April, complete, tortoise |
| | ou, u | cautious, circus |

[a]Diacritical marks do not appear on this chart because they vary by dictionary. Fill in your own from the dictionary in your classroom.

provide a way to integrate it with other aspects of the language arts and with other curricular areas. A good spelling program can be a good vocabulary program and can provide an additional mode of instruction to accompany methods that are suggested in Chapter 10.

## *REFERENCES*

HORN, T.D. (1947). The effect of the corrected test on learning to spell. *Elementary School Journal, 47,* 277.

KEAN, J.M., & PERSONKE, C.R. (1976). *The language arts: Teaching and learning in the elementary school.* New York: St. Martin's Press.

PERSONKE, C., & KNIGHT, L. (1967). Proofreading and spelling: A report and a program. *Elementary English, 44,* 768–784.

PERSONKE, C., & YEE, A.H. (1966). A model for the analysis of spelling behavior. *Elementary English, 43,* 278–284.

PERSONKE, C., & YEE, A.H. (1971). *Comprehensive spelling instruction: Theory, research, and application.* Scranton, PA: International Textbook Co.

## *SUGGESTED READINGS*

KEAN, J.M., & PERSONKE, C. (1976). *The language arts: Teaching and learning in the elementary school.* New York: St. Martin's Press. The spelling chapter in this book, already referred to in this chapter, contains very useful lists of phoneme-grapheme correspondencies, derivational morphemes, and common phonograms of English.

MCELWEE, G.W. (1974). *Systematic instruction in proofreading for spelling and its effects on fourth and sixth grade composition.* Unpublished doctoral dissertation, University of Wisconsin at Madison. Although doctoral theses are sometimes hard to obtain, they are available for purchase through University Microfilms, Ann Arbor, Michigan. This thesis has complete copies of the proofreading lessons described in this chapter.

SMITH, R.W.L. *The wordsmith: Intermediate grade language arts.* This public television program may be available on your local PBS station. Although not a spelling program, it nonetheless supplies a great deal of etymological information you might use. Teacher's manuals are available from the Agency for Instruction T.V., Box A. Bloomington, IN 47401.

VENEZKY, R.L. (1970). *The structure of English orthography.* The Hague: Mouton. This is a very exhaustive, yet readable, examination of the phoneme-grapheme relationships of English. A shorter version is available in: "English orthography: Its graphical structure and its relation to sound," *Reading Research Quarterly* (Spring, 1967), 75–105.

# EIGHT
# HANDWRITING AS A LANGUAGE ART

Although language and speech have enabled people to share thoughts, ideas, and recollections, to tell of happenings and situations, and to narrate stories, it was the invention of writing that allowed knowledge concerning the life of people to be communicated even after the lapse of thousands of years (Fairbank, 1970). Today, people continue to use writing for sharing thoughts and ideas, for expressing feelings and emotions, and for keeping records. In context, writing continues to serve as a fundamental means of historical communication.

As a tool of communication, *handwriting* is a means of encoding and sharing thoughts, the emphasis being upon what is written. In handwriting, or penmanship instruction, the focus of attention is on how the message is written, the main concern being legibility and efficient production of graphic symbols. The primary goal in teaching penmanship is to produce efficiently a free flow of ideas or thoughts onto paper with a minimum of attention to mechanics. The purpose of this chapter is to suggest concrete instructional procedures that are practical and educationally sound for developing children's skills in handwriting.

Handwriting, as a perceptual motor activity, requires a high degree of fine-motor coordination (Herrick, 1963), especially coordination of eye and hand movements (Frostig, Miller, and Horne, 1966). Therefore, your children, especially pre- and beginning writers, should participate in exercises that develop their eye-hand coordination. Such development may occur as you use either a direct or incidental approach to instruction.

By general educational definition, *direct instruction* is a form of teaching in which the lesson objective is projected into the experience provided for the learner. Direct instruction presents sequenced specific learning experiences in a formal schedule with definite time allocations for specific skill activities. Instructors using the direct teaching approach depend upon objective evaluation of pupil progress to plan for continued instruction in the sequence of the curriculum. *Incidental instruction* is a form of teaching with purpose arising from experiences rather than specifically planned from a scope and sequence chart. Incidental instruction integrates learning experiences based on the interests and needs of the participants and allows practice through informally scheduled large blocks of time. When you use the incidental approach you generally present the skill to be developed embedded in interdisciplinary experiences and depend upon subjective evaluation of pupil progress through the experiences.

The following activities provide samples of exercises that directly or incidentally help children develop eye-hand coordination for better handwriting. The lists are composed of activities typically presented in pre- and beginning writing programs and in many school handwriting curriculum guides.

## ACTIVITY SUGGESTIONS FOR DIRECT INSTRUCTION OF EYE-HAND COORDINATION

Fairchild (1979), adapting Canadian handwriting curriculum (Kinney, 1964), proposed activities such as those that follow for teachers endorsing direct instructional strategies:

1. Flying on the Ground: While the child is lying on his or her back on a carpeted floor, for two minutes at each exercise, the child will
   a. move the arms from the sides of the body to over the head while keeping the movement close to the floor.
   b. practice moving the legs together and apart, keeping the movement close to the floor.
   c. move the arms from the sides of the body to over the head while simultaneously moving the legs together and apart.
   d. move only his or her right arm and right leg in the practiced motion.
   e. move only his or her left arm and left leg in the practiced motion.
2. Balloon Patterning: While the child is standing without touching other children, for two minutes at each exercise, he or she will
   a. use either hand to continuously bat a balloon into the air.
   b. use only the dominant hand to bat a balloon into the air.
   c. use only the subdominant hand to bat a balloon into the air.
   d. alternately use the right and left hands to bat a balloon into the air.
   e. bat a balloon into the air five times with the right hand, then five times with the left hand, and continuously on the pattern of alternating hands.
3. Target Toss: While the child is standing four feet from a target "X" on the chalkboard, as often as comfortably possible in two minutes, he or she will
   a. toss a beanbag at the target, retrieve it, and toss it again.

b. use only the subdominant hand to toss a beanbag at the target, retrieve it, and toss it again.
c. use three beanbags and three targets in a row to toss one bag at each target beginning with the leftmost target and moving to the right.
d. use one ball and three targets in a row to toss the ball at each target, beginning with the leftmost target and moving to the right.

Using the exercises similar to those listed above, construct lessons appropriate to the individual's physique, character, personality, age, mental ability, and perceptual maturity. In addition, because beginning writing experiences involve use of the finer muscles, they need to be of a simple nature and of short duration, gradually increasing in difficulty and length as the individual approaches neuromuscular maturity (Page, 1964).

## ACTIVITY SUGGESTIONS FOR INCIDENTAL DEVELOPMENT OF EYE-HAND COORDINATION

Children's manipulations of typical play materials and art activities, which are reflected in the following ideas, are proposed for teachers endorsing incidental strategies.

1. Shaving Cream and Powdered Tempera (finger painting)
   Purpose: to explore making designs with fingers stroked in varying substances
   Procedure: Encourage children to finger-paint on colored paper to which shaving cream has been applied. The shaving cream may be colored by adding powdered paint. Purchasing a cream with mint or another scent provides an olfactory experience for children.
2. Torn Paper (collage making)
   Purpose: to give children opportunity to express creatively with tearing
   Procedure: Lead children to tear various sizes and types of available paper and glue them to a mounting sheet in any design. Allow picture construction and free design.
3. Junk Sculpture (sculpting)
   Purpose: to explore sculpting with junk materials collected from the children's environments
   Procedure: Allow children to explore making creations by arranging "junk" materials into free or structured forms. By gluing the objects together, junk sculpture is created. Try similar exercises with pieces of sponges or wood.
4. Sawdust and Wheat Paste (modeling)
   Purpose: to give children the opportunity to use the medium of sawdust and wheat paste to create and express
   Procedure: Add just enough water to moisten sifted sawdust. Sprinkle in wheat paste to thicken. Knead with hand until the mixture can be molded like clay. Squeeze out excess water. Allow children to model freely with the mixture. If left to dry for several days the modeled pieces may be painted and decorated with items glued to the model. Pup-

pet heads, baskets, pencil holders, or similar items can be molded for use in school or as gifts. Let the children create whatever they choose whether it is recognizable to you or not.

5. Glass Monoprints (printing)
   Purpose: to explore printing with paper pressed on liquid designs
   Procedure: Allow children to apply paint with any tool to the surface of a glass square or mirror. While the paint is still wet, carefully press paper on the painting. Different amounts of pressure will give different results. Carefully peel the paper from the glass or mirror and examine the project. Pressed prints may be used again to add printing of another color or design. Let your children decide what arrangements they want to explore.
6. Chalk in Water on Dry Paper (drawing)
   Purpose: to create with chalk dipped in water
   Procedure: Allow children to draw with chalk. Suggest, by giving each child a small pan of water, that he or she experiment with dipping the chalk in water before stroking it on the paper. Other liquid substances may be substituted for water to examine their effects. Buttermilk and condensed milk have interesting effects on the chalk. White chalk is fun to dip in liquid paints as a substitute paintbrush.
7. Creamy, Chalky, Shiny Paints (painting)
   Purpose: to explore painting with substances of varying textures
   Procedure: Allow children to paint pictures or free designs using paints provided. Make available three containers of paint, each the same color. To produce creamy paint, mix powdered paint with liquid laundry starch. Provide a chalky painting experience by mixing buttermilk with powdered paint. Use condensed milk with powdered paint instead of water to make shiny paint. The use of only one color encourages the children to focus on the paint gloss rather than the color.
8. Meat Plate Design Stitchery (sewing)
   Purpose: to give children the opportunity to explore stitchery as a means of expression while getting acquainted with the medium
   Procedure: Allow children to sketch a simple design on styrofoam meat trays. Poke holes about one inch apart along the design drawn. Instruct the children to stitch along their drawing by sewing through the holes with yarn of any color selected.

## THE COMPONENTS OF HANDWRITING

At some point in children's development it becomes necessary to prepare them for actual letter and numeral formation through experiences aimed at introducing the components of handwriting. A program exposing children to basic handwriting strokes, to letter formation, size, and proportion, and to spacing, alignment, and line quality should foster growth in readiness for the more formal handwriting programs of elementary schools. Children may be directly introduced to the components of handwriting or incidentally meet them through manipulation of typical early childhood materials.

When using didactic instructional strategies, your children should practice basic handwriting strokes in the following sequence as you draw their attention to size, proportion, spacing, and alignment.

1. Basic chalkboard practice with circular and straight lines
2. Vertical strokes on upright surfaces
3. Horizontal strokes on upright surfaces
4. Diagonal strokes on upright surfaces
5. Circular strokes on upright surfaces
6. Basic strokes practiced on horizontally positioned surfaces

If children are given time, space, and materials to draw, color, and "write," they will incidentally practice basic handwriting strokes and will move easily into experimenting with combinations of the lines. Such experimentation indicates a beginning awareness that print conveys a message, that talk can be written down, and that "writing" can only be read by others when it somewhat resembles the adult sign-symbol system. Recently, the work of Marie Clay (1975) suggested that such experimentation initiated by the child who is, therefore, personally involved is a valuable teaching/learning technique for learning to write. Through such self-motivated exercises, children personally develop concepts of size, proportion, spacing, and alignment. Your responsibility is to provide an environment conducive to experimentation with handwriting.

## FORMAL HANDWRITING INSTRUCTION

Once children are assessed as ready, they enter a program of handwriting instruction through participation in teaching-lessons and practice-lessons. In teaching-lessons they meet new material and develop skill in using the material through practice-lessons. The cycle of teaching, practice, diagnosis, teaching, practice, and so on represents the basic elementary school handwriting program typical of language arts classes.

Instructional strategies appropriate for teaching handwriting are varied. Some programs traditionally used include discussion, drill and practice, performance-based learning packages, laboratory approach, learning centers, and independent study plans. Regardless of the instructional strategy used, effective lessons are developed around the following considerations about instruction and practice.

### CONSIDERATIONS ABOUT INSTRUCTION AND PRACTICE

1. Knowing the purpose for an activity tends to affect positively the performers' participation (Powell, 1976).
2. Visual demonstrations by teachers or other children serve adequately to help children see specifically what is to be practiced (Cratty, 1969).

3. Children who can verbalize a task before performing it show greater improvements in acquisition (Livesey & Little, 1971; Lombard & Stern, 1969).
4. The number and the spacing of practice sessions are important in skill acquisition. Adequate rest and mass, but distributed, practice are beneficial.
5. Analyzing the motor task to be practiced in order to identify small, teachable steps permits children to master parts of the activity prior to execution of the whole movement after they have explored its wholeness.
6. Reinforcement encourages continued practice, especially for children who are not intrinsically motivated in these psychomotor areas.
7. Giving children knowledge of the results of their practice is generally recognized as contributing to enhancing instruction. Teach them how to evaluate their own progress.

### GENERAL MANUSCRIPT AND/OR CURSIVE SUGGESTIONS AND ACTIVITIES

1. Surround students with models of good writing.
2. Teach correct pencil-hold position; if position is already formed, allow it and make recommendations if you diagnose that the position interferes with writing.
3. When presenting instruction, group letters into families of distinctive features.
4. Provide a variety of writing tools and surfaces—chalk on sidewalks, water on chalkboards, pens, felt markers, lined and unlined papers of various colors, and so forth.
5. Provide practice that uses letters in context after the basic formation has been studied.
6. Teach handwriting through instruction in all learning modes; use a multisensory stimulation approach.
7. Expect good writing outside the handwriting class—making signs and labels for projects; doing crossword puzzles; writing posters, letters, and reports, etc.
8. Do not use handwriting as discipline.
9. When beginning cursive instruction, be sure children can read cursive writing.
10. Be consistent with letter-formation instruction in class and in next grade.
11. To develop awareness of individual strokes or letters, use pictures that stimulate the image.
12. Make practice enjoyable.
13. Help children write individual letters on paper and draw the letter into a picture.
14. Help children find basic letter-formation strokes or letters in the environment; when possible, fasten cutout paper letters on those real objects.
15. Have children write in cursive and color the closed spaces or just outside of those spaces.
16. Have children hold a small square mirror to their writing to explore reverse images.
17. Have children do "skywriting"—moving the hand in the air to form letters or words.
18. Brainstorm lists of words with particular patterns such as double *t* or double *l* words (better, dolly, etc.) or any letter pattern you want to explore; practice writing those words.
19. Have children plan practice assignments for their peers, possibly on problems they themselves have been having in writing.

20. Practice through writing concrete poetry, limericks, puns, riddles, or other interesting forms of literature.
21. Help children write words that can become a picture where the picture demonstrates the meaning of the word.
22. Give children practice words with letters omitted that they will insert; see how many words they can find that fit the pattern; choose words containing practice on letter forms they need.
23. Allow children to correct and/or redo writings with obvious errors you present.
24. Have children create nonsense words and meanings to be written correctly.
25. Give practice with particular groups of words such as homonyms and antonyms.
26. Present a letter challenge of the day posted on the chalkboard or in a special enrichment corner.
27. Have children write and execute fingerplays; both the writing and the doing will be helpful for their coordination.
28. Have children research the history of handwriting, then write about the future of handwriting.
29. Allow children to create other symbol-code systems and communicate using them; these too are forms of writing.

## SUMMARY

With careful instruction, guidance, and practice that are both meaningful and enjoyable, children can develop, improve, and use effective, legible handwriting as a tool of communication.

### *REFERENCES*

Clay, M.M. (1975). *What did I write?* Portsmouth, NH: Heinemann.

Cratty, B.J. (1969). *Movement, perception and thought.* Palo Alto, CA: Peek Publications.

Fairbank, A. (1970). *The story of handwriting.* New York: Watson-Guptill.

Fairchild, S. (1979). *The effects of sequenced eye-hand coordination experiences on the young child's ability to reproduce printed symbols.* Unpublished doctoral dissertation, The Pennsylvania State University, University Park, PA.

Frostig, M., Miller, A.M., & Horne, D. (1966). *Developmental program in visual perception.* Chicago: Follett.

Herrick, V.E. (1963). *New horizons for research in handwriting.* Madison: University of Wisconsin Press.

Kinney, M.C. (1964). *Teaching handwriting—A teacher's guide to developing skills in handwriting.* Regina, Saskatchewan: School Aids and Text Book.

Livesey, P.J., & Little, A. (1971). Sequential learning by children. *Journal of Genetic Psychology, 118,* 33–38.

Lombard, A., & Stern, C. (1969). Effect of verbalization on young children's learning of a manipulative skill. *Research in Education* (ERIC Document Reproduction Service No. ED 035 447).

Page, S.M. (1964). What's involved in getting ready to write? *The Instructor, 74,* 44–74.

Powell, M. (1976). What research tells the practitioner about skill acquisition (ERIC Document Reproduction No. ED 124 531).

## *SUGGESTED READINGS*

BARBE, W.B., LUCAS, V.A., & WASYLYK, T.M. (1984). *Handwriting: Basic skills for effective communication.* Columbus, OH: Zaner-Bloser. This book deals with the issues facing the teacher of handwriting: the role of manuscript writing; when to make transition to cursive; integrating handwriting into the language arts curriculum; evaluating writing; and adapting handwriting instruction for students with special needs. A review of significant research on handwriting from the past 50 years is included. The articles in this text are intended to give teachers and teachers-in-training an insight into the status of handwriting in the modern curriculum.

GETMAN, G.N. (1983). About handwriting. *Academic Therapy, 19,* 139–146. Children need the opportunity to learn the motor patterns involved in handwriting; thus, Getman describes a sequence of chalkboard activities to promote these necessary skills.

GREGORY, A. (1982). Handwriting instruction and art education in early grades. *Art Education, 35,* 42–45. Art educators can reinforce handwriting skills in classroom art activities. Gregory suggests why and how.

YAWKEY, T.D., ASKOV, E.N., CARTWRIGHT, C.A., DUPUIS, M.M., FAIRCHILD, S.H., & YAWKEY, M.L. (1981) *Language arts and the young child,* pp. 146–180. Itasca, IL: F.E. Peacock Publishers. This chapter of a language arts methods and activities textbook for pre- and in-service teachers of young children focuses on instructional strategies, including teaching handwriting vocabulary, evaluation of handwriting skills, and explanation of the development of writing as a process.

# NINE
# SPEAKING AND WRITING ABOUT VISUALS IN THE LANGUAGE ARTS

Visual images are everywhere. Over 80 percent of the information we process comes through our eyes (Debes & Williams, 1974). Visual messages become important early in life. Before young children learn to interpret print messages by reading, they learn to interpret visual messages by looking.

Therefore, it is logical to link visual and print messages as young children learn to write. Useful composing experiences can be based on the process of moving from visuals to words. Among the types of experiences teachers can provide are:

1. Adding words to wordless picture books.
2. Writing about artist's paintings.
3. Writing story lines from films.
4. Comparing variant editions of the same story.
5. Making statements of preference.

## WORDLESS PICTURE BOOKS

Many experts have recommended having children dictate or write a story line depicted in the sequential pictures in wordless books (Herman, 1976). The built-in story structure provided is helpful, especially to young writers just beginning to develop some intuitive grasp of how stories are made. Providing the picture structure allows ample opportunity for imagination, yet it gives beginning writers an organizational framework within which to write.

A second-grade teacher used *Time to Get Out of the Bath, Shirley* (Burningham, 1978). The book, not technically wordless, features a minimal story line on left-hand pages, while on the right-hand pages, Shirley embarks on a fantasy journey.

The teacher read the book to children, who then translated the pictures into words. One of the students, Lindsay, dictated:

> Shirley went down the pipe and she's going into the bricks. The wood is holding the tub up. The soap seems like it is slippery. There's a box under this part, right here.
>
> She came out into the swamp through the pipe. There's a horse under the tree. She came out of the brick wall into a greenish kind of river.
>
> It's in the afternoon. Shirley jumped off the duck and hung onto the tree, or else she would have gone down the waterfall. The duck went down the waterfall. People are riding on horses. There's a king on one of the horses.
>
> There's three witches, and Shirley is riding on the horse with the man. And it's night and the moon is out. There's an owl on the tree.
>
> Now it's morning. The trees are full of leaves. There are two flags. One man is holding them. There's a princess with the prince. They're having a race.
>
> They're going to jump. They're on the castle. Shirley's duck is down in the river. There are two cows near the duck. The green clouds are out. The sun is out.
>
> The people are blowing balloons, and the balloons are ducks. The princess and the king are blowing them up.
>
> The king is on the duck with the punching glove on a stick. His shoes are in the water. There's a person over on the castle stairs catching fish. There are lily pads. The princess is about to punch Shirley.
>
> Shirley punched the princess off her duck into the river. The frogs are swimming, trying to get away from the princess and Shirley.
>
> Shirley punched the king off the duck headfirst. And Shirley is still on her duck.
>
> Shirley was dreaming.

The teacher takes down the child's oral language, encoding more sophisticated vocabulary and syntax than Lindsay herself would be able to enscribe in print. The story shows some admirable language use:

specificity: ". . . under this part, right here."
causality: ". . . or else she would . . ."
temporality: "Now it's morning."
variety: sentences vary from 3 to 19 words.

In this, as in other activities suggested later, the teacher encodes, sometimes pausing to comment upon one of the enscribing conventions, while a child, or the group, sees oral language being converted into print. Later the language can be read aloud (reconverted into sound), making a conscious link between oral and written forms.

Single pictures present a more sophisticated visual and language challenge. Instead of a sequence, the child, confronted with a single visual, must extend the action backward or forward in time, inventing plot and detail to make a complete unit only suggested by the illustration.

## COMPOSING FROM PAINTINGS

Children can write about artists' paintings; large reproductions are available at reasonable cost. Share a reproduction with children, encouraging them to tell what they see, responding positively or negatively to the painting. Following this group oral-language experience, children choose a painting they like and make up a story about it.

In one second-grade classroom, the teacher introduced "Girl With a Watering Can" by Renoir, and children responded orally. The picture itself is a placid, realistic presentation of a young girl dressed rather formally. After initial discussion, the class dictated this group story:

> Once there was a little girl. Her name was Carol. She had blond hair. She was impossible! She sticks out her tongue at her mom! She's always running away from home! She hits her dad! She hates her mom!
>
> One day she bought a red ribbon and she tried to strangle somebody. And somebody tried to strangle her back.
>
> That didn't kill her so she bought a present for her grandmother. It was a pop-up snake in a box, and it scared her grandmother out of her wits. Then the little girl went home and cried. Then she got punished.
>
> That's why she's impossible.

We adults might not see the active, indeed aggressive, events in such a calm painting. Nonetheless, these students clearly understood (albeit unconsciously) the way a single picture can become a departure point for a generated fiction story.

In another classroom, Brenda dictated to her teacher the following about a Picasso painting, "Two Acrobats with a Dog":

> There is a girl and a boy and a dog and they are gymnastic people. They are going to gym. Their house is in back of them; there are trees by it. The boy's name is Larry and the girl's name is Brenda. The doggy's name is Dusty and he is a cocker spaniel. It is winter out and she has bare feet. Brenda has a blue leotard and blue tights and Larry's got all different color tights and all different color sleeves and a blue leotard. He has a sack over his back and she is petting the doggy. In the bag there are hers and his tap-dancing shoes, dog biscuits, milk in case they get thirsty, and a blanket. He has a key in his hand to open up the gymnastic place. Doggy's wagging his tail. The girl has brown hair and the boy has blackish-brownish hair. They are standing and in a while they'll be walking. After they go to the gymnastic place they will go home. They will lock the gym-

> nastic place and unlock their house door. Then, they will take the dog in and wipe off its feet because it's all dirty and muddy.
>
> Thank you for reading my story.

Notice how skillfully Brenda uses the painting as a departure point. Starting from this single, static moment, she develops an entire plot, rich with small, significant detail.

"The Country School" is by the American genre painter, Winslow Homer. Homer worked early in his career as a magazine illustrator, which affected the strongly realistic character of his later work. About this painting, second-grader Lori wrote:

> Once upon a time there was a little schoolhouse. There were only 12 kids not including the teacher. I think that it is reading time because everybody is reading. I bet they have a super time at recess time because it's so beautiful. I think a little boy is crying because he can't pronounce a word. The teacher saw someone doing something wrong and is giving him a hard stare. Someone brought the teacher flowers today. Perhaps it was her secret admirer.

Lori's story clearly shows how students can be led to make writers' inferences about a painting, in the process creating a vividly detailed story.

## COMPOSITION FROM FILMS

A more difficult task is writing a story line from a film. The structure is provided by the sequence of visual images, which cannot be varied. What makes the task difficult is the transitory nature of the images. Because of this, such film dictation should occur after children have had several opportunities to write about still pictures.

To motivate first graders, we used an animated version of Hans Christian Andersen's story "Thumbelina" (Coronet Films). The teacher showed the film, telling her children before viewing that later they would retell the story in their own words. Showing the film with the sound turned off encouraged students to focus on the task: encoding in their own words the film's visual images. Children talked about the film and then viewed it a second time to make sure they understood the action. Following this, Aamir dictated:

> Once upon a time there was a girl named Thumbelina. First she put her feet in the water. Then this frog came. He was trying to eat her. Thumbelina ran. She jumped in a clam. Then the frog got the clam. He went under the sea. Thumbelina got out of the clam and then she called a fish. She said, "You push me," and the fish said, "Yes." Thumbelina said, "Thank you." She was far away, and then the frog came. He was wondering where she was. Thumbelina was floating. A bee picked her up. The other bees were laughing at her. The bee was mad. He said, "Stop that," and the bees laughed. So the other bee pushed her off the leaf.

> Thumbelina landed on a spider web. She thought it was a swing. The spider saw it, and he cut the spider web. Thumbelina landed on a flower that had some white things that were flying. Then she caught one and she was flying. She dropped it, and landed in a flower. The flower closed. Thumbelina was safe, but then there was a big wind. The leaves were flying off, and Thumbelina fell down.
>
> She went near to this cave, and she was knocking on this other flower to open, but it wouldn't open. This mother beaver took Thumbelina in her cave, and showed her around. And then she showed her to a bird. Thumbelina wanted to go to the bird, but the mother beaver said, "Don't care about him." Then they went downstairs.
>
> Thumbelina and mother beaver were cleaning up, and mother beaver fell asleep. Thumbelina went upstairs. She was looking at the bird and petting him. Father beaver came and wanted some tea. He said, "Where's my tea?" Mother beaver said, "Thumbelina, come here." She came downstairs. She was frightened of the father beaver, so she went upstairs to the bird. Then father beaver came, and he was going to get Thumbelina, so the bird flew away with Thumbelina.

Notice that Aamir's story is coherent, able to stand independently from the film that inspired it.

In Rachel's retelling, details are different. Nonetheless, the film's sequence enabled her to recreate the story accurately, yet with imagination.

> The bird was singing, "Tweet, tweet." The little girl was in a flower, and then a bee came to knock at the flower. The girl opened the flower, but the bee did not like her. Then the bee went away.
>
> Thumbelina went to a pond. She went splash with her legs. A green frog came out of the pond and he wanted to eat her. She ran away but the frog got her. She was hiding in a nut shell. The frog took the nut shell with her in it. He put it on a green leaf. She wanted to get off the green leaf.
>
> A fish came and blew her back to the dry land. Then a bug took her. But the bugs did not like her very much. The king or queen, whichever (I don't know) threw her down on the spider web, and then she got into big trouble.
>
> She went to a mouse hole. She rang the bell. The mother mouse took her into her house. She went to sleep. The next morning, the mother said, "Clean up this room." She looked at mother mouse and said, "Is that it?" "Yes, go on." The mother was doing a little dress for her. The mother was real tired. The mother opened her eyes and then closed her eyes. She went to sleep.
>
> The little girl saw her sleeping. She went upstairs. That was the sleeping bird. The mother said, "That's nothing—just a bird that always sleeps." But it wasn't, and when the mother got to sleep, the girl went upstairs to the bird. She petted the bird.
>
> When the father got home she came down, because she was scared of him. The mother and father ran after her. The girl was under the bird's wing, and then the bird flew back out. The bird let her out on a flower, and the little girl took the flower with two hands. She flew back to her own flower. The bird was on her tree, and she was singing "Tweet, tweet" again.

In the preceding examples, details are different. Each child fleshed out the plot skeleton with imaginative language different from that of other children. Yet the organizing framework gave structure to the dictation, resulting in a coherent story that makes sense out of context. The stories would make more sense if we read them while also viewing the film, but they are independent enough to stand alone as literary retellings.

## VARIATIONS

A more sophisticated skill is comparing variations of the same story (Stewig, 1978). Many folk tales are available in different editions, varying in language, plot structure, or in the accompanying illustrations. It is easy to locate a pair of books, share them with children, and encourage students to point out likenesses and differences.

One first-grade teacher used two variants of an old tale. *The Five Chinese Brothers,* with illustrations by Kurt Weise, is well-known (Bishop, 1938). Less familiar is *Six Chinese Brothers,* illustrated with scissor cuts (Hou-tien, 1979). The teacher read the first book one day and encouraged students to react. The following day she read the Hou-tien version, and again the class discussed the book. Then they drew up a list of comparisons, including:

The books are the *same*
- both were about brothers who had talents
- both begged to say good-bye
- in both, someone tried to kill the sons
- no names in either story
- both tried to chop off the heads

The books are *different*
- brothers had different powers in each story
- one had a mother, the other had a father
- one had skin so hard, steel bounced off, and the other had an iron neck
- their clothes were different
- they had different ways of asking to go home and to say "good-bye"

The lists represent impressive observation skills by children who had never before participated in such a comparing/contrasting experience. Such activities lay needed groundwork for high-level thinking and responding skills.

## MAKING CHOICES

Making preference statements involves going beyond simply noting likenesses and differences, to more sophisticated expression of reasons for liking one of the books or films. Second graders, after seeing both books, gave reasons for their choices:

> I liked *The Five Chinese Brothers* because it had funny pictures like when the third brother got thrown off the boat. The powers were gooder because the legs could stretch farther. I like the boats better because the boats were not fancy. (by Ian)

Among responses to the *Six Chinese Brothers* was:

> My favorite book was *The Six Chinese Brothers* because I liked the pictures. It was exciting and thrilling. It was sad and happy. I liked it because they are smaller and I like small people. I was sad because the King wanted to kill the first brother. It was exciting because when the doctors said, "You will have to get the King's pearl and boil it in water." That was exciting because I've never heard of that cure. (by Lori)

## FILM PREFERENCES

Children can also express preferences about films. Many traditional tales are available in more than one version. By careful advanced scheduling, teachers can secure a pair of films in contrasting style to show children, who can choose their favorite and write a reason.

Third graders saw two versions of "Thumbelina." One was the four-color, animated version mentioned earlier. The second was a black-and-white version with silhouettes cut by Lotte Reiniger (Contemporary Films). After seeing each, children wrote about the one they liked best.

Among those who chose the four-color version was this:

> I liked the cartoon version much more than the silhouette version, because the cartoon had a lot more colors. The silhouette was just plain black and white. All my life I liked cartoons more than silhouettes. (by David)

Among the responses from children choosing the silhouette version was:

> I liked the silhouette better because it was pretty hard to make that black and white. Also because there wasn't any noise except the author's voice. In both stories there were likenesses and differences. Anyway, the silhouette was longer. (by Randy)

Of 32 students involved, 17 preferred the four-color, animated version, whereas 15 preferred the black-and-white silhouette film, a more even distribution than the teacher and I had anticipated. Given the pervasive four-color nature of television, we thought fewer children would choose the black-and-white film, but this was not the case.

Children can indeed perform the rather sophisticated task of looking at two films and articulating a preference. Although these primary-age children had never before done this task, their writings were coherent, conscientious responses. Their writing should become even more fluent as they encounter even more opportunities to respond to film. Intermediate-grade children generate even more sophisticated language after they have had several opportunities to work with this sort of composition experience.

## SUMMARY

Visuals can be an effective stimulus to composition. Students of all ages can indeed write fluently about: (1) wordless picture books, (2) artists' paintings, (3) story lines in films, (4) variants in the same story, and (5) their preferences.

These boys and girls responded enthusiastically to the five composing experiences, and the ideas can work equally well with your students. Will you give children an opportunity to try?

### *REFERENCES*

BISHOP, C.H. (1938). *Five Chinese brothers.* New York: Coward, McCann.

BURNINGHAM, J. (1978). *Time to get out of the bath, Shirley.* New York: Thomas Y. Crowell.

DEBES, J.L., & WILLIAMS, C.M. (December, 1974). The power of visuals. *Instructor,* 32–38.

HERMAN, G.B. (1976, July). Books without words: Picture stories bring thought, imagination, delight. *Wisconsin Library Bulletin,* 151–152.

HOU-TIEN, CHENG. (1979). *Six Chinese brothers.* New York: Holt, Rinehart & Winston.

STEWIG, J.W. (1978). Book illustration: Key to visual and verbal literacy. In J.W. Stewig & S. Sebesta (Eds.), *Using literature in the elementary school* (pp. 35–50). Urbana, IL.: National Council of Teachers of English.

# TEN
# DEVELOPING VOCABULARY IN THE LANGUAGE ARTS

For many years researchers have attempted to unravel the complexity of reading comprehension. A primary emphasis of the research has been to isolate the discrete skills that enable readers to comprehend. Davis (1944, 1968), after surveying the literature to determine the skills involved in reading comprehension, performed a factor-analytic study of comprehension skills and found that *word knowledge* is clearly the most important factor in comprehension.

Nevertheless, O'Rourke (1974) concluded that there is no systematic general approach to vocabulary instruction in schools and that no attempt has been made to look at vocabulary development as an integral part of the language system. He suggested that a systematic design for vocabulary instruction across all curriculum areas would result in greater breadth and depth of learning.

O'Rourke also asserted that vocabulary instruction has typically been viewed in a narrow context and taught in an unstructured, incidental, or even accidental manner. He commented that, while teachers are concerned with the mechanics of vocabulary instruction, they do not appear to know why they use a specific teaching technique for helping students learn to use vocabulary meaningfully. O'Rourke explained that this is particularly true for instruction in vocabulary development that is part of a reading lesson from a basal series textbook. Stauffer (1971) pointed out that teachers rely on a very limited repertoire of activities that are presented in the basal manual when they could be creating their own activities or choosing others that might be more useful for some students or more appropriate for certain types of reading.

Recently, attention has been given to an instructional strategy that provides an alternative to many of the traditional activities that are typically included in basal reading series. This strategy, *semantic mapping,* draws its strength from the activation of students' prior knowledge bases.

## SEMANTIC MAPPING

*Semantic mapping,* developed by Johnson and Pearson (1978, 1984), is a categorical structuring of information in graphic form. It is an individualized content approach in that students relate new words to their own experiences and prior knowledge. Semantic maps are diagrams that help students see how words relate to one another.

Although the semantic mapping procedure may vary somewhat according to individual teacher objectives, the procedure generally includes a brainstorming session in which students are asked to verbalize associations to the topic or particular words as the teacher maps (categorizes) them on the chalkboard. This phase of semantic mapping provides students with the opportunity to engage actively in a mental activity that retrieves prior knowledge, as well as to see the concepts they are retrieving. It is through the semantic mapping process that students learn the meanings and uses of new words, see old words in a new light, and recognize the relationships among words. Through discussion, the students have the opportunity to verify and expand their own understandings of concepts. They share their own experiences, relating new concepts to their own background knowledge. The known words they retrieve and offer are reinforced as they get immediate feedback from their peers and teacher.

According to Lindsay and Norman (1972) all information in the memory system is interrelated; new relations link to old concepts. The process of semantic mapping capitalizes on the way the brain hypothetically stores information both hierarchically and categorically, building upon the prior knowledge of students. More simply stated, semantic mapping takes advantage of what the child already knows in order to learn new words and concepts. Because semantic mapping is usually performed in group discussion, each child gains the benefit also of what each other child already knows.

In addition to being an effective strategy for vocabulary development, semantic mapping has been demonstrated to be a good alternative to traditional activities used before reading a new passage (prereading), as well as after reading a passage (postreading). In this application, the semantic-mapping process can be used not only to introduce the key vocabulary words from the passage to be read but also to activate the students' prior knowledge of the topic, thereby preparing them better to understand, assimilate, and evaluate the information in the material to be read. Following the reading of the selection, the discussion of the semantic map can be refocused to emphasize the main ideas that were presented in the written material.

The application of semantic mapping as a strategy to enhance comprehension is a logical one because the semantic-mapping procedure draws heavily on the activation of prior knowledge. Comprehension, similarly, is defined by Pearson and Johnson (1978) as "the building of bridges between the new and the known." Underlying this assumption is the premise that comprehension is a mental dialogue between the writer and the reader, an active process wherein the reader interprets and processes what is read in accordance with what is already known. According to this perspective, it is difficult for a reader to learn something new until it can be tied to something already known. The skilled reader actively engages in the reading act by linking the knowledge and experiences already stored.

Recent research has confirmed that there are several effective applications of the strategy of semantic mapping. The two most commonly used applications of the semantic-mapping strategy are (1) for general vocabulary development, and (2) for pre- and postreading. A description of both of these applications of the semantic-mapping procedure is presented below.

## SEMANTIC MAPPING AS A STRATEGY FOR GENERAL VOCABULARY DEVELOPMENT

Perhaps the most widely known procedure for employing semantic mapping as an instructional strategy for general vocabulary development is the one suggested by Johnson and Pearson (1978, 1984). The following steps constitute their procedure:

1. Choose a word or topic related to classroom work.
2. List the word on a large chart tablet or on the chalkboard.
3. Encourage the students to think of as many words as they can that are related to the selected key word and then to list the words by categories on a sheet of paper.
4. Students then share the prepared lists orally and all words are written on the class "map" in categories.
5. The joint effort of the class might resemble Figure 10–1, a map developed by a fourth-grade class for the topic *Stores*.
6. Students can gain further practice in classification by labeling the categories on the semantic map: (a) People, (b) Kinds, (c) Problems, (d) Expenses of Owning, (e) Prices.
7. Discussion of the semantic map is perhaps the most important part of the lesson. The purpose of the exercise is to encourage students to become aware of new words, to gather new meanings from old words, and to see the relationships among all the words. (Adapted from Johnson & Pearson, 1984, pp. 12–13).

## SEMANTIC MAPPING AS A STRATEGY FOR PRE- AND POSTREADING

Semantic mapping can also be used in pre- and postreading situations. In this application, have students develop a map of the topic of a story prior to read-

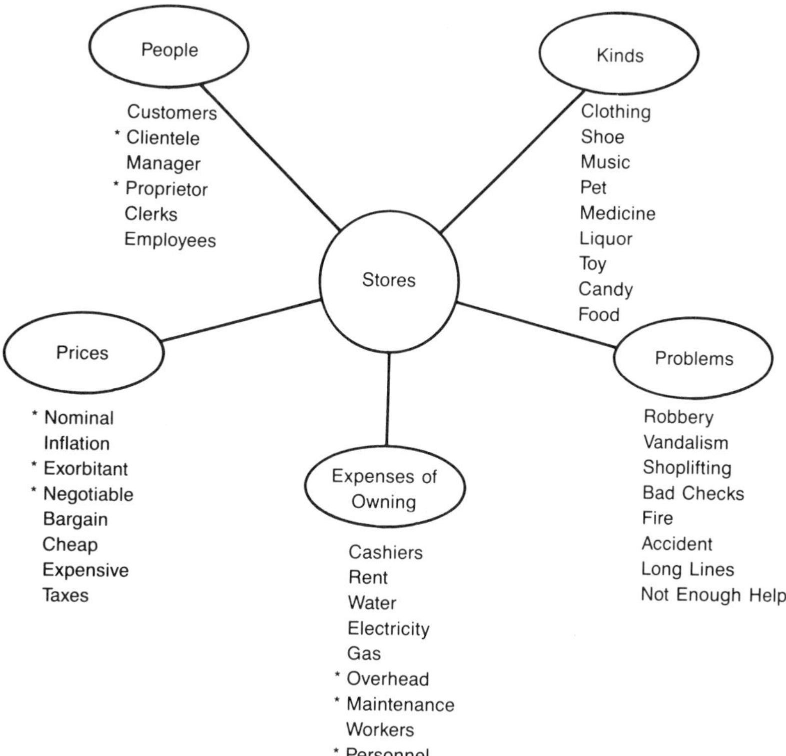


**FIGURE 10-1** Semantic Map for Stores (General Vocabulary Development)

ing the story in order to learn the key vocabulary words necessary for comprehension as well as to activate their prior knowledge bases regarding the story topic. The semantic-mapping exercise also serves to motivate the students to read the selection.

As the story is read, or after reading the story, students can add words and new categories to their own copies of the map. In the final phase of the semantic-mapping procedure, which is a class discussion, an opportunity is provided for the identification and integration of the new information. This class discussion can also serve as a comprehension check for the teacher. Following are two semantic maps of the topic *Sharks*. The first is a prereading map. The second, a more elaborate map, is an example of one done after students had read a chapter about sharks. (See Figures 10–2, 10–3).

You will find that semantic mapping as a pre- and postreading strategy is effective with basal and other reading materials. You can successfully adapt it to content instruction as well. As a postreading activity, semantic mapping affords students the opportunity to recall, organize, and graphically represent the pertinent information read.

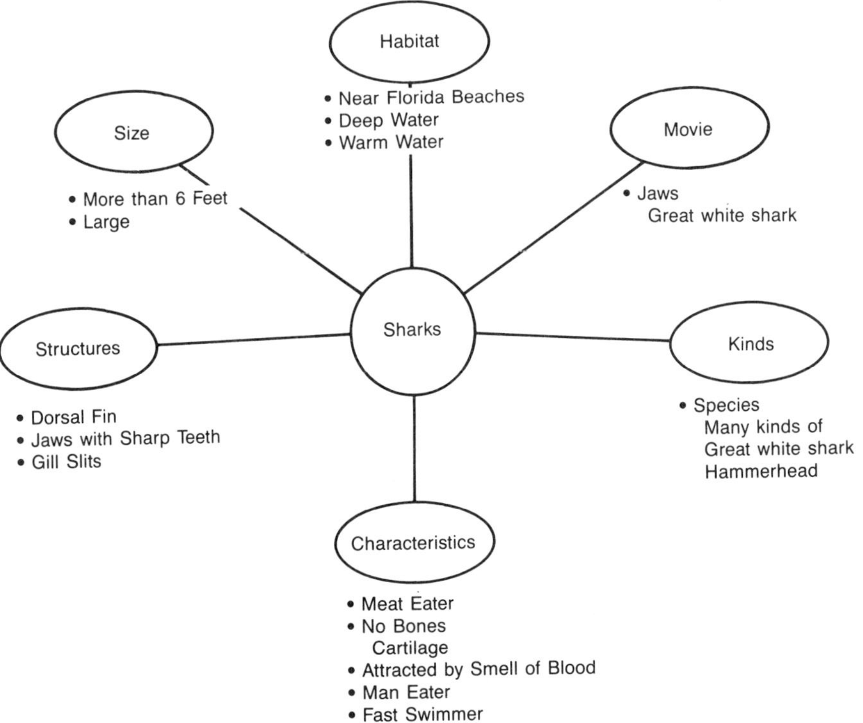


**FIGURE 10-2** Prereading Semantic Map for *Sharks.*

## SUMMARY

Semantic mapping has been used successfully by teachers with students of all grade levels. It has been found to be useful with students who are learning disabled, students in remedial reading classes, and illiterate adults. Semantic mapping appears to motivate highly students of all age levels and to involve them actively in the thinking-reading process.

Based on observations of student reaction while conducting pilot sessions using semantic mapping, Hagen (1978) suggested that semantic mapping may have great potential as a motivator. She reported that students involved in the mapping process showed a higher level of interest: eyes brightened, hands shot up readily as words were volunteered for the map, and oral comments were made. Hagen stated that even students who were initially reluctant to participate in what was, to them, a novel process contributed eagerly after a short time, and they continued their active involvement throughout the semantic-mapping sessions.

It has also been suggested that semantic mapping could also be used to help children organize ideas prior to writing or reading activities both in lan-

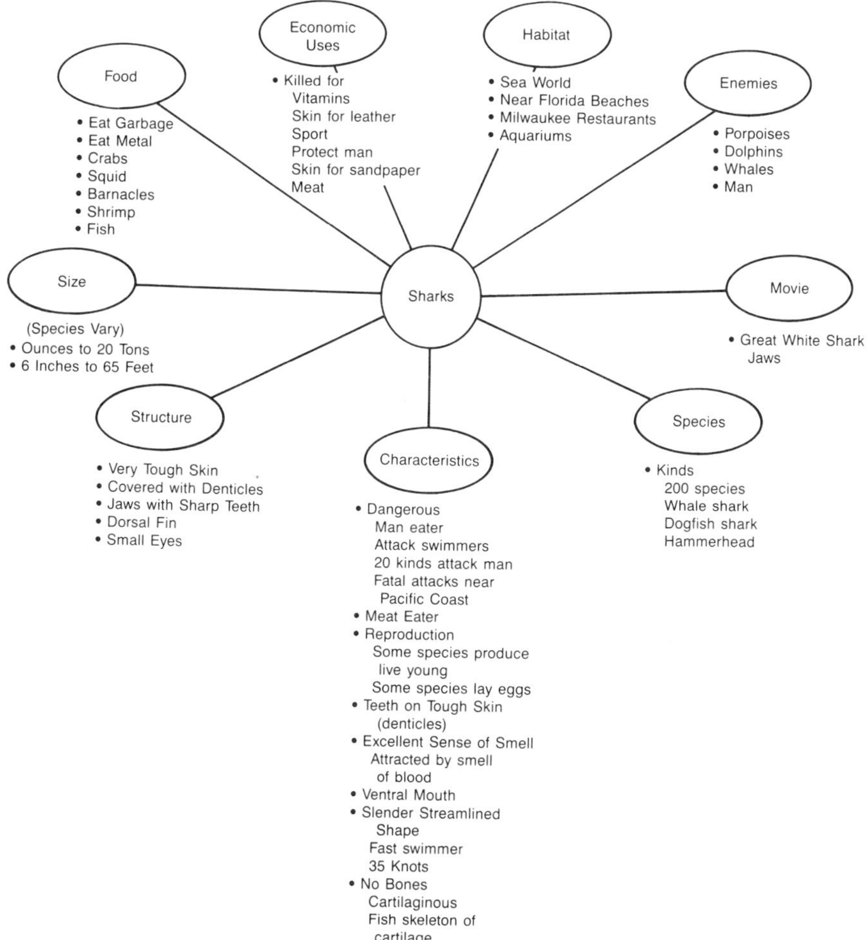


**FIGURE 10-3** Postreading Semantic Map for *Sharks.*

guage arts classes and in the content areas. As an aid in story and report writing, the semantic-mapping process affords the student the opportunity to organize thoughts and information. A complete map can easily serve as a guide by which to structure a story, with the category headings serving as topic sentences or main ideas for the paragraphs and the underlying details serving as the content to be included.

Semantic mapping can also be used to illustrate the relationships between content areas in a major instructional unit. For example, if art or music projects were part of a social studies unit on the Civil War, a semantic-mapping activity could be done to bridge the relationships of all the content-related information to the Civil War. This map might then be displayed in the classroom to demonstrate the relationships of the separate content area projects to the central idea of the whole unit—the Civil War. The map would provide a synthesized focus of the diverse classroom activities and could be used in final summarizing and review of the unit.

In summary, semantic maps are diagrams that aid discussion, which in turn helps children see how concepts and ideas are related to one another. The procedure can be used for general vocabulary development and as pre- and postreading activities. The procedure has been shown to be highly effective and popular with both students and teachers.

## *REFERENCES*

Davis, F.B. (1944). Fundamental factor of comprehension in reading. *Psychometrika, 9,* 185–197.

Davis, F.B. (1968). Research in comprehension in reading. *Reading Research Quarterly, 3*(4), 499–545.

Hagen, J.E. (1980). The effects of selected pre-reading vocabulary building activities on literal comprehension, vocabulary understanding, and attitudes of fourth and fifth grade students with reading problems. *Dissertation Abstracts International, 40,* 6216A. (University Microfilms No. 80–07, 553)

Johnson, D.D, & Pearson, P.D. (1984). *Teaching reading vocabulary* (2nd ed.). New York: Holt, Rinehart & Winston.

Lindsay, P., & Norman, D. (1972). *Human information processing.* New York: Academic Press.

O'Rourke, P.J. (1974). *Toward a science of vocabulary development.* The Hague, Paris: Mouton.

Pearson, P.D., & Johnson, D.D. (1978). *Teaching reading comprehension.* New York: Holt, Rinehart & Winston.

Stauffer, R.G. (1971). Slave, puppet or teacher? *The Reading Teacher, 25,* 24–29.

## *SUGGESTED READINGS*

Baumann, J.F., & Johnson, D.D. (1984). *Reading instruction and the beginning teacher: A practical guide.* Minneapolis: Burgess. This collection of practical essays written especially for beginning teachers contains several chapters that focus on vocabulary instruction. Several prior-knowledge board approaches are described and exemplified.

Johnson, D.D., & Pearson, P.D. (1984). *Teaching reading vocabulary* (2nd ed.). New York: Holt, Rinehart & Winston. This volume posits the belief that vocabulary is the key to comprehension. Its 10 chapters cover all aspects of vocabulary instruction, including sight vocabulary, meaning vocabulary, and word identification skills and strategies both in basal reading programs and in the content areas.

Sauntesanio, R.P. (1983). *A practical approach to content area reading.* Reading, MA: Addison-Wesley. This text presents an articulate description and exemplification of story mapping and other graphic aids that help students comprehend text.

# ELEVEN
# SENTENCE AND PARAGRAPH BUILDING IN THE LANGUAGE ARTS

The purpose of this chapter is to provide the teacher of the intermediate and middle-school grades with a selection of teaching strategies, techniques, and activities for teaching basic sentence and paragraph structures. Although there is much more to the writing process and the composition component of the language arts, the fact is that sentences and paragraphs represent the foundation of all writing structures. It is obvious that inability to write a complete sentence prevents any extended composition writing. Perhaps somewhat less obvious is that the ability to relate sentences to each other and to organize them logically into a paragraph is just as important if one is to compose anything other than lists. Yet, after a decade of assessing the writing abilities of 9- , 13- , and 17-year-olds in the United States, the National Assessment of Educational Progress concluded that the three most profound composing problems our students have are deficiencies in the:

1. ability to write sentences that relate directly to those that either precede or follow;
2. ability to write paragraphs that are logically related to those that precede them;
3. ability to perceive revision as a part of the ongoing writing process rather than a matter of simply correcting noted mechanical, spelling, usage, or grammar constructions. (*Writing Achievement, 1969–79,* Vols. I–III, National Assessment of Educational Progress, 1980.)

Notice that two of the three problem areas relate to matters that are a function of intersentence relationships rather than simply internal sentence construction problems.

This is not to say that sentence-writing ability is any less important, however. In fact, the need to construct reasonably elegant sentences is the major reason that the majority of elementary-grade basal language arts texts are primarily devoted to teaching the elements of sentence structure. Lessons in grammar, usage, spelling, and sentence mechanics generally make up the bulk of the instruction in writing in these texts.

The role of grammar instruction in particular has typically been one that is assumed to be central to writing. This is in spite of the fact that there has been little support over the years to show any significant correlation between knowledge of formal traditional grammar and ability to write (Sherwin, 1969).

Since the late 1960s a substantive body of research indicates that selected activities in grammar instruction, such as sentence-combining, can be beneficial in learning to write more structurally sound and sophisticated sentences (Mellon, 1969; Vitale, King, Shontz, & Huntley, 1971; O'Hare, 1973; Perron, 1974; Combs, 1976).

In addition, many authorities, researchers, and teachers concur that knowledge of grammatical structure and ability to use the language, terminology, and grammar significantly increases instructional ease in later grades. The middle-grades and high-school language arts teacher can confer with the student writer knowing that there is a common core of language and knowledge present and all grammatical matters do not have to be explained in detail every time a paper or composition is written. It is not direct application of the knowledge of formal grammar that is helpful as much as the common language and knowledge of appropriate referents that help to facilitate the writing instruction.

The same situation is true to some extent in paragraph writing. Experiences in writing different kinds of paragraphs—becoming familiar with different paragraph structures, stylistic features, and techniques—require immersion in paragraph-building and paragraph-production exercises. Knowledge of the nomenclature, for example, discourse mode, narrative, exposition, argumentation, etc., is helpful for conferring, for responding to the writing, and to some extent for classroom instruction. But ultimate success in effective paragraph writing is dependent upon the writer's ability to relate knowledge of paragraph structures, sentence structures, and the logical development of both to the purpose and the audience to be addressed.

Because we cannot address all matters of sentence and paragraph production in this one chapter, it appears reasonable to choose and highlight those few that are either the most critical or that lend themselves to the limited bounds of chapter length. To do this somewhat systematically, the remainder of the chapter will address strategies, techniques, and/or activities in each of the following categories: sentence-experimenting, sentence-combining, and paragraph types and structures.

You should remember that these ideas are intended to be examples or models of strategy, techniques, or activity type that can be effective in the classroom. Also, they are not intended to be construed as either the content of a total writing program or even indicative of the basic approach to instruction for all of the program. Given these restrictions, however, they can be effective and useful tools.

Most of the ideas that follow are based upon a few important generalizations that the author has inferred from both contemporary research and ongoing successful teaching practices. They are:

1. Sentence and paragraph analysis can be helpful to the learner. However, sentence and paragraph production is what we want, and activities that incorporate production are most desirable.
2. Modeling is one of the more effective means for teaching writing skills in the areas of sentence and paragraph structure. This modeling should include writing by peers and student dialogue about their writing.
3. Both sentence structure and paragraph structure are most effectively learned in instructional approaches that emphasize the teaching of necessary writing skills within a meaningful and functional language context.
4. Any skill instruction in writing must take place within the larger contexts of the writing process. In particular, there is assumed at least a minimal writer fluency so that there is the capacity for some written productivity that can be worked with.

## SENTENCE-EXPERIMENTING

By *sentence-experimenting* we mean activities or approaches that place the learner in the position of examining, manipulating, or otherwise working with sentences in ways that help the learner acquire a feel for structure and the relations that hold between sentence structure and sentence meaning.

### Inferring Sentence Structure

Use the following experimental format in developing sentence-structure inference ideas:

#### GIVEN:

1. The dog ate the bone. → The bone-eating dog.
2. The car drinks gas. → The gas-drinking car.
3. The well pumps oil. → The oil-pumping well.

#### MATERIAL:

1. The dog chased the wagon. →
2. The bugs ate the banana. →
3. The boy spilled the milk. →

#### DIRECTIONS:

Change each of the sentences in the *Material* section the same way the sentences were changed in the *Given* section. Remember to use hyphens.

1. __________(answer: the wagon-chasing dog.)
2. __________(answer: the banana-eating bugs.)
3. __________(answer: the milk-spilling boy.)

**CONCLUSION:**

Are the new constructions you have produced still sentences? (No. You have changed sentences into noun phrases that can be used in new sentences.)

**APPLICATION:**

Make up three new sentences using the three sentence parts you produced in the *Directions* section of this experiment.

**EXTENDED PRACTICE:**

Make up three sentences using the following verbs: "sniff," "eat," "write." Exchange your sentences with another student. See if you can change the sentences that student produced the way we did those in the *Material* section of this experiment.

Notice that this format can be used to teach any important grammatical structure: adjectives in phrases, relative clauses, subordinate clauses, extended sentence modifiers, etc. For example:

**GIVEN:**

1. __________is my friend. → *The new boy* is my friend.
2. The boy is new.
3. __________left quickly. → *The old car* left quickly
4. The car is old.

**MATERIAL:**

1. __________was sad. →
2. The girl is little.

**DIRECTIONS:**

Change the sentences under *Material* the way those were changed in the *Given* section.

**CONCLUSION:**

What is one way to build a bigger sentence? (We can combine two or more shorter ones. And we make certain systematic changes.)

**APPLICATION:**

From what two sentences does this sentence come?

"The tired monkey ate the pear."

The answer most likely should be:

1. __________ate the pear.
2. The monkey is tired.

   or

1. The monkey ate the pear.
2. The monkey is tired.

This particular experimenting format possesses a number of important advantages for teaching sentence structure.

1. The inductive process involves higher-level inferential applications by the learner. The focus is on the deep-structure features of sentences central to their meaning and final structural evolution rather than mere surface features.
2. This format can be used with or without formal grammatical terminology; thus, it presents a wider range of curricular-type applications.
3. There are opportunities to explore many of the optional "appropriate" grammatical constructions that occur in our language without the unnecessary attention to "correct" and "incorrect" answers in many traditional grammar lessons.
4. Students and teacher are encouraged implicitly in the overall design of the experiments and explicitly in the *Conclusion* and *Application* sections to use oral language in talking about responses and answers and procedures.
5. There is a range of instructional strategy potentials with this format. Materials can be photocopied as handouts; overhead transparencies can be used for group instruction, etc.

## SENTENCE-COMBINING

One of the most effective measures at our disposal for teaching more effective and fuller grammatical exploitation of sentence structures is through *sentence-combining*. We got into a little of that in the experimental format presented earlier. However, a more comprehensive use of sentence-combining needs to be made. The following options are presented for the teacher to consider.

### Open-Ended Sentence-Combining

This type of sentence-combining simply asks the student to combine a series of short, choppy sentences into one sentence, dropping or changing word forms where necessary or appropriate. For example:

Combine the following:

1. The Porsche 914 roared around the corner.
2. The corner was sharp.
3. The Porsche was white.

Possible result:

"The white Porsche 914 roared around the sharp corner."

Another example:

1. The student did poorly on the test.
2. The student didn't study.

Possible result:

"The student did poorly on the test because he didn't study."

(Notice how there is implicit pressure on the writer to use a word such as "because" when combining this pair.)

The open-ended sentence-combining method encourages an open and nonprescriptive approach to teaching grammar. Often there are a variety of acceptable sentences the student can possibly produce. For example, many students will probably produce, "The student who didn't study did poorly on the test," rather than a sentence with "because." However, either is a worthwhile syntactic construction.

### Slotted Sentence-Combining

This sentence-combining method is different in that it identifies one sentence to be the "consumer" or "container" sentence whereas others are to be altered before being "inserted" into the container-sentence slot. For example: Combine the following:

1. __________knew the secret of the lost treasure.
2. The man was old.

Possible result:

"The old man knew the secret of the lost treasure."

Notice that this type of sentence-combining activity gives the writer less flexibility than the open-ended type. This method, however, provides the teacher with the opportunity to focus more readily upon specific grammatical structures. The same is true of the third type, called *cued* sentence-combining.

### Cued Sentence-Combining

This fairly directive method requires the student to employ specific grammatical structures. The cue is typically presented as a word or word part in parentheses immediately following the sentence to be altered prior to combining.

Combine the following:

1. The man is my uncle.
2. The man is driving the car. (who)

Result:

"The man who is driving the car is my uncle."

Or, combine the following:

1. The bugs flew into the screen.
2. The bugs were little.
3. The bugs gasped their last. (ing)

Possible result:

"The little bugs, gasping their last, flew into the screen."

Variations include the open, slotted, and cued sentence-combining in combination after students have had practice with each type; pulling paragraphs from a text students are using, breaking the sentences down into short basic ones, and then having students combine them; scrambling a list of short sentences, asking students to reorder them, clustering them, then combining them to produce a paragraph. After using sentence-combining, you will think of many other uses.

## PARAGRAPH TYPES AND STRUCTURES

Learning to write effective paragraphs involves mastery of skills similar to those necessary for effective sentence writing. Paragraphs have structural attributes and content attributes. Further, there are unique relationships that hold between these two categories of attributes according to paragraph type. For example, a simple descriptive paragraph, one that provides a straightforward objective description of a thing, an event, a game, etc., would be an *expository paragraph.* The vocabulary, sentence structures, and organization of the paragraph would be different from a very subjective description, which might appear in a novel or story.

Expository paragraphs, especially those designed to be persuasive in character, reflect both a tight organizational structure and pattern. Very often this is a three-part organization that moves from a *thesis,* or *claim sentence,* that appears first, to *support sentences* in the body of the paragraph, to a final *conclusion sentence,* which often summarizes or paraphrases the content of the claim sentence. For example, consider the following:

We should buy a new car. The one we have now is nearly seven years old. The engine is knocking, and the suspension system is gone. The tires, brakes, and body are all in bad shape. A new car seems to be the best answer.

or,

*Claim Sentence:* We should buy a new car.

*Support Sentences:* The one we have now is nearly seven years old. The engine is knocking and the suspension system is gone. The tires, brakes, and body are all in bad shape.

*Conclusion Sentence:* A new car seems to be the best answer.

Although within the support sentences, especially in longer paragraphs, there is abstraction-level movement, it is not as varied or central as in narrative paragraphs.

Expository paragraphs and *narrative paragraphs* are the two most important kinds of paragraphs students must learn to write. There are many ways to describe the nature of these paragraph types, for example, comparison-contrast paragraphs, paragraphs by definition, and so forth. There are many sets and subsets of specific concepts and skills the effective writer must master, for example, types of unity and coherence, various kinds of sequencing strategies, transitional devices, etc., and a host of other things such as interparagraph structures and relationships in larger compositions. However, many of these are advanced skills that go beyond the scope and purpose of this chapter, which is to address only "basic" writing skills and concepts. The ideas that follow derive from this assumption.

Find examples of brief expository and narrative paragraphs (three or four of each), mix them up on handouts, put students in pairs, and ask them to jointly decide which ones are expository and which ones are narrative. Talk about why they categorized each as one or the other.

Present the following model paragraphs (or others that you write or find in other resources) to students:

(P1). The Senator said the farming bill was necessary. Farmers were in financial trouble and needed support. It was the responsibility of the government to see that they were accorded their fair share. They shouldn't have to work for nothing. Farming was the backbone of American society.

(P2). The Senator said the farming bill was unnecessary. Farmers were overpaid and needed no help. It was the responsibility of the individual to see that he carried his own weight. The government shouldn't provide everything. Farmers had always been a drain on American society.

Using these two examples as models, provide students with different topics, for example, need for an indoor pool in their school, the rights of the poor, whether the class should go on a field trip, etc. Then ask them to write two brief paragraphs, nearly identical in structure but presenting opposite points of view. Talk about some of these paragraphs in class. Choose particularly good examples and make transparencies for use on the overhead projector.

> Present the class with a handout of the following paragraph or one you design. Ask them to choose pairs of adjectives or adverbs for each blank, one designed to present a positive picture, one a negative.
>
> The ________ balloonist looked ________ at the ________ crowd. He thought they looked ________ as they talked about his flight. They knew he was ________. And, he was ________.

Talk about how choice of descriptive words in a paragraph can shape the reader's attitude or understanding of what has actually happened.

> Present students with the following models, asking them to complete the handouts where sentences are missing.

A. *Claim Sentence:* I think I should have a new bike.
*Support Sentences:* My old one is in bad shape.
I need one for my paper route.
I can get more exercise with a new one.
*Conclusion:* Therefore (or So), ________________.

B. *Claim Sentence:* Our school needs an indoor swimming pool.
*Support Sentences:* ________________.
*Conclusion:* It would improve our whole school program.

C. *Claim Sentence:* We need a longer summer vacation.
*Support Sentences:* ________________.
*Conclusion:* ________________.

After working through each of these three models, discuss with students the reasons for appropriateness of sentences for each slot. Point out specific characteristics of appropriate sentences, differences in vocabulary types in each, and so forth.

With enough practice, the three-part character of the expository persuasive paragraph should be mastered with enough facility for you to begin direct instruction in the more sophisticated and often subtle skills for paragraph writing that are necessary for more elegant writing.

*Note:* Remember that the focus of this chapter has been upon the development of basic sentence- and paragraph-building skills, and even that in a limited way. The ideas offered should not be seen as substitutes for other strategies for fluency and skill development. Their purpose is to enhance a writing program more comprehensive in nature. Used in this way, they can make your program more varied, versatile, and effective.

## REFERENCES

COMBS, W. (1976). Further effects of sentence-combining practice on writing ability. *Research in the Teaching of English, 2,* 137–149.

MELLON, J. (1969). *Transformational sentence-combining.* NCTE Research Report, No. 10, Champaign, IL: NCTE.

O'HARE, F. (1973). *Sentence-combining.* NCTE Research Report, No. 15. Champaign, IL: NCTE.

PERRON, J. (1974). *An exploratory approach to extending the syntactic development of fourth-grade students through the use of sentence-combining methods.* Unpublished doctoral dissertation, Indiana University.

SHERWIN, S. (1969). *Four problems in teaching English: A critique of research.* Scranton: International Textbook Company.

VITALE, M., KING, R., SHORTZ, D., & HUNTLEY, G. (1971). Effects of sentence-combining exercises upon several restricted written composition tasks. *Journal of Educational Psychology, 62,* 521–525.

*Writing Achievement 1969–79, Vols. I–III.* (1980). Denver, CO: National Assessment of Educational Progress.

## SUGGESTED READINGS

KLEIN, M. (1985). *The development of writing in children: Pre-K through grade 8.* Englewood Cliffs, NJ: Prentice-Hall. This volume moves from a review of contemporary theory and research in writing development to a presentation of suggested teaching strategies, techniques, and activities through the eighth grade.

TIEDT, I., et al. (1983). *Teaching writing in K–8 classrooms: The time has come.* Englewood Cliffs, NJ: Prentice-Hall. This book is the result of work done in the South Bay Writing Project. It focuses upon practical teaching ideas in all of the major areas of writing-instruction concerns, including writing forms, the writing process, writing evaluation, and others.

STRONG, W. (1981). *Sentence-combining and paragraph-building.* New York: Random House. Although aimed at upper-middle grades and high-school level, the sentence-combining and paragraph-building models presented have useful application as models for intermediate grades as well.

MOFFETT, J. & WAGNER, B. (1983). *Student-centered language arts and reading, K–13.* Boston: Houghton Mifflin. Through several editions, this book continues as a near classic in offering imaginative ways for teaching writing at all levels and in a variety of ways.

# TWELVE
# TEACHING READING COMPREHENSION IN THE LANGUAGE ARTS

A reading lesson should prepare the student for comprehension of a text's content by activating the reader's prior topic knowledge and experience and by orienting the student to the structure of the selection. It should help students apply these prior learnings, or schemata, to the reading content as they reconstruct meaning and/or generate new understandings (McNeil, 1984). We are aware that prior knowledge regarding a reading topic facilitates the learning of new information and that new knowledge increases and modifies prior knowledge (Pearson & Johnson, 1978). Likewise, we know that experience with and introduction to the internal organization of a reading selection influences its comprehension (Smith & Hesse, 1969). At the same time, we are aware that content familiarity and structural schemata vary from student to student. As a result, it is unlikely that two students would come to a reading session with exactly the same preparation. We are likewise cognizant that these differences in the backgrounds of individuals who read a common selection frequently result in a variance in the understanding, interpretation, and application of meaning derived from that exercise.

The meaning derived from reading a selection thus is intrinsic in and peculiar to the reader (Lee, 1984; King & Watson, 1984). This being the case, it would be incorrect for teachers to assume that there is only one manner of comprehending a text. Beyond the accurate recall of factual information about the reading, the higher-order comprehension components of drawing conclusions, and deriving learnings and application of the concept to one's own life are all open to individual interpretation. There is no right or wrong interpretation, only *varied* interpretations. Consequently, it may therefore be more useful to view comprehension as a process of deriving and/or generating meaning from reading a text rather than that of approximating a single understanding and interpretation established as correct by an instructor or teaching guide. Comprehension assistance, then, should help students actively seek out and reconstruct meaning, explore and experiment with interpretation of content, and discover that thread of purposefulness which ties the content together. It should provide opportunities for expression of the individual's understanding of the interrelatedness of ideas as they help in making sense out of the world. This means that the reading selection will not and should not be comprehended in the same way by all readers because of individual differences among the readers. It means that students will learn to value their own opinions and to test them with those of other students; they will learn the process of meaning generation and interpretation, and they will learn to determine relatedness of content to the world in which they live. You, as a teacher, can facilitate reading comprehension by focusing not on a predetermined understanding of content but by allowing and guiding students to experience the process of comprehension.

This chapter describes an integrated approach to reading comprehension assistance. With this type of reading assistance, you can help students to derive a learning from the reading selection and to verify its adequacy according to their own background. In these comprehension sessions, students are allowed to interact with each other. They are guided to holistic understanding of the reading selection and the discovering of new learnings from their reading. Together, students work out solutions to discussion problems that are posed. Using this procedure, the audience for the problem solving becomes other students. Your role changes from that of information provider and verifier to that of discussion facilitator.

In ensuring content familiarity, you can discuss students' current understanding of the topic of their reading. This session is designed not to test what students have as background knowledge related to the topic of the reading selection but to help them recall what they already know. Because students are not always aware of what they know about a topic, your role in facilitating this recall is important. The following is a guide to this effort:

1. *Ask your students to share previous experiences or background knowledge relating to the assignment's topic and/or to speculate about the content of the reading selection.* First, realize that comprehension is facilitated by such recall. Second, help your students realize that they already know something about the reading topic that can help facilitate their interaction with the text. If you determine that students are lacking in background knowledge or experiences related to the topic of the selection, you are then aware of a need present among your students that should be addressed prior to the reading.

As students share what they already know about the topic, they will often use terms aloud that they will encounter when they read the selection. These individual words are reflective of their current understanding of the topic and can be listed by you on the blackboard for later study.

2. *Allow your students to interpret their own information about the topic.* Because prejudgments are difficult if not impossible to avoid, they can be incorporated into this prereading preparation session for study prior to the reading. You can encourage your students to share opinions and value statements regarding the topic in the text because these will reflect your students' current thinking and preconceptions about the text's subject. A worthwhile prereading exercise is to allow students to express their preconceptions and to differentiate these judgments from facts known about the topic.

3. *Relate this information to your students' lives.* Help your students recognize the relevance of the topic they are about to read. You can increase motivation by guiding students to explore the relationship of the study of the content of a selection to that which is familiar to them—their own lives and interpretation of the world. New information will thus become more meaningful to your students when it is anchored to material already familiar to them.

4. *Summarize the collective knowledge as it relates to the reading selection to be assigned.* Because students don't always realize what they know or what they don't know about a topic, you can help them realize the extent or limitations of their collective knowledge through this activity. Through this summary, you can orient your students to thinking about the content or information in a reading selection by identifying their collective prior knowledge, pointing out preconceptions they hold about that content, and focusing their attention on any informational gaps present.

Following this schema discussion, you can take vocabulary items recorded in item 1 above along with other important content terms identified in the text and graphically arrange them on a blackboard to depict the relationships and ordering of concepts inherent in the selection. This display provides an indication of the general organizational structure of the reading selection for students. This structured overview (Smith & Hesse, 1969) is a type of cognitive organizer that orients the students to preview a map of concepts involved in the lesson.

The procedure for developing a structured overview is relatively simple and involves the following steps. Analyze the reading selection for its major ideas or concepts. Once identified, important content vocabulary items are classed together and listed to show relatedness to the major ideas in the diagram. Thus, this structure depicts the interrelationships and ordering of concepts. Graphically present the global aspects of a story deductively by structuring the vocabulary in such a way that the items identify and outline the concepts contained within the reading as suggested in Chapter 10. Attributes of new and unfamiliar vocabulary are discussed along with this diagram prior to reading the selection. By highlighting the diagram that depicts the overall structure of the reading selection and by using a statement or two sketching the general topic outline of the reading, you can orient students to the structure of the text they are then assigned to read.

*Then ask the student to read the selection.*

Following this reading of the text is the postreading session. At this time, students are guided through the process of comprehending the assigned reading. Testing is avoided and exploration and experimentation of student ideas are encouraged. In these comprehension sessions, allow students to interact. Guide them to holistic understanding of the reading selection and the discovering of new learnings from their reading. Together, students can work out solutions to discussion problems you pose. Using this procedure, the audience for the problem solving becomes other students.

Guide questions that you can use in accomplishing the above are uncomplicated and can be easily followed. Four hierarchical levels of inquiry, which are set forth below, are suggested for this postreading session. Notice that each requires a different intellectual effort. You serve as a facilitator who moves the discussion from a literal recall, to interpretation, to conceptualization and to application. A complete discussion at each level of inquiry is suggested before moving onto the next. Remember that these questions are suggested only to facilitate discussion at each level of inquiry and thus enact the process of comprehending. They do not constitute a test to determine students' accuracy in responding to predetermined questions and answers. Your tasks involve helping your students understand what they read, orienting them to thinking about and reacting to its content, and guiding them as they clarify the concept of the text and apply it to their own lives.

1. *What was the story about? What happened?* Encourage your students to verbalize their understanding and recall of the text's contents. Don't encourage or insist on complete recall; instead, emphasize holistic understanding. Information at this level of inquiry is descriptive, literal, and factual. Thus, accuracy of response at this level of inquiry is verifiable through reference to the text. What students recall from reading the text is important only as that content information is useful in facilitating discussion and inquiry beyond this base level. Discussion of this factual content from the text then becomes the basis for subsequent levels of inquiry.

2. *What do you think about the story? Why did these events occur? Why was it written?* Allow your students to interpret the reading selection by reacting to it. Allow opinions to be expressed. You can probe for clarity in the communication of the value statements offered by students. A student's response at this level of inquiry is likely to reflect his or her prior experiences and learnings as well as his or her response to the new information from the reading assignment. "Correctness" in interpretation is idiosyncratic and should be beyond judgment by others. Most important at this level of inquiry and discussion is for the students to think about the reading and to experiment with the expression of their reaction to that text.

3. *What did you learn from reading this selection? What is the message?* The moral, or thesis, of the selection can be discussed by students, and consensus achieved. The intent of this level of inquiry and discussion is to help your students learn to derive and articulate their own learnings stimulated by the reading assignment. A synthesis that directly matches your own experience and interpretation should not be imposed. The thinking that results when discussion is encouraged in this way can be as exciting as it is active.

Similarly, you can help your students understand the concepts presented in their reading. A *concept* is an abstract idea that evolves from a singular situation or collection of facts. A *concept category* includes those items that conform in attributes or distinguishing qualities to those that identify that concept. You can help students clarify a concept from a reading selection by helping students identify how it is developed in a text, by exploring how it manifests in the reading selection, and by ascertaining its application in other contexts. The attainment of a concept can be demonstrated by having students verbalize that concept and determine membership of examples and exclusion of nonexamples in that concept category.

4. *How can we use this learning? Suppose that. . . . If. . . . then. . . .* By guiding students to apply the learning in situations with which they have some familiarity, you can help "set" the learning. This application can vary in abstractness from its concrete manifestations in your students' everyday life to its application in hypothetical and abstract problem solving. Discussion involving conjecture, supposition, and hypothesizing are appropriate activities at this level of inquiry.

What follows is a sample reading lesson. Included is an abbreviation of the interactions between students and teacher. The two major sections of prereading and postreading are elaborated for you. This particular story dealt with the cooperative lifestyle of the Pueblo Indians.

### EXAMPLE OF PREREADING COMPREHENSION SESSION (Abbreviated)

Teacher: This story is about life among Indians, a special type of Indian: The Pueblos. What do you know about the lives of Pueblo Indians? [This helps the students recall any prior background information relating to the topic, namely, the Pueblo Indians. In addition, pictures from the text were referred to as aids to schema activation.]

Student 1: Weren't they the Indians who lived in large houses?

Student 2: Yes, like in Taos. They live in a big apartment house made of adobes.

Student 3: Many Indians lived together.

Teacher: Why do you suppose so many chose to live together? [This seeks to discover an understanding of societal needs to group together for mutual benefit.]

Student 4: To protect themselves from their enemies.

Student 3: The Pueblo buildings made it easier to defend themselves.

Student 1: Also, so that they could grow corn and hunt together.

Student 2: Yes, they did many things together.

Student 3: That way, if one hunter or farmer did not have enough to eat, others would give his family food.

Student 2: A friend of mine who came from a Pueblo in New Mexico said that everyone helped each other all the time.

Teacher: Are there ways that people in your neighborhood help each other out? [This relates the general concept of the story to the community in which the students live. This anchoring establishes a link between the text and the students' own experiences.]

Student 1: Yes, people in my apartment building are always taking food to their neighbors.

Student 2: In my neighborhood, my neighbors watch us until my parents come home from work.

Teacher: Yes, there are many parallels, ah, similarities, in our own lives in the way Pueblos live. I want us to take a look at vocabulary words we will encounter in the story. They are arranged in a diagram depicting the structure of the story you are to read. [The following diagram is provided for the students. Each vocabulary item is discussed and its relationship to the general diagram is explored. Additionally, through this review, students have an opportunity to associate meaning to words they are learning to visually recognize and phonemically decode.]

**Pueblo Indians: A Sharing Lifestyle**

| LIVES | WORKING TOGETHER |
|---|---|
| apartment buildings | sharing |
| clans | hunting |
| extended families | food gathering |
| crowding | community fields |
| Southwest deserts | common good |

Teacher: I want you to read this story. It discusses the lives of Pueblo Indians and the many things they do together. When you have finished the story, we will discuss how life in the Pueblo is similar to or different from our own. [This advance organizer introduces the topic of the reading selection. It provides a general outline of the information to be encountered—for example, individual lives and doing things together.]

Students are then asked to read the selection.

In the postreading session that follows, the teacher begins by having the students recall the story. This is followed by inquiry, which helps students interpret the story, determine the major learnings and further understand the concept, and apply this understanding to other situations.

#### EXAMPLE OF POSTREADING COMPREHENSION SESSION (Abbreviated)

Teacher: What was the story about? [A recall of the major thrust of the story is sought first.]

Student 1: It's about Indians.

Student 2: Yeah, Pueblo Indians.

Student 3: It tells us how they live.

Student 1: They share everything.

Student 2: Like work, they work together. They cooperate.

Teacher: In what way did they benefit from working together? [This furthers the discussion of the concept of cooperation.]

Student 3: They get more done. They get along with each other.

Teacher: Who can summarize the story? [Asking the students to determine the most salient points of the story thus limits the total recall of inconsequential information that might otherwise be offered.]

Student 2: This story is about Pueblo Indians. It tells us that they share work and cooperate together. This way they get more done.

Teacher: What do you think about people working together, cooperating, as the Indians did in the story? [This question solicits the students' interpretation of and reaction to the text's content. There obviously is no right or wrong answer to this type of inquiry. What is important is that students begin to think about the generalization of cooperative existence found among the Pueblo Indians.]

Student 2: It worked well for the Pueblo Indians.

Student 3: It would never work in [name of town].

Teacher: Why would it not work in [name of town]? [The teacher goes from the story, to interpreting the generalization of cooperation, to the students' own experiences. At this point, the teacher attempts to have students think about the story's content with no fear of judgment as to "correctness of response."]

Student 3: People are too independent. They believe they should not work together.

Student 2: No, most people work together. Else, they would not accomplish much.

Student 1: Sometimes it is better for people to work together. Like when the snows melted in Salt Lake City, people worked together in building dikes to prevent flooding.

Student 2: Yes, and at my mother's office, people work together on projects. That way, they accomplish more.

Student 3: Yes, people work together. There are times when it is better to work alone. I like to work alone. Working with other people takes more time and I accomplish less than if I work alone.

Teacher: What did we learn from this story? [This introduces the discussion leading to the concept of the story. The moral or thesis of the story is discussed. Again, there is no right or wrong response.]

Student 1: It is better to cooperate.

Student 2: The Indians worked together to get things done.

Student 3: Cooperation is good for the Indians, but it isn't right for us.

Teacher: Can we put those three ideas together? [Synthesis of ideas generated is sought, thus forming a thesis statement, which represents each student's "learnings" from the reading.]

Student 2: Some people work together to get more things done.

Student 3: While some people work together to get more things done, sometimes it is better to work alone.

Student 1: There are times when cooperation is good. There are times when independent work is necessary.

Teacher: Let us determine when it is important for people to work together and when they should work alone. Let us list activities and together determine if and when it is better for people to work on them alone or with others.

[This exercise helps "set" the learning of the nuances of the concept. Concept attainment is established by having students identify those activities that are examples of cooperation. Each of the suggested items is listed on the blackboard. Discussion is delayed until after the brainstorming is completed.]

Student 1: Doing homework is best done with another person.

Student 3: An airplane model should be built by oneself.

Student 1: Cooking—they say too many cooks spoil the broth.

Student 4: Practicing the piano by oneself is best.

Student 3: Two friends helping deliver newspapers makes it easier.

Student 2: Tests have to be taken by themselves.

Student 4: It takes a group to plan a picnic.

Student 1: I study best for an exam when I do it with my friends.

Student 2: Mowing the lawn is easier if someone else helps.

Teacher: Okay, let us discuss each item on this list. It is apparent that several of the suggestions may not fit easily into either category of cooperative or individual accomplishment. What do you think? [Discussion of each item continues as students are asked to weigh the extent of cooperation in each example in determining its placement into either the cooperative or individual accomplishment column. Consensus can be achieved by the group as demonstration that the concept of cooperation is understood by the students.]

Teacher: We have seen how the benefits of cooperation outweigh the disadvantages in some but not all situations. [This is a final summary of the learning derived from the lesson. The teacher now realizes that the students understand the concepts of cooperation and competition, not only in the context of the stories they read but also beyond the text in their own lives.]

Many follow-up activities can be planned at this time with the students. You could, for example, have students read about a competitive lifestyle of another group of people. Of course, in the prereading session, reference would be made to the cooperation evidenced among the Pueblo Indians. A contrast between the two stories can then be made. In the postreading session of the competitive story, students are then involved in a discussion of competition similar to that provided in the example above.

Assignments involving writing, drama, investigative work, historical analysis, or sociological study could culminate either reading exercise. Such assignments go beyond the reading experience and involve the student in employing the language arts to explore the concept further.

Reading in such a comprehensive lesson becomes the beginning of a wealth of learning that may follow from subsequent activities. Students are prepared for the reading by helping remind them of the information they already know about a topic and are oriented to the general structure of the selection. Further, they are guided through a discussion of the salient points of the selection. Additionally, they are encouraged to think through implications, concepts, and applications of these understandings. Finally, they are holistically allowed to integrate meaning from these activities into their own lives.

## *REFERENCES*

KING, D.F., & WATSON, D.J. (1984). Reading as meaning construction. In B.A. Busching & J.I. Schwartz (Eds.), *Integrating the language arts in the elementary school.* Urbana, IL: National Council of Teachers of English.

LEE, D.M. (1984). Language experience. In B.A. Busching & J.I. Schwartz (Eds.), *Integrating the language arts in the elementary school.* Urbana, IL: National Council of Teachers of English.

MCNEIL, J. (1984). *Reading comprehension—New directions for classroom practice.* Glenview, IL: Scott, Foresman.

PEARSON, P.D., & JOHNSON, D.D. (1978). *Teaching reading comprehension.* New York: Holt, Rinehart & Winston.

SMITH, R.J., & HESSE, K.D. (1969). The effects of prereading assistance on the comprehension and attitudes of good and poor readers. *Reading in the Teaching of English, 3,* 166–167.

# THIRTEEN
# TEACHING STUDY SKILLS IN THE CONTENT AREAS

Because study skills are the "learning how to learn" skills, they are taught most naturally and effectively as part of the content areas, such as social studies, science, mathematics, and so forth. Instruction in study skills ought not be an end in itself, but a means to help children learn content in all subject areas. Although the foundation for study skills needs to be laid in the early primary grades, the point at which students need to use content area textbooks and other resource materials is the best time for instruction in study skills. If skills are applied immediately in real tasks, transfer from instruction to application occurs naturally.

## CONTEXTS FOR STUDY SKILLS INSTRUCTION

Before suggesting specific activities to develop selected study skills, we will describe several contexts in which study skills instruction and application can take place. If students can read the content area textbook, then comprehension can be enhanced by use of study guides, and study skills can be taught using the textbook. Often, however, the textbook is too difficult and some sort of modification is necessary (Askov & Otto, 1985).

Assuming a heterogeneous classroom for content area instruction, a more appropriate context for instruction may involve the use of the textbook as only one of a variety of sources of information rather than as the sole vehicle for providing information about the content area study. The textbook becomes a tool in the curriculum rather than the curriculum itself.

### Unit Plan

In preparing a *unit,* you should first *identify the objectives* for instruction. For example, in a social studies unit relating to Native Americans, the objectives might include the history and customs of specific tribes as well as a sensitivity to Native American culture today. The objectives should also include at least one study skills objective, such as notetaking from oral and written sources. Only after the teacher formulates the objectives are materials sought. In using a unit plan the content area textbook may be one of the sources of information for those students who can read it.

Because the elementary teacher should have information about students' reading abilities, you should locate *learning materials* at the various reading levels represented within the classroom. Although students are often placed in homogeneous groups by reading level for reading instruction, groups for content area instruction are generally heterogeneous, based on topics within the content study (such as a group studying Native American battles and subsequent migration). Reading materials at a variety of levels also need to be supplemented by other media, such as films, audiotapes, and photographs.

You must also *determine the learning strategies* that best fulfill your objectives for instruction. For example, students might hear a guest speaker, engage in independent library research to write a paper related to their topics, or create a diorama. Study skills instruction is incorporated in the learning strategies. For example, if notetaking is the focus, instruct the students in how to take notes from an oral presentation before they apply the skill when the guest speaker arrives. Likewise, they should learn a system for taking notes from written materials before they go to the library to read written sources in preparation for writing a research paper.

The next step is *evaluation.* You should decide how mastery of each objective for instruction is to be assessed. Some objectives lend themselves to paper-and-pencil evaluation, whereas others, such as cultural sensitivity, may have to be evaluated by observation. Test questions should reflect what has actually been taught and should clearly measure the objectives for instruction.

The last step in the unit plan is *teacher self-evaluation,* which involves modification of objectives, materials, learning strategies, and student evaluation. A more complete description of the unit plan may be found in Dupuis and Askov (1982).

### Learning Activity Packages (LAPs)

LAPs, which include objectives for instruction, preassessment, learning activities, and postassessment of mastery, are appropriate for independent skill instruction. Although LAPs usually are designed for use by students deficient in a skill area, it is possible for some aspects of a LAP to involve group discussion, interaction, activities, and checking.

An advantage to using LAPs is that once they have been created and duplicated, they may be reused in the future. Most of the drawbacks to LAPs involve their use. Although you could assign only specific parts of a LAP for use with a particular student, or provide for partial use through pretesting, the tendency is to use the complete LAP with all students, regardless of level of skill development. Furthermore, because LAPs usually are in mimeographed form, it is tempting to include strictly paper-and-pencil activities. However, used creatively, LAPs can contain more involved activities such as collecting a set of data or constructing tables or graphs to present the data.

## STUDY SKILLS

Now we will suggest some activities for teaching study skills in the content areas. These activities would have to be adapted not only for the particular content area but also for the reading abilities of the students. (A more complete array of study skills teaching ideas may be found in Askov and Kamm, 1982.)

## EXPLORE: A STUDY TECHNIQUE

Basic to all student learning from printed material is the need for a *study technique.* It is through the use of a study technique that students can unlock content area reading tasks. Two popular techniques that are often cited in the literature are *SQ3R* (Robinson, 1961) and *PQRST* (Spache, 1963). Another similar study technique that we have developed is *EXPLORE,* a four-step procedure which students in elementary schools can use to explore their content reading assignments. Each step in this technique is designed for student self-monitoring; it is a tool that students can utilize to control their own learning from content assignments. The four steps are outlined below.

### Step 1: Examine

Students are first taught to *examine* their assigned reading task. To do this, students read the chapter headings and subheadings. Marginal notes are read. All graphic aids, pictures, maps, charts, tables, etc., are "read" or examined. The introductory paragraph and the concluding paragraph are read. Any italicized or special print is noted. From this examination, or overview, students are prepared for the next step.

### Step 2: Plan

In step 2, students are ready to *plan* what they will learn from the reading assignment. To plan, students should take a piece of notebook paper and jot down questions they have developed from the headings, the subheadings, the pictures, maps, or any other graphic aids. Any chapter questions, either introductory questions or concluding questions, should be included on the notebook page.

### Step 3: Absorb

With the list of questions in hand, students are ready for step 3, *absorb;* they are ready to read the assignment and absorb the information. As the students read they should jot down a key word or two as answers to the questions developed in the planning stage (step 2).

### Step 4: Evidence/Express

Having completed step 3, the students are ready to *provide evidence of their learning.* Complete answers to the questions in step 2 can be expressed by the students. An adequate logical answer is expected for each question. The notebook page of questions should now contain complete answers. The question-and-answer sheet should be saved for later review of the content reading and student self-checking of the learning.

Through the use of a study technique like *EXPLORE,* students are ready to learn from their content area reading assignments.

## BOOK UTILIZATION

Because textbooks are primary tools used in the learning process, students need to become familiar with them and their many features. All content area teachers have the responsibility of teaching students to use textbooks efficiently and effectively. What are the features of a textbook about which students need to learn?

### Title Page

Students need to know the title of the textbook and how *this* particular textbook will be related to the class. Certainly students should learn to recognize the author or editor and the difference that each serves. The year of publication is also essential, especially in the sciences, because students need to begin making judgments on the "newness" or "current status" of the information contained in the book.

### Table of Contents

Through a review of the table of contents, students will have a road map or plan for the book. They will begin to develop a cognitive framework of what they will be studying and learning from the textbook. Have students determine the organization of the book. Does it follow a time line? Is it organized around topics or themes? Is the information presented in a simple-to-complex progression? Have students predict what they will learn from the textbook or develop a series of broad questions they would like to explore through the use of the text. Games and activities can be developed from the table of contents. Finally, through the exploration of the table of contents, students are exposed to a type of organization, or outline, a format that is an important study tool.

### Glossary

Does the textbook contain a glossary? What is a glossary? Have students explore the glossary to determine what terms are included; are abbreviations listed; are synonyms provided; is a pronunciation guide included? Many dictionary-usage games and activities can be adapted to a textbook glossary.

### Index

What do students need to know about an index? Students should recognize that the index is a detailed alphabetical listing of the topics covered in the text. Information can be located quickly through the use of the index. It is easy to determine how well a topic is covered by noting the number of references made to a topic. Students need to know what each of the following entries indicates:

| | |
|---|---|
| polar bears 89 | (one page) |
| polar bears 89,97,102 | (three pages) |
| polar bears 89–96 | (seven pages) |

Additionally, teach students to recognize that the italicized or bold, dark printed page numbers often indicate the page(s) on which the topic is defined or explained succinctly. Finally, students are often confused when the index includes: "polar bears (see bears)" or "See also." They need to learn the procedures for use of these designations.

### Appendix

Often the most overlooked book part is the appendix. Have students explore the appendix of the textbook. Does the appendix contain maps, tables, charts, samples, or government documents?

### Additional Aids

Some textbooks contain additional aids with which students need to become familiar. Marginal notes often are found and serve as guides to reading. Visual aids such as maps, pictures, diagrams, charts, and tables all serve the important function of providing additional information. You need to teach students the importance of the visual aids and how to read or interpret them. Boxed or shaded or colored areas can be found in many books. These special areas provide rules, formulas, definitions, or principles. Students need to learn that this special information is important and has been purposely set off or highlighted.

## NOTETAKING

*Notetaking*[1] is another important skill that students need to acquire. Perhaps a more appropriate term would be "note making," for students must learn to make notes. The notes must be made in the students' own words for the process to have meaning and to ensure greater learning; the information from a textbook or speaker must be processed cognitively and translated into notes that are meaningful for the student.

Students need to acquire several basic concepts that will facilitate "note making." Among the concepts are *chronological order, comparison and contrast,* and *simple listing.*

*Chronological order,* or the time line of events, is an important concept for students to learn. Students need to recognize what happened first, second, third. Encourage students to build their own time lines, which list their daily activities; steps in a science experiment; events leading to the Boston Tea Party; planning a trip; and, events from the *Tale of a Fourth Grade Nothing.*

*Comparison and contrast* is another concept students need to acquire. From the different content areas, have students compare and contrast:

*Social Studies:* two countries, type of government, climate, occupation of people, and customs.

*Science:* the nutritional value of two foods and physical appearance of two fish.

*Language Arts:* two poems on the same topic, two characters from a story, and treatment of a news story from two different newspapers.

*Math:* shopping for a particular item in two different stores or buying two small cans of the same item versus buying a large can.

*Simple Listing* is another important concept students need to acquire. This can be accomplished through the description of an item:

*Science:* qualities of a mineral.

*Social Studies:* the wigwams of an Indian tribe.

*Language Arts:* the physical description of a character.

When students have acquired these concepts, learning "note making" will become more natural.

Notetaking, or "note making," should be taught as a skill to help mem-

[1]This information has been adapted from a series of "Reading in the Content Areas" workshops presented during 1978 by D. A. Evans and J. T. Heller, Williamsport (PA) Area School District.

ory and as a means of saving time and effort. Well-taken notes can serve as a memory jogger and help students avoid rereading of content materials. Notetaking can assume many forms: outlining, mapping, and summarizing are some formats. Students should be encouraged to develop their own style of notetaking.

Some basic teaching ideas include providing students with sentences, paragraphs, and, finally, longer selections. Have the students read or listen to the sentences, paragraphs, and longer selections and then, in their own words, briefly write or tell what the selection was about. As students gain in skill and confidence, progressively longer and more difficult materials can be assigned.

When students have acquired basic notetaking skills and are applying the skills, a few additional points need to be made. Students need to follow these steps or procedures for notetaking to be effective:

Step 1: Develop their notes from the reading or from the speaker.

Step 2: After making their notes, "complete" their notes. Read the notes and fill in any vague or unclear areas. Accuracy and clarity are the goals in this step.

Step 3: Relate their notes to previous learning. (How does this information help me better understand the topic?) Search for relationships.

Step 4: Review their notes frequently. Try to recall as much information about the topic as they can through the use of their notes.

## OUTLINING

*Outlining* is used most frequently as a tool for developing a speech or a written report. Students need to begin learning outlining skills in the intermediate grades. A prerequisite skill to outlining is identification of a main idea and details. Teachers at all grade levels should teach this skill. When students are ready to begin outlining, several ideas can be used to teach this skill:

1. Provide students with a partial outline and have them complete it from a list of related subtopics or details.
2. Provide students with a scrambled outline. Have the students organize the outline.
3. Provide students with a partial outline and a reading selection. Have students read the selection and complete the outline.
4. Collect several brief, one-page articles or stories related to a content area topic. When students are studying that topic, have them read the article and develop an outline.
5. Have students identify a topic of interest to them that is related to a unit and begin to develop a report on the topic. Have students generate a series of questions on the topic. An example might be a talk on a hobby, like photography. Some questions that might be addressed could include:
    a. Why do I like photography?
    b. What equipment do I need?
    c. How do I care for my equipment?

d. Are there any special effects/tricks I can do with my camera?
e. Could my hobby become a career?

Have the students change their questions into outlining headings or topics. Have them organize the headings into a logical sequential presentation. Students should now read to complete their outline. From the detailed outline, students will be ready to develop their oral or written reports.

## LIBRARY SKILLS

As you plan your units of study for students, the school library serves as a tremendous resource center. Students need to become familiar with the many resources available in the library. Consider learning to use the school library as an important set of study skills.

### Dewey Decimal System

Most school libraries use the Dewey Decimal System for arranging books. Therefore, you should teach students to use this system. Making posters with information about the Dewey Decimal System provides students with a guide for exploring the library. Games such as "Guess Where You'll Find Me?" can be developed. With this game you should provide titles for books or descriptions of books/materials and ask students where the books/materials would be found. Assigning topics for reading of content materials provides another avenue for exploring the Dewey Decimal System. The students could use sources from several different categories when doing the American Indian unit plan. The categories of history, arts, myths, literature, and generalities should provide a variety of resources for exploring the topic.

### Card Catalog

When students have begun to understand the general arrangement of the library, it is time for them to learn how to use the card catalog. The card catalog is a tool used to research topics for information. Students need to learn to use:

| Author Card: | Jones, Brian<br>The American Indian<br>Smith Publisher, Inc. 1984 |
|---|---|

| Title Card: | The American Indian<br>Jones, Brian<br>The American Indian<br>Smith Publisher, Inc. 1984 |
|---|---|

| Subject Cards: | Indians, American<br>Jones, Brian<br>The American Indian<br>Smith Publisher, Inc., 1984 |
|---|---|

| Cross Reference: | American Indian Folk Tales<br>*See*<br>Folk Tales American Indian |
|---|---|

Sample cards provide students with a general introduction to the variety of cards. As you plan your teaching units, you can devise particular activities for the units which will require students to use the card catalog. Through actual experiences with the card catalog, students will learn to use this resource. An example from a unit on American Indians might be:

1. Read one folk tale from/about American Indians.
2. Construct/draw an Indian village.
3. Compare and contrast an Indian tribe from northeastern United States with a tribe from southwestern United States.

Not only will students have practice with and learn about the card catalog and other library resources, but the activities will be completed in the context of learning content area knowledge, the most effective basis for teaching study skills.

### Other Reference Books

*Encyclopedias.* At the intermediate-grade level, the encyclopedia should become an important resource for information. Yet, as teachers, we must recognize that the reading level of most encyclopedias is quite high. Therefore you need to give assignments based on students' reading ability. A set of junior encyclopedias, written on a lower level, is a good resource for all school libraries. Students should be taught that information in an encyclopedia is arranged in alphabetical order. Activities that require students to find the specific volume where information can be found are good ideas. For example, ask such questions as:

1. Where would I find information about the first manned space flight?
2. Where would I find a chart that shows the equivalence of a mile to kilometer; a pound to grams?

Another activity would be to provide students with specific questions on a topic. To answer the questions—for example, questions on American Indians or bears or photography—the student would need to read the encyclopedia article. Finally, as they prepare their own oral or written reports, students should read all related information on the topic, written on the appropriate reading levels, including encyclopedias.

Almanacs, which update information annually, and atlases, which contain maps, are other resources available in school libraries. You need to introduce students to these resources as they are needed in content area studies. The use of centers or LAPs can focus on use of these resources.

To guarantee maximum effectiveness, instruction on study skills must be provided in the context of content area instruction. Study skills need to be applied immediately in real tasks to facilitate transfer from instruction to application. Through content area instruction, which incorporates study skills instruction, students will be "learning how to learn" in the most efficient and productive manner.

## REFERENCES

ASKOV, E.N., & KAMM, K. (1982). *Study skills in the content areas.* Boston: Allyn & Bacon.

ASKOV, E.N., & OTTO, W. (1985). *Meeting the challenge: Corrective reading instruction in the classroom.* Columbus, OH: Chas. E. Merrill.

DUPUIS, M.M., & ASKOV, E.N. (1982). *Content area reading; an individualized approach.* Englewood Cliffs, NJ: Prentice-Hall.

ROBINSON, F.P. (1961). *Effective study* (rev. ed.). New York: Harper & Row.

SPACHE, G. (1963). *Toward better reading.* Champaign, IL: Garrard.

## SUGGESTED READINGS

CHEYNEY, A.B. (1984). *Teaching reading skills through the newspaper* (2nd ed.). Newark, DE: International Reading Association.

EARLE, R. (1976). *Teaching reading and mathematics.* Newark, DE: International Reading Association.

LUNGSTRUM, J. & TAYLER, B. (1978). *Teaching reading in the social studies.* Newark, DE: International Reading Association.

MOORE, D.W., READENCE, J.E., & RICKELMAN, R.J. (1982). *Prereading activities for content area reading and learning.* Newark, DE: International Reading Association.

THELEN, J. (1984). *Improving reading in science* (2nd ed.). Newark, DE: International Reading Association.

# FOURTEEN
# TEACHING WRITING STRATEGIES FOR THE CONTENT AREAS

The purpose of this chapter[1] is to describe three strategies for improving content area learning by integrating writing and reading.

## WRITING: BRIDGE BETWEEN READING AND LEARNING

Just as a bridge can span a waterway and connect two separate pieces of land, so can writing connect reading and learning. We know that about 80 percent of what we read is forgotten and about 20 percent is remembered. As a teacher, one of your tasks is to help students remember more than 20 percent of what they read. Integrating writing activities with content area reading can help students learn to identify important information in print and remember it better. Key-word notetaking, outlining, and précis writing are based on several ideas from learning theory:

> Active involvement in processing print (physically and cognitively) aids learning.
>
> Manipulating language to construct or generate meaningful text after reading enhances learning.

[1]Some of the ideas in this chapter derive from an article by Karen D'Angelo, "Précis Writing: Promoting Vocabulary Development and Comprehension." *Journal of Reading, 26* (March 1983), 534–539.

Visual representation of material aids recall.

Organized information is more easily stored and remembered.

Results of current research and practice also indicate that when key-word notetaking, outlining, and précis writing accompany content area reading they can promote learning for students in middle and upper elementary grades. Vocabulary growth, comprehension, and retention can be positively affected when reading is reinforced with these writing strategies.

## BEFORE INSTRUCTION: SOME CONSIDERATIONS

You should be aware that even those students who possess well-developed fundamental skills in reading and writing may not possess effective content area reading and writing skills. Content area learning calls for special reading and writing skills not usually taught in basal reading programs. Unlike basal readers, content material, such as science and social studies, is expository (written to explain) and factual (containing technical words and various organizational patterns). Training students in reading and writing activities to promote their learning of content material is important.

It is critical that students understand the *purpose* of any strategy *before* it is taught to them. Group discussions will help students identify the reasons for learning a certain strategy, the uses they will have for it, and the advantages this strategy has for helping them learn and remember information. Further, it is important for you to realize that careful training over a long period of time is necessary in order to learn a new strategy. Often a teacher will underestimate the amount of time students need to spend working together in order to be able to work independently with success. Training in any one of the strategies described here should probably cover a time period of two or three lessons a week for a month or more before most students can be expected to work successfully on their own.

In summary, when you and your students understand the importance and *purpose* of a particular writing strategy, then the teaching and learning of that strategy will be easier. When you can help students understand "why" something will benefit them, then teaching the "how" is not a problem.

## KEY-WORD NOTETAKING

*Notetaking* is one way that students can learn to record important information from a book or lecture for later use. Traditionally, notetaking has served as a way of studying for tests, but when a notetaking system is learned and used consistently by students it can aid in organizing, outlining, and writing written reports and research papers. Most students, at all grade levels including college, do not know how to take good notes because they have never understood the purpose of notes and they have not been taught a system that makes sense to them. The following describes a format for teaching one notetaking strategy.

### Set Purposes

Some obvious purposes follow. You may wish to add others that emerge from your discussion with students.

To identify important information in text and reinforce this information by writing it.

To provide a written record for later use (either to study for a test or to write a report or research paper).

### Identify Key Words

Students must first learn to identify "key" words in print. Just as a metal key can unlock a door, so can a key word unlock the meaning of a sentence. Just as all doors cannot be opened by the same key, so too the meaning of all sentences cannot be unlocked by the same key word. A sentence may have one or more key words. A key word is:

A critical word that clues or signals meaning.

Basic or essential to an idea in the sentence.

Needed in order to restate or paraphrase the sentence.

Personally important and helps the individual remember what the sentence is about.

Students will need several lessons to practice identifying key words. Suggestions for group activities follow in sequence. Students can:

1. *Look at* a series of pictures or slides and *determine* one word from each that best describes it.
2. *Listen to* a series of sentences and *decide* which word is most important in that sentence.
3. *Look at* a series of sentences on a transparency using an overhead projector and *choose* key words in each sentence. For example:
   a. *Sea otters* were *nearly extinct* 100 years ago.
   b. The *forward movement* of an airplane is called *"thrust."*
   c. In the U.S. we *celebrate* the 4th of July with *fireworks.*
4. *Discuss* these activities as a small group or as a class to *develop* the concept of key word as the most important word.

### Restate Ideas

When you have determined that students can identify key words, learning to retell or restate the idea the key word stands for is next. Students can:

1. *Listen to* a short selection and *write* any key word heard. Lists should be reviewed and clarified by adding or deleting words.
2. *Orally restate* the message of the selection with a phrase or sentence for each key word. Students should be encouraged to paraphrase and put ideas into their own words.
3. *Look at* a short selection on a transparency and *underline* key words. For example:

   ***Daddy Longlegs*** A daddy longlegs has *eight* long, thin *legs.* A daddy longlegs has *four pairs* of legs. A daddy longlegs can travel very *fast.* Daddy longlegs spend much of their time cleaning or "*preening*" their long legs. The body of a daddy longlegs is round or *oval.* Behind the front legs there are two *odor glands.* Daddy longlegs are *related* to *spiders,* but are not true spiders.
4. *Write* the key words and *orally restate* the selection by looking only at the key words.

Restating or paraphrasing ideas is often difficult for students. They should be taught to use their own words and supply synonyms whenever possible. A dictionary or thesaurus can be helpful in learning this skill.

### Writing Notes From Key Words

Once students can identify key words and orally restate ideas by expanding key words into phrases and/or sentences, it is time to extend these skills by writing notes from key words. Again, the use of an overhead projector can be helpful to show visually how key words and expanded notes can be generated. Several group lessons of this type should be carried out with a short selection before students begin to work independently. Students can:

1. *Listen to* the teacher read a content area selection, *record* key words, then *convert* these words to phrases.
2. *Silently read* a content area chapter or selection, *write* key words notes, and *convert* these words to notes. For example:

   ***Computers*** Computers are machines. They are fast and accurate and have amazing memories. People have to decide which facts to put into the computer. They have to plan the program that tells the computer what to do with the facts. People have to interpret and use the information that comes out of the computer.

#### KEY WORD EXPANSIONS:

| | |
|---|---|
| computers | Computers are machines. |
| fast | They are fast and can remember. |
| memories | |
| facts | Facts are put into computers by people. |
| programs | People program the computer to use the facts. |
| interpret | People decide how to use the information. |

In the format suggested here, key words are written vertically down the left side of the page, leaving the remainder of the page for expanding the words into phrases and sentences. As students gain skill in writing key-word notes, they should realize that information in a particular selection may be reorganized. Not all writers of content materials organize their work in the best or most understandable way. Students should also realize that when key-word notes are reviewed some may not be critical and can be deleted. Keeping notes short by extending only the most important key words to brief phrases or idea units should provide students with enough material to recall what the selection was about or what to study for a test.

Key-word notes also lend themselves to report writing in content areas. Key-word notetaking actively involves students as they read, discourages verbatim copying, and encourages personal written work.

## OUTLINING

*Outlining*—the identification of main ideas and supporting details from a text and the representation of this information in a specified format—can also improve content area learning. An outline is a summary of a subject consisting of a systematic listing of its most important points. Two types of outlining often taught in elementary school are *sentence* and *topic* outlines. In a topic outline, which will be described here, key words and phrases from the text represent main ideas and supporting details.

The form of a topic outline reflects the degree of importance of included ideas. The following form can be used with your students:

I. Main idea (most important or general topic)
    A. Subtopic (important idea about general topic)
        1. Detail (fact to support subtopic)
        2. Detail.
    B. Subtopic (second important idea)
        1. Detail
        2. Detail
II. Another main idea (main ideas begin with Roman numerals)
    A. Subtopic (subtopics are indented and require capital letters)
    B. Subtopic
        1. Detail (details are indented again and need numerals)
        2. Detail

When students learn to make topic outlines as they read content material, these outlines can be used to study for tests. Topic outlines can also be expanded to sentence outlines and used to guide students in writing reports or research papers. Clearer, better organized, and coherent paragraphs and reports/papers will be the result, with fewer revisions and less time spent in rewriting as well.

As with notetaking, outlining can probably best be taught by using a chalkboard, chart paper, or overhead projector so that students can see the form of the outline. The following steps describe a suggested sequence of activities for teaching outlining:

### Set Purposes

Several purposes for learning how to outline should be discussed with students, who will add to the discussion just as they did with notetaking. These purposes are intended to:

Tell the difference between main ideas and supporting details.
Provide information that can be used to study for a test or to write a paper.

If students have first been taught to identify key words this should make main ideas easier to find. Comparing an outline to a tree may also help students see that just as the trunk and branches represent the biggest parts of the tree, in an outline the main ideas and subtopics represent the biggest or most important parts of text content.

Three questions can help students find main ideas in paragraphs:

What or who is the paragraph about?
What is most important or interesting about the paragraph?
What particular "big" idea or topic does the author want you to remember or understand?

### Identify General and Specific Words

A few lessons in identifying "general" and "specific" words are necessary for your students first. You may need to use different vocabulary depending on the ability of your students. Students can:

1. *Look at* sets of three words and *determine* one word from each that is the most general word or main idea:

| | | |
|---|---|---|
| group | Galaxy | Big Mac |
| team | Ford | lunch |
| Yankees | car | sandwich |

2. *Put* each set of three words *in order* from general to specific:

| | | | |
|---|---|---|---|
| relatives | night | fruit | whisper |
| brother | twilight | Ida Red | communicate |
| siblings | 6:30 P.M. | apple | speak |

### Supply General and Specific Words

Once students can identify and tell the difference between general and specific words the next step is to help them verbally supply words that fit these two categories. Students might:

1. *List* specific words to fit under each general word:
   sports dogs rock groups
2. *Name* the general word for each set of specific words:

| fly<br>ladybug<br>mosquito<br>gnat | maple<br>beech<br>oak<br>aspen | elephant<br>tiger<br>alligator<br>kangaroo |
|---|---|---|

3. *Supply* details for a main idea such as:
   I enjoy summer vacation for many reasons.
   *Group* details into two or three subtopics like:
   Things to do outdoors Things to do indoors
   *Write* an outline of the information. For example:
   I. Summer vacation
      A. Things to do outdoors
         1. Swim
         2. Ride a bicycle
         3. Fish
4. *Relate* the terms "general" and "specific" to "main idea," "subtopic," and "detail" using the outline above.
5. *Make* outlines of information for other main ideas such as:
   Faces can show many emotions.
   Many types of living things can be found on the Earth.
   Our solar system is made up of several different bodies.

### Write Brief Outlines

When students are proficient in the above skills you can present them with short passages to read and outline. Students can:

1. *Listen to* short selections as they are read. On a blank outline, together *identify* in writing main ideas and details.
2. *Look at* a short filmstrip or movie of suitable content. On blank outlines have students *fill in* important ideas and details.
3. *Read* short selections and *write* brief outlines of information contained in the selections.
4. *Look at* the outlines written in the above activities, *retell* what was read or heard, and make oral reports from outlines.
5. *Write* summaries of selections using only outlined information.

## PRÉCIS WRITING

Students' memory for and comprehension of content material can be improved as a result of *précis writing* (Bromley, 1985). The ability to write a précis is an important skill that can promote vocabulary growth and comprehension. A *précis* is an abstract or summary of an original composition. It is a paraphrase of someone else's writing, a condensation that retains the information, emphasis, and point of view of the original (Ebbitt & Ebbitt 1978). Usually a précis is less than one-third the length of the original and it involves reading and understanding a sample of text by selecting and rejecting ideas, and also paraphrasing and writing ideas.

Students who learn to write a concise and accurate précis possess a skill that is useful for report writing, research papers, and studying for tests. As each chapter in a content text is read, a précis of it can be written and these summaries kept for review and study before a test.

As with notetaking and outlining, précis writing can effectively be taught using an overhead projector so that students can see the change that the original selection must undergo in the formation of a précis. The following steps describe a suggested format for teaching précis writing.

### Set Purposes

Writing a précis or summary can serve several purposes for students. A précis represents one of the most difficult writing exercises a student will tackle in school, but on the other hand précis writing can help to develop some very sophisticated reading and writing skills. You might want to share with students the fact that pupils in grades two to nine in British and French schools write a précis at least twice a week, and this is seen as an exercise requiring high-level thinking skills. As with notetaking and outlining, the purposes of précis writing should be conveyed first:

To identify main ideas in topic sentences.

To paraphrase main ideas and condense an original work.

To provide a written statement, communicating the essence of the original, that can be reread and studied for a test.

### Identify Main Ideas

Selecting the main ideas of paragraphs is often difficult for both teachers and students. Donlan (1980) found that most teachers consistently identified the first sentence of the paragraph as the main idea, whether or not the main idea appeared there. When the main idea was not given in the first sentence, they generally could not locate it! So we know it is a skill that both teachers and students need to learn. Students must be able to locate the important ideas in a passage before writing a précis. They need to know that a main idea is often expressed in a topic sentence, which

states the central thought or main idea of the paragraph;
can appear anywhere in the paragraph;
is supported by other sentences in the paragraph.

One way to teach topic sentences is to show students graphically how paragraphs are organized. Burmeister (1974) suggests that teachers use five geometric shapes to illustrate possible location of topic sentences:

▽ topic sentence at beginning of paragraph
△ topic sentence at end of paragraph
⧖ topic sentence at beginning and end
◇ topic sentence within paragraph
○ topic sentence not stated

Several lessons in identifying main ideas will be important before teaching précis writing. Understanding overall paragraph organization is a necessary first step. Students can:

1. *Listen to* a series of paragraphs and after each is read *identify* the sentences that contain the most important ideas.
2. *Look at* a series of paragraphs on transparencies and *underline* the topic sentences.
3. *Draw* the geometric shape beside each paragraph that illustrates the location of that paragraph's topic sentence.
4. *Underline* topic sentences on copies of text material, and draw shapes to illustrate locations of topic sentences.

### Paraphrase Ideas

After students can identify topic sentences in content paragraphs, restating or paraphrasing these ideas is next. This step is critical because at this point students must process text by supplying their own words rather than merely copying the words of the author, as is the case in outlining. Better comprehension may result when students process information more deeply by using their own words to elaborate on the text and paraphrase its important ideas. Students can:

1. *Listen to* a series of sentences and *identify* one or two key words to change so that each sentence can be reworded.
2. *Look at* a series of sentences and *determine* words for which synonyms can be substituted so that sentences can be rephrased. (At this point much oral practice is necessary before you ask students to actually write a précis. If this part of the teaching sequence is omitted, students will likely have trouble.)
3. *Underline* topic sentences on copies of content selections, *identify* words to be changed, and *write* synonyms.

| | |
|---|---|
| favorite | Stamp collecting is one of the (most popular |
| pastime | hobbies) in the (United States.) Collectors enjoy |
| U.S. | looking at stamps and learning about them. |
| several | There are (many) ways to (get) stamps for your |
| obtain | collection. You can buy issues of stamps at the |
| | post office and older unused stamps at a stamp |
| | store or from catalogues. But they are expensive! |
| lots | (Many) people (collect) used stamps. There are |
| save | ways to get used stamps at little or no cost. One |
| purchase | way is to (buy packages of used stamps). These |
| them | are inexpensive and they contain many stamps. |
| keep | Another way to get used stamps is to (save |
| letters | envelopes) that come in the mail. Tear off |
| | the corner of the envelope with the stamp. Be |
| | careful not to tear the stamp! |
| take | Now you need to (remove) them (from) the |
| off | envelope corners. Put some cool water (hot water |
| | will fade some stamps) into a bowl. Drop a few |
| | corners with stamps into the water. Let them soak |
| | until the stamps slip off easily. Place them face |
| | down on a newspaper or towel to dry. Then place |
| | them between the pages of a book. When the stamps |
| | are dry and flat, you can arrange them. |
| saving | (Collecting) used stamps is a good inexpensive |
| cheap | way to enjoy a great (hobby). |
| pastime | |

From the *Holt Basic Reading* series, level 13: TIME TO WONDER by Evertts et al. Copyright © 1980 by Holt, Rinehart and Winston, Publishers. Reproduced by permission.

**FIGURE 14-1** Paraphrasing Examples

### Write Précis

If students can identify topic sentences in paragraphs and paraphrase these ideas, writing the précis is the next step. Actually showing students an example of a finished précis so that they know what it is they are expected to do is a good idea. Students can:

1. *Write* a précis from material they have used to identify main ideas and practice synonym substitution. For example:

   Stamp collecting is a favorite pastime in the U.S. There are several ways to obtain stamps. Lots of people buy used stamps. Another way is to take stamps off envelopes that come in the mail. Soak envelopes in cool water until stamps come off. Dry them on a towel and flatten them in a book. Collecting used stamps is a cheap way to have a fun hobby.

2. *Look at* a précis and compare it to the original selection; *discuss* ways that it is similar and ways that it is different.

3. *Write* a précis from actual content area material that is being read in science or social studies.

When students become comfortable with the précis writing process it may not be necessary for them to underline and use geometric shapes. When they are proficient at this task, students will be able to do it quickly and correctly. If précis writing is used consistently with content material then students will have a record of the most important material that they can use to study for tests. You should not overlook the possibility of allowing students time in class to review and reread their précis before taking a test. It is in this way that précis actually will become relevant for your students!

Research with fifth-grade students suggests that précis writing and outlining are equally as effective in promoting content area learning, and students enjoy using both strategies (Bromley, 1985). Research also tells us that students' spelling of content vocabulary improves when they are engaged in summary writing (Cunningham & Cunningham, 1976).

## SUMMARY

We know that key-word notetaking, outlining, and précis writing can enhance retention, comprehension, vocabulary growth, and learning in general. In addition, the strategies provide students not only with skills that promote the writing of reports and research papers but also personalized material to study for tests.

You should adapt the suggestions contained in this chapter whenever necessary, especially if they do not fit your students' needs and there is a more effective way to teach something. Remember that it is critical to spend most of your time engaged in the prewriting activities suggested here. In this way you will ensure that when students are expected to accomplish the writing task independently they have had sufficient oral practice in a group setting to understand well what it is they are to do and then be successful at it.

### *REFERENCES*

BROMLEY, K.D. (1985). Précis writing and outlining enhance content learning. *The Reading Teacher, 38,* 406–411.

BURMEISTER, L. (1974). *Reading strategies for secondary school teachers.* Reading, MA: Addison-Wesley.

CUNNINGHAM, P., & CUNNINGHAM, J. (1976). SSSW, better content writing. *Clearinghouse, 49,* 237–238.

D'ANGELO, K. (1983). Précis writing: Promoting vocabulary development and comprehension. *Journal of Reading, 26,* 534–539.

DONLAN, D. (1980). Locating main ideas in history textbooks. *Journal of Reading, 24,* 135–141.

EBBITT, W.R., & EBBITT, D.R. (1978). *Writer's guide and index to English.* Glenview, IL: Scott, Foresman.

# FIFTEEN ORGANIZING THE CLASSROOM FOR LITERATURE STUDY

As you begin the daily task of teaching children to read and to enjoy their reading, you will become acutely aware of the need to make the reading personal for each child. You will recognize the necessity of building an individualized program of literature in which the unique needs of each child are met. However, unless you also understand *how* to organize and implement such a plan, the program will forever remain an ideal rather than a reality.

The purpose of this chapter is to examine specific techniques for initiating and maintaining a classroom reading program that focuses on library books. It will describe such basic procedures as setting up the library center and using children as librarians. It will offer you help in directing student book selection, independent reading, book sharing, and record keeping. It will also feature competent ways of interviewing students and conferencing with parents. Self-rating instruments are included in the chapter to assist you and your students in evaluating the effectiveness of the literature program.

## PREPARING THE CLASSROOM

The first requirement of a library-centered reading program is a collection of appealing books close at hand from which students may choose at will. No certain number of books is required for such a classroom reading center, but there certainly should be an ample number of titles to give students a wide selection according to their individual preferences and reading abilities.

**FIGURE 15-1** Two kindergarten girls discuss the illustrations in a Caldecott Award book from their classroom library center. From Coody, Betty, *Using Literature with Young Children* 3rd ed. © 1979, 1983. Wm. C. Brown, Publishers, Dubuque, Iowa. All rights reserved. Reprinted by permission.

You will find the central library in your school the best single source of books for your classroom collection. Needless to say, it pays to establish a good working relationship with the school librarian if you are to check out dozens of books to be kept for several weeks at a time. As the literature teacher, it is your responsibility to select the books for your classroom and to check them out from the central library. You will also be responsible for transporting them to the classroom and for arranging them into a few easy categories such as "Poetry," "Animal Stories," "Sports," etc. The classifications will change as students grow and mature in reading. The shelves will need to be restocked from time to time with new titles. Moreover, by featuring seasonal and holiday books on a regular basis the collection can be given a new and updated look. You will do well to appoint a rotating committee of students to assist with each aspect of the operation. Students can relieve you of many tedious details, and you have the added benefit of a keener interest in the library program.

A student-interest inventory should be taken periodically to help you in determining what books your students can and will read. Open-ended questions similar to the ones given below will provide a great deal of useful information to guide you in checking books from the central library:

1. What is the name of your favorite book?
2. What do you like best about our reading class?
3. Which library book are you now reading?
4. What is the next book you plan to read?
5. What are your hobbies?
6. What is your main hobby?
7. Do you collect anything? If so, what?
8. What games or sports do you like?
9. What is your favorite television program?
10. What is the best movie you've ever seen?
11. Who is your favorite author?
12. What do you like best about reading books?

Once you have decided on a series of questions, ask them a few at a time and make notes on the children's responses. Use the findings to choose books for classroom use and for recommending titles to parents who request help in book selection.

Once reading interests have been determined, another essential factor to consider in book acquisition is the readability level of each book—the relative ease with which the sentences may be read and understood. In general, the books should range from very easy to rather difficult in order to suit the varied reading abilities to be found in your class. Some obvious features to look for in selecting easy-to-read books are plenty of white space around words and sentences, large bold print, realistic illustrations, ample dialogue among characters, and interesting subjects. Never underestimate the ability of the students themselves to choose books they can read comfortably. When plenty of time for browsing is permitted and encouraged, the problem of readability seems to solve itself.

The popularity of the library center in the classroom depends to a large extent on its beauty, order, and eye appeal. Children's books are attractive in their own right and should be displayed to their best advantage with as many covers showing as possible. You might consider using some of the successful display techniques employed by professional booksellers such as colorful posters, book-related sculpture and artifacts, green plants, art prints, and other materials that serve to enhance books. In addition to the books and book shelves, the center should contain a library table, a few comfortable slip-covered chairs, and perhaps some pillows and an area rug. An attractive, well-organized library center often becomes an oasis in a busy, crowded classroom, and in the long run this pays rich dividends in reading interest and achievement.

## THE SYSTEM IN OPERATION

A successful literature program always allows students time to browse leisurely and to read independently. It takes time to scan, ponder, reject, and finally decide on a book to check out for further reading. As students grow in the skill of self-selection, fewer and fewer errors are made, and students become very efficient at choosing books they can read and will read.

Once the right book has been chosen, the student needs time to read silently and independently in an uninterrupted fashion on school time. The period need not be a lengthy one, but long enough to whet the appetite for further reading and to show that you the teacher fully support independent, self-selected reading. Bookmarks should be provided and students encouraged to continue reading any time a few spare minutes present themselves. Reading in spare time has a tendency to cut down on behavior problems caused by sheer boredom, and thus it becomes a classroom-management practice. The

**FIGURE 15-2** The Library Center

main benefit, however, is that reading in spare time has a way of becoming a lifelong habit.

An important feature of the individualized literature program is the student reading-record chart. It provides you and the student with a graphic picture of achievement and encourages further reading. To make such a reading-record chart, attach a series of pockets to poster board or plywood or to a bulletin board. The pockets may be made of small boxes or sturdy envelopes. As each library book is completed, the student writes its title, author, and the date of completion on a small card and files it in his or her special pocket that has been numbered or coded in some other manner. Enjoyment comes first in reading the book and secondly in watching the card pack grow. The reading-record chart should be recognized as a motivational device to be abandoned when a child no longer needs it, or to be omitted altogether for the child who reads widely in many books but has no interest in keeping a written record of such reading.

A few basic criteria should be followed in constructing a student reading-record chart. It should first of all be colorful, attractive, and appropriate to the age level of your students. Because it will remain on view for many months at a time, it should be a decorative beauty spot for the classroom wall. The chart should always contain a caption that promotes books and reading—a title that tells a story of the chart's purpose to all passersby. Obviously, the reading-record chart should be durable. Because it is to be posted at eye level and used daily by the children it needs to be well constructed of sturdy materials. Each pocket on the chart becomes a child's personal and private storage space. The only competition involved is the student's own past reading record.

Even though the main purpose of a reading-record chart is motivational, the card pack of titles is very useful in parent–teacher conferences. It tells parents how many books have been read independently, the student's level of reading, and provides a clue as to individual taste and preferences in literature. This kind of information is not readily available elsewhere and certainly not to be found on the traditional report card.

A favorite feature of the individualized literature program being described in this chapter is the planned and scheduled sharing of books. The next best thing to reading a good book is telling someone else about it, and students agree that the most enjoyable book reports are those made orally. Lively, informative book-sharing sessions are beneficial for many reasons. They promote further independent reading because students have a strong tendency to read books recommended by their peers. In fact, they very seldom select total "strangers" off the shelf for independent reading. In an informal way, quality book discussions teach boys and girls about plot, theme, characterization, style, and other literary elements that develop in them a lasting sense of story. A program of successful book sharing helps to build positive attitudes toward books and reading—attitudes that tend to build lifelong readers.

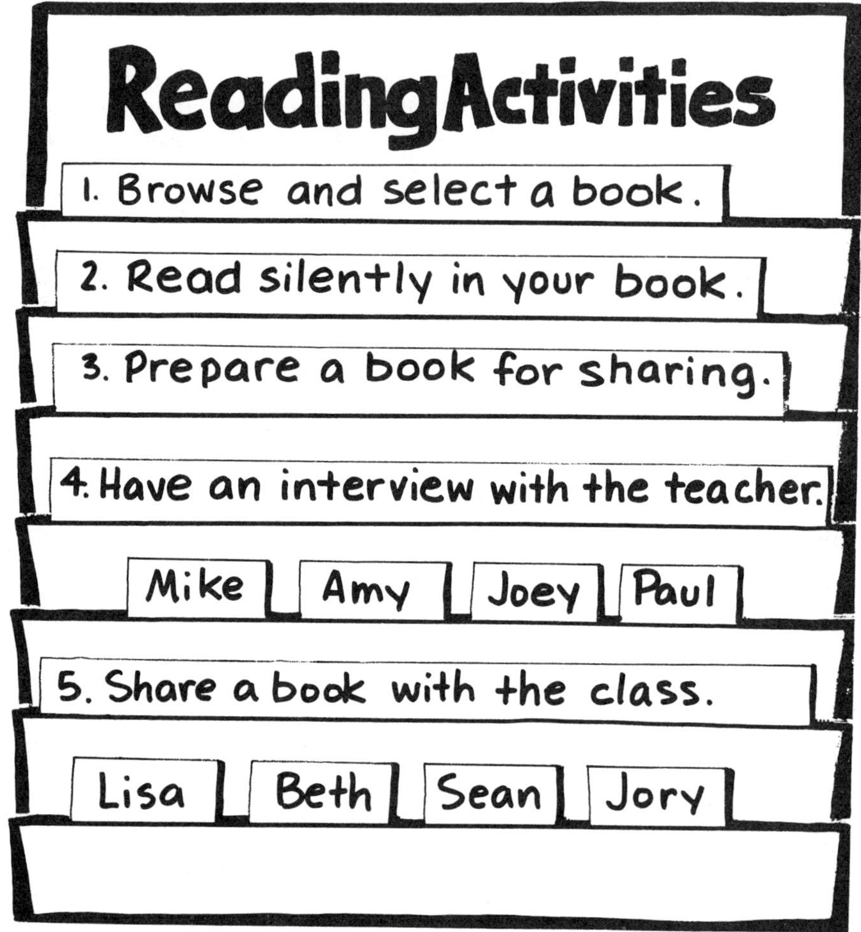

Reading Activities
1. Browse and select a book.
2. Read silently in your book.
3. Prepare a book for sharing.
4. Have an interview with the teacher.
Mike
Amy
Joey
Paul
5. Share a book with the class.
Lisa
Beth
Sean
Jory


**FIGURE 15-3** Reading Activities

An easy and effective way to organize the book-sharing sessions is to use a pocket chart for rotating the names of students who are prepared to report on a favorite book. Students place their own name cards on the chart when a report is ready. At a glance you are able to see how many students wish to make a report and how much time you need to allot to the session. As reports are finished, names are removed. If time runs out before all reports are completed, the remaining names come up first at the next scheduled session. This system is fair and impartial, and no student is overlooked.

In order for your students to derive maximum benefit from the time spent on oral book reporting, you will need to develop the art of asking provocative questions at times when a student is suddenly at a loss for words or when the group discussion lags.

To illustrate how your questions may proceed from surface questions to higher-level ones that call for personal involvement, Peter Spier's book *People* (1980) will serve as an example. It is a factual story about people the world over, their customs, traditions, languages, religions, games, hobbies, and pets. The book is illustrated with numerous fascinating details that lend themselves to class discussion. Some suggested discussion questions follow:

### RECOGNITION AND RECALL

How many human beings live on this earth?
Are there any two people exactly alike?
What are the three main religions?
Is "cricket" a game popular in China, Great Britain, or the United States?

### DEMONSTRATION OF SKILLS

Show me how "sukatan" is played.
Locate Italy on the globe.
Spell your name in sign language.

### COMPREHENSION AND ANALYSIS

Why do people live in different kinds of homes?
Why do people have different tastes in art and music?
Why do some people excel at things others could never do?
Why do some people cry at weddings while others smile?

### SYNTHESIS

What would the world be like if all people were exactly the same?
What if you were one of the millions of people who cannot read or write?
What would it be like if you could never have any privacy?

### OPINION

Why are some people who want to work unable to find a job? What is your opinion?
Why do you think some people are rich and powerful while most are not?
Why do you think we still remember people like Benjamin Franklin?

### ATTITUDES AND VALUES

How do you feel when you hear people speaking a language you cannot understand?
Why are most people both wise and foolish?

Why do people everywhere love to play and laugh?
How do you feel about a religion other than your own?

## THE TEACHER-STUDENT INTERVIEW

Students tend to read many more library books and have more enthusiasm for the reading program in classes where teachers find time to talk with them privately about their personal reading. Such a task may seem impossible at first, but if the session is kept brief, and if you follow a plan, it can be managed. A few minutes two or three times a month of your undivided attention focused on the student's independent reading can be extremely encouraging. You may wish to use the same pocket chart in which you schedule book-sharing sessions to keep yourself and the students apprised of upcoming interviews.

While the rest of the class is engaged in independent work of various kinds, set up an interview station in the quietest corner of the classroom and begin the series of interviews with the child whose name appears first on the chart.

In a short period of time, five minutes or so, you should ask several pertinent questions about the current library book being read by the student, listen to the reading of a passage from the book (chosen and prepared in advance by the child), and make recommendations for further reading. On completion of the interview, you will wish to make notations on your impressions, on problems that might need corrective measures, and on points that call for follow-up in future interviews. Believe it or not, this routine can become a smooth and efficient operation that brings pleasure to both you and your students. Your notebook (with dated notations) becomes a kind of handbook for problem solving and a graphic record of reading achievement.

## PARENTS AS PARTNERS IN READING

Many teachers working with the individualized approach to literature study have found that face-to-face conferences with parents have done much to dispel any misgivings about time allotted to independent reading in the classroom. Actually, such meetings have been a key factor in creating a feeling of goodwill about the method. Through the scheduled conference at school, teacher and parents (often teacher, parents, and child) compare views regarding independent reading and literature. A wholesome relationship is established in which the child becomes even more fully aware that important and respected adults in his or her life are interested in the youngster's reading progress and are in agreement on the best way to bring it about.

As you plan conferences with parents in which the literature program is to be discussed, you might wish to keep in mind the following suggestions:

1. Be prepared to explain how the program is organized and how it works day in and day out.
2. Have on hand a folder containing notations made during interviews with the child being discussed.
3. Be prepared to make specific suggestions as to ways parents can help with the child's independent reading.
4. Allow parents plenty of time to ask questions and to make comments. Give a complete and thoughtful answer to each question.
5. Do not compare the progress of children in the class; focus on only one child at a time.
6. Show that you know the child's taste in literature by discussing specific titles that have been read. (The reading-record chart helps to provide this information.)
7. Make certain that the child, if present at the conference, is prepared to participate. Ask the child to read orally a short passage from a library book—a selection that has been chosen by the child and prepared in advance. You guarantee three-way satisfaction as you, the child, and parents listen to really effective oral reading.
8. After approximately 20 minutes, begin the closure of the conference. Make plans for any future meetings with parents and assure them you will keep in touch.
9. End the conference on a positive note. You may wish to invite the parents to visit the class at a time when book sharing is in progress. Allow them to go away feeling that they are actually *in* on their child's reading development.
10. Once the conference is over, analyze it as to its relative effectiveness. Ask yourself what went right and what went wrong. Use such observations to improve the quality of the next conference.

Parent–teacher conferences are now a major method of reporting all areas of student progress to parents, but to the teacher of individualized reading, they are an absolute necessity. Not only do the parents need to know how and why you use this approach but you also need their approval and cooperation for it to be completely successful. Conferencing skills can be learned. They are improved and refined only with practice, but you will find them well worth the effort as you see wholesome attitudes and feelings toward books and reading being developed in your classroom and you realize that those feelings and attitudes will remain with the children throughout life.

## RATING THE CLASSROOM LITERATURE PROGRAM

As you progress in developing your own classroom literature program, you will want some means by which you can do periodic self-assessments. Table 15–1 is a self-rating instrument that was designed to give you an informal method of ranking the classroom literature program by using a set of recommended criteria.

**TABLE 15-1 Developing Appreciation for Literature Inventory (DALI)[1]**

FOR PRIMARY TEACHERS

Circle the numeral on each five-point scale below that best describes the teaching practices under consideration. (One (1) is the lowest rating and five (5) is the highest.) Add total points and refer to key.

| | | | | | |
|---|---|---|---|---|---|
| 1. Do you provide a wide collection of books in the classroom that range from easy to difficult? | 1 | 2 | 3 | 4 | 5 |
| 2. Do you schedule a period each day for independent reading? | 1 | 2 | 3 | 4 | 5 |
| 3. Do you conduct private conferences with students in regard to self-selected reading? | 1 | 2 | 3 | 4 | 5 |
| 4. Do you provide students with an efficient record system for keeping a personal account of self-selected reading? | 1 | 2 | 3 | 4 | 5 |
| 5. Are your students given an opportunity for creative "reporting" on favorite books? | 1 | 2 | 3 | 4 | 5 |
| 6. Do you invite resource persons to your classroom to discuss literature? | 1 | 2 | 3 | 4 | 5 |
| 7. Do your students make use of puppetry to enhance literature? | 1 | 2 | 3 | 4 | 5 |
| 8. Do you read aloud to students on a regular basis? | 1 | 2 | 3 | 4 | 5 |
| 9. Do you use the procedure of storytelling on a regular basis? | 1 | 2 | 3 | 4 | 5 |
| 10. Do you study children's books and reviews of children's books on a regular basis? | 1 | 2 | 3 | 4 | 5 |
| 11. Do your students frequently write and illustrate their own books? | 1 | 2 | 3 | 4 | 5 |
| 12. Do you discuss with students the parts of a book and the people who work to make a book? | 1 | 2 | 3 | 4 | 5 |
| 13. Do you have an organized plan of parent involvement in the literature program? | 1 | 2 | 3 | 4 | 5 |
| 14. Do you help select books for the school library and do you have a voice in determining library policy? | 1 | 2 | 3 | 4 | 5 |
| 15. Do your students read widely and do they appear to enjoy the literature program? | 1 | 2 | 3 | 4 | 5 |
| Total______ | | | | | |

Interpret your total score as follows:

| | |
|---|---|
| Below 50 | You definitely need to enrich your literature program. |
| From 50 to 65 | Your literature program is about average. |
| From 65 to 75 | You have an excellent literature program. |

[1]Betty Coody, *Using Literature with Young Children*, 3rd ed., p. 219. Copyright 1983 by Wm. C. Brown Company Publishers. Used by permission.

## SUMMARY

In order for the literature program to meet the unique needs of each child, you as a teacher need to be aware of the basic components of a personalized program of independent reading. Such an approach calls for a collection of library books in the classroom, time for boys and girls to browse and select their own reading material, time for independent reading, a system of student record keeping, routine book-sharing sessions, scheduled teacher–student interviews, and a plan for parent involvement. A self-rating inventory is offered as a guide for monitoring and evaluating the program.

## *SUGGESTED READINGS*

Coody, B. (1983). *Using literature with young children* (3rd ed.). Dubuque, IA: Wm. C. Brown.
Cullinan, B.C. (1981). *Literature and the child.* New York: Harcourt Brace Jovanovich.
Norton, D.E. (1983). *Through the eyes of a child.* Columbus, OH: Chas. E. Merrill.
Petreshene, S.S. (1978). *Complete guide to learning centers.* Palo Alto, CA: Pendragon House.
Spier, P. (1980). *People.* New York: Doubleday.
Veatch, J. (1978). *Reading in the elementary school.* New York: John Wiley.

# SIXTEEN ENCOURAGING CREATIVE-THINKING ABILITIES THROUGH CHILDREN'S BOOKS

The purpose of this chapter is to introduce you to creative thinking and to identify ways in which creative-thinking skills can be promoted through the use of children's books. We define creativity, describe basic creative-thinking abilities, and identify elements of the classroom environment that foster creative-thinking abilities. We then provide examples of creative-thinking lessons and activities based on specific literature selections.

## WHAT IS CREATIVITY?

Numerous definitions of *creativity* have been offered by individuals interested in the subject. One of the most widely used definitions is by Renzulli (1979, p. 2):

> Creativity is the production of an idea or product that is new, original, and satisfying to the creator or to someone else at a particular point in time, even if the idea or product has been previously discovered by someone else or if the idea or product will not be considered new, original, or satisfying at a later time or under different circumstances.

Another widely accepted definition was formulated by Torrance and Myers (1970). They state that creativity is a type of problem solving in which the learner becomes sensitive to problems, identifies a particular problem, hypothesizes solutions, tests those solutions, and finally communicates the results.

From these definitions, it is evident that creative thinking is both a process and a product. When engaging in activities for fostering creativity, an individual thinks divergently to seek ideas or solutions to problems. The thinking produces results that are unique and satisfying to the individual and perhaps to others.

According to Torrance and Myers (1970) creative potential can be developed by planned activities. We believe creative-thinking activities related to literature can both develop creativity and offer potential for improving it.

## BASIC CREATIVE-THINKING ABILITIES

Four specific creative-thinking abilities have been identified by Renzulli (1979, p. 2):

> Fluency—the ability to generate a ready flow of ideas, possibilities, consequences, and objects.
>
> Flexibility—the ability to use many different approaches or strategies in solving a problem; the willingness to change direction and modify given information.
>
> Originality—the ability to produce clever, unique, and unusual responses.
>
> Elaboration—the ability to expand, develop, particularize, and embellish one's ideas, stories, and illustrations.

Examples based on familiar fairy tales may clarify these four creative-thinking abilities. *Fluency* is called for when pupils are asked to tell other ways Hansel and Gretel might have marked the trail through the woods. Posing the question "Could Cinderella's Prince have found her in any other way? How?" calls for *flexibility.* Asking pupils to act out a new conversation between the mirror and the stepmother in *Snow White* entails *originality.* In the story *Goldilocks and the Three Bears,* having pupils think of items other than the bears' food, chairs, and beds—which Goldilocks might have tried—and having pupils tell whether or not Goldilocks liked each item draws upon the thinking skill of *elaboration.*

These four basic thinking skills—fluency, flexibility, originality, and elaboration—provide a framework for structuring activities that promote creative thinking.

## THE ENVIRONMENT FOR FOSTERING CREATIVE THINKING

As you begin, be sure to establish a classroom environment that fosters creative thinking. Consider these key elements as an initial base:

> Establish an atmosphere of respect and acceptance that values the ideas of each pupil.

Provide opportunities throughout the day for pupils to engage in divergent thinking.

Minimize the threat of teacher evaluation.

Recognize individual differences by accepting a wide range of responses.

Become an active participant in the creative process by engaging in the activities with your pupils.

## INSTRUCTIONAL PLANS WITH CREATIVE THINKING FOLLOW-UP ACTIVITIES BASED ON CHILDREN'S BOOKS

In the following section are presented sample lesson plans that use children's books to encourage creative thinking. We also identify other books, and we briefly suggest possible activities that are listed in Table 16–1 at the end of the chapter.

As you read our plans and suggestions, keep in mind the following points:

Many types of books can be used to promote creative thinking.

Most books can serve a range of grade levels, depending on the activities and the pupils.

Many of the activities foster more than one thinking skill.

Different grouping options can be employed in using the plans—as a whole group, small group, or individually.

Some lessons and activities may require more than one day.

One further word: Don't be discouraged if your first efforts in trying creative-thinking activities aren't highly successful and/or pupils' responses aren't what you expected. Fostering creative-thinking skills takes time, and pupils do become more skillful with experience. Keep trying!

### Instructional Plan 1

*A Snake Is Totally Tail,* by Judi Barrett

Genre: Concept/Language (Picture Book)

Level: Primary, Middle

Creative-Thinking Skills Emphasized: Fluency, Originality

*Summary of Book:* This picture book with single-sentence alliterative text for each page suggests distinctive characteristics of both familiar animals and less familiar ones such as the toucan and anteater.

### Teaching Plan:

*Prereading:* As you name an animal, ask pupils to "think in their heads" of words that describe the most important things about that animal. For example, indicate that when you say *dog* they might think *bark*. Have pupils name the words they thought of for *dog*. Continue with several other examples such as *bird, mouse, cat,* and conclude with *snake*.

*Reading:* Share the book title and have pupils compare their responses for *snake* to the words in the title, that is, *totally tail.* Then read the book aloud, sharing the illustrations on each page.

*Creative thinking follow-up activities:* Select one or more of the following activities:

1. Point out the alliterative words used in the book to identify characteristics of each animal, for example, totally tail, piles of prickles, oodles of odor. Reread the story and have pupils contribute alliterative words to complete each sentence. For example: A snake is curvy and cold; a snake is scaly and slimy.
2. Have pupils name animals not mentioned in the book. After listing the animals, have pupils brainstorm key characteristics of each. Accept all responses without evaluation, and if necessary question to elicit key characteristics. Then, using the pattern of *A Snake Is Totally Tail,* have pupils select from among the animals and write and illustrate several pages for an original class book. Select one child's statement and use it as the title.
3. Suggest some categories that pupils could use for creating individual books using the pattern of *A Snake Is Totally Tail.* Encourage pupils to think of other categories that they might wish to use. Foods, toys, space, and vehicles are among those that would lend themselves well to the activity.

### Instructional Plan 2

*The Aminal,* by Lorna Balian
Genre: Realistic Fiction (Picture Book)
Level: Primary, Middle

**FIGURE 16-1** Two Pages from a Third-Grade Pupil's Book, *Apples Are Rosy Red*

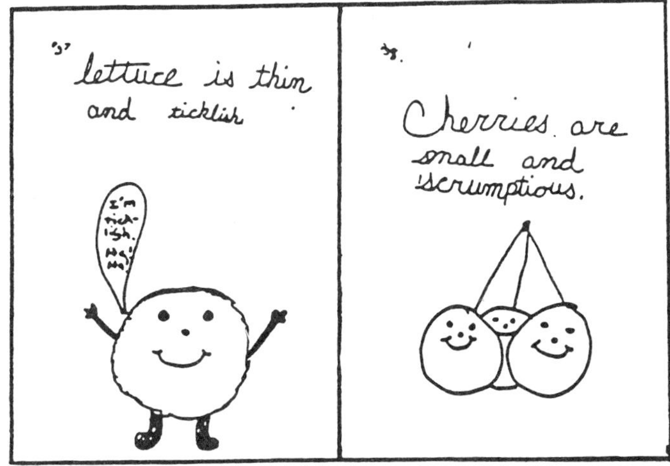


-- by Mandy

Creative-Thinking Skills Emphasized: Flexibility, Originality, Elaboration

*Summary of Book:* While having a picnic, Patrick caught a creature. He put it—the Aminal—in his lunch bag and started for home. When he met Molly, he described the Aminal to her. Molly in turn tells Calvin, and as the description travels from child to child, the Aminal's reputation grows and becomes more ferocious. When the Aminal disappears, Patrick's friends try to find it and discover the Aminal is really just a friendly turtle.

**Teaching Plan:**

*Prereading:* Read the title of the book and have pupils speculate about what kind of creature the Aminal is.

*Reading:* Rather than reading the story straight through, involve pupils in the following activity as the story is being read. Distribute drawing paper. Have pupils fold their papers to make a total of six squares. Ask them to number the squares from 1 to 6. Read the story, stopping after Patrick puts the creature in his lunch bag; in square 1, have pupils make a pencil drawing of the "it" they think Patrick put in his lunch bag. Continue reading the story, stopping after each description of the Aminal, and ask pupils to make a drawing from the description. (Do not show the book's illustrations.) Before reading the ending, which reveals what the Aminal is, have pupils show their illustrations. Then finish reading the story. Reread the story a second time, showing the illustrations from the book.

*Creative thinking follow-up activities:* Select one or more of the following activities:

1. Before starting this activity, caution pupils to keep their drawings secret. Ask them to make a drawing of a common animal. After the drawings are completed, ask pupils to think about a description of the animal. (With older pupils you might have them write down their descriptions.) Then divide the class into groups of five or six pupils. Starting with one pupil in each group, have that pupil whisper the animal description to the next child. That child then whispers what was heard to the next child. Continue around the group until the last child is reached. Have that child recount the description aloud. The child who started with the description can then display the illustration of the animal. Compare the final description with the original one and with the illustration. Follow this procedure until all pupils have had a chance to display their drawings.
2. Have pupils imagine that there is a creature like an Aminal, create a drawing of it, and write an original description. (Older students could imagine that their Aminal is lost and write their description as a Lost-and-Found item for the newspaper.) As time permits, let pupils take turns reading aloud their descriptions while others make drawings. Compare the illustrations.
3. Have pupils recall that Patrick used his lunch bag as a first home for the Aminal. Have pupils brainstorm uses for a lunch bag. To get pupils started, suggest some ideas such as: fire starter, rain cap, wrapping paper. Encourage unique ideas.

### Instructional Plan 3

*I Unpacked My Grandmother's Trunk,* by Susan Ramsay Hoguet

Genre: ABC (Picture Book)

Level: Primary, Middle, Intermediate

Creative-Thinking Skills Emphasized: Fluency, Originality

*Summary of Book:* Improbable objects beginning with each letter of the alphabet are taken from grandmother's trunk. All objects are repeated in the text and illustrations as the next object is added. Split-page illustrations add interest and excitement.

### Teaching Plan:

*Prereading:* Have pupils name things that might be packed in a big trunk.

*Reading:* Read the book. Take time to have pupils name and identify each object and enjoy the lively illustrations.

*Creative thinking follow-up activities:* Select one or more of the following activities:

1. Have pupils list objects for each letter of the alphabet that they would like to find in a trunk. Then let them make their own alphabet book of these objects.
2. Have pupils brainstorm other things that could be unpacked; for example, spaceship, van, and truck. Individually or in small groups, pupils can then create "unpacking" alphabet books. Older students can be encouraged to develop a thematic alphabet book. For example, if they choose a spaceship to unpack, objects for each letter of the alphabet could be related to something associated with a spaceship. Older students could design their alphabet book in the shape of the object to be unpacked and/or use the split-page technique.
3. Have pupils write, tell, or dramatize original stories about two or more of the items shown in the book. You could suggest such topics as how the items came to be in the trunk, or what the two items talk about at night when the trunk is closed.

### Instructional Plan 4

*The Book of Pigericks,* by Arnold Lobel

Genre: Poetry

Level: Middle, Intermediate

Creative-Thinking Skills Emphasized: Fluency, Originality, Elaboration

*Summary of Book:* Thirty-eight witty limericks about all kinds of pigs—young, old, warm, cold, plain, stout—are presented. Detailed illustrations accompany each limerick.

**Teaching Plan:**

*Reading:* Over a period of several days, read aloud the limericks. Reread the ones that pupils especially enjoy.

*Creative thinking follow-up activities:* Select one or more of the following activities:

1. Discuss the word "Pigericks" and compare it to the word "limericks." Guide pupils in concluding that "Pigerick" is a created term for limericks about pigs. Have pupils think of all the other words that could be coined to mean limericks about a specific animal; for example, "catericks," "frogericks," "birdericks." List all the new terms coined.
2. In preparation for having pupils write their own limericks about an animal they select, display two or more of the Pigericks on the chalkboard. Guide pupils in examining the rhyme scheme. Working as a group, elicit pupil ideas and compose a limerick together about an animal other than a pig. Then let pupils work individually, with a partner or in a small group, writing and illustrating books of "catericks," "frogericks," or some other type of limerick about animals.
3. Provide pupils with an inkblot or incomplete drawing. Using crayons, have pupils develop the inkblot or drawing into the most unusual animal they can imagine. Have them write one or more limericks about their animal.

---

***Poor Lucky***

I found a young kittin named Lucky
Who loved to play with his ducky
He fell in the lake
Not his piece of cake
Now he thinks duckies are yucky.
—by Heather

---

(Published by permission)

**FIGURE 16-2** A "Kitterick" Written by a Fifth-Grade Pupil

## SUMMARY

Creativity is a divergent thinking and problem-solving process that results in the development of ideas or products that are new, original, and satisfying. Renzulli's four basic creative-thinking abilities—fluency, flexibility, originality, and elaboration—provide a framework for lessons and activities designed to promote creative thinking based on children's books.

We encourage you to adapt and/or modify our lessons and activities, select other books, and design your own activities for stimulating creative thinking. Enjoy the satisfaction that results from using children's books to promote creative thinking.

## *REFERENCES*

RENZULLI, J.S. (1979). Thinking things up: Training for creativity. *Reading Newsletter,* No. 7. Boston: Allyn & Bacon.

TORRANCE, E.P., & Myers, R.E. (1970). *Creative Learning and Teaching.* New York: Dodd, Mead.

**TABLE 16–1 Suggested Creative Thinking Follow-up Activities for Selected Books**

| GENRE | TITLE | LEVEL* | | | CREATIVE-THINKING SKILLS | | | |
|---|---|---|---|---|---|---|---|---|
| | | P | M | I | FLUENCY | FLEXIBILITY | ORIGINALITY | ELABORATION |
| *WORDLESS* | *Bubble Bubble* M. Meyer | X | X | | | The boy's bubble playmate finds himself left behind and totally alone. Have pupils tell what he does to solve his problem. | | Have pupils create a new bubble creature for the boy OR a new character finds the boy's discarded bubble-maker. What happens next? |
| | *A Special Trick* M. Meyer | X | X | X | Before reading the complete story, have pupils suggest what might happen if Elroy touches something on the magician's table and lets loose those magic powers. | | Elroy was searching for a spell that would fix things. Have pupils create a new spell for the magician's book. What happens when the magician reads it? | Have pupils develop their own book of spells. The book could be indexed and spells arranged by categories. |
| *ABC BOOKS* | *On Market Street* A. Lobel | X | X | X | Have pupils predict what could be bought on Market Street (items for each letter of the alphabet). Compare the predictions to those used in text. | Have pupils create a dramatization or art work showing what the friend did with the items that were purchased on Market Street. Were they put to unusual uses? Could they be combined in any way? | Have pupils develop their own "shopping" book for a new specialty area such as the supermarket, toy store, hardware store, school cafeteria, etc. | Have pupils design illustrations for each page of an original book using the items "purchased" to elaborately dress each character that will appear in their book. |

*P = primary; M = middle; I = intermediate.

| | | | | | | | | |
|---|---|---|---|---|---|---|---|---|
| | *Q Is For Duck* M. Elting and M. Folsom | X | X | X | Have pupils contribute alliterative words and phrases, beginning with two words and then increasing the number. | Have pupils make up questions for an alphabet guessing game based on a principle other than facts about animals. For example: position of letter in a word: *t* is for cat and *r* is for paper. Why? | Have pupils write and illustrate their own alphabet guessing game book. | |
| CONCEPTS | *Is It Rough: Is It Smooth? Is It Shiny?* T. Hoban | X | X | | Have pupils name everything they can think of that is rough, smooth, shiny. Continue by combining categories, i.e., rough and shiny, smooth and shiny. | | | Have pupils create their own books of rough, shiny, and smooth using actual materials/objects. Encourage them to combine categories and include other concepts in unusual ways. |
| | *Summer Is. . .* C. Zolotow | X | X | X | Have pupils brainstorm their associations with the four seasons. | | Using the pattern of the book, have pupils create their own books around categories such as holidays around the year, months, or days of the week. | Have pupils imagine that they can add a fifth season to the year. What would they name the season? What would the weather be like? What special holidays would they celebrate? |

(continued)

**TABLE 16-1 Suggested Creative Thinking Follow-up Activities for Selected Books (continued)**

| GENRE | TITLE | LEVEL | | | CREATIVE-THINKING SKILLS | | | |
|---|---|---|---|---|---|---|---|---|
| | | P | M | I | FLUENCY | FLEXIBILITY | ORIGINALITY | ELABORATION |
| *CONCEPTS (cont'd)* | | | | | | | | Have pupils write or tell about their new season. |
| | *What's Left?* J. Barrett | X | X | X | Have pupils suggest their own ideas of what's left for each item in the book. | Have pupils collect pictures of what's left after something happens. Can they or others suggest what came before? | | Have pupils make their own "What's Left" books with illustrations. |
| | *The Look Again. . . and again, and again, and again book* B. Gardner | X | X | X | Before reading aloud the four captions for each page, have pupils view the illustrations giving as many captions as they can think of. | Provide a group of objects that suggest different things when viewed from different perspectives, e.g., upside down, turned backwards. Have pupils brainstorm words and phrases describing what each object looks like from each viewpoint. | Have each pupil make an illustration with four different captions (i.e., top, bottom, left, and right sides) as in the book. | |

| | | | | | | | | |
|---|---|---|---|---|---|---|---|---|
| *LANGUAGE* | *Eight Ate: A Feast of Homonym Riddles* M. Terban | | X | X | Guide pupils in listing as many homonyms as they can think of. | | Working with a partner, have pupils develop and illustrate homonym riddles for a class book. | |
| | *The Giggle and Cry Book* E. Spinelli | X | X | X | Have pupils list as many antonyms as they can. | Individually have pupils compile lists of all the different ways they would try to make someone giggle. Encourage far-out ideas. They may illustrate and/or act out some of their ideas. | Have pupils choose two antonyms and create their own books, e.g., mean and nice, pretty and ugly. | |
| | *The King Who Rained* F. Gwynne | | X | X | Have pupils develop a class list of figurative phrases (idioms), e.g., "raining cats and dogs," and multiple meaning words, e.g., "trunk." | | Have pupils secretly select idioms to illustrate literally. Share by having the class guess the idioms from viewing the illustrations. | |
| *POETRY* | *The Baby Uggs Are Hatching* J. Prelutsky | | X | X | Have pupils brainstorm words that they know which convey their meaning through sound. | Guide pupils in creating new words which somewhat convey their meanings and/or characteristics by the sound of the words | | Have pupils draw one straight line and one circle on their papers. Ask them to add on to create new kinds of animals. Have them |

(*continued*)

**TABLE 16–1 Suggested Creative Thinking Follow-up Activities for Selected Books (continued)**

| GENRE | TITLE | LEVEL | | | CREATIVE-THINKING SKILLS | | | |
|---|---|---|---|---|---|---|---|---|
| | | P | M | I | FLUENCY | FLEXIBILITY | ORIGINALITY | ELABORATION |
| *POETRY (cont'd)* | | | | | | themselves (as the character names in the book, e.g., Smasheroo). Pupils may write stories about one of the words created. | | give their animals a name and write a poem (either in rhyme or free verse) telling about them. |
| | *Street Poems* R. Froman | | X | X | Have pupils list all the things that can be seen on their streets. | | Ask pupils to each select one thing that can be seen on their street and write a concrete poem about it. | |
| *FOLKLORE* | *Beauty and the Beast* D. Apy | | X | X | Have pupils brainstorm all the associations they make when hearing the terms "beauty" and "beast." | | Have pupils pretend that they are Beauty alone all day long. What new things would they do to keep from being lonely? Have them write or tell their ideas. | Have pupils make up stories telling what the Beast does during the daylight hours. |
| | *Little Red Riding Hood* T. S. Hyman | X | X | X | Have pupils name as many items as possible which Little Red Riding Hood could take in her basket to Grandmother. | | | Have pupils modify and rewrite the story by creating an additional character, e.g., a twin sister for Red Rid- |

| | | | | | | | | |
|---|---|---|---|---|---|---|---|---|
| | | | | | | | | ing Hood, or changing the setting, e.g., from the woods to the city. |
| | *Jack and the Beanstalk*<br>L. B. Cauley | X | X | X | Have pupils think of all the ways Jack might go up the beanstalk other than climbing up. | Using a shoe box, have each pupil design a room in the giant's house which has at least two unusual places for Jack to hide. Have them share their creations. | | Have each pupil think of at least one "get-rich-scheme" to suggest to Jack. Have them explain their scheme to Jack in a role-playing situation. |
| | *Mr. and Mrs. Pig's Evening Out*<br>M. Rayner | | X | X | | Have pupils create new ways for the little piglets to capture and/or escape from Mrs. Wolf. | | Have pupils rewrite the story in the style of a newspaper article or an editorial. |
| *F A N T A S Y* | *The Amazing Bone*<br>W. Steig | X | X | X | Have pupils brainstorm the advantages of having magical talking bones in their pockets. They could also brainstorm objects that have magical powers to bring good luck. | Have pupils suppose that for one day all inanimate objects could talk. Have them choose the object they would talk to, and list four questions they would ask the object. | Have pupils create individual adventures of going home from school with talking bones in their pockets. | Have pupils write the bedtime conversation between themselves and their talking bones. |
| | *Flat Stanley*<br>J. Brown | X | X | X | Have pupils brainstorm the advantages of being one-half inch thick. | | Have pupils imagine that Stanley became one-half inch tall rather than one-half | Have pupils think of numerous ways in which they could be changed, e.g., |

(*continued*)

**TABLE 16–1 Suggested Creative Thinking Follow-up Activities for Selected Books (continued)**

| GENRE | TITLE | LEVEL | | | CREATIVE-THINKING SKILLS | | | |
|---|---|---|---|---|---|---|---|---|
| | | P | M | I | FLUENCY | FLEXIBILITY | ORIGINALITY | ELABORATION |
| *FANTASY (cont'd)* | | | | | | | inch thick and then write his adventures. Ask them to include the happening that restored him to his original size. | height, weight, age, three hands. Have them select the way in which they wish to change and write a story about a day in their new life. |
| | *The Magic Sled* N. Benchley | X | X | X | Have pupils brainstorm all the items they could have that would require special conditions to use. i.e., kite/wind, ice skates/ice, surfboard/waves. | Have pupils add a new character to the story. How did this character happen to be out in the snow? Why can't the bear eat him? What happens when the snow melts? Does this character influence the outcome of the story? | | Have pupils suggest all that might happen if they wished for special conditions so that they could use their magic item. |
| | *Tooth-Gnasher Superflash* D. Pinkwater | X | X | X | | Have pupils think of new ways to improve upon the modern-day automobile. | Have pupils design on paper a new vehicle with unusual qualities, give their vehicle a name, and write an adventure they had in their new vehicle. | Have pupils think up three new inventions by combining two or more objects or inventions, and then convince others of the advantages of the new combinations. |

| | | | | | | | | |
|---|---|---|---|---|---|---|---|---|
| | *The Whingdingdilly*<br>B. Peet | X | X | X | | Have pupils discuss how the world would be different if there were no dogs. List their ideas. | Have pupils combine characteristics of two or more animals to create a new animal in a drawing. Ask them to name their animal, and describe its characteristics, e.g., where it lives, what it eats, its uses. | |
| *REALISTIC FICTION* | *From the Mixed-Up Files of Mrs. Basil A. Frankweiler*<br>E. L. Konigsburg | | X | X | | Present pupils with a baffling antique or art object. Have them decide who created or used it, prove their ideas, and/or create a drama or display about it. | Have pupils plan an adventure for themselves. Their plans could include where they will go, what they will need, and how they will make their escape. | Have pupils decide which of a museum's many rooms would be the most exciting for them. What would be found in that room? What could happen while they are there? |
| | *Miss Rumphius*<br>B. Cooney | X | X | X | Have pupils brainstorm objects/items in the environment that they would like to see beautified. | Select a common item from the environment (such as a trash can) and have pupils tell or show in a drawing what they would do to make the item more beautiful. | Have pupils write stories about one thing they would each do to make the world more beautiful. | Give students a blank sheet of paper and ask them to beautify it in some way, e.g., with crayons, scrap pieces, paints. Have them show and describe the beautifications. |

*(continued)*

**TABLE 16-1 Suggested Creative Thinking Follow-up Activities for Selected Books (continued)**

| GENRE | TITLE | LEVEL | | | CREATIVE-THINKING SKILLS | | | |
|---|---|---|---|---|---|---|---|---|
| | | P | M | I | FLUENCY | FLEXIBILITY | ORIGINALITY | ELABORATION |
| *REALISTIC FICTION (cont'd)* | *Mrs. Frisby and the Rats of NIMH* R. O'Brien | | | X | Have pupils consider the advantages of developing a society of intelligent long-lived creatures. Will the advantages vary according to the special characteristics of the creatures? Construct charts detailing the ideas. | Have pupils design several methods of recapturing the rats of NIMH. They may wish to draw, make, or act out their method. | Have pupils consider the other animals who might have been subject to the experiments at NIMH. What experiments were these? Did the animals escape? What difficulties will they present to the humans who must recapture them? | |
| | *The Snail's Spell* J. Ryder | X | X | | Have pupils list animals that might be found in a garden. | | Have pupils pretend that they are an animal in the garden, e.g., rabbit, bird, grasshopper. Let them create narration including size, movement, eating habits, and other characteristics. They can then direct others to "become the animal" in a dramatic activity. | |

# SEVENTEEN
# TEACHING READING WITH TRADE BOOKS

The purpose of this chapter is to present ideas for using complete works of literature in the intermediate classroom to create in children a love and appreciation for the printed word and to help them become more perceptive readers. All ideas in the chapter have been used by Arlys Caslavka and me at Crestwood Elementary School in Madison, Wisc.

## READING INSTRUCTION USING TRADE BOOKS

Using complete works of high-quality literature is paramount in achieving the goal of developing young readers who read with mature understanding, and who see reading as a major way to learn things they want and need to know and to enjoy reading.

If the literature selected is appropriate to the reading and experience level of the students, trade books can be used for *all* children in the classroom. Teachers can select books that meet the interest and skill needs of their students. Instructional materials can be designed for a particular small group, which will enhance understanding of the literary qualities of the book. This approach may be used either to supplement and enrich a basal reading program or to replace it and thus become the total instructional reading program. We have used this approach as our total instructional reading program at Crestwood Elementary School since 1974.

### Key Elements of the Instructional Program

*Complete works of literature.* Start building your instructional library by purchasing six to eight copies of a single title. Before purchasing a book, read it yourself and, if possible, discuss it with your school librarian. Review the book for its treatment of racial, social, economic, and ethnic groups. Consider both the appropriateness of the language for your school population and the reading needs and interests of the students. Look for respected contemporary authors. Consider a variety of literary genres: biography, fantasy, science fiction, historical fiction, mystery, poetry, short story, factual pieces, and contemporary fiction. Include themes of interest to your students such as animals, survival, and interpersonal relations. Remember, these trade books also can be used to extend and supplement other areas of the curriculum.

*Small-group instruction.* Divide the class into groups of four to eight students according to their skill needs and/or interests. In the early fall, we administer an informal reading inventory to assess each child's reading abilities. Our first groups are established based on information gained from the inventory. Groups might change during the year because using trade books allows for flexibility in grouping (students can move easily from one group to another at the end of each book), and it offers unlimited opportunities to expand the interests of an individual or small group.

Each child within a small group will be reading the same title. It is conceivable you may be working with three or four small groups at a time, each group reading a different title. Plan to spend from two to five weeks on each book depending on the length of the book, complexity of the story, and skills of the students in the group.

Each week assign a given number of pages to be read and discussed within the group. The number of pages to be read will vary depending upon the needs and abilities of the group and complexity of the story, but you might consider seven to fifteen pages a day as reasonable. Books usually present natural breaking points that you will want to plan around. Remember, this is instructional reading. Provide time to read and reread, to reflect, and to analyze the assigned passage. The volume of reading is not as important as reflective time.

Plan to meet with each small group two to three times a week for group discussion. During the first prereading time, "read" the book cover, title page, and contents. Scan the book to study the illustrations and make interpretations. Make predictions and form hypotheses about the story. All of these reading-readiness activities help to set a purpose for reading and provide a reading guide for the students. Each small-group session should provide some hypothesizing and purpose setting for the upcoming reading assignment.

Many other comprehension, vocabulary, and study skills can also be modeled and practiced during the small-group time. Children can be taught to evaluate characters, to question motives, and to make judgments. They can be taught to recognize bias and causal relationships. Students can practice discriminating between fact and opinion, the real and the fanciful. You can help to build awareness of emotionally laden words and the author's techniques in creating a certain mood in the story. Interpretation of figurative language, idioms, ambiguous words, and analogies can be clarified. Students should be encouraged to draw and test inferences of many kinds, including interpretations, predictions, and conclusions. Opportunities should be provided to summarize a situation or compare it to another. Relate current happenings in the lives of the children, the classroom, and the world to the reading experience. This oral interaction, modeling, and questioning time is a critical component of comprehension instruction!

*Written comprehension/vocabulary questions.* Write questions that help to guide the reading experience and that focus on understanding the assigned segment. In writing such work sheets, provide opportunities for personal opinion, imaging, predicting outcomes, and relating the literary experience to one's own. Questions on the work sheets should stimulate thinking about the author's message. Ask the children to compare, predict, and order events, but also include questions requiring higher-level thinking skills such as analyzing the author's purpose and style, supporting opinions, and applying concepts to new situations. Include vocabulary questions, especially where children use the new words in familiar personal situations. Require answers to be written in sentence and paragraph form. In the following examples taken from units we have developed, watch to see how these questioning goals are met.

Sample questions used with *Boris,* a book of historical fiction by Jaap ter Haar:

> What does it mean to be *evacuated?* Tell of a situation in the USA where people have been evacuated.
>
> How did the author set the mood for the dangerous adventure?
>
> How did you feel as Nadia dropped down in the snow?
>
> Using context of the English words, "guess" what the Germans were saying.
>
> Close your eyes. Imagine the snow falling on Leningrad.
>
> What is Boris' reaction to this natural happening?

Sample questions used with *The Cricket in Times Square,* by George Selden:

> Close your eyes and picture Sai Fong's shop. What do you smell? What do you see? Describe Sai Fong's shop.
>
> Compare Tucker's and Chester's feelings as to the use of the talent.
>
> It's your opinion. Chester's short visit to Times Square seems to have affected the lives of many people in different ways. Which single person do you feel changed the most as a result of the cricket's visit to the Bellinis' newsstand? Give as many reasons as you can to defend your choice.

*Silent reading.* Make reading an important part of each day by providing time to read. Schedule a period for silent reading 20 to 30 minutes a day. This should provide ample time for the students to complete their trade book reading assignments and to pursue their individual reading interests. As the teacher, you should model the reading habit by also reading during this period. This will help to generate a community feeling and to establish a classroom climate favorable to reading.

*Related language activities.* "A good reading program cannot separate reading from all the other language arts. . . . An integrating reading program uses writing, creative dramatics, speaking, listening and similar activities in conjunction with children's exploration of books" (McClure, 1982, p. 785).

With literature as the stimulus, related language activities abound. The students will often suggest ideas, but you should also plan for language extensions that require students to extend their problem-solving and thinking abilities.

1. *Research.* Some books lend themselves to doing research. Before reading *Mr. Popper's Penguins,* by Richard and Florence Atwater, ask each child to collect five facts about penguins and share them in the small group. Record them for use while reading the book to help the children discriminate between fact and fantasy. In preparing to read *Secret of the Andes,* by Ann Nolan Clark, ask the students to study maps of Peru and reproduce a map to be referred to while reading the book. After reading this book, research the Incas to find out more about the lost treasure and the people who created such an advanced early culture.

2. *Writing.* Writing in many forms can help to extend the reading experiences. While reading *Genie of Sutton Place,* by George Selden, write magical incantations such as those that Tim used in the story. Write free verse expressing the dreams, feelings, and special strengths of Sadako in *Sadako and the 1,000 Paper Cranes,* by Eleanor Coerr. Keep a diary of observations and feelings such as the diary that Esther may have kept in *The Endless Steppe,* by Esther Hautzig. Write messages to each other using secret codes after reading *Alvin's Secret Code,* by Clifford Hicks. You or a student might design a treasure hunt written in code.

During the reading of stories such as George Selden's *The Cricket in Times Square,* have each child keep a record of information about a single character on a character card. After completing the book, use these notes to write a paragraph about each character with supporting information from the story. Examples of children's responses to these activities are contained in Figure 17–1.

Write letters to authors and *mail them.* Your local city library should be able to aid you in finding current addresses. In writing to an author, comment on specifics in the book, offer suggestions, and ask a few questions. See Figure 17–2.

Ask each child to choose a book that has at least one strong character. At the end of a set period of time, the child writes a five-line poem (cinquain)

Magic incantations: *The Genie of Sutton Place*

Crystal ball, clear as ice.
Tell me everything precise.
Tell me what my future be,
Crystal ball what do you see?
Susie Malek

Ball of glass, crystal clear
Spirits come to me here
Bring me wisdom, give me strength
Let me live a long length.
Lisa Kunes

Vase, oh Vase upon my stand,
Please give me a helping hand.
Please help me when I work and play,
And guide me day by day.
Scott Seavey

SADAKO. . .
A runner, rushing like a whirlwind
always in a hurry
A worrier, afraid of being late for events
of causing sadness for her family
A believer, in superstitions
in herself
A helper, shares her love by helping at home
raised Kenji's hope as he neared his death
A considerate helping family member,
thinks of others, not only herself.
A group poem
*Sadako and the 1,000 Paper Cranes*

Harry Cat

Harry Cat is a very nice cat and other than Chester, I think he is one of the nicest characters. Harry Cat likes opera because he is a cultured cat, but he also likes other songs. Harry Cat enjoys Chester's singing in Times Square and whenever there is an opera in the theater, he sneaks in to listen. According to Tucker, Harry Cat is not a very good singer. He knows a lot about New York because he's lived there a long time.

Mike Coats

**FIGURE 17-1** Student Writing Samples

about a character from the book. Because the poem has a limited number of words, the child must be selective about vocabulary. Each word must tell important characteristics about the character.

A suggested form for this *character cinquain* is:

1. name of character
2. two words describing the character
3. three words relating actions of the character
4. a four-word phrase telling a happening or a relationship from the book
5. name of character.

2021 Forest Lane 10/4/84
Fayetteville, G.A.
30214

Dear Mr. Burch,

I am from Crestwood School in Madison, Wisconsin. Our reading group has read your book called Ida Early comes over the Mountain. We all loved it and wanted to write to you. We thought a sequal to your second book which I believe is called Christmas with Ida Early, would be neat. We even thought of the title of The Secret of Ida Early. We thought that Randall or Ellen, or even the twins could find a ring in her bag while trying to write another note. Then tell of the supposedly strange man she was to marry. We don't know how this story will fit with your second book because we haven't read it yet, but I think we've got a good idea. We would certainly appreciate it if you would write back to us, but it would make us even happier if you used our ideas in your next book. Thanx's

Your new friend,
Jenny Brightbill

P.S.
Please write back!

FIGURE 17-2 Student Letter to Author

Student examples from our fourth and fifth graders are contained in Figure 17-3.

A teaching friend, Shirley Steinbach, first introduced me to the following book report idea. Ask each child to choose a biography to read in order to prepare a report entitled *The Ghost I'd Most Like to Meet.* This is an op-

Squanto
Strong, brave
Builds teepees, fishes, hunts
Friend of the Pilgrims
Squanto
Dan Urben
From the book: *Squanto*

Mr. Popper
Penguin lover, untidy
Dreams, reads, paints
People think he's crazy
Mr. Popper
Valerie Bridger
From the book: *Mr. Popper's Penguins*

Stuart
Small, intelligent
Explores, drives, sails
Searches for best friend
Stuart Little
Russell Nelson
From the book: *Stuart Little*

Eliphaz's ghost
Evil spirit, powerful
Smells of wet ashes, leaves messages,
Appears in Lewis' dream
Terrifies Lewis
Ghost of Eliphaz
Shawn Johnson
From the book: *Figure in the Shadows*

**FIGURE 17-3** Student Samples of Character Cinquain

portune time to involve parents in helping children to make a choice that has some special interest for them. We sent this letter home to parents:

> Dear Parents,
>
> This note is to inform you of a class project and to ask your help in preparing for it. *The Ghost I'd Most Like to Meet* is a project integrating reading, writing, speaking, and social studies.
>
> During the next four weeks, your child will have his/her own GHOST! Each child will choose from the list, *The Ghost I'd Most Like to Meet.* A biography will be selected from our library. This will be done in privacy with Mrs. Austad. Each book will be wrapped to keep its subject a secret. During the next two weeks the biography will be read in school and at home. Notes will be recorded in the structured-notes folder. Following the note-taking process, a rough draft and final copy report will be required. We will share our written reports orally with the whole class.
>
> Tonight, you and your child need to discuss *several* of these possible choices.

Many times a child enjoys studying about someone who had the same interests as he/she does. On Thursday and Friday we'll make the final choices with Mrs. Austad. Secrecy is important!

Thank you for your continued cooperation. This should be an exciting unit for all of us.

Set a given amount of time for the children to complete the reading of their biography. As students read, assign them to take notes about their "ghost" in the "Notes" folder prepared by you. Sample questions might include:

Important dates in the life of ______________________________.

What kind of family background did your ghost have?

How was your ghost's education different from yours?

Why is your ghost well-known or famous?

What contribution did your ghost make to the world about it and to our life today?

Important happenings during your ghost's life: Did any one person or event have a great effect on the life of your GHOST?

Could this person be famous today? Explain why or why not.

Pretend your GHOST is living and you are preparing for an interview. Write at least three questions you would be sure to ask.

After reading the book, assign each child to write a report using the notes collected during the reading of the biography. Reports may be shared in writing and/or orally. We prepared a book of reports that we presented to the Kids Shelf in the Instructional Media Center, and we shared our reports orally in class. See Figure 17–4.

3. *Creative dramatics.* Children love to pretend, and they enjoy sharing their experiences with others. After reading a book such as *Ramona the Brave,* by Beverly Cleary, have the students act out a favorite episode. Dialogue may be modified from the book, but the children will be freer to act if they create their own dialogue to express the scene. Chapter 2 in this text provides a detailed description of ways to use creative dramatics in your program.

4. *Field trips.* Some pieces of literature lend themselves naturally to small-group field trips. Have group members prepare questions prior to the trip and brainstorm what they want to find out. They might compose their own parent-permission letters including all necessary information. Following such field trips, thank-you notes are usually written.

Consider your particular teaching community. Visit an art museum such as the one Claudia and Jamie did in *From the Mixed-Up Files of Mrs. Basil E. Frankweiler* and watch for places to hide. Perhaps you'll be lucky to visit a secret part of the museum, that is, if the guide also knows the story by E. L. Konigsburg that is cited above. After reading *Champion Dog Prince Tom,* by Jean Fritz and Tom Clute, take the reading group to a dog show or obedience class. Students will appreciate the accomplishments of Prince Tom even more after such a visit.

*A Great Inventor*
By Scott Storch

Hello, I'm Scott Storch reporting for NBC news. Today we take a look at great inventors. We look at a specific inventor who was born January 17, 1706 in Boston. We now go to Boston to ask a few questions to this great inventor.

*Was it hard being an inventor in your day?*
No, it wasn't because everything I invented people really needed, things like stoves that kept heat in and the smoke out. I also invented the Almanac and I made it so the people back then and the people today could check out books from the library. Back then you had to stay in the library to read the book you wanted. I made it so you could check it out and go home and read it.

*What kind of family background do you have?*
Well, I was the 15th child out of 17 children. I was in school for two years, then my father pulled me out of school and made me work for him as a soap and candle maker. I was bored being a soap and candle maker so after a few years my father asked my brother to teach me printing. I became a printer's apprentice at the age of 12.

*What was it like working for your brother?*
He was a good teacher and I learned a lot. I began to write articles under another name which my brother printed until he found out it was me. Then he stopped printing them. After that we argued a lot until at the age of 17 I went to Philadelphia. I worked as a printer until I was able to own my own print shop where I began publishing the Pennsylvania Gazette.

*With all that hard work did you ever have fun?*
I certainly did. I married my landlady's daughter, her name was Debby Read. We had three children. I also enjoyed swimming.

*What do you think are your best accomplishments?*
Well, I proved that lightning is electricity and I made all of your homes safer by inventing the lightning rod. I was very proud to have organized the first city hospital and to have invented bifocal eye glasses. One of my proudest moments was when I saw the United States become an independent nation. I was one of the signers of the Declaration of Independence.

An interview with Benjamin Franklin

**FIGURE 17-4** Student Biography Report

5. *Other activities.* Bake "Ida's magic muffins" (popovers) after reading *Ida Early Comes Over the Mountain,* by Robert Burch. While the popovers are baking, play tiddlywinks. The children will come to appreciate Ida and her skills even more.

After reading *No Such Thing as a Witch,* by Ruth Chew, cook Maggie's Magic Fudge. (Any nummy recipe will do.) When the children share the fudge with the entire class, they can retell the story and relate the effects of the fudge on people who eat it.

Invite a speaker to visit the class. We invited an expert on mammals from the Department of Natural Resources to talk about foxes. Students who had just completed Betsy Byars' *The Midnight Fox* prepared questions to guide the speaker's presentation. Another time our school custodian talked to the group and told of his experiences as a hunter. His views presented alternatives to the antihunting thoughts expressed in *The Great Dane Thor,* by Walter Farley.

Plan an art activity. After reading *The Door in the Wall,* by Marguerite DeAngeli, and/or *Castle,* by David Macaulay, the reading group might build a castle. Another group might make Chinese kites that they have read about in *Little Pear,* by Eleanor Lattimore.

The options for relating language activities with the reading experience are limitless. As you become familiar with more books, more ideas will present themselves. The oral language, planning, and problem solving that go on during these activities are priceless.

## SUMMARY

High-quality trade books provide experiences that both satisfy the intellect and the emotions and motivate students to seek out other books that will do the same. Throughout the reading experience the major emphasis in teaching is on *synthesis of meaning.* Continually ask students to bring together their literal comprehension, intuitions, feelings, and aesthetic responses into a complete understanding of what the writer is trying to say and do with his work (Yatvin, Sloup, & Stamm, 1979).

After spending several weeks reading and sharing a story, the children will enter the world of the book. They will begin to identify with the characters and to place themselves within the setting. The reading experience becomes meaningful and important in their personal lives.

## RECREATIONAL READING

If the paramount goal of your reading program is to develop young readers who read with mature understanding, who see reading as a major way to learn the things they want and need to know and who enjoy reading, the payoff should be seen in the students' recreational reading habits. Easy access to the school Instructional Media Center (IMC) is important, as well as providing books and magazines in the classroom. Sharing recreational reading experiences on a personal basis stimulates reading for enjoyment and self-satisfaction. Many suggestions for these types of activities are contained in Chapter 15 of this book.

## READING ALOUD

In addition to students' own reading, it is important that adults also read to children daily. Kimmel and Segel (1983) remind us, " . . . reading aloud to children from literature that is meaningful to them is now widely acknowledged among experts to be the most effective, as well as the simplest and least expensive, way to foster in children a lifelong love of books and reading. The task now is to pass this word along to individual parents, school administrators, and classroom teachers."

Reading aloud to students provides time for you, the teacher, to model expressive reading. Children love it when the reader "becomes many a character" through voice change, varied expression, and lively language. When reading to children, vary your pace, your voice tone and pitch, and enjoy the story itself. What a time for you to express a love for literature too!

In reading aloud, you can choose books of high quality and appeal to children, even though some books may be beyond the reading abilities of your students. In so doing, literary horizons of the children can be extended through the reading and follow-up discussions.

### Preparation for Reading Aloud

The read-aloud experience will be more successful if you have read the book before sharing it with your students. Watch for sensitive areas, parts that require emphasis, and key stopping points.

Before starting a book with the children, provide background information on the author and content of the story, and suggest points to listen for.

Once started, read the book with a minimum of interruptions to preserve the integrity of the selection, but do not hesitate to stop to clarify a concept or word you know may be unfamiliar to many of the children or to answer a question.

### Selecting Read-Aloud Books

A good read-aloud book should (1) be fast-paced in its plot, allowing children's interests to be hooked as soon as possible; (2) contain clear, rounded characters; (3) include crisp, easy-to-read dialogue; and (4) keep long descriptive passages to a minimum, at least at the start (Trelease, 1982, pp. 73–75). Books that include conflict, strong character development, and humor are pleasers for classroom reading.

Remember, reading aloud is important to children and may be integrated with all areas of the curriculum. Make it an important part of each day in your classroom.

## *REFERENCES*

KIMMEL, M., & SEGEL, E. (1983). *For reading out loud!* New York: Dell Publishing.

MCCLURE, A. (1982). Integrating children's fiction and informational literature in a primary reading curriculum. *The Reading Teacher, 35,* 784–789.

TRELEASE, J. (1982). *The read-aloud handbook.* New York: Penguin Books.

YATVIN, J., SLOUP, M., & STAMM, A. (1979). *Group reading with tradebooks: A responsible alternative to a basal program.* Madison, WI: An unpublished study.

## *SUGGESTED READINGS*

CHAMPLIN, C., & KENNEDY, B. (1982). *Books in Bloom.* Omaha, NE: Special Literature Press. Champlin and Kennedy present many ideas for developing creativity through literature. Activities in this book are based on Benjamin Bloom's "Taxonomy of Learning."

REASONER, C. (1972). *Where the readers are.* New York: Dell Publishing.

——. (1975). *When children read.* New York: Dell Publishing.

——. (1976). *Releasing children to literature.* New York: Dell Publishing. The three books by Reasoner provide an excellent source of ideas for using literature in the classroom.

## *LITERATURE REFERENCES*

ATWATER, R., & ATWATER, F. (1981). *Mr. Popper's penguins.* New York: Dell Publishing.

BABBITT, N. (1983). *Tuck everlasting.* New York: Bantam.

BURCH, R. (1982). *Ida early comes over the mountain.* New York: Avon.

BYARS, B. (1982). *The midnight fox.* New York: Penguin, Puffin Books.

CHEW, R. (1971). *No such thing as a witch.* New York: Scholastic Book Services.

CLARK, A.N. (1976). *Secret of the Andes.* New York: Penguin, Puffin Books.

CLEARY, B. (1975). *Ramona the brave.* New York: Scholastic Book Services.

COERR, E. (1983). *Sadako and the 1000 paper cranes.* New York: Dell Publishing.

COLLIER, J.L., & COLLIER, C. (1974). *My brother Sam is dead.* New York: Scholastic Book Services.

DAHL, R. (1966). *The magic finger.* New York: Harper & Row.

DEANGELI, M. (1975). *The door in the wall.* New York: Scholastic Book Services.

FALL, T. (1972). *Canalboat to freedom.* New York: Dell Publishing.

FARLEY, W. (1980). *The great dane Thor.* New York: Dell Publishing.

FRITZ, J., & CLUTE, T. (1958). *Champion dog Prince Tom.* New York: Scholastic Book Services.

FRITZ, J. (1982). *Homesick: My own story.* New York: Putnam's.

GRAHAME, K. (1981). *Wind in the willows.* New York: Dell Publishing.

HAUTZIG, E. (1968). *The endless steppe.* New York: Scholastic Book Services.

HICKS, C.B. (1963). *Alvin's secret code.* New York: Scholastic Book Services.

KEY, A. (1974). *The forgotten door.* New York: Scholastic Book Services.

KONIGSBURG, E.L. (1974). *From the mixed-up files of Mrs. Basil E. Frankweiler.* New York: Dell Publishing.

LANGFORD, C. (1975). *Winter of the fisher.* New York: A Manor Book.

LATTIMORE, E. (1959). *Little Pear.* New York: Harcourt, Brace & World.

MACAULAY, D. (1977). *Castle.* Boston: Houghton Mifflin.

MOREY, W. (1972). *Canyon winter.* New York: Dutton.

SELDEN, G. (1976). *The cricket in Times Square.* New York: Dell Publishing.

——. (1974). *Genie of Sutton Place.* New York: Dell Publishing.

TERHAAR, J. (1971). *Boris.* New York: Dell Publishing.

WHITE, E.B. (1945). *Stuart Little.* New York: Harper & Row.

# EIGHTEEN
# UNDERSTANDING AND APPRECIATING FOLKLORE

Climbing an enchanted beanstalk and outwitting a ferocious giant ("Jack and the Beanstalk"), emerging from the ocean as a fully grown goddess and living on Mt. Olympus ("Aphrodite"), or battling the monster Grendel and fighting the dragon Firedrake (Beowulf) are a few of the vicarious experiences available to readers of folklore. Traditional tales of great heroes, humorous simpletons, and magical objects are among the most beloved and remembered stories from childhood. Children will not, however, enjoy these vicarious experiences unless folklore is a valued part of the school curriculum. (Folklore, as used in this chapter, includes the traditional tales that have been handed down from generation to generation by word of mouth. The traditional tales emphasized in this chapter include folktales, myths, and legends.)

The purpose of this chapter is to identify the values gained from sharing folklore with children; to describe the basic components of a literature program that emphasizes folktales, myths, and legends; and to develop methods and sample lessons that increase children's understanding of and appreciation for folklore. Specific instructional methods and sample lessons are designed to help children distinguish the differences among folktales, myths, and legends; to compare different versions of the same folktale found in different countries; and to use folktales from a single country or culture to learn about that country.

## THE VALUES OF SHARING FOLKLORE WITH CHILDREN

Pleasure, amusement, and delight are among the earliest values that young children gain from folklore. Sharing simple folktales such as "The Three Little Pigs" fosters an appreciation for literature and serves to encourage a lifelong interest in books. Older children may experience pleasure in vicarious fantasy experiences as they follow the exploits and adventures of mythical heroes.

This same folklore stimulates language development. For example, as young children listen to the repetitive language in "The Three Little Pigs," they frequently join in as the wolf declares, "I'll huff and I'll puff and I'll blow your house in." When older children read the more complex folktales, myths, and legends, they are introduced to varied literary forms and to symbolic and artistic use of language.

Cognitive development is also enhanced through sharing folklore. The tightly written plot developments in folktales encourage children to develop an understanding of story structure, to organize a plot into a logical sequence, and to hypothesize about what will happen in the story. Analytical skills are strengthened when older children first identify the characteristics found in folktales, myths, and legends, and then analyze whether a specific piece of literature is a folktale, a myth, or a legend.

Folk literature provides a marvelous material source for developing world understanding and appreciation for the contributions of diverse cultures. When teachers share and discuss numerous folktales from a single country or culture, children discover the important beliefs or values of the people, the cultural contributions of the country, the geographic characteristics of an area, and the social institutions of the time period. If used correctly, folklore is a powerful tool that increases cultural respect and understanding. In addition, children may acquire a heightened self-esteem as they discover the traditional values and the literary contributions that are characteristic of their own backgrounds.

Variations in folktale motifs such as the one found in "Cinderella" are found in more than 500 versions from around the world. Sharing different versions of the same tale helps children understand that humans throughout the world have experienced similar needs and problems, that people and their stories have moved throughout history, and that oral stories reflect the culture in which they are told.

Pleasure, language development, world understanding, appreciation for the contributions of others, and improved self-esteem are all important reasons for sharing folklore with children. If these objectives are to be met, the literature collection must contain a variety of folklore from many countries and cultures.

### Components of the Literature Program

If the previous values of sharing folklore are to be gained, the teacher will need a wide variety of excellent sources. The teacher should balance the collection according to folklore types, to cultural backgrounds, to highly illustrated volumes, and to folklore collections. First, the folklore collection should include all of the types of traditional literature: folktales, fables, myths, and legends. Within folktales there should be cumulative tales, humorous tales, magic and wonder tales, *pourquoi* tales, and realistic tales. Second, the collection should reflect a wide variety of cultures and countries. For example, the collection should include European tales, Asian tales, Hispanic tales, Jewish tales, Russian tales, African tales, and Native American tales. Within the North American tales, the literature should reflect the diversity of American culture by presenting stories of Native Americans and Eskimos, stories of Black Americans, stories brought to America by European immigrants, and American tall tales. Third, the collection should include highly illustrated single tales in which the illustrations reflect careful historical and cultural research. Fourth, the collection should include anthologies that provide excellent sources for comparative studies and appreciative listening and reading.

## INSTRUCTIONAL METHODS FOR SHARING FOLKLORE

The methods developed in the following section encourage children to appreciate, understand, and analyze folklore. The specific strategies suggested in the activities include both *charting* and *webbing.*

### Distinguishing Differences Among Folktales, Myths, and Legends

The study of folklore is a respected adult profession. College courses, advanced degrees in folklore, and university professors who specialize in folklore attest to the importance of this subject. (This information may increase the interest of your older students in a study of folklore.) *Folklorists,* specialists who study traditional beliefs and folklore of the people, have developed ways of collecting, identifying, defining, and categorizing different types of folklore. Older students may develop and practice some of these specialized skills as they explore the various forms of folk literature found in the library.

Instructional activities that encourage children to read and discuss various types of folklore, to develop a definition for each folklore type, and to analyze folklore according to these definitions will improve older children's appreciation of folk literature and increase their analytical abilities. You may include the following procedures when you develop this activity with a class.

1. Collect numerous examples of folktales, myths, and legends. Try to choose your examples from different countries and diverse cultures.
2. Explain to the children that many folklorists define different types of folklore according to whether the original storytellers and their audiences believed the stories to be true. In addition, folklorists consider the time when the stories occurred (that is, anytime, the remote past, or the recent past), the setting in which

the stories took place (that is, any place, another or earlier world, or the world of today), the attitude of the stories (secular or sacred), and the characteristics of the main characters (human or nonhuman). Ask the children to consider each of these topics and to think of a definition as you read them an example of a folktale, a myth, and a legend. Good literature examples for this activity include "Snow White and the Seven Dwarfs" (folktale), "Cupid and Psyche" (myth), and "Robin Hood" (legend).

3. After the children have developed their own definitions for folktale, myth, and legend, share with them the following definitions developed by folklorist William Bascom (1965). *Folktales,* according to Bascom, are regarded as fiction by the original storytellers and their audiences. In addition, folktales take place at any time or in any place, are not considered to be history or religious dogma (that is, they are secular, not sacred), and include human and nonhuman characters. *Myths* are considered by the original storytellers to be true accounts of happenings in the remote past. They are accepted on faith; they are taught to be believed. Myths are usually sacred and the main characters are gods and goddesses. *Legends* are also regarded as true stories by the original storytellers and their audiences. They are set in a more recent past. The human characters may lead lives that are either secular or sacred.
4. Place definitions on the chalkboard or on a large chart. Choose headings similar to those shown in Table 18–1.
5. Read an example of a folktale, a myth, and a legend to the class. After each reading, discuss the particular folklore and place the appropriate example from the folklore onto the chart. The folklore examples shown in Table 18–1 include Emoke de Papp Severo's (1981) *The Good-Hearted Youngest Brother* (folktale); Catherine Sadler's (1982) "Shooting the Moon" found in Sadler's *Treasure Mountain: Folktales from Southern China* (folktale); Gerald McDermott's (1984) *Daughter of the Earth* (myth); Olivia Coolidge's (1951) "The Hammer of Thor," from *Legends of the North* (myth); Harold Courlander's (1982) "Liongo, A Hero of Shanga," found in *The Crest and the Hide: And Other African Stories of Heroes, Chiefs, Bards, Hunters, Sorcerers, and Common People* (legend); and Rosemary Sutcliff's (1981) *The Sword and the Circle: King Arthur and the Knights of the Round Table* (legend). This final selection is a longer book. For this activity you may want to read only the beginning chapter.
6. Continue this activity over several class periods. The initial reading and discussion should be a teacher-led group activity. Later, students may add information to the chart from either individual reading or from small-group interaction.

### Comparing Different Versions of the Same Folktale

Studying variants of the same folktale found in different countries and cultures encourages children to develop an understanding of both cultural diffusion and common needs and problems. For this activity, collect all of the variations of one folktale that you can locate. For example, you might locate "Cinderella" stories from France, England, Germany, Italy, China, Vietnam, and America (Native America). You can also find different versions of "Rumpelstiltskin," "The Lad Who Went to the Northwind," and "Little Red Riding Hood."

After you have located several versions of the same tale, discuss the concept of folktale variations with the children. Ask them to consider why folk-

**TABLE 18-1 Characteristics of Folktale, Myth, and Legend**

| FORM & EXAMPLES | BELIEF | TIME | PLACE | ATTITUDE | PRINCIPAL CHARACTERS |
|---|---|---|---|---|---|
| FOLKTALE | FICTION | ANYTIME | ANYPLACE | SECULAR | HUMAN OR NONHUMAN |
| 1. *The Good-Hearted Youngest Brother* (Hungarian) | fiction, magic, & enchantment | "Once there was. . ." | "beyond where the bob-tailed piglet roots" | secular | three human brothers; three enchanted princesses; little man with magical powers |
| 2. "Shooting the Moon" (China) | fiction, magic, & transformations | "Long ago, in ancient times. . ." | in a mountainous land | secular | a fine human archer, and a good human woman |
| MYTH | CONSIDERED FACT | REMOTE PAST | OTHER WORLD OR EARLIER WORLD | SACRED | NONHUMAN |
| 1. *Daughter of Earth* (Roman) | considered fact | "When the world was divided into three kingdoms. . ." | earth, Pluto, underworld kingdom | deities | Nonhuman gods and goddesses: Ceres, Proserpina, and Pluto |
| 2. "The Hammer of Thor" | considered fact | remote past | Asgard, home of the gods | deities | Nonhuman, Norse god Thor, who. . . |
| LEGEND | CONSIDERED FACT | RECENT PAST | WORLD OF TODAY | SECULAR OR SACRED | HUMAN |
| 1. "Liongo, A Hero of Shanga" (Africa—Swahili) | considered fact | recent past, "a time of heroes" | "In the old city of Shanga" | secular | Human, "hero of heroes" |
| 2. *The Sword and the Circle* (British) | considered fact; believed by many to be a real king | recent past; time of chivalry | world of today; Britain | secular | King Arthur and the Knights of the Round Table |

tales with similar story lines might be found in locations that are far apart. Although names may vary, magical objects may change, and settings may differ, the basic plots remain the same. Next select one type of variant tale and follow the steps listed below:

1. Choose at least three or four versions of a folktale. The examples for this activity include several versions of "Little Red Riding Hood," namely: a French version located in *Perrault's Complete Fairy Tales* (1961); a German version, *Little Red Riding Hood,* retold by Trina Schart Hyman (Grimm Brothers, 1983); a Chinese version, "The Chinese Red Riding Hoods," located in *Chinese Fairy Tales,* by Isabelle Chang (1965), and in Sutherland's and Livingston's *The Scott, Foresman Anthology of Children's Literature* (1984); and another French version, "The True History of Little Golden Hood," found in *The Red Fairy Book,* edited by Andrew Lang (1960).
2. As you read each story, ask the students to compare the different versions of the tales according to specific events in the story, to similarities and differences in plot and characters, to similarities and differences in language and style, and to similarities and differences in the morals stated in the stories.
3. Place the major categories for comparison on a chart similar to the one in Table 18–2, which sets forth some of the major similarities and differences found in these versions.
4. Discuss these similarities and differences with the class. Divide the class into smaller groups and have each group prepare one of the tales as a creative drama. Share the dramas with the class.
5. This activity should be extended by having the class analyze other folktales that have several variations. Encourage your students to develop a list of plot occurrences, characters, character traits, settings, and themes that could be compared in each version.

### Using Folktales From a Single Country or Culture

In addition to providing pleasure and enjoyment, folktales are excellent sources for obtaining supplementary information about a country or a culture. Disliked human characteristics, admired human characteristics, disliked animals, admired animals, traditional social structures, cultural customs, common occupations, common names, and geographical characteristics are frequently included in the tales. If the illustrations reflect authentic traditional settings, you have another source for study and enrichment. Such illustrations encourage children to discover information about the architecture, the fashions, the lifestyles, the geography of the area, and the time period illustrated in the folktale.

*Mapping folklore from one country.* Each semester my university students develop instructional units around some aspect of children's literature. Brainstorming ideas and drawing semantic maps or webs are excellent first steps when developing instructional units. This approach is equally beneficial when developed with children. For example, you and your class may identify

**TABLE 18–2 Comparisons of "Little Red Riding Hood" Variants**

| | FRENCH:PERRAULT | GERMAN:GRIMM | CHINESE:CHANG | FRENCH:LANG |
|---|---|---|---|---|
| *Comparison to Investigate* | "Little Red Riding Hood" | "Little Red Riding Hood" | "The Chinese Red Riding Hoods" | "True History of Little Golden Hood" |
| *What is taken to Grandmother?* | Cake and pot of butter | Loaf of fresh bread, sweet butter, bottle of wine | Not told; Mother visits Grandmother | Piece of cake |
| *Where does Grandmother live?* | In another village "yonder by the mill" | In the woods "by the three big oak trees, right next to blackberry hedge" | The mother's house is at the edge of the woods | At the other side of the wood, in the village, "near the windmill" |
| *Who discovers the Wolf's deception?* | No one | Huntsman | Felice, the oldest daughter | Grandmother, "The brave old dame" |
| *What happens to Little Red Riding Hood?* | Wicked wolf "leapt upon Little Red Riding Hood and gobbled her up" | She is eaten and then jumps out of the wolf after huntsman cuts wolf open | The three girls outwit the wolf | Wolf tries to eat her but she is saved by the magical hood that burns the wolf's throat |
| What happens to the Wolf? | He eats Grandmother and Little Red Riding Hood and escapes | He is killed by the huntsman who skins the wolf and nails the pelt to the door | The girls drop him from a basket that is high up in a tree | Grandmother catches him in a sack, "runs and empties it in the well, where the vagabond, still howling, tumbled in and drowned" |

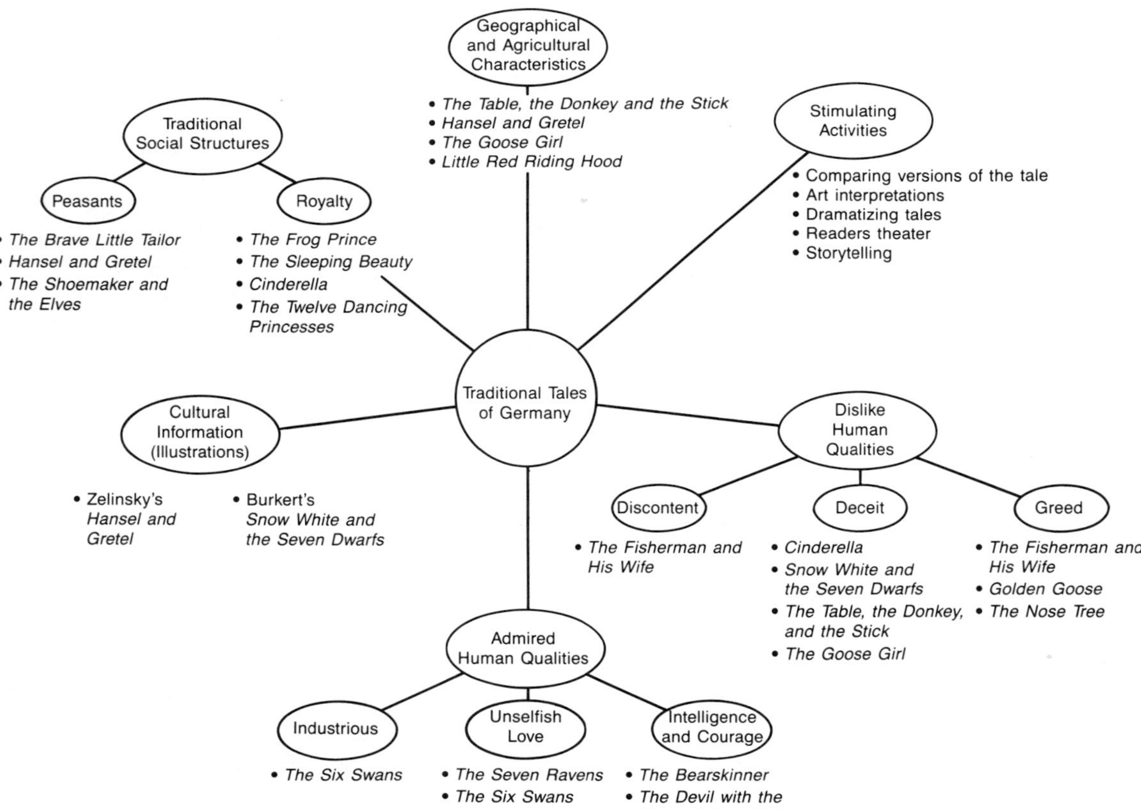


**FIGURE 18-1** Traditional Tales from Germany.

a specific country in the center of your web and then identify areas that you and your class would like to investigate or activities that you would like to include.

Next, collect as many folktales as you can find from the country you have identified. As the tales are either read by or read to the children, the webs are completed. (An alternate approach at the university level is first to complete the webs with a group of your peers then later to use the webs to help you develop instructional tasks with your classes.) Figure 18–1 illustrates this approach with a partially completed web highlighting folktales from Germany. (The books identified on the web are listed under Grimm in the reference section at the end of this chapter.)

If the web is placed on a bulletin board, information may be added throughout the study of a country. This approach frequently stimulates interest in other nations. You may use a similar approach to analyze and to enjoy folktales from around the world. Folktales from Africa, Russia, China, France, England, Japan, Norway, Poland, Hawaii, and the United States (Native American, tall tales, Black folktales) are just a few of the sources for developing world understanding.

## SUMMARY

Vicarious experiences, pleasure, language and cognitive development, world understanding, and improved self-esteem are important reasons for sharing folklore with children. The activities developed in this chapter foster these values.

Distinguishing the differences among folktales, myths, and legends encourages language and cognitive development. In addition to cognitive and language development, comparing different versions of the same folktale encourages the development of world understanding and cultural respect. These values are further enhanced through analysis of folktales from a single country or culture.

All of the folklore activities include reading, listening, and discussing. The specific techniques of charting and webbing were also developed in the chapter. Charting included charting the characteristics of folklore and charting comparisons of folktale variants. Webbing included mapping folklore for a study of traditional German tales.

### *REFERENCES*

BASCOM, W. (1965). "The forms of folklore: Prose narratives." *Journal of American Folklore,* 78: Jan-Mar, 3-20.

CHANG, I.C. (1965). *Chinese fairy tales.* New York: Crown.

COOLIDGE, O.E. (1951). *Legends of the north* (Illustrated by Edouard Sandoz). Boston: Houghton Mifflin.

COURLANDER, H. (1982). *The crest and the hide: and other African stories of heroes, chiefs, bards, hunters, sorcerers, and common people.* New York: Coward, McCann and Geoghegan.

GRIMM, BROTHERS. (1978). *The bearskinner* (Illustrated by Felix Hoffman). New York: Atheneum.

——. (1981). "The Brave Little Tailor." In L. Owens (Ed.), *The complete Brothers Grimm fairy tales* (pp. 75–82). New York: Avenel.

——. (1981). *Cinderella* (Illustrated by Nonny Hogrogian). New York: Greenwillow.

——. (1983). *The devil with the three golden hairs* (Retold and illustrated by Nonny Hogrogian). New York: Knopf.

——. (1978). *The fisherman and his wife* (Translated by Elizabeth Shub; illustrated by Monika Laimgruber). New York: Greenwillow.

——. (1936, 1964). "The Frog Prince." In *Tales from Grimm* (Translated and illustrated by Wanda Gag). New York: Coward, McCann & Geoghegan.

——. (1964). *The goose girl* (Illustrated by Marguerite de Angeli). New York: Doubleday.

——. (1969). *Grimm's golden goose* (Illustrated by Charles Mikolaycak). New York; Random House.

——. (1982). *Hansel and Gretel* (Translated by Anthea Bell; illustrated by Otto S. Svend). New York: Larousse.

——. (1984). *Hansel and Gretel* (Retold by Rika Lesser; illustrated by Paul O. Zelinsky). New York: Dodd, Mead.

——. (1983). *Little Red Riding Hood* (Retold and illustrated by Trina Schart Hyman). New York: Holiday.

——. (1974). *The musicians of Bremen* (Translated by Anne Rogers; illustrated by Otto S. Svend). New York: Larousse.

——. (1981). *The nose tree.* (Retold and illustrated by Warwick Hutton). New York: Atheneum.

——. (1981). *The seven ravens* (Translated by Elizabeth Crawford; illustrated by Lisbeth Zwerger). New York: Morrow.

——. (1981). "The Shoemaker and the Elves." In L. Owens (Ed.), *The complete Brothers Grimm fairy tales.* (pp. 161–162). New York: Avenel.

——. (1973). *The six swans* (Illustrated by Adrie Hospes). New York: McGraw-Hill.

——. (1979). *The sleeping beauty* (Illustrated by Warwick Hutton). New York: Atheneum.

——. (1972). *Snow White and the seven dwarfs* (Translated by Randal Jarrell; illustrated by Nancy Ekholm Burkert). New York: Farrar, Straus & Giroux.

——. (1976). *The table, the donkey and the stick.* New York: McGraw-Hill.

——. (1980). *The twelve dancing princesses* (Illustrated by Errol LeCain). New York: Viking.

LANG, A. (1960). *The red fairy book* (Illustrated by Reisie Lonette). New York: Random House.

MCDERMOTT, G. (1984). *Daughter of the earth.* New York: Delacorte.

PERRAULT, C. (1961). *Perrault's complete fairy tales.* Translated by A. E. Johnson, illustrated by W. Heath Robinson. New York: Dodd, Mead & Co.

SADLER, C. (1982). *Treasure mountain: Folktales from Southern China* (Illustrated by Cheng Mung Yun). New York: Atheneum.

SEVERO, E. DEPAPP. (1981). *The good-hearted youngest brother* (Illustrated by Diane Goode). Scarsdale, NY: Bradbury.

SUTCLIFF, R. (1981). *The sword and the circle: King Arthur and the knights of the round table.* New York: Dutton.

SUTHERLAND, Z., & LIVINGSTON, M.C. (1984). *The Scott, Foresman anthology of children's literature.* Glenview, IL: Scott, Foresman.

## SUGGESTED READINGS

NORTON, D.E. (1983). *Through the eyes of a child: An introduction to children's literature.* Columbus, OH: Chas. E. Merrill. Chapter 6, "Traditional Literature," provides selection criteria, book discussion, and techniques for using folklore with children.

NORTON, D.E. (1985). *Language arts activities for children* (2nd ed.). Columbus, OH: Chas. E. Merrill. Chapter 9, "Multicultural Activities," includes numerous activities developed for using African, Native American, Hispanic, and Asian folklore.

PURVES, A.C., & MONSON, D.L. (1984). *Experiencing children's literature.* Glenview, IL: Scott, Foresman. Chapter 2, "Folk Tales, Popular Literature, and Myth," includes a discussion on selecting and presenting folklore.

# NINETEEN
# MAKING AND USING MEDIA AS A LANGUAGE ART

*Media* can mean many things, from a hieroglyphic message carved in stone millions of years ago to a mainframe computer ready to process the information of the millenium. But all media are made by people for purposes of communication and for recording and processing information, for self-expression, and for the retention and retrieval of meaning. The purpose of this chapter will be to show why and how children should have experiences in making media, not only because of the relevance this may have for today's media-oriented youngster growing up in a media-oriented world culture, but also because helping children learn to use and make media is one of the most forceful means teachers have available to them to give children access to this powerful means of communication and language learning.

But just exactly how do you go about making media? Many schools, libraries, and media centers today are well equipped with the very latest equipment such as video, instructional television, sound-recording systems, and computers. Thus, all teachers should be just as well versed in the use of these media as they expect their students to be as they prepare them to participate as adults in a world forever changed by the advent of the electronic media. Some of the most direct accesses to media, in the self-contained elementary classroom, are those that do not require any equipment or other hardware to create and communicate in that particular media form. For example, several of the visual media that use acetate as raw material—and all film is made of acetate—can be made by teachers and students without cameras or other equipment. These include: films, filmstrips, slides, and transparencies. Children can create in all of these particular media by drawing and writing directly on clear acetate with pens and pencils made specifically for this purpose. All the materials to create draw-on films, filmstrips, slides, and transparencies are easily obtained or made, and they are also inexpensive. Most can be found in schools or solicited from parents. All the equipment needed to show the final product is readily available in all schools: 16mm film projectors, filmstrip projectors, slide projectors, and overhead projectors. These all share a similar sequential teaching approach and developmental learning process for children from kindergarten through upper elementary grades.

## A SEQUENCE FOR MAKING DRAW-ON FILMS, FILMSTRIPS, SLIDES, AND TRANSPARENCIES WITHOUT A CAMERA

All of these acetate media for making meaning and learning language can be approached through the same developmental sequence of steps that can be applied to the teaching of filmmaking (Cox, 1985), or any other of the visual and/or auditory forms.

1. Envisioning a Medium. Children can find ideas and visions for media-making anywhere, both in the classroom—group activities and experiences, field trips, and content in other subject areas, holidays, etc.—and out of the classroom—personal activities and experiences, trips, events, or dreams. Experiences with children's literature, both shared in class or through personal reading, are an excellent starting point for making media. Encourage children to seek and find their own visions and their own reasons for expressing them through media. This will always be more successful than using media-making as a way to show others what you have tried to teach children. Center media-making around children, their ideas, and their language.
2. Arranging a Medium. Once children have a vision in mind, they must begin to expand and clarify it as they seek to understand what they mean through arranging their medium in their mind. Children working in groups will brainstorm in discussion sessions and take notes in writing and drawing as they begin to record and sketch their visions. Children working alone will discuss their ideas with the teacher as they struggle simultaneously to expand their original idea and narrow it down to an arrangement that can be transcribed into a script in preparation for media production.
3. Transcribing a Medium. After children have arranged their ideas for media production in their minds through brainstorming, discussion, and notetaking, they will transcribe these ideas. They will probably already have noted and sketched a central idea on paper. They must then break this idea up into meaningful chunks of images and action, and record these on a storyboard that will become a script for final production. Storyboards can be dittoed sheets with three or four squares down the center for images, and space on either side for a description of the content, production notes, or narration, music, or dialogue for sound to be added later on tape.
4. Translating a Medium to Medium Form. After a successful storyboard has been composed, drawn, and written, children can translate the storyboard directly onto blank film, filmstrips, slides, or transparencies, or on gauges the size of the

medium. These drawings on the gauges should look exactly the way the children would like the final product to look. They may then place the acetate for each medium over the gauge, secure it with masking tape, and trace over the gauge onto the acetate with the pens or pencils designed for use on acetate.

5. Editing a Medium. Most of these media will not require editing because the gauge represents the final product. If changes are to be made, however, films and filmstrips can be rearranged and edited with splices. Splices can be made with transparent tape; however, better and more lasting splices are accomplished by using quite inexpensive splicers available in many film stores or through film catalogs. Editing a series of slides or transparencies requires simply rearranging the order in the slide tray, or the order of showing the transparencies, or creating new slides and transparencies to make changes.
6. Presenting a Medium. Presenting a medium is an important part of the creative composing process of communication. Film, filmstrips, slides, or transparencies shown may be publicized and presented by the children to other children in the class, other classes in the school, and parents and other members of the community.

## MATERIALS FOR MAKING DRAW-ON FILMS, FILMSTRIPS, SLIDES, AND TRANSPARENCIES WITHOUT A CAMERA

For all acetate media:

pens and pencils designed to draw and write on acetate.

For each specific acetate media:

| FILMS | FILMSTRIPS | SLIDES | TRANSPARENCIES |
|---|---|---|---|
| clear 16mm film | clear filmstrip; or 35mm film roll | 35mm negatives or film roll; or blank transparency | blank transparency |
| 16mm reel & can | filmstrip can | plastic slide mounts | mounts |
| 16mm film gauge | filmstrip gauge | slide gauge | |
| 16mm film projector | flimstrip projector | slide projector | overhead projector |

## MAKING FILMS WITHOUT A CAMERA

Children can make 16mm films without a camera by drawing directly on clear film leader with pens designed for use on acetate. Clear film leader can be purchased where art supplies are sold. However, often you can get discarded films free at television stations or media centers. These may be soaked and cleaned of the film emulsion in a solution of bleach and water. Wipe the clean film dry, roll around a film reel, and it is ready to use.

Children then may work as a whole class, in small groups, or individually to create a draw-on film. For kindergarten and primary children, the whole class film project can be done in the following way. Cover a table with newspaper. Pull a strip of film the length of the table and attach the reel at one end by anchoring it in a blob of modeling clay. Secure the film in a few places with masking tape. Young children may then draw in small groups from both sides of the table. Their images will tend to be very abstract and very free; namely, colorful squiggles, doodles, and dots. When they have finished a length of film, loosen the reel and drop the finished section of film in a clean bag on the floor at the end of the table. Pull a new strip of film and let a new group of children draw on it.

Older children may also work in groups or individually in a filmmaking center. They may create abstract images like the younger children, or they can learn to do draw-on animation by drawing the same image enough times so it will appear on the screen when the film is shown. Sixteen frames of one image will show one second on the screen when using silent speed projection. Words should be reversed and written from right to left so they will show from left to right on the screen. You simply reverse the film when winding it in order to obtain correct screen image. These images or words may also be moved slightly horizontally in each frame so they will move horizontally on the screen. Children love to experiment with this medium, and with practice they will be able to draw and animate fish that swim, flowers that bloom, faces that smile, and words that dance. Music, narration, dialogue, and sound effects may be taped on a cassette and played when the film is shown.

A kindergarten class created the "Color Me Film" in one morning. Because it was close to Valentine's Day, the film was filled with tiny attempted hearts and a few initials in hearts by those who could write them—their own and those of their valentine.

When the film was completed, the children watched it with delighted cries of "That's mine," or "There's me." They viewed, discussed, and interacted with each other and with their film for many weeks. They played records to it, sang with it, drew pictures of themselves as filmmakers, wrote about it, sometimes "danced" with it by standing between the projector and the screen so the squiggles covered their bodies, and presented it to family and friends at the May art show.

Two fourth-grade girls developed elaborate storyboards detailing each sequence they used to create the draw-on film "Yours, Truly You." They timed each design experiment with a stopwatch and built a carefully executed abstract film of color and light with concrete images and short written messages interspersed throughout. For example, a drooping flower, a stop light flashing green, yellow, and red, a fish swimming, and words and sentences such as "HELP," "STOP," "Three or four inches of a word makes it show," and "We thank Carole for all her help" (love notes to the teacher can appear in the most unexpected places, and make it all worthwhile).

One of the young filmmakers, Gretchen, commented on her film:

> YOURS, TRULY YOU, an exciting film about scribbles that make you use your imagination. You make the film. You dream up what you think.

Obviously Gretchen is aware of the nature of the film medium, the abstract nature of this particular film, and the interaction between the filmmaker and the viewer for she suggests that the viewer "make" the meaning of the film.

*Resources:* There are many fine films that use the draw-on animation technique and can be shown to children who make draw-on films (Cox, 1980). The work of Canadian filmmaker Norman McLaren popularized this technique with films like "Begone Dull Care" (International Film Bureau) and others. All of his films, which are produced by drawing directly on film, are distributed by International Film Bureau, 332 South Michigan Avenue, Chicago, Illinois 60604.

### Making Filmstrips

Children can make filmstrips by drawing directly on blank filmstrip that can be purchased where art supplies are sold or from discarded filmstrips from a library or media center. The strips should be cleaned with a solution of bleach and water in the way described to clean 16mm film. You can also use a roll of 35mm exposed film (ask a photographer or go to a newspaper office) or an unexposed roll of film (outdated is fine). Clean in the same way as the old filmstrips (the unexposed film will be harder to clean). The size of a roll of 35mm film is the same as a filmstrip. Store the cleaned strip of film in an old filmstrip container.

When children have brainstormed an idea and developed a storyboard, they can transfer their idea and images to a filmstrip gauge dittoed on paper and the exact size of the actual strip of film. Leave some film for leader at the beginning and then mark off frames with a black acetate pen. You may also want to have a frame that says FOCUS, another with START TAPE (if you plan to use one), and a TITLE. Place the filmstrip on the gauge, secure with masking tape, and transfer the drawing by tracing directly over the gauge with the acetate pens. Caution children to stay inside the marks where the sprockets will go. If they don't, what they draw won't show when the filmstrip is projected.

To add sound or music, help children develop their ideas for narration, dialogue, or music on the storyboard, matching sounds and words with images

**FIGURE 19–1** Filmstrip gauge with frames indicated. Frames will not show on new filmstrip material or old filmstrips or 35mm film that has been cleaned of emulsion.

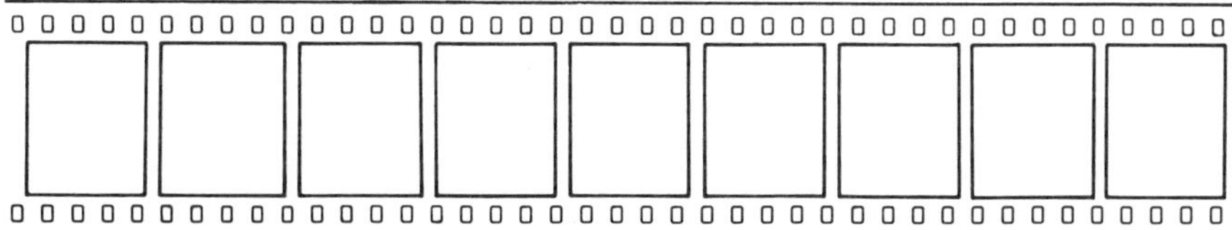

in the correct sequence. When taping, use a bell or other sound to signal a frame change to the projectionist. Don't rush the taping. Count to five before and after each bell to leave time to turn to the next frame and for the viewer to process the message.

"*If You've Never,* a Halloween Poem Filmstrip" was produced by Marion Harris, a first-grade teacher at Southside Elementary School in Denham Springs, Louisiana. After sharing poems about Halloween, the class discussed and planned the making of a filmstrip, divided into groups to brainstorm and write storyboards, and made several filmstrips in response to the poems.

Children had a chance to choose a poem, draw a frame for lines for each poem, and record their voices on a tape to accompany the filmstrip as they read the lines to match their drawing.

*Resources:* A bibliography on filmstrips and other media for sharing and responding to children's literature is Mary Alice Hunt's (1983) *A Multimedia Approach to Children's Literature.* Blank filmstrip material can be ordered in reels from Hudson Photographic Industries, Irvington-on-Hudson, New York, and in a "U" Film Kit from Miller, Brady Productions, Inc., 342 Madison Avenue, New York, New York 10017.

### Making Slides Without a Camera

Children can make slides without a camera by drawing and writing directly on clear acetate. You can use exposed 35mm negatives from prints, which come in strips of three or four negatives. Cleaned with a solution of bleach and water in the same way you would clean old film or filmstrips, each of these strips of negatives could be used for one or two slides. You might also use a whole roll of exposed 35mm film cut into pieces, or blank transparencies cut to the inside dimensions of a slide mount.

When children have brainstormed and discussed ideas, and drawn and written a storyboard, they can make a gauge from the inside dimensions of a slide mount to draw and write on, then lay the clear film over the gauge, secure with tape, and trace over the images with the acetate pens. It will be easier for them to draw the slides first and cut them later. Be sure they cut the size of the film larger than the interior dimensions of the mount to create the border needed to secure the finished slide in a mount. Plastic slide mounts are available at camera stores, or ask children to ask their parents for old slides with plastic mounts they no longer use.

My third- and fourth-grade class one year wrote a script and produced a "slape"—their acronym for a slide-tape presentation. The script idea emerged from discussions and writing they had done in response to a book that I had read aloud to them, *Mystery of the Haunted Mine,* which described a search for Spanish treasure in the Arizona desert. It was written by Western novelist Gordon D. Shirreffs, who is also my father. After he had visited the class and talked to them about writing, as well as hunting treasure, they talked and wrote voluminously on both subjects. They also began to imagine and draw maps leading to imaginary treasures. In the end, all this activity came together as the class wrote a script and produced the "slape" "Mystery of the Ancient Treasure," a tale of an underwater search for the lost treasure of a Seahorse King. It featured a brother and sister as main characters, a computer robot that could fly, and fantastical creatures such as an evil sorcerer, and talking sea horses and sea dragons.

They also recorded narration, music, sound effects, and dialogue on tape and presented their "slape" to other classes in the school, parents, and members of the community.

### Making Transparencies

Children can make their own transparencies by drawing and writing on blank transparencies available in most schools. This is an extremely simple project because these blanks do not need to be cleaned off as do the other acetate media, and they are much larger and easier to work on than films, filmstrips, or slides.

Children can use transparencies quickly and easily for a variety of purposes: storytelling, book sharing, or reporting research. They can use them as a visual aid to an oral presentation or they can use a tape for recorded sound. They can draw separate images to show one at a time, or create a transparency triptych. This may be made by starting with a basic image in a transparency mount and then adding two more, one on each side of the mount, by attaching them with tape so that when they are each laid over the first image, each will add more detail to the final picture.

Mounts made especially for transparencies may be found in your school or where school supplies are sold, or children can make them of different sizes and shapes by cutting a frame from poster paper, light cardboard, etc., and taping the transparency inside the mount. If they cut a frame in one side of a manila folder, the other side may be used for notes, a script, a story, etc., and the transparency can be kept in its own folder.

Two of my undergraduate students in a preservice language arts methods class developed a unit on ways to encourage children in the classes where they were doing their field experiences to respond to literature through media. One of the fifth-grade students in the class chose to share the book *Pippi Longstocking*. My students showed her how to make a transparency tryptych, which she used as she told an episode from the story to other children in the class.

| | |
|---|---|
| Transparency 1 | A picture of Pippi with two children watching her. |
| Transparency 2 (laid over 1) | An overturned bucket and water spilled all over the floor. |
| Transparency 3 (laid over 2) | Pippi says, "Who needs a holiday to scrub floors!?" in a balloon caption, and two scrub brushes are attached to her feet like skates as she cleans the floor. |

This fifth-grade student also used this transparency for storytelling with a first-grade class and shared her response to literature through media with younger children.

## Making Media and the Language Arts

In addition to being forms of visible language themselves, media such as film, filmstrips, slides, and transparencies provide meaningful contexts within which children and teachers may use and learn language and practice all forms of the language arts. Children who make media must first view and listen to media that not only present them with content and information on many topics, or present traditional literature or media versions of children's books, but also encourage them to think and respond to these media and this information by sharing what they are thinking through talking, drawing, writing, dramatizing, dancing, singing, and any other means children have to express their ideas through language and other expressive forms.

Children who make media must generate ideas and brainstorm together—through discussion with each other and the teacher, making and taking notes, and drawing and writing rough drafts of their ideas as they begin to compose in the media form, and in other forms of language as well. They must then begin to revise and refine their ideas through more discussion, interaction with each other, and more notetaking, writing, and drawing as they write and draw storyboards or scripts for making media. They must learn to organize and arrange their ideas in sequential order, make smooth transitions, consider their purpose and audience, refine what they want to communicate, and then make it concrete as they produce a final draft on a storyboard. They must then record, transcribe, and translate this storyboard script onto the acetate medium, working alone or in groups to create and communicate their visions and ideas. Finally, they must present what they have done to others, as they learn to make media and meaning while learning and using language.

Many specific language arts skills are required to produce media successfully: reading for ideas, researching topics, notetaking, spelling, writing and symbol making. The subjects of children's creative media experiences can be closely related to ideas in literature: storytelling and folk literature, picture books for younger children and novels for older children, film literature. Above all, making media offers children a means to learn language in *use* rather than mere language *usage,* and it offers the teacher a means to making language arts teaching meaningful.

### REFERENCES

Cox, C. (1980). Making films without a camera. *Language Arts, 57* 274–279.

Cox, C. (1985). Filmmaking as a composing process. *Language Arts, 62* 60–60.

Hunt, M.A. (1983). *A multimedia approach to children's literature: A selective list of films (and video cassettes), filmstrips, and recordings based on children's books* (3rd ed.). Chicago; American Library Association.

Lindgren, A. (1950). *Pippi Longstocking.* New York: Viking.

Shirreffs, G.D. (1965). *Mystery of the haunted mine.* New York: Scholastic.

### SUGGESTED READINGS

Gaffney, M., & Laybourne, G.B. (1981). *What to do when the lights go on: A comprehensive guide to 16mm films and related activities for children.* Phoenix, AZ: Oryx Press. A very complete look at 16mm films for children, including preschoolers: Filmography, film sources and programming, and encouraging children's responses to film—including making media—are discussed in this text. Lists and describes several draw-on films with follow-up activities.

LAYBOURNE, K., & CIANCIOLO, P. (1978). *Doing the media: A portfolio of activities, ideas and resources.* Chicago: American Library Association. This source book includes many ideas for making films and slides without a camera, and creating filmstrips and transparencies, as well as other forms of media. An excellent and comprehensive guide to media in schools.

MORROW, J., & SUID, M. (1977). *Media & kids: Real-world learning in the schools.* Rochelle Park, NJ: Hayden Book Company. Contains excellent rationale, approaches, and specific activities for involving children with media and integrating a great variety of media—drama, print, design, photography, radio, film, and television—into the curriculum.

# TWENTY
# USING THE VCR IN THE LANGUAGE ARTS

> Hey, let's see that again. We were really wild in that one.
>
> Look at John; he made it sound just like a king.

The comments above are by second graders after viewing their video production of *Where the Wild Things Are* (Sendak, 1963). Their teacher has provided them with a perfect opportunity for using and practicing language to communicate in a way that is highly motivating and meaningful. In addition, she has capitalized on the instant playback capabilities of video recording to extend and enrich that language experience. Her second graders not only produced purposeful language but also naturally reflected on their action and language and its effectiveness in communicating a story. The purpose of this chapter is to show you how to use video to enhance oral-language activities. Included in the chapter are ideas for many activities suitable for video recording. The equipment you will need for a video production is described, as is its operation. Finally, you will find some practical suggestions for using the video equipment in your classroom along with a sample video lesson.

## WHAT ARE THE BENEFITS OF USING VIDEO?

Oral-language activities such as storytelling, improvisation, puppetry, role playing, interviewing, and reporting have always been important avenues for children's language growth. These activities allow children to communicate naturally in ways that are meaningful to their experiences. As children participate in them, they become more effective communicators to a wider range of audiences for a wider variety of purposes. Given the accepted value of improvisation, interviewing, and other language activities, why add video? That is, why include the extra complication of setting up video equipment to record what is probably, for example, already a wonderful dramatic response to literature? The answer is that the video component actually strengthens and extends children's language growth during the stages of planning, experiencing, and reflecting back on their language experience.

Baity (1978) noted that creating a video recording requires discipline and structure. Children develop a sense of responsibility as they practice following directions and directing others. Preparing for a "live" dramatic enactment or interview also demands cooperation and planning. But in order to capture the performance on video camera (which cannot go as quickly or everywhere that the eye can), all aspects of the enactment must be even more well thought out. This maximizes student participation as well as creative involvement (Phillips, 1982).

The playback capability of video allows participants to relive their dramatic experience again and again. The feelings created when reliving the dramatic moment seem to enhance the experience (Laybourne, 1978).

The playback capability also creates another advantage. It allows children to study both the elements of the dramatic structure they have created as well as their own performance (Laybourne, 1978). Children can focus on aspects of narratives such as characterization, mood, plot, and point of view as they view and review their own productions. They can also become more sensitive to how well their performance reflected audience awareness and focus as they sharpen their interviewing and debating skills. This frequent feedback—not only from the teacher and others but also from one's self—can greatly enhance self-image and presence (Morrow & Suid, 1977).

## WHAT ACTIVITIES ARE APPROPRIATE FOR VIDEO RECORDING?

In actuality, the types of activities suitable for video recording are limited only by your imagination. Any of the regular classroom language activities—show and tell, book reports, discussions—make good subjects for video productions (Baity, 1978). In addition, the medium itself suggests other activities perhaps not so commonly practiced in the classroom—candid camera skits, quiz shows, and news programs, for example. However, all video-recorded activities fall into two basic categories: dramatic/improvisation and documentary/journalistic activities (Laybourne, 1978). Dramatic/improvisation activities allow children to explore the world of make-believe, to speculate on what was or what could be, and to enjoy language as a means of self-expression. Documentary/journalistic activities focus children's attention on facts and reality as they use language to get jobs done.

### Dramatic/Improvisation Activities

Laybourne (1978) suggested that the easiest and most nonthreatening activities with which to initiate video recordings are pantomimes. These activities have the added benefit of helping students attend to what *they* are doing rather than to what the *camera* is doing. Several pantomime activities should take place before videotaping begins. Begin with the entire class acting out a scene together. The teacher might describe a scenario which the children act out. For example, each student pretends that he or she is a burglar climbing in a window, stepping on the family dog, and tripping over a table. Students then pretend to fill a bag so that it is very large and heavy. Next they act out trying to climb out of the window again. Once the class gets the feel of pantomimes, each student can act out an action individually. This can be done like charades where one student mimes—eating a hot dog, for example—while the rest of the class tries to guess the action.

Video recordings of more extensive pantomimes of everyday scenes can be an easy initial encounter with video. Small groups of children can work together to enact a visit to the dentist, going to the beach, or shopping for new shoes. Phillips (1982) argued that students should select their own material for video production, and everyday pantomimes provide students with just this opportunity. Discussion of domestic, social, or business scenes such as going to a drive-in bank, or a father helping with homework, should help students create ideas for video pantomimes.

Improvisations of children's favorite stories are also good subjects for video recordings. Preplanning of scenes and dialogue is required, but script reading is not necessary or even desired. Not using a script assures spontaneity and freshness (Phillips, 1982). Children could also improvise stories they have created. Puppet improvisations of favorite or children's own stories make good video creations. Morrow and Suid (1977) suggested that older children might produce video puppet shows for younger students.

Video improvisations make wonderful extensions of content study. Children could role-play driving the golden nail connecting the first transcontinental railroad or discovering the smallpox vaccination. Teachers who have used video drama as a vehicle for learning subject material find that students come to "know" the material in ways that bring it more alive and make it more personally meaningful.

There are a variety of TV show formats that can be adapted for video activities. Students can stage their own variety shows, quiz programs, and even candid camera skits. These formats are also suitable for extending content study. For example, a quiz show could be developed to test knowledge of a current science topic or a variety show planned to illustrate the talents of Colonial American men and women.

### Documentary/Journalistic Activities

Documentary/journalistic activities help children learn to use language more effectively to accomplish goals. Videotape is a perfect complement to these activities because television is an important source of information and persuasion for both children and adults. Viewing their own video productions has potential not only for strengthening children's communicative power but also for sensitizing them to the subtle ways language is used to influence and manipulate.

Even young children can conduct video interviews. They can interview students, school staff, or students impersonating famous persons. The interviews should have a clear focus, and students should be prepared with probing questions. Again, a script is not desirable. The interview is probably one of the easiest activities to videotape because the performers stay essentially stationary. This activity provides an excellent opportunity for students themselves to operate the camera.

Older students could prepare more in-depth interviews or documentaries. Similarly, a memorial program documenting the life and accomplishments of a famous person or a classmate makes a good video production (Laybourne, 1978). Finally, students could videotape a debate over current or historical issues.

Another familiar format that can be adapted for classroom purposes is the news program. Students studying the causes and measurement of weather conditions could produce their own weather show. Or, a news program could be developed for a day from history under study. Children would enjoy creating news events and stories depicting a day in the Middle Ages or a day in their own school life.

One activity especially appealing to youngsters is videotaping their own commercials (Phillips, 1982). Children gain a better appreciation of the appeals used in TV commercials as they plan their own productions. This activity could be tied to a study of nutrition or safety, as well as of propaganda, if children produce food or toy commercials.

Finally, children can create video recordings designed to exchange with children from another area of the state or country (Mack, 1975).The purpose of these recordings is to communicate information about the students, the school, the community, and the state. These recordings can be used much like the traditional pen pal activities.

## WHAT IS INVOLVED IN CONDUCTING A VIDEO ACTIVITY?

Getting reading for and conducting a video activity includes gathering and assembling the video equipment, planning how to organize your students and classroom, operating the equipment to produce the video, and leading your students in a follow-up discussion of their activity. Although this sounds like a lot to do, most teachers find it takes no more time to get ready than the time it takes, for example, to gather materials and prepare for a science demonstration. Similarly, practicing and recording a language activity does not take much more time than that required to accomplish the activity without the video component. Because of the media boom of the 1970s, many elementary schools are stocked with video equipment, and librarians are familiar with its operation. You may be surprised to find that some of your students have video equipment at home and are quite expert in its use.

### Setting Up the Video Equipment

The equipment you will need to make and play back a video recording is very simple and easy to set up. First, you will need a video recorder/player. This looks like a large cassette player. In the newer versions, the recorder/player uses a video cassette (VCR) while the older versions use a videotape (VTR), or reel-to-reel type. Next, you will need a monitor. This looks like a television set. In fact, by using an adapter, a regular TV set can be used as a monitor. Be careful, however, for some monitors allow you to record only your own productions from a camera. Others also allow you to record a TV show. Most schools have large rolling carts specially made to hold the monitor and recorder/player.

You will also need a video camera. Older cameras are stationary (they sit on a tripod and are connected to the recorder/player by a length of wire). Newer cameras are called *Portapaks.* They are portable (can be hand held) and do not need to be connected to the recorder/player if a battery-operated recorder is strapped to the back of the camera operator. If your school is very up-to-date you may have a *Camcorder.* These small, lightweight cameras are completely self-contained. The small cassettes play from 20–60 minutes and may be played back on your VCR or dubbed onto standard size cassettes. Most cameras have built-in microphones, but some have an optional plug-in microphone that you can place closer to the actual enactment. Finally, you will need tape or a cassette. These come in various sizes (3/4 inch or 1/2 inch, Beta, and VHS) depending on the format required for your particular recorder/player.

You will find that in most schools the librarian or principal will help you set up the equipment. Connecting the plugs can prove complicated, however. The directions that come with the video equipment are the best source of assistance in completing the connections. If you borrow some equipment from the parents of your students, the parents or students themselves will be able to provide the assistance.

### Organizing Students and the Classroom

Before bringing the equipment into the room, the teacher should divide the class into groups of up to 10 students. Each group will create its own video production. The groups should have a clear idea of what their production will be—improvisation, puppet show, interview, etc.—as well as be thoroughly familiar with the subject of their production—children's literature selection, content material, creative story, and so forth. If some of the students are going to act as director and camera operators, they should be identified. Once the groups are formed and jobs assigned, the students should have time to plan their production. The amount of teacher guidance in planning will depend on the age and experience of students.

Once you set up the video equipment, you will want to leave it in your room for a few days. It is best to set up the equipment in a corner or nook where it will be away from the flow of normal classroom activities. The desks or tables near the set-up should be movable so the area can be cleared during the recording. Some teachers prefer to set up the equipment so the area they shoot into will have a wall or bulletin board as a backdrop.

Early on, all the children need to look through the camera into the area where the action will be recorded. This helps calm initial excitement about the video project and allows them to visualize the space requirements of recording their enactment. A rotation system for each student to view through the camera can be established while other activities are going on in the classroom.

Each group will need time to practice in the actual space where the recording will take place. This practice time should be kept at a minimum to maintain spontaneity. Then students should be ready to record. This is the only time that the class must be absolutely quiet. Any noise will be picked up on the recording. Some teachers plan the recording so that the other groups will be out of the room—outside for recess or visiting the library. Because videotaping requires that the enactment be recorded in its entirety from beginning to end, the recording time is actually very short. It is a good idea to start with a practice run with the camera being operated but not turned on. Then two enactments can be recorded. More than two trials is not necessary; the quality of the recordings seems to deteriorate after this point.

### Operating the Video Equipment

Operating a VCR is not hard to learn, and the user's manual will explain exactly what to do. Remember to caution everyone that the machines are expensive and hard to replace. Everyone must be careful to treat the equipment with respect. A good rule of thumb is to handle the VCR equipment with the same reasonable common sense you would use when handling a good stereo or TV.

First, you and your students should become familiar with the controls on the recorder/player. These controls are very similar to those on a cassette recorder: play, rewind, fast forward, stop, and eject. Many models have a pause button to freeze the action of the tape and give a still picture. Your machine may also have a power button for on-off control and perhaps a timer. Finally, the recorder/player should have a set of channel buttons to select the TV station that coincides with the channels on your monitor. Playback is generally done on channel 3 or 4, and the monitor channel must be set on the same channel as the recorder/player.

Becoming familiar with the camera and what it can do will come with practice. First, be sure the lens cover is removed. Once the camera is plugged into the recorder/player, press *play* and *record* together. On some equipment, especially newer models, a single button is used for each. Learn about your equipment before using it. Then press the camera trigger switch once. Look into the viewfinder of the camera to see if you can find a little red light. This means the camera is on and you should see what you are shooting on the monitor. To stop the camera, push the trigger once more. Before you actually start to record, you need to focus the camera. This is done before pushing the trigger on the camera to record. Focus on some far object by opening and closing the camera aperture. Next turn the zoom ring until the object is as large as possible. Focus on the object again. Now zoom out and you are focused and ready to record. You will also notice that the camera will swivel on the tripod up and down and side to side. Practice making these motions slowly and smoothly. Then try pivoting the camera as you zoom in and out. As you and your students practice these movements, you may want to introduce some of the specialized vocabulary associated with video recording such as pan, dolly, and zoom in (see Morrow & Suid, 1977; Laybourne, 1978). To play your recording back, you must rewind the tape and then push *play.*

### Following-up Video Activities

When all the recordings are completed, they are viewed and enjoyed by the class. A discussion then follows, which allows students to respond to the activity and their product. These discussions and viewings are important to children's continued language growth. But because the "most innocuous, casual comment can resonate deeply with a child, what is said during playback and discussion is important" (Laybourne, 1978). Unfocused feedback can be unnecessarily scary if students are not prepared with some rules.

Laybourne (1978) suggested several rules for video discussions that can be adapted in any classroom. First, teach children to separate fact from opinion. Children need to be able to distinguish what they see and hear from how they feel about what they saw and heard. Teaching them to use a format such as "I saw_________, and that made me feel_________" will help them separate fact from opinion (Laybourne, 1978). Second, children need to be sure they understand each other's comments during the discussion. Helping students learn to paraphrase someone else's comment before agreeing or disagreeing will accomplish much toward assuring accurate listening. Finally, the focus of the discussion must always be positive. Children should identify and amplify strengths by saying something good about everyone.

If you plan to have your class participate in other video activities, part of the discussion might focus on improving the technical quality of the video. For example, students may note that camera movements were too swift or important action was missed off camera. When to zoom in for close-ups can also be considered. Remember that your students will be less critical than adults. They should be proud of their video product whatever the quality. After all, it is the language that went on before, during, and after the recording that is of significance, not the quality of the recording.

## A SAMPLE VIDEO ACTIVITY: USING VIDEO TO CAPTURE FANTASY WITH REALISTIC FICTION

One type of children's literature that lends itself particularly well to the combination of drama and video is realistic fiction with a fantasizing motif. One of the earliest examples of this type of literature is Maurice Sendak's *Where the Wild Things Are* (1963). In this story, Max fantasizes a trip to the land where the "wild things" are to cope with being sent to bed with no supper. Realistic fiction with a fantasizing motif usually involves a realistic character living in the real world who fantasizes (dreams) either to cope with problems or to satisfy a need. Two narratives are simultaneously told within the one story: the real life narrative and the fantasy narrative. Here is where video fits in. Children can dramatize the fantasy *on video*. The fantasy is played on the monitor *while* the students dramatize the real-life narrative live. In this way, the instant playback capability of the video enables children to participate simultaneously in both the real story and the fantasy story.

The first step is to decide on an appropriate selection of realistic fiction with a fantasizing motif. An annotated bibliography of this literature is available in C. Craig Roney's article "Fantasizing as a Motif in Children's Realistic Literature (*Language Arts,* April 1983, pp. 447–455). Some selections that are especially easy to record are *Come Away from the Water, Shirley* (1977), by John Burningham; *Can I Keep Him?* (1971), by Steven Kellogg; *Where the Wild Things Are* (1963), by Maurice Sendak; and *I'll Fix Anthony* (1969), by Judith Viorst.

The next step is to read the selection (or selections) to each group of students. Discuss the selection with them, focusing on realism versus fantasy. Now the students are ready to plan the fantasy enactment for the video recording. Students should recall the events of the fantasy and plan out how they will enact these events. Drawing pictures on the board or writing scenes may help. Dialogue should be planned as well. Simple props and backdrop for the recording can be included. The students will want to fine-tune their enactment as they practice. Now bring the video equipment into the room and allow students to make their final preparations for the recording. If your students are ready, allow them to operate the camera.

The next step is to view the recording of the fantasy narrative and decide on how to dramatize the realistic story. Here the children need to plan carefully because the videotape of the fantasy will be playing during the enactment of the real story. Timing is important. That is, the enactment played on the monitor is to be seen as the thoughts of the character while he or she is going through real life.

Finally, you are ready to put it all together. Practice only a few times with the recording. Then invite an audience to share your dramatic masterpiece—video and drama. For example, in *Come Away from the Water, Shirley,* Shirley goes to the beach with her parents. She spends an entirely uneventful day. In contrast, she fantasizes she sees a pirate ship, fights to gain a treasure map, and discovers a chest of gold. The fantasy of the pirate adventure is shown on the monitor while Shirley and her parents enact "live" the dull day at the beach.

The follow-up discussion of this activity should help children gain a better awareness of the contrast between the outer and inner lives of characters. Often children focus on the actions of a story rather than the thoughts, motivations, dreams, feelings, and desires of characters and how these influence the story. Videotaping the inner life of a character allows the children to understand how this aspect of the character sheds new meaning both on the character and on the story.

## CONCLUSION

Video activities can bring language classrooms to life because they are especially appealing to today's visually oriented youth. Through planning, enacting, and thinking about video productions, children are using language in appealing new ways. When they finish with their activity, they have a language product they will be happy to share again and again.

### *REFERENCES*


Baity, J. (1978). Studio television. In K. Laybourne & P. Cianciolo (Eds.), *Doing the media.* Chicago, IL: American Library Association.

Burningham, J. (1977). *Come away from the water, Shirley.* New York, NY: Thomas Y. Crowell.

Hick, S., Hughes, G., & Stott, C. (1982). Video analysis and correction of learner performance. In M. Geddes & G. Sturtridge (Eds.), *Video in the language classroom.* London: Heinemann Educational Books.

Kellogg, S. (1971). *Can I keep him?* New York, NY: Dial Press.

Laybourne, K. (1978). Doing videotape. In K. Laybourne & P. Cianciolo (Eds.), *Doing the media.* Chicago, IL: American Library Association.

Mack, T. (1975). Videotape exchange. *Media & Methods, 12,* pp 50–51.

Morrow, J., & Suid, M. (1977). *Media & kids.* Rochelle Park, NJ: Hayden.

Phillips, E. (1982). Student video production. In M. Geddes & G. Sturtridge (Eds.), *Video in the language classroom.* London: Heinemann Educational Books.

Sendak, M. (1963). *Where the wild things are.* New York: Scholastic Books.

Viorst, J. (1969). *I'll fix Anthony.* New York: Harper & Row.


### *SUGGESTED READINGS*


Geddes, M., & Stutridge, G. (1982). *Video in the language classroom.* London: Heinemann Educational Books.

Haratonik, P., & Laybourne, K. (Eds.). (1974). *Video & kids.* New York: Gordon & Breach.

Laybourne, K., & Ciaciolo, P. (Eds.). (1978). *Doing the media.* Chicago, IL: American Library Association.

Morrow, J., & Suid, M. (1977). *Media & kids.* Rochelle Park, NJ: Hayden.

Ray, M. L. (1982). Videotaping: You and your kids can do it. In J. Thomas (Ed.), *Nonprint media in the elementary curriculum.* Littleton, CO: Libraries Unlimited.

# TWENTY-ONE
# USING TELEVISION IN THE LANGUAGE ARTS

## WHY USE TELEVISION ACTIVITIES IN LANGUAGE ARTS?

A fact of life for any language arts teacher is that kids watch a lot of TV. What effect a large amount of television watching has on the life of a child is a subject of considerable controversy. Television has been blamed for having harmful effects on the language abilities of school-aged youngsters (as well as on most other facets of their lives). Research studies abound, and the controversy rages. It seems likely that children who spend a lot of time watching television will be influenced by it.

Because television viewing looms large in the lives of many pupils, our suggestion begins with the old saying, "If you can't beat 'em, join 'em." Consider the information and language habits acquired by your pupils from many hours spent in front of TV sets. Such TV experience provides useful starting points for many worthwhile language arts lessons.

However, simply "joining 'em" is not a completely satisfactory answer. You must use pupils' present knowledge of TV programs as a base upon which to build activities for extending their language skills. Therefore, the purpose of this chapter is to give you reasons, teaching principles, and classroom activities for using pupils' knowledge and experience with television in your language arts instruction.

### The Media Mandala

To illustrate why you should use children's knowledge of commercial television as a part of language arts instruction we have devised the *Media*

*Mandala.* A mandala is a graphic symbol of the universe, in this case the "universe" of television and the language arts. See Figure 21-1.

The Media Mandala shows thought and language intertwined at the core of the Language Arts: listening, speaking, reading, and writing. Surrounding the language arts are the main divisions of the popular media, of which TV is currently the most popular. Note that listening, speaking, reading, and writing surround the inseparable duo—language and thought. To be used for communication, thoughts must be encoded in language. It seems to matter little to the brain which of the language arts is engaged at any moment; if it is processing language, it is developing. Each of the media, shown in the outer circle of the Media Mandala, employs all of the language arts and is ultimately linked to the language and thinking abilities of its creator.

Our position is that if a child's mind is actively engaged in processing language to gain a clearer understanding of the world, any medium will serve.

**FIGURE 21-1** The Media Mandala

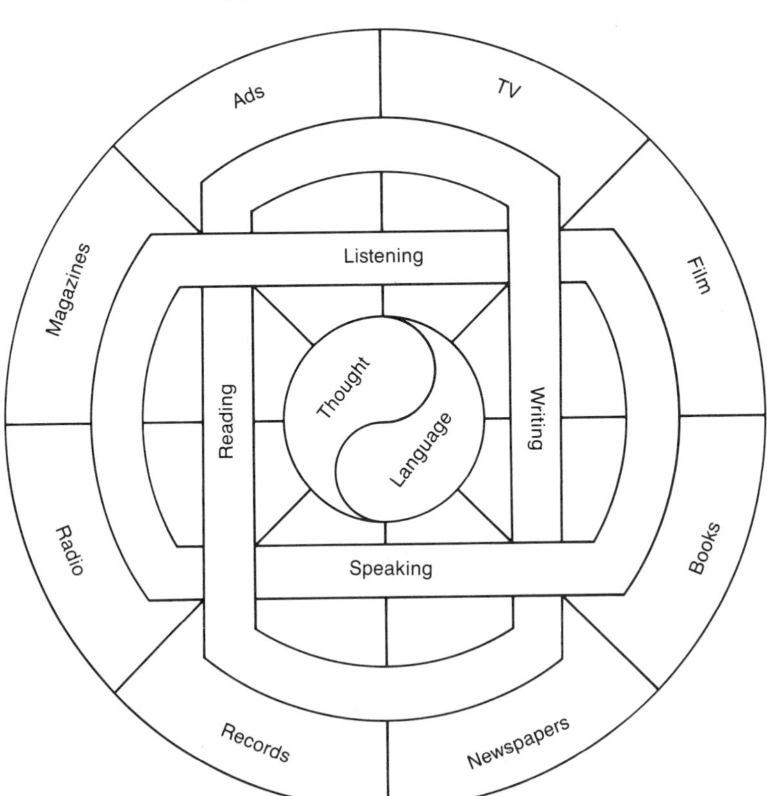

The key seems to be in the term "actively engaged." Language arts teachers who are attuned to the "active" use of popular media in the classroom may have greatest impact upon the development of language skills of their pupils.

One of the best reasons to use children's knowledge of commercial television in language arts classes is simple: Children like to watch TV. Furthermore, it is likely that they have stored in their minds a lot of information about TV programs, formats, plots, characters, commercials, etc. You will find they are willing to share this information readily and that it can be used in productive study of the language arts.

### Memory, Curiosity, Imagination

Children's knowledge about commercial television can be used to develop memory, curiosity, and imagination. Even very young pupils will gain skill as they recount from memory the plot sequence and character details of favorite Saturday morning cartoons. Older pupils can recount TV stories and compare them with real-life experiences. Knowledge and memory of word meanings become more attractive when new and unfamiliar words are uttered by memorable characters from favorite TV programs.

Also, TV programs are useful in arousing curiosity. The most lethargic pupils may be willing to discuss, read about, and write about new experiences, people, places, ideas, and actions they have seen depicted in television programs. Curiosity, whether about the new and strange or about the commonplace and familiar, is more readily aroused when pupils have a strong personal interest in the content. Use television activities to stimulate pupils' imagination. Ask them to devise new endings, new characters, unusual settings, appropriate dialogue, and even new situations. Never underestimate what your pupils know and can do relative to TV. It is a powerful motivator.

## TEACHING PRINCIPLES FOR USING TV ACTIVITIES

To make the best use of television activities in your language arts classes, here are a few things to keep in mind:

### Watch TV, Teacher

First, find out what television programs your pupils watch regularly. Then, watch them yourself. You need not watch every episode of every series for most have quite predictable formats. However, you should become aware of TV characters and general plot situations familiar to your pupils. Thus you will have common topics to talk about with pupils, and you will gain insights into the breadth and depth of their knowledge and skills in language arts.

### Teach for Active Viewing

The principle of *active viewing* cannot be stressed enough. Active viewing, rather than passive viewing, seems to be the key to overcoming TV's depressing effects on thought processes and language-skill development. Becoming actively involved—working at understanding the message—results in increased comprehension and memory of specific messages, whether in print or on a TV screen.

### Use the Series, and Prepare for Specials

When you have become acquainted with general plots and characters appearing in your pupils' favorite programs, it is a relatively simple matter to design language arts activities around such information. Regular use of TV favorites in classroom discussions, and as a basis for reading and writing assignments, will do much to perk up many lessons.

However, to derive most benefit from special TV programs, you should prepare both yourself and your students. Mini-series of famous literary works, biographies of men and women who have influenced the world, accountings of scientific discoveries, and so forth appear frequently on both commercial and public television channels. Scan the TV sections of news magazines and newspapers to find out about upcoming "specials." Prior to a special program, find books and articles appropriate to the topic and to the reading abilities of your students and have these ready for use. A day or so before the program, hold discussions with the pupils (1) to find out what they already know about the topic, (2) to present them with necessary background information, and (3) to give them some specific questions to guide their viewing.

### Watch Your Attitude!

Do not adopt the attitude commonly held by many "educated" adults that all commercial television is dreadful. A familiar argument against TV watching runs like this: "Most commercial television programs could be labeled inane, insipid, shallow, or stupid. But they are popular, and as long as they remain so, TV networks will continue to broadcast them."

The focus of this chapter is that classroom teachers, especially in language arts, can face the challenge. Children can learn to recognize quality. If enough children (and adults) reject TV's poorer offerings, programming will change.

Use this time-honored principle: The teacher must find out where the pupils are and begin at that point. Do not begin by belittling your pupils' TV viewing choices and habits or you may lose their confidence. Of course your standards are higher! You're an educated adult. If you become too critical of pupils' choices, you are likely to confront a large bloc of pupils who have developed the attitude: "Teacher may know what's good for us, but he[she] doesn't know what we really like!"

## TV ACTIVITIES FOR LANGUAGE ARTS CLASSES

The activities in this section focus on using your pupils' knowledge about commercial television in language arts classes to develop pupils' communication skills.

### Learning About Our TV Habits

Learn as much as you can about your pupils' knowledge, perceptions, and experiences with television. As you learn about your pupils' TV habits, so they will learn about themselves and about a subject that looms large in their lives.

*Surveys.* Have pupils fill out survey forms during class time to gather general knowledge about their viewing habits. Be sure to discuss the tabulated results and lead pupils to draw valid conclusions from any surveys. After pupils have completed a number of surveys, they may be willing to venture further. Some upper-grade classes have created schoolwide TV surveys to assess the viewing habits and preferences of an entire school.

**CLASSROOM TV SURVEY**

Name ______________________ Grade __________ Room ______________

1. Does your family have a TV set? (circle) yes no
2. If yes, how many TV sets does your family have? (give numbers)
   Color Sets__________ Black & White Sets______________________
3. Do you have your own TV set? (circle) yes no
4. Do you watch TV before school? (circle) yes no
   If yes, what?______________________________________________
5. Do you watch TV as soon as you get home from school? yes no
   If yes, what?______________________________________________
6. About how many hours do you watch TV each day?_______________
7. What is your favorite commercial?____________________________
8. Who is your favorite TV personality?_________________________
   Why?______________________________________________________
9. Do your parents let you watch whatever you want? yes no
10. List three of your favorite TV programs.
    a. ______________________________________________________
    b. ______________________________________________________
    c. ______________________________________________________
11. About how many hours a week do you read (not school work)?__________
12. How many books have you read since school started this year?__________

*Viewing logs.* A *viewing log* is a work sheet that directs pupils to consider specific ideas or issues related to the programs they watch at home. Logs may be checklists, charts, continuums, or sentence-completion formats. They may be used during or after viewing. After pupils have worked with a few viewing logs, they may like to devise their own formats around common themes or topics. Here are two samples to get you started:

**Viewing Log: Lower Grades**

Name ____________________ Grade: __________ Room: ____________________

THE BEST TV PROGRAMS I WATCHED THIS WEEK

For each day, tell. . .

-What TV program you liked best.
-What time it was on.
-What channel it was on.
-What you especially liked about it.

(It's all right to ask a parent to help you, but you should give the answers yourself.)

| DAY | BEST PROGRAM AND WHY YOU LIKED IT | CHANNEL | TIME |
|---|---|---|---|
| *SUN* | | | |
| *MON* | | | |
| *TUE* | | | |
| *WED* | | | |
| *THU* | | | |
| *FRI* | | | |
| *SAT* | | | |

What was your favorite program this week? Explain why.

**Viewing Log: Upper Grades**

Name: ____________________ Grade: __________ Subject: ____________________

Title of Program Evaluated ________________________________________

| Day | Date | Time | Channel | Network |
|---|---|---|---|---|
| ________ | ________ | ________ | ________ | ________ |

Type of Program: (check one)

__________ action-adventure series
__________ children's program
__________ comedy series
__________ drama
__________ educational program
__________ mini-series
__________ movie
__________ news program
__________ quiz program
__________ "soap"
__________ "Special"
__________ sports event
__________ other (describe) ________________________________________

| Your rating of this program (circle one): | ★★★★ excellent | ★★★ good | ★★ fair | ★ poor |
|---|---|---|---|---|

On the back of this sheet, explain the reasons for your rating. Be specific and include examples to back up your reasons:

---

*Questionnaires and discussion starters.* Another way pupils develop insights into the powerful influence of TV on our lives is through the time-honored method of *discussion.* There are endless variations on this method, so each teacher needs to develop his or her own style for leading discussions. Here is one possibility.

### *BRAINSTORMING*

Choose any of the TV-related topics suggested below for a brainstorming session. Tell your class that you are going to give them a word (or phrase) that has something to do with television. When they see it, they are to tell you what other words and ideas it makes them think of. Then write the TV term on the chalkboard or on an overhead projection transparency. As pupils give oral responses, write them for all to see.

Get as many responses as you possibly can—no matter how far off the topic they may seem to be. However, it is fair to challenge or question a pupil's response that is not clear, or that you understand but believe some pupils may not. Simply ask the pupil to explain why that particular response was given. Work for communication and clarification. Teachers trying this activity for the first time are often impressed by the number and quality of pupils' responses generated by a TV-related word.

As pupil responses run out, move to the next phase. Have pupils work in pairs to categorize the many responses generated in the first phase, devising category headings as needed. Each pair of students presents its groupings to the other members of the class. After some practice, pupils learn to suggest a wide variety of categories. To end the discussion, try to get the class to agree on the "best" or most workable set of categories.

Then, move to the third and final phase of this activity. Ask the pupils what they have learned about themselves and about this TV topic from listing and categorizing their responses.

Some suggestions for Brainstorming topics:

| **FOR YOUNGER PUPILS (GRADES 1–3)** | **FOR OLDER PUPILS (GRADES 4–8)** |
|---|---|
| cartoons | "soap operas" |
| animal characters | car crashes |
| station breaks | news/weather/sports |
| weather reports | sponsors |
| *TV Guide* | "specials" |

## Learning about Types of Programs and How to Evaluate Them

Children need ways of coping with the transitory nature of television programming. Help them to understand more about the nature of TV programming by examining such topics as: (1) basic formats and types of programs, (2) the reason for TV ratings systems, and (3) the influence of TV ratings on sponsorship. By having pupils view TV programs, discuss them openly, and read and write about television topics, they develop skills in communication and critical thinking.

Use the following sets of questions for class discussions or debates, or, for written activities, as work sheets or viewing logs.

### ACTION-ADVENTURE SERIES

1. Name a show you've seen several times.
2. Briefly describe the usual action or plot.
3. About how long has this series been on? Weeks? Months? Years?
4. Are the main characters always heroes or heroines? Explain.
5. Describe the specific plot of the most recent episode. (Opening incident, rising action, climax, falling action, and conclusion)
6. Do programs on this series usually have happy endings?
7. What emotions do you feel as you watch this series?

### SITUATION COMEDY SERIES

1. Where do the characters in this comedy live? City? Suburb? Rural area? In what part of the U.S.? Another country?
2. What is the setting of most situation comedies this season?
3. Who are the main characters in this series? What do you know about them? Where do they work? What do they eat? Do they watch TV? How do they spend their leisure time? Are they generally happy? How do they compare with your family?
4. What sorts of problems do the characters usually have on the programs? How do the problems get solved? Is one character usually the problem solver, or does it vary?
5. Why do you think so many programs are about families?
6. What things would you like to know about the characters that the program hasn't told you?
7. Do you like the people in this series? How are they different from people you know? Do you laugh at the silly things these people say and do because they are so stupid? Or do you laugh with them because you have done similar things yourself?

### NEWS PROGRAMS

1. Name the local news, weather, and sports programs in your area. What times and channels are they on? Who are the commentators?
2. How is each show arranged? What comes first, second, third, etc.?

3. About how many news stories are contained in a half-hour program?
4. What kind of room are the commentators in? Do they sit behind desks? Do they read the news from a script or do they seem to be looking at you?
5. How do various news programs differ? Have you ever watched the same news event covered on several channels? How do they differ?
6. How does TV news differ from newspaper coverage of the same event?
7. When might TV news coverage be better than that of a newspaper?

You and your pupils can devise similar questions about other types of TV programming such as game shows, variety shows, "soap operas," talk shows, cartoon shows, children's shows, musical shows, etc.

### Learning about TV Advertising

If you doubt the power of TV to plant product names and ideas in children's minds, try this quiz with your pupils:

#### THE COMMERCIALS CONNECTION

1. Fly the friendly skies of____________________
2. Aren't you glad you use____________________?
3. Don't leave home without it.____________________
4. Wouldn't you really rather have a____________________?
5. You deserve a break today at____________________
6. Let your fingers do the walking through the____________________
7. Own a piece of the__________(Company?____________________)
8. It's the real thing.__________is.
9. We're__________Airlines, doing what we do best.
10. Aren't you hungry for__________now?
11. Oh, oh, oh, what a feeling!____________________
12. "Look, Mom! No cavities!" tells us the toothpaste is____________________

Because commercials support most of television, they are unlikely to disappear. You can help pupils understand commercials and prepare some defenses against them. This can be done by analyzing commercials to understand the language devices they use.

### TV Activities Using Commercials to Increase Listening Skills

Make audiotape recordings of several current and popular TV commercials and play them for your class. Without the video portion, pupils' attention is more focused on the words and they will listen more closely if they are given specific things to listen for.

Younger pupils can listen to your audio recordings to identify the following:

| | |
|---|---|
| commercials: | (How many of you know this commercial?) (What pictures go with it?) |
| products: | (What is this commercial trying to sell?) |
| well-known people: | (Whose voice is this?) |
| sound effects: | (Who can tell what this sound is?) |
| moods: | (Does this voice sound happy? sad? angry?) |
| new words: | (Raise hands when you hear the word "fun.") |
| sight words: | (Each pupil has a card with a sight word printed on it. When the sight word is spoken, the pupil with that word holds up the card.) |

Older pupils can listen to your audio recordings of commercials to identify and classify types of words:

| ADJECTIVES | ACTION VERBS | RHYMING WORDS AND ALLITERATION |
|---|---|---|
| new | save | no muss, no fuss |
| improved | performs | fly the friendly skies |
| bright | dazzles | no-wait rebate |
| **MOOD WORDS** | **"-ING" WORDS** | **"INVENTED" WORDS AND SPELLINGS** |
| family | lasting | manwich |
| heart | introducing | playskool |
| tender | conditioning | lymon |

### Using Commercials to Increase Reading, Writing, and Speaking Skills

*1. Logging commercials:* Middle- and upper-grade pupils can learn much about commercials by keeping logs of the ones they watch.

What types of products are advertised during prime time?
During Saturday A.M.? Early morning? Dinner time?
About how many commercials are shown each hour?
How much time is taken by commercials during an hour?
How long (in seconds) are most commercials?

*2. Classifying commercials:* Producers of television commercials are very creative, constantly devising new ways of making product names stick in our minds. First, have pupils list as many different commercials as they can. Then have them try to sort the commercials into categories. Usually they will "discover" such types as these: humorous, animated cartoon, famous person, shouting, luxurious, expensive, demonstration, before & after results, etc.

*3. Producing commercials:* After pupils have gained some experience in viewing and classifying commercials, have them create, write scripts, and produce their own commercials to present "live" to the rest of the class. Working individually or in pairs, pupils create a commercial for some simple object: a styrofoam cup, a plastic spoon, pencil, paper clip, eraser, rubber ball, etc. Each commercial is to be exactly 30 seconds long. Pupils can invent slogans, write copy, use pictures, demonstrations, interviews, or any other commercial technique they wish as long as they don't exceed the strict time limit. Allow a few minutes over several class periods for creating and rehearsing. Set a definite due date for performance. Afterwards, hold a discussion to evaluate the commercials. Focus on clarity, words used, reasonableness of appeal, whether or not pupils would buy the product, and so forth.

The activities described in this section are but a few of the countless television-related ideas you might use in language arts classes. Once you begin to use TV activities suggested in this section, you will quickly develop many more ideas of your own.

## SOURCES OF MATERIALS FOR USING TELEVISION IN THE LANGUAGE ARTS

In recent years, many TV-related educational materials have been developed and published. Here are a few sources that you may find useful.

### BOOKS AND KITS:

1. Becker, G.J. (1973). *Television and the classroom reading program.* Newark, DE: International Reading Association.
2. Cheyney, A.B., & Potter, R.L. (1980). *Video: A handbook showing the use of the television in the elementary classroom.* Stevensville, MI: Educational Service, Inc.
3. Potter, R.L., Faith, C., & Ganek, L.B. (1979). *Channel: Critical reading/tv viewing skills.* Freeport, NY: Educational Activities, Inc.

### AGENCIES AND INFORMATION SOURCES

CBS Educational Relations
51 West 52nd Street
New York, NY 10019

International Reading Assn.
800 Barksdale Road
Newark, DE 19711

Scholastic Magazine
50 West 44th Street
New York, NY 10036

ABC Community Relations
1330 Avenue of the Americas
New York, NY 10019

Prime Time School Television
120 South LaSalle Street
Chicago, IL 60603

Teacher's Guides to Television
699 Madison Avenue
New York, NY 10021

Of course, the best sources of TV-teaching information are your pupils and yourself. Because of the ever-changing nature of television, what interested your pupils last year probably will be of less interest to this year's class. So a final reason for using TV activities in your language arts classroom is that it will keep you attuned to the current interests of your pupils, thus providing a chance to keep your teaching always fresh.

# TWENTY-TWO
# USING THE NEWSPAPER IN THE LANGUAGE ARTS

Teaching language arts can be exciting and interesting. Searching for new and creative ideas in presenting listening, speaking, reading, and writing activities can be demanding and challenging. Relating this instruction to today's world is one way of making learning come alive. The newspaper is an excellent vehicle for helping children see language arts at work on a daily basis. As you search for innovative ways to provide experiences for your children you will find that the newspaper is a ready source. It is important, however, for you to determine specific ways in which the newspaper can be used. You must decide on the skill or concept that is the focus of your lesson, and you must identify the technique for accomplishing your goal.

The purpose of this chapter is to present ideas and activities for incorporating the newspaper into the language arts program of your classroom. Suggested teaching/learning strategies for the primary, intermediate, and upper-grade levels will be described. These techniques will supplement and reinforce the skills within the language arts strands—listening, speaking, reading, and writing. Tips will be given for organizing your classroom for using the newspaper and for integrating it into your communication arts program. Some roadblocks and limitations will be outlined as well as some advantages and disadvantages.

## ORGANIZING FOR INSTRUCTION

As you begin your use of the newspaper, you should determine if you are going to subscribe to a local newspaper, if articles are to be clipped by the children and brought to school, or if you are to be the primary source of the news items. Any one of these procedures could be followed. In any event, keep in mind that the children should always be active participants in the process, but the responsibility for directing the teaching/learning experiences of the children rests with you. You should be certain that you know (1) the purpose of the lesson, (2) for whom the activity is intended, and (3) the way in which you will make it an integral part of the language arts lesson. Include the newspaper experiences in your daily and/or weekly lesson plans; base them on the ongoing language arts program. Be specific. Avoid substituting the reading of article after article as a "time filler." Do not use the newspaper as a substitute for your regular program. Carefully select an article to satisfy the needs of the day's objective. You should also be alerted to the fact that children, especially older ones, are sometimes very clever in diverting your attention away from the lesson by pretending to pursue newspaper study further. Limit the teaching/learning strategy to the time needed to accomplish your purpose. Another caution is to adjust the lesson for the grade level(s) intended.

You might want to consider the suggestions listed below in setting the stage for using the newspaper as an adjunct to your language arts program.

Decide on the source(s) of the news items (your file, student articles, and/or classroom newspaper subscriptions).

Be sure the articles fit the purpose of the lesson.

Determine the methodology you will use (teacher-directed, brainstorming, discussion, committee presentation in reports, or the like).

As you give the newspaper its rightful place in your language arts curriculum, you will want to consider each of the sources of articles mentioned previously. If there are no funds available in your general fund, you may wish to solicit funding for the subscription of a local paper from local parent groups or other community agencies. You will also want to keep a file of newspaper articles and activities that are especially interesting and helpful. This file should be updated frequently. Whatever the major source, you should have children bring in articles. This will help to ensure that the children are reading the newspaper and it will aid in building lifetime reading habits.

Once the initial planning for using the newspaper has been made, it is essential that diversified grouping patterns are explored so that motivation can be continuous and instructional techniques can be meaningful. Some procedures may include the following:

Organizing the class into committees or interest groups. These groups could select articles of a given type such as cartoons, want ads, sports section, etc., and then present their articles to the class.

Pairing students and using a question/answer format.

Dividing the students into teams to compete in giving answers based on articles.

Setting aside a given day for individual students to report on articles.

Using games to report on articles.

The physical setting of the classroom should be considered as an integral part of the newspaper program of instruction. A bulletin board is one excellent way for displaying articles. News notebooks can be kept by each student and displayed along the chalkboard ledge, on the reading table, or in a teacher-made news file box covered with contact paper, newsprint, construction paper, and/or colored in a collage fashion by the students. You may wish to consider arranging the furniture so that there is a designated space for a "News Corner."

## INTRODUCING THE NEWSPAPER

Setting the stage for integrating the newspaper into the regular language arts program is extremely important. You must be a powerful salesperson as you convince your class of the significance of gaining information via the print media when the news and other information can be gotten so easily and entertainingly from television. One of the first activities is to introduce the newspaper in a step-by-step and systematic way. Using a newspaper, walk the children through the parts of the paper in each section. You will want to acquaint the children with the index to the newspaper as one initial step. This study skill will assist the children in locating articles quickly and will be transferred into their daily assignments in other subject areas.

Children should become familiar with the news section, the feature section, entertainment features, editorials, want ads, comics, radio and TV sections, sports pages, advertisements, book, film, drama, and play reviews, travel section, special interest columns, financial news, and other sections, as well as the newspaper's production and distribution process.

It is also important to introduce the newspaper vocabulary. The definition of terms such as the ones listed at the end of this chapter can serve as a vocabulary "starter list" for the children. As the year progresses and new words are discovered, they, too, can be added to the list.

Understanding the use of the five W's, that is, Who, What, When, Where, and Why in the writing and/or reading of an article can prove to be an aid to children at all levels. You may also want to introduce the "H" question, *How.* This question will complete and crystallize the ideas the writer is attempting to convey. Eliciting the answers to the questions mentioned above can ensure that the children are gleaning the main ideas and details from the articles.

Another idea is to provide the students with other general tips that can be used in reading the paper. These may include the use of captions, pictures, type of print, tables, abbreviations, and so forth. Some mention should be made of the diverse articles that appear in the newspapers and the types of writers who contribute to the vast numbers of news items. Reading the newspaper is no different from reading other materials. Understanding a news item, like understanding other materials, requires the reader to know the purpose, the author's style, and the prescribed format of the selection. For example, a well-written news story is factual and the most important material is given in the beginning of the story. An editorial, on the other hand, usually states the purpose of the article toward its beginning; an editorial is the opinion of the writer. Knowledge of the intricacies of style, purpose, and the like can help children focus on key items when reading the newspaper. Some classes will not need as thorough an introduction as others. At any rate, assess the maturity and background of the students and adjust your instruction accordingly.

## EMPHASIZING THE LANGUAGE ARTS SKILLS

The newspaper can be used to teach or reinforce many language arts skills. You can determine the skill(s) that is best suited for your lesson objective(s). The skills listed below are but a few that can be easily presented via the newspaper.

Choosing the main idea and details
Outlining
Differentiating between fact and opinion
Answering literal questions

**TABLE 22-1 Skills/Article Selection Correlation Chart**

| LANGUAGE ARTS SKILL AREA | TYPES OF ARTICLES |
|---|---|
| Main idea/detail<br>Outlining<br>Literal questions | News articles<br>Headlines/who, what, when, where, why (how) |
| Fact and opinion | News articles/editorials |
| Charts, graphs, maps | Weather, sports |
| Sequential order | Comics, news stories |
| Writer's purpose | Feature articles, editorials, news articles, special interest articles |
| Categorizing | Want ads, advertisements |
| Cause/effect | News articles |
| Writing skills<br>Critical listening<br>Summarizing | Rewriting all types of articles |

Reading charts, graphs, maps
Understanding sequential order
Developing vocabulary
Recalling facts
Determining the writer's purpose
Categorizing
Understanding cause and effect
Developing writing skills
Developing critical listening skills
Summarizing.

Once you have identified the language arts area being highlighted, a determination of the type of article or section of the newspaper that could best facilitate instruction should be made. Table 22–1 gives a few examples of skill areas and the type of articles to be chosen.

## SELECTED ACTIVITIES FOR USING THE NEWSPAPER IN LANGUAGE ARTS

There is nothing more helpful to a teacher than having a repertoire of techniques for teaching a skill or concept. A bank of activities can save time for the busy teacher and serve as a springboard for extending language arts experiences to other content areas. For these reasons, several teaching/learning strategies for the primary, intermediate, and upper grades are listed on the pages that follow. It must be emphasized, however, that a myriad of possible activities exist that a teacher may employ in the quest to make the newspaper a viable tool for teaching the communication arts. The suggestions here are presented to whet your appetite.

### FOR THE PRIMARY GRADES

Read selected cartoons to the children; have them tell the main idea of the cartoon. Have the children draw pictures of the cartoon; alert them to draw their pictures in the correct sequential order.

Read words selected from the newspaper to the children; have them tell the beginning and/or ending sounds of each word.

Locate children's activities in the paper and guide the children in completing them.

Use pictures as a way of having children tell a news story in their own words.

Use letters, words, or pictures to have children develop the concepts of big-little, tall-short, up-down, over-above, etc.

Have the children cut pictures from the paper and paste them under various categories such as fruits, clothing, furniture, cartoons, games, sports, etc.

Read an article from the newspaper and have the children look at television news to see how the story is reported.

Use pictures from the newspaper; have the children create their own stories and tell them to the class.

Have the children make a "pictionary" by cutting pictures from the newspaper and pasting them under the correct alphabet letter.

Have the children design original advertisements using the newspaper as a model.

## FOR INTERMEDIATE GRADES

Have the children peruse the newspaper to determine the way in which it is organized. Discuss the major sections of the newspaper: news section, sports pages, want ads, travel section, etc.

Locate the index of the newspaper and find selected sections; point out the importance of using the index as an aid to improve study skills.

Role-play a reporter and interview another student or teacher on an item reported in the paper. From this information have him or her rewrite the news story based on the interview. Have the news stories read to the class and discuss them.

Make a list of vocabulary words associated with the newspaper. Using the words, have the students complete the activities below:

Write antonyms and synonyms

Use the words in sentences.

Write paragraphs using the words.

Make a list of unfamiliar words found in their reading of the newspaper. Play charade games using these new words. Let other children in the class guess the words being demonstrated.

Read a news story out of sequence. Rewrite the story in the correct sequential order.

Write a new heading for two or three articles.

List the different kinds of things that appear in the want ads. Discuss the ones listed.

Write a review of a movie or play seen recently.

Choose a topic and collect news clippings based on it.

Discuss the meaning of editorial cartoons.

Discuss the intent of editorials.

Use a weather map to answer specific questions.

Use the sports section to find answers related to sports heroes.

Bring in articles about astrology and advice columns; discuss the articles to bring fun and variety to news study.

## FOR THE UPPER GRADES

Discuss the selected genres such as fiction, nonfiction, biography, autobiography, poetry, short story, etc. Find sections in the newspaper which are similar to these genres. Use these articles as a basis for discussions.

Read articles that have a historical link with the past (articles related to the Viet Nam War, the Summit Meeting, and so forth). Have students research the topic and write an expository essay based on their findings.

Organize a class and/or school newspaper. Use the newspaper as a vehicle for teaching writing skills, grammar, usage, style, etc.

Have the students complete the crossword puzzles; review the answers with the class. Study the etymology of new and unfamiliar words.

Use the editorials, news articles, feature articles, etc., as a background for debates and group discussion.

Choose a current topic about a country or issue and do research. Encourage the students to present their findings via a panel discussion and/or through written reports, projects, or displays.

Summarize the information given in an article by writing one or two sentences that give the main idea of the article.

Have students rewrite articles in their own words.

Use sociodrama, dramatization, or improvisation as a way of demonstrating the contents of articles.

Discuss the role of advertising as it relates to the economy.

Use news articles to trace the history from the present to the past.

Write original editorials that support or refute ideas on an issue.

Using study guides is still another way for helping children read the newspaper as an independent activity. The guides could be used in class or they may be used as a homework activity.

A few guides are outlined in Figures 22-1, 22-2, and 22-3.

Other activities might also be used for the generation of more study guides. Some of these are listed below; you might want to add some of your own.

Paste an editorial on a sheet of paper. Rewrite the editorial using a different point of view.

Draw a time line to illustrate a chronology of an article that has a historical perspective. Trace the facts for a period of 20 years or more.

Use the skeleton on the next page to outline a news article.

**FIGURE 22-1** Generic Study Guide: Primary Grades

<u>My Newspaper Study Guide</u>

Tell what kind of story you read and draw a picture of a face that fits the story.
Draw a picture that tells about the story.
Mark the picture that fits.

My Newspaper Study Guide

Answer these questions about your story:

Who are the people in the story?
What happened in the story?
When did the action take place?
Where did the action take place?
Why did the action take place?
How did the events happen?

Complete the chart(s).

Choose an Appropriate Article

| | Name of Article |
|---|---|
| Byline | |
| Type of article | |
| Purpose of article | |
| Main idea | |
| Lead | |

**FIGURE 22-2** Generic Study Guide: Intermediate and Upper Grades

*Title of Article*

I.
    A.
    B.
II.
    A.
    B.
III.
    A.
        1.
        2.
    B.
        1.
        2.

## SUMMARY

There is no way that one could delineate all ways in which the newspaper could be used to teach the language arts. What I have done is to tap the fertile news soils from which new plants may grow. As you begin to use this most vital publication, you will no doubt discover many more new methods. This chapter

| My Newspaper Study Guide |
|---|
| Locate an Appropriate Article |
| Fact |
| Opinion |
| Drama/Play Review |
| Special Interest Article |
| Feature Article |
| Cartoon |

**FIGURE 22-3** Generic Study Guide: Intermediate and Upper Grades

has offered ideas for organizing your newspaper study and techniques for gearing your instruction to primary, intermediate, and upper-grade students. We have intended it as a how-to instructional aid. With these guidelines and activities you can go on to make the newspaper an integral part of your language arts program.

## *VOCABULARY STARTER LIST*

**ads:** public notices; advertisements designed to arouse an interest in buying a product or service
**byline:** bylines identify the writer of an article
**captions:** words written beneath pictures that give information about the picture
**cartoon:** a design or drawing that comments on a political, social, or public issue
**columns:** a special feature in a newspaper or periodical
**comic strip:** a group of sequential cartoons designed to tell a story
**drama–book reviews:** a drama or book review gives a critical opinion of a play or book

**editor:** a person who writes editorials
**editorials:** a newspaper or magazine article that states the editor's or publisher's opinion
**headlines:** words set at the top of a newspaper story or article, usually printed in large letters and intended to give the main idea of the article
**international news:** worldwide news
**lead:** the introductory part of a news story
**local news:** news related to the locale in which one lives
**reporter:** a person employed by a newspaper or magazine to gather news and write articles
**state news:** news related to the state in which one lives
**special section heads:** special section heads identify recurring features

## *SUGGESTED READINGS*

BURNS, P.C., & BARSETT, R. (1982). *Language arts activities for elementary schools.* Boston: Houghton Mifflin. Suggestions and variations of suggestions are given on ways of providing students with practice in writing newspaper items that parallel actual newspaper items. Functional writing and locational skills related to the newspaper are also addressed.

Chicago Tribune Educational Services. (1977). *Activities to do with your newspaper.* Chicago: Chicago Tribune Educational Services. This packet of materials offers you practical ideas for developing specific skills in reading, writing, language, and literature through newspaper use. Color-coded and presented on individual cards, the activities may be incorporated as part of a total group, small group, or individualized activity.

GITELMAN, H. (April, 1983). Newspaper power. *Reading Teacher, 36,* 8, 831. This short selection offers a strategy for using the newspaper in conjunction with open-ended questions to address all the areas of language arts.

# TWENTY-THREE
# USING MICROCOMPUTERS IN THE LANGUAGE ARTS CLASS. I

## INTRODUCTION

This chapter describes the effective use of computers in English-language arts instruction at the elementary school level. Particular attention is given to the computer as a tool in the teaching of writing. The chapter examines how the distinct yet recursive stages of the composing process, that is, prewriting, writing, and rewriting, are enhanced by microcomputer use. Examples of commercially available software and files that teachers can create for language arts instruction are offered.

## PREWRITING

The importance of the *prewriting* component of composing has been emphasized by researcher Donald Murray, who estimates that the bulk of the writer's time is spent in prewriting (85 percent), whereas 1 percent is spent in composing and 14 percent in revision (Murray, 1982). Teachers use varied instructional strategies to aid students in prewriting; these include class discussions, use of art materials, and listening to recorded music and stories.

The microcomputer offers unique opportunities for prewriting activities, creating an individualized and personalized environment for the young writer. Increasing numbers of prewriting programs designed for learners of diverse needs, ages, and learning styles offer choice and flexibility for students. Programs take many forms, including commercial prompting-type programs specifically prepared for prewriting; teacher use of word processors for file creation; word processing packages that contain prewriting modules; and programs containing graphics and music capabilities.

Software containing prompts provide open-ended questions concerning student writers' purpose, audience, form, and voice. Students type answers to questions, print the results of their dialogue with the computer, and use this material in composing their essay, letter, or report. Early efforts in prewriting programs, such as Hugh Burns' *TOPOI* (Wresch, 1984), were designed for college and high school use; however, new products offer the same opportunities to elementary school students. One publishing company, for example, markets a set of three prewriting modules as a supplement to its elementary school word processing package. These programs (Milliken) permit students to brainstorm and organize ideas on disk, print the results of the thinking, and proceed to write with pen and paper or merge the ideas with their files on the word processor. Software such as these provide both individualization of instruction and the opportunity for young writers to experience a social, almost conversational, interaction concerning their ideas.

The prewriting portion of William Wresch's *The Writer's Helper* (Conduit) offers middle-school and high-school students numerous choices of activities to generate, organize, and rework their ideas. Included is a comparison of the student's topic with unusual images, an activity called *visual synectics* (Rodrigues & Rodrigues, 1984). A sample question might be "How is composing on a computer [your topic] like a subway train?" Students are encouraged to see commonplace concepts and articles in a fresh way and create unusual metaphors for their work. This package also includes programs for use in editing activities.

Prewriting activities are also provided by two volumes of the *Bank Street Writer Activity Files* (Scholastic). These files present both structured and open-ended files for writing. These include code-breaking, poetry writing, peer-editing, and directed prewriting fantasies in Volume 1 in addition to position statement, sequencing, writing of letters for business, invitation and thank-you purposes, and composing of dialogue and character description in Volume 2.

Teachers can use word processors to create shells or scaffolds for the unique needs of their classes. Teachers can do this by writing activities on a disk, saving them, and providing students with information about the help they provide. Students can then use the activities or assigned work or can go to special files should they have a specific problem. Examples of files teachers can create include activities for sentence-combining, the format for report of a science experiment, varied book report forms, short story elements, and research report models. Specific files can be developed for brainstorming ideas about the subject, purpose, audience, voice, and form of any writing. Students may also enjoy creating questions and activities for peers to use. These files serve as a reminder to students concerning the form of their prospective compositions and encourage independent problem solving.

Teachers can use commercial packages prepared for this purpose as well. A program called *Quill* (D. C. Heath) is designed to help teachers and students create shells, or banks, of questions and forms for across-the-curriculum activities. Teachers are given detailed instructions for creation of shells for movie and restaurant reviews, classified advertisements, and student-authored encyclopedia entries. The shells and the student writing attached to them are then available for storage and peer viewing in the library module of the program. Students and teachers can also communicate via *Quill*'s Mailbag, an electronic bulletin board. *Quill* provides both prewriting help and enlarges the audience for student writing.

Graphics and music programs offer entry to writing via the arts. Young artists and composers create banks of pictures and music for private pleasure and sharing with classmates. Whereas crayons and paper have traditionally been allied with the language experience approach to teaching reading and writing, computer software extends the possibilities for artistic idea generation of primary-grade and intermediate-grade students.

## COMPOSING

Students respond with excitement and anticipation to *composing* with the word processor. This phenomenon, which has been called "writing with light," soothes the fearful author with its ease of erasure and revision and the crisp, professional appearance of the copy produced. Young writers are particularly intrigued with the fluid movement of their text and the polished quality of the printed copy. The many benefits of providing word processors for young writers include the following:

1. First drafts can be written with major attention on getting down the ideas and minor attention on spelling, mechanics, and style.
2. First drafts are easily revised without need for tedious recopying or retyping. This encourages the student who is reluctant to revise because of lengthy and laborious recopying. Further, the word processor frees teachers to require changes without concern for time wasted in that recopying.
3. Students whose negative attitudes about composing were based upon difficulty in producing manuscript or cursive text are freed from the burden of this production. New attitudes are formed based upon the task of composing rather than the rigors of handwriting. In addition, the computer is a valuable tool for those students whose physical disabilities have prevented them from communicating in print. Special equipment is available to help disabled students use the computer.
4. Word processors make possible experimentation with multiple printed formats for a single piece of writing. Adjustments in type font, margins, and boldface text are easily accomplished and meet the needs of varied audiences.
5. The transition from writer to reader is made with greater ease and speed. The appearance of typed text on the screen or printed copy moves the writer to a role of reader/audience/editor at a faster pace.

Use of the word processor for activities known as *invisible writing* (Marcus & Blau, 1983) and *paired writing* (Marcus, 1983) also provides help for student authors. Invisible writing occurs when the computer monitor is darkened and students no longer view what they are writing. This activity appears particularly helpful in first drafts, where students concentrate on getting down their ideas without concern for spelling and mechanics. Writers using the invisible writing technique (Marcus, 1984) say that not seeing the text appearing on the screen allows them greater freedom to express ideas.

Paired writing activities involve students who switch monitors as they compose. Each student sits at a computer and writes while the partner responds to the text moving across the screen. Students who are "stuck" for the appropriate word choice or who desire feedback about the clarity of their message receive help from the partner viewing their work. This activity frees the young author from the hindrance of concern with mechanics in the first draft and provides a real audience for the work.

In addition to word processors, many programs dedicated to story writing are available for elementary school use. These programs vary on a number of dimensions:

1. Programs differ as to targeted age and presumed composing skill of users. *That's My Story* (Learning Well) offers story starters for students from grades one through eight on one master disk. It is suggested that each story starter be transferred to a separate disk where students write "what if" or "choose your own adventure" type stories. These can be read by peers who choose varied paths determined by the writer. Programs like this offer a good value for schools because writers of varied grade levels have access to material geared to their interests. It should be noted that the procedure for writing the "what if's" remains the same for all users of the program. A variety of interest and reading levels have, however, been accommodated on this one disk.

2. Some story-writing programs provide combinations of graphics and text while others offer text only. An example of an engaging program for the primary-age child is *Kidwriter* (Spinnaker), which artfully combines text and graphics. Children use the keyboard to choose among 99 pictures, numerals, and alphabet letters for screen placement on any of nine different colorful backgrounds. Space for story writing is available on the lower half of the screen. However, students may use the picture creation portion of the program as a form of prewriting and move to pencil and paper to compose their story. This would enable more children to use the program in any single time period.

Another program featuring a combination of text and graphics is *Story Maker: A Fact and Fiction Tool Kit* (Scholastic), which offers selection of multiple type fonts, drawing capability, and use of "galleries" of pictures for students' use. Children create illustrated stories, save them, and print them. This program requires use of a joy stick, mouse, or Koalapad. There are many ways to give information to the computer; using the keyboard is one, and these devices attached to a computer offer alternative means of operating a program.

3. Programs vary as to ability to print the text produced and saved on disk. For example, the *Kidwriter* program mentioned above does not allow for printing, and all stories must be saved on disk. When the disk is full, stories are deleted to make room for new ones. *Story Tree* (Scholastic) is another example of a program with a choose-your-own-adventure format. It provides four sample stories, uses of the program on a story disk, and detailed directions (in the documentation) for producing stories, as well as across-the-curriculum uses. One fine example of a nonstory use of this program is one's ability to use the story-writing shells for student-written book reviews. These reviews on disk can then be available for peer perusal in book selection. *Story Tree* stories may be printed. When the story disk provided is full, writers copy stories they wish saved to their own initialized disks, leaving the story disk free for others' use.

4. Programs also vary as to amount of time they assume that the user will work directly on the computer. Both *That's My Story* and *Story Tree* are programs that demand careful planning away from the computer for there are a number of branching possibilities available for any one section of the program.

A program called *Storymaker* (Bolt, Beranek, & Newman) was developed with the express purpose to free young writers from the problems of handwriting, spelling, and mechanics. Therefore, students work directly on the computer, linking various branches of stories and printing them. In this task, young writers combine their choices from the bank of story parts on the computer and same and print their compositions.

The best story-writing programs offer students stimulating opportunities for composing. They provide interesting environments for writing and are easy to use. The best story-writing programs lead students to exploring options in composing. They increase the purposes and audiences for student work.

## REVISING AND EDITING

The art of revising is best learned through practice. It is an arduous task, one that most students would prefer to ignore and avoid. If students do edit, they are most likely to make surface-level corrections of spelling and mechanics. This is due, in part, to the amount of time students are given to write; the length and kinds of assignments given; and the audience and response they receive for their work. Assignments growing from real purposes, offered to interested audiences who respond with more than just correction, encourage revision.

Given a purpose and an audience for their work, student use of word processors provides motivation for writing and encourages redrafting. Word processors allow students to add, delete, or move pieces of text on the screen with ease. Revising no longer means recopying.

In addition, the computer provides exciting opportunities for peer-editing. Students find it easier to read and comment on one another's work when it is in clearly printed form instead of handwritten, which is often difficult to decipher.

Special software is also available to aid students with problems of mechanics and spelling. Many word processing packages now have electronic spellers that highlight words not found in their dictionaries. Students are told that the words indicated deserve attention as they may be misspelled. These programs enable students with some spelling ability to check for errors and search the program's dictionary for suggested alternative spellings of the word(s) in question. It should be noted, however, that poor spellers may not find significant aid in such software, for they must decide which of the choices presented are correct.

Increasing numbers of programs offer editing modules that check word-processed text for use of passive language, length of sentence and paragraph, and common errors of usage. These programs provide suggestions to students for improving their writing.

## SOFTWARE SELECTION

Teachers are faced with an increasing array of choices of programs for use in the language arts classroom. While the programs mentioned in this chapter are examples of available materials, technology is becoming increasingly sophisticated. This does not necessarily mean that software will automatically become better. Teachers must exercise care and judgment in software selection. Checklists and guidance are available from numerous resources, including those listed below:

1. MECC (Minnesota Education Computing Consortium)
   2520 Broadway Drive
   St. Paul, Minnesota 55113
   (612) 638-0600
   MECC does not evaluate software, but does provide a number of services including: development and distribution of software; inservice teacher training; technical support; and newsletters.
2. RICE (Resources in Computer Education)
   Northwest Regional Laboratory
   300 Southwest Sixth Avenue
   Portland, Oregon 97204
   (503) 248-6800
   This is a database accessed via the ERIC system. It offers descriptions and evaluations of software.
3. MicroSift (Micro Computer Software and Information for Teachers)
   Northwest Regional Laboratory
   300 Southwest Sixth Avenue
   Portland, Oregon 97204
   (503) 248-6800
   MicroSift is a service providing 27 evaluation sites across the United States, each

staffed by two teachers and a computer technician. MicroSift uses the following criteria for evaluation: instructional quality, areas of content, and technical quality. Reviews are acquired by writing or phoning the service or by accessing RICE.

4. EPIE Institute
   Teachers College
   Columbia University
   Box 27
   New York, New York 10027

The National Council of Teachers of English Committee on Instructional Technology has also produced a list of cautions and suggestions for software used in the language arts. Teachers may obtain this work sheet by writing NCTE Headquarters, 1111 Kenyon Road, Urbana, Illinois 61801.

However, the best source of review is the teacher and student working with a program. Many software publishers now provide free preview of programs. Teachers need to take advantage of these opportunities and lobby other publishers to provide such service.

Selection of software for composing purposes should primarily be concerned with provision for: easy use, the loading of the program into multiple computers for simultaneous use by many students, back-up copies, and most important, an environment conducive to writing for the age and needs of the learner.

## ISSUES OF CONCERN

Despite the promise of the new technologies, many problems remain in their implementation and use. These include questions concerning keyboarding, lack of equipment in schools, quality of software, and need for staff development in the use of the hardware and software.

Although this chapter offers numerous examples of the benefits of word processing and story-writing software, many questions and cautions still remain. One unanswered question concerns whether children need keyboarding (typing) skills before using software for composing purposes. Teachers appear to be divided on this issue. Although some voice concern over the slow "hunt and peck" method of typing by young children, others remain convinced that hands too small for "proper" hand positioning find their own successful methods of coping with the keyboard. Recent publication of software offering drill and practice typing activities, and books on the same subject, give teachers of children in grade 3 and up (the age hands seem large enough for positioning on the keyboard) options for teaching typing. No studies exist that offer conclusive answers to this question. However, teachers continue to offer students who lack formal typing training the opportunity to use the software, and children seem to benefit from the experience.

An additional concern, and as yet unresolved question, is whether the polished quality of the printed copy leads writers to make surface proofreading and formatting changes as opposed to deeper-level editing. Students may also lose a sense of the flow of their entire theme as they glimpse a screen filled with text or split-screen views of a composition.

Another concern is whether computer use enhances or reduces student interaction and communication. Initial speculation concerning computer use was that students sitting in front of computers would lose contact with one another as they became engrossed in interaction with the machine. Reports from teachers, however, indicate that students do a great deal of chatting and sharing with one another as they work at their individual monitors. Teachers can also encourage such activity through directed peer-writing and editing activities.

In addition to questions about the selection, production, and use of technology are issues of equity. Increasing numbers of families are purchasing home computers, yet a substantial number of students lack the financial resources for computer ownership. School resources remain scarce and access to computers at school varies greatly. Once students use the machinery and reap its benefits, it is difficult for schools to meet the great demand for computer use. The gap between those with and without access to microcomputers/word processors has potential influence on students' motivations and school performance. The lack of access to technology becomes the lack of access to knowledge in our students' future.

## CONCLUSION

Computers provide an additional resource for the teacher of language arts. Computers offer especially promising assistance for the teaching of composing. They are tools to assist the writer at each part of the composing cycle: prewriting, writing, and rewriting. Teachers of the language arts have joined hands with technology to produce an exciting environment for student authors. Studies of students working at the computer on language-related tasks will continue to provide new directions and assistance for the teacher of language arts.

### *REFERENCES*

BURNS, H., MAJOR (1984). Recollections of first-generation computer-assisted prewriting. In W. Wresch (Ed.), *A writer's tool: The computer in composition instruction* (pp. 15–33). Urbana, IL: National Council of Teachers of English.

DAIUTE, C. (1983, May). The computer as stylus and audience. *College Composition and Communication, 34*(2), 134–145.

——. (1984). Computers and the teaching of writing. In D. Peterson (Ed.), *Intelligent schoolhouse-readings on computers and learning* (pp. 108–116). Reston, VA: Reston Publishing.

MARCUS, S. (1983). Real-time gadgets with feedback: Special effects in computer-assisted instruction. *The Writing Instructor,* A publication of the University of Southern California Freshman Writing Project, Los Angeles, CA: Sumner, 156–164.

——. (1984). *Computers and the teaching of writing: A resource guide.* Cupertino, CA: Apple Education Affairs.

MARCUS, S., & BLAU, S. (1983, April). Not seeing is relieving: Invisible writing with computers. *Educational Technology,* 12–15.

MURRAY, D.M. (1982). *Learning by teaching: Selected articles on teaching and writing.* Boynton/Cook Publishers.

RODRIGUES, R.J., & RODRIGUES, D.W. (1984, February). Computer-based invention: Its place and potential. *College Composition and Communication, 35*(1), 78–86.

SHOSTAK, R. (1983). Computer-assisted composition instruction: Some promising practices. *The Best of Pipeline, 8*(2), 19–22.

## SUGGESTED READINGS

BERTELSON, S., CHRISTENSEN, S., JOHNSON, S., REITER, T., SCOTT, K., & SMART, J. (1983). *A guide to using the computer in the writing process.* Madison, WI: Wisconsin Writing Project. This guidebook is written by English-teacher participants in the Wisconsin Writing Project, part of the National Writing Project network. It offers clear and easily read advice and information for teachers beginning to use computers.

CHANDLER, D. (Ed.). (1983). *Exploring English with microcomputers.* Leicester, UK: Council for Educational Technology. Chandler is an English teacher who offers practical advice and information concerning computers in the English curriculum.

DAHMAN, D., FISCHER, L., GOMEZ, M.L., GRISHAM, M., & HAAS, J. (1984). *A guide to using the computer in the writing process, part 2.* Madison, WI: Wisconsin Writing Project. This guidebook is written by English-teacher participants in the Wisconsin Writing Project, part of the National Writing Project network. It offers information for teachers beginning to use computers and includes many examples of software for use in the language arts curriculum.

RUBIN, A. (1983). The computer confronts language arts: Cans and shoulds for education. In A. C. Wilkinson (Ed.). *Classroom computers and cognitive science* (pp. 201–219). New York: Academic Press. Andee Rubin discusses four issues concerning the role of computers in language arts education: the level of text on which the program focuses, the role of feedback, the possibility of providing opportunities for learning by doing, and the social environment supported by the software.

SCHWARTZ, H.J. (1985). *Interactive writing-composing with a word processor.* New York: Holt, Rinehart & Winston. This book was written as a textbook for an upper-level secondary or college-level composition class. It is a comprehensive volume offering information about the writing process, computers, and computer-based activities for the composition classroom.

SHOSTAK, R. (1984). *Computers in composition instruction.* Eugene, OR: International Council for Computers in Education. Shostak's monograph offers many brief chapters concerning software to support the writing process and courseware selection and design.

STANDIFORD, S., JAYCOX, K., & AUTEN, A. (1983). *Computers in the English classroom: A primer for teachers.* Urbana, IL: National Council of Teachers of English. This book is an easily read introduction to computer use in the English classroom. The authors provide scenarios in which fictional teachers learn about computers and composition.

WRESCH, W. (Ed.). (1984). *A writer's tool: The computer in composition instruction.* Urbana, IL: National Council of Teachers of English. This text provides chapters written by the directors of major computer and composition projects in the United States. Although most projects described are oriented toward the secondary-level, the text is a valuable resource for anyone concerned with computers and the teaching of writing.

ZINSSER, W. (1983). *Writing with a word processor.* New York: Harper & Row. William Zinsser details his initial encounter with and use of a word processor.

# TWENTY-FOUR
# USING MICROCOMPUTERS IN THE LANGUAGE ARTS. II

## INTRODUCTION

This chapter examines three roles of the computer in the language arts classroom: that of teacher, student, and tool. As a teacher, the computer can build skills (spelling, grammar, punctuation, etc.), present concepts about the writing process, and model invention heuristics. As a student, the computer can be used to aid the drafting, revising, and analyzing of student writing.

In this chapter, we relate these roles of the computer to four stages of the writing process—pre-prewriting, prewriting, writing, and revising—and suggest activities appropriate to these stages.

These symbols identify which role the computer plays in each activity:

Teacher  Student  Tool 

## PRE-PREWRITING STAGE

### Communication Skills

Communication-apprehensive students can benefit from computer applications in *pre-prewriting*. These applications give students an opportunity to build writing skills, develop vocabulary, increase reading comprehension, and play with dialogue, all of which should be considered as enabling rather than as primary goals of instruction. Although the computer activities do not teach the enabling goals directly, the nature of computer–student interaction requires that the student learn them in order to use the computer effectively.

### Activity 1—

There is a genre of computer programs called "adventure" or "dialogue" games that involve the student as a participant in a story or adventure, in a conversational setting. The student types responses either as answers to direct questions or as reactions to developing situations. The program is designed to scan each response and to determine if it matches a predetermined remark germane to a keyword or phrase. If it does, the computer replies with a predetermined remark germane to a keyword or phrase. If no match is found, the computer remark is usually a noncommittal but encouraging reply to "please go on" or to "tell me more." A sample dialogue is illustrated in Figure 24–1. The matched words have been underlined.

Communication skills are enhanced by more than just students' interactions with a computer program. Frequently, dialogue games cannot be completed within a single class period because of the time required to explore multiple options. Students often tell each other about paths explored that were not fruitful. Although the games are designed for individual use, the outcomes are achieved frequently through group effort. This shared communication among students is an additional benefit.

**FIGURE 24-1** Sample Dialogue Using *Doctor* (Krutch, 1981)

(computer) Please state your problem:
(student) ? I DON'T LIKE COMPUTERS.

(computer) Do computers worry you?
(student) ? A LOT.

(computer) What does that suggest to you?
(student) ? NOT A THING.

(computer) Please go on.
(student) ? YOU REMIND ME OF MY UNCLE.

(computer) In what way?
(student) ? I AM AFRAID TO TALK TO HIM.

(computer) Is it because you are afraid to talk to him that you came to me?
(student) ? YES. CAN YOU HELP ME?

(computer) You believe I can help you, don't you?
(student) ? . . .(and so on)

**Activity 2—**

Students may want to try writing their own adventure game. To write dialogue that a computer can recognize, begin with a set of index cards. The students identify the basic vocabulary words needed for the game and write each word on one side of a card. On the back side of the card, students should write the response triggered by the vocabulary word. Remind students that synonyms get the same response as the original word.

After the students have created a set of vocabulary cards, the cards are classified by type and arranged in a specific order. Because a computer will be programmed to react to the first word it finds, the ordering is important. Related words are ordered from most to least specific. For example, the words *pet, beagle, dog* should be ordered *beagle, dog, pet.* This is done to ensure that a phrase that includes related words of different specificity (such as "pet beagle") elicits the more specific reply.

Once the cards are ordered, test the "dialogue." To do this, one student plays the role of the computer and a team of students plays the role of the participant. The "computer" sets the scenario. When the participant responds, the "computer" goes through the cards, finds the first keyword or phrase, and reads the response on the back of the card. As dialogue continues, several difficulties could emerge: not enough vocabulary, inappropriate order of responses, or insufficient noncommital remarks for the computer to use when none of the participants' response words are recorded on the cards.

After modifications have been made, the dialogue is tested until it is satisfactory. The cards are numbered and the scenario formalized. These cards can be used in the activity that follows.

**Activity 3—**

We have included a simple program (Figure 24–2) that illustrates the principles in the previous activity. Enter this program directly on an APPLE (II, IIplus, IIe, or IIc) microcomputer. With minor modifications, the program will run on any microcomputer that uses the BASIC programming language. After it is entered, it can be modified to reflect the dialogue that your students have written.

*Grammar.* We believe that grammar is best taught in context. For that reason, we have not included tutorial and drill or practice grammar activities. Rather, we will describe some activities in which the student can use the computer to "mess about" with a language-free grammar in a manner described by Michael Sharples, an Australian researcher in artificial intelligence (Sharples, 1983).

**Activity 4—**

Students can teach the computer to recognize *categories* of words and to draw samples from those categories. Examples of categories might be parts

```
10 NP=47
100 HOME
110 PRINT "A CONVERSATION ABOUT PETS"
125 PRINT "-------------------------------------"
130 PRINT "WHAT KIND OF PET DO YOU HAVE?"
135 PRINT:PRINT
140 INPUT SA$
150 IF SA$="" THEN PRINT "PLEASE SAY SOMETHING":GOTO 140
151 TRIES=TRIES+1
152 PRINT
153 L=LEN(SA$)
155 RESTORE
160 FOR I=1 TO NP
170 READ KW$,JU
180 K=LEN(KW$)
190 FOR J=1 TO L-K+1
200 IF KW$=MID$(SA$,J,K) THEN GOTO 600
210 NEXT J
220 NEXT I
230 GOTO 500: REM NO MATCH FOUND
300 DATA NONE,1,NO ONE,1,NOBODY,1, EVERYONE,2,EVERYBODY,2,EVERY ONE,2,EVERY BODY,2
320 DATA MOTHER,3,MOM,3,FATHER,3,DAD,3,SISTER,3,BROTHER,3,FRIEND,4,PAL,4
340 DATA SITUP,5,SIT UP,5,SITS UP,5,ROLL OVER,5,PLAY DEAD,5
345 DATA PLAYS DEAD,5,SHAKE,5,HEEL,5, STICK,6,BALL,6," CAR ",7
360 DATA TRUCK,7,BICYCLE,7,BIKE,7, YARN,8,STRING,8, TRICK,10
400 BATH TRAIN,10, BATH,11,FEED,11,WALK,11,GROOM,11,BRUSH,11,CARE  OF,12, PLAY,13
430 DATA COLLIE,14,GERMAN,14,MUTT,14,SPANIEL,14,  SIAMESE,14,TABBY,14
450 DATA DOG,15,CAT,15,BIRD,15, SNAKE,17, GERBIL,18,HAMPSTER,18,SPIDER,18
500 RN=INT(RND(1)*3+1)
505 IF TRIES>15 THEN PRINT "IT WAS NICE TALKING TO YOU. I HAVE TO WALK MY ROBOT. BYE.":END
510 ON RN GOTO 520,530,540,550
515 GOTO 500
520 PRINT "THAT'S INTERESTING. PLEASE GO ON.":GOTO 135
530 PRINT "REALLY? TELL ME MORE.":GOTO 135
540 PRINT "IS THERE ANYTHING ELSE?":GOTO 135
550 PRINT "CAN YOU TELL ME MORE?":GOTO 135
600 ON JU GOTO 610,620,630,640,650,660,670,680,685,690,700,710,720,730,740,750,760,770
610 PRINT "NO ONE? WHO WOULD YOU LIKE TO HELP YOU?" :GOTO 135
620 PRINT "EVERYONE? COULD YOU BE MORE SPECIFIC?":GOTO 135
630 PRINT "TELL ME MORE ABOUT YOUR FAMILY.":GOTO 135
640 PRINT "TELL ME MORE ABOUT YOUR FRIEND.":GOTO 135
650 PRINT "WHO HELPED YOU TEACH YOUR PET?":GOTO 135
660 PRINT "THAT'S A LOT OF EXERCISE FOR BOTH OF YOU. WHO HELPS YOU?":GOTO 135
670 PRINT "THAT SOUNDS DANGEROUS. WHAT DO YOU DO WHEN THAT HAPPENS?":GOTO 135
680 PRINT "THAT CAN BE FUNNY. WHO HELPS YOU CLEAN UP?":GOTO 135
685 GOTO 135: REM NO CORRESPONDING NUMBER TO GET HERE
690 PRINT "WHAT KINDS OF TRICKS?":GOTO 135
700 PRINT "WHO HELPS YOU TAKE CARE OF YOUR PET?":GOTO 135
710 PRINT "WHAT DO YOU DO TO TAKE CARE OF YOUR PET?":GOTO 135
720 PRINT "HOW DO YOU PLAY WITH YOUR PET?":GOTO 135
730 PRINT "I HAVE A ROBOT "KW$".":PRINT "WHAT DO YOU AND YOUR "KW$" LIKE TO DO?":GOTO 135
740 PRINT "WHAT KIND OF "KW$" DO YOU HAVE?":GOTO 135
750 PRINT "WHAT KIND OF PET DO YOU HAVE?":GOTO 135
760 PRINT "YECHHH. HOW DO YOU TAKE CARE OF A SNAKE?":GOTO 135
770 PRINT "I DON'T KNOW ANYTHING ABOUT "KW$"S. TELL ME MORE.":GOTO 135
```

**FIGURE 24-2** Modified *Doctor* (Krutch, 1981) Program

of speech such as noun, verb, adjective, or adverb. The student can put examples in each category. For example,

NOUN tree, typewriter, video game, cat
VERB shout, walk, draw, get, climbs
ADJECTIVE red, huge, bold
ADVERB Quickly, slowly, carefully, loudly

Once the computer has been taught the categories and the examples, the student can instruct the computer to complete a pattern. For example, given

PATTERN: the ADJECTIVE NOUN and ADJECTIVE NOUN VERB

the computer might respond with the HUGE VIDEO GAME and RED CAT SHOUT. The student, of course, could type what we might consider to be nonsense patterns such as VERB NOUN ADJECTIVE ADVERB and get as a response DRAW CAT BOLD SLOWLY. The teacher can guide the student to discover the structure of English grammar. For example, the use of singular nouns (as above) reveals some difficulties. Observe,

PATTERN: the ADJECTIVE NOUN VERB
the BOLD TREE WALK.

Such an example reveals the need for a singular form of the verb. The student can remedy that by entering the ADJECTIVE NOUN VERBs (the final S supplied by the student) to produce the BOLD CAT CLIMBs (it might even make sense). The verb can be changed to past tense by supplying an "ed." For example, the ADJECTIVE NOUN VERBed might produce the RED VIDEO GAME WALKed, but it might also result in the RED VIDEO GAME DRAWed. Now the student realizes that the computer must distinguish verb forms. This can be done by teaching the computer new categories for the different forms (let the student choose the category names but look for "regular" and "irregular" distinctions).

Categories of categories are possible. For example, the category SENTENCE could have as instances NOUN VERB or ADJECTIVE NOUN VERB. Then the pattern the SENTENCE might result in the CAT DRAW or the RED TREE CLIMB. The pattern mrs. jones' SENTENCEs might result in mrs jones' BOLD VIDEO GAME WALKs. We have included a simple program written Applesoft BASIC to be used by your students. The program is shown in Figure 24–3.

**Activity 5—**

*Modeling* is a frequent writing activity. Samples of authors' works are often studied for style, organization, and vocabulary choice. The program described here can be used to generate writing samples to model a particular

```
10 DIM N(20), O$(20,30), PS$(20), U(20,30)
49 PARTS = 0
50 PARTS = PARTS + 1
55 READ PS$(PARTS)
60 IF PS$(PARTS) = "*" THEN PARTS=
      PARTS-1: GOTO 300
70 N(PARTS)=0
80 READ O$(PARTS, N(PARTS))
85 IF O$(PARTS, N(PARTS))="*" THEN
      N(PARTS)=N(PARTS)-1: GOTO 100
90 GOTO 70
100 GOTO 30
300 HOME
310 PRINT "PATTERN - ENTER * WHEN FINISHED."
315 POKE 34,2
316 PRINT
319 N=0
320 N=N+1
325 INPUT "PATTERN: ";A$(N)
327 IF A$(N) = "REPEAT" THEN ANS$=OA$:
      GOTO 400
330 IF A$(N) = "*" THEN N=N-1:A$(N)="":
      GOTO 350
335 IF RIGHT$(A$(N),1)<>"*" THEN GOTO 320
340 A$(N)=LEFT$(A$(N),LEN(A$(N))-1)
350 IF N=1 THEN ANS$="": GOTO 380
355 FOR J=1 TO N-1
360 ANS$=ANS$+A$(J)+ " "
370 NEXT J
380 ANS$=ANS$+A$(N)
390 OA$=ANS$
400 FOR K=1 TO PARTS
410 L=LEN(PS$(K))
415 FOR J=1 TO LEN(ANS$)-L+1
420 IF MID$(ANS$,J,L)=PS$(K) THEN
      GOSUB 100: GOTO 400
430 NEXT J
440 NEXT K
450 PRINT
470 GOSUB 2000
480 GOSUB 3000
490 INPUT " ";P$
500 GOTO 316
599 END
999 REM KEY WORD FOUND
1000 TRY = 0
1010 R=INT(RND(1)*N(K))+1
1020 TRY = TRY + 1
1030 IF TRY > N(K) THEN FOR Q=1 TO N(K):
      U(K,Q)=0: NEXT Q
1040 IF U(K,R) = 1 THEN GOTO 1010
1050 IF J = 1 THEN M1$ = "": U(K,Q) = 0: NEXT Q
1060 M1$ = LEFT$(ANS$,J-1)
1070 M3$ = ""
1080 IF J<>LEN(ANS$)-L+1 THEN M3$=RIGHT$(ANS$,
      LEN(ANS$)-J-L+1)
1090 M2$=O$(K,R)
1100 U(K,R) = 1
1110 ANS$=M1$ + M2$ + M3$
1120 RETURN
1999 REM LINE SPACING - NO WRAP
2000 IF LEN(ANS$) < 40 THEN PRINT ANS$: RETURN
2010 FOR J=38 TO 1 STEP - 1
2020 IF MID$(ANS$,J,1)=" " OR MID$(ANS$,J,1) =
      "." THEN PRINT LEFT$(ANS$,J): ANS$=
      RIGHT$(ANS$,LEN(ANS$)-J)
2030 NEXT J
2040 GOTO 2000
2999 REM INITIALIZATION SECTION
3000 FOR J=1 TO 20
3010 FOR K=1 TO 30
3020 U(J,K)=0
3030 NEXT K
3040 NEXT J
3050 RETURN
4000 REM DATA SECTION
4010 REM BOX 1 NAME
4020 DATA NOUN
4030 REM BOX 1 EXAMPLES
4040 DATA TREE, TYPEWRITER, VIDEO GAME
4050 DATA CAT, *
4060 REM USE * TO SIGNAL END OF BOX
4070 REM BOX 2 NAME
4080 DATA VERB
4090 REM BOX TWO EXAMPLES
4100 DATA SHOUT, WALK, DRAW, GETS, CLIMBS, *
4110 REM USE * TO SIGNAL END OF BOX
4120 DATA ADVERB
4130 DATA QUICKLY, SLOWLY, CAREFULLY, LOUDLY
4140 DATA *
4150 DATA ADJECTIVE
4160 DATA RED
4170 DATA BOLD
4180 DATA HUGE
4190 DATA *
4200 REM USE * TO SIGNAL END OF ALL BOXES
4210 DATA *
```

**FIGURE 24-3** BASIC Program: Language-Free Grammar

author. The use of the program requires that the students label word types (categories), select examples of those types choosing vocabulary used by the author, and identify the sentence patterns used by the author. For example, if William Shakespeare's 29th sonnet were chosen as a model, vocabulary for each category would include:

ADJECTIVE sweet, thy, such, rememb'red, sullen, deaf, bootless
NOUN love, wealth, state, king, disgrace, fortune, heaven, fate
VERB bring, scorn, change
ADVERB then, most, least, haply.

The sentence patterns for the last couplet of the sonnet:

for ADJECTIVE ADJECTIVE NOUN VERBed ADJECTIVE VERBs
that ADVERB I VERB to VERB my NOUN with NOUNs.

might read:

for SWEET THY WEALTH SCORNed SULLEN CHANGEs
that HAPLY I BRING to CHANGE my HEAVEN with FATEs.

Students have the opportunity to "mess about" and become comfortable with the language of authors whom they may otherwise have found intimidating.

**Activity 6—** 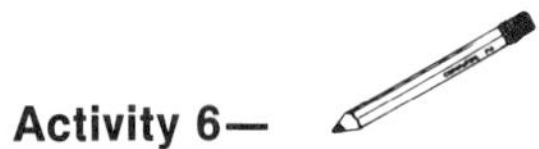

You could also use the program in Figure 24–3 to help students examine their own writing styles. If you have identified trite or overworked words or phrases, you could define each as a category. Examples in the categories could be alternative words or phrases. For example, suppose that your students overuse words such as "awesome." You might have them enter the following in the program (depending on formal, colloquial, or slang use):

FORMAL: impressive, striking, imposing
COLLOQ: terrific, out of this world, tiptop
SLANG: swell, bang-up, nifty

Adding other words and phrases (at the same level of formality) would permit the student to type a sentence and study a computer-generated alternative. In addition, students could define their own thesaurus. The possible sentence construct might read:

his new car was totally AWESOME.

Using the SLANG version, it might produce alternative sentences such as:

his new car was totally swell.
his new car was totally nifty.

## PREWRITING STAGE

The *prewriting stage* of the writing process is one in which a student should spend time gathering information, thinking about ideas and how they interrelate, and trying voices. The computer can help the student explore topics, express ideas, and, in general, get ready to write.

### Getting Information

Students frequently find it difficult to locate information about a topic. The use of information databases can help a student locate information and narrow a topic so that it isn't overwhelming. *Databases* are like electronic filing cabinets used to store information in a specifically designed format. For example, magazine article citations (including title, author, key ideas, and summary) entered in a database could be searched for all articles that satisfy some preset criteria.

**Activity 7—**

Software designed for other subject areas are often appropriate programs for a language arts classroom. A database program designed for social studies, for example, could be used in a language arts classroom to help students learn search strategies for finding specific information. Searching databases such as MECC Dataquest: The Presidents, which contains information about the 40 U.S. presidents, gives students practice with defining criteria and combining sets of criteria. A sample search might be to find all presidents who did not have a college degree *and* who served in Congress.

**Activity 8—** 

Students can design their own database using one of several commercial electronic file programs for the microcomputer such as PFS:File or MECC Stuff and Fetch. Students select the information, design the layout, and explore a variety of search strategies to cull information from the database. Students could work in teams to design their databases and then challenge other teams to answer questions with information culled from their database.

**Activity 9—** 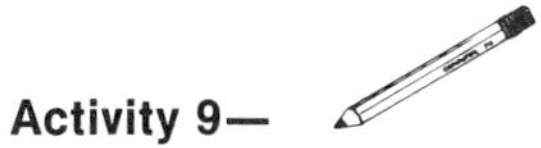

Using computer database such as one designed by the Educational Resource Information Centers (ERIC) or any other commercial database available through such services as DIALOG or CompuServe, the student can have additional practice learning appropriate search strategies and can experience how sophisticated databases are designed. For example, the commercial database Magazine Index could be used to locate information about the impact of computers on society. Using a computer with a micromodem, a local telephone number could be dialed to connect with GTE Telenet, one of several telecommunications networks, which in turn connects to the database. Once connected, the search could focus on computers and (society or social issues). If informed that there were more than 80 magazine article citations, students could experiment with several ways of modifying the topic to a more reasonable number of "hits." Several commercial databases can be searched at reduced cost or at no cost to new subscribers. Using a computer with a telephone modem, you can demonstrate use of a commercial database at little expense. Teaching students how to access computerized information systems often motivates them to take more seriously their research report assignments.

*Narrowing a topic.* Students frequently choose topics that are too broad and have difficulty in identifying a smaller, more manageable subtopic. *Invention heuristics,* such as Aristotle's *topoi,* Burke's *pentad,* and Young, Becker, and Pike's *tagmemic matrix,* have helped writers identify an appropriate topic. Hugh Burns, an early pioneer in computer heuristics, wrote his *Tagi* and *Topoi* programs while at the U.S. Air Force Academy. These programs are adaptations of invention heuristics for computer use. As long as students are willing to enter appropriate answers to the open-ended questions these programs present, they are rewarded with abundant prewriting material.

**Activity 10—** 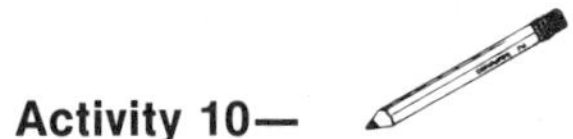

Following the popularity of Burns' work, several commercial programs have been designed to explore a topic with a student. For example, *Writer's Helper,* by William Wresch (1984b) and Mimi Schwartz's *Pre-Write* (1984) use a variety of formats to encourage the student to look at a subject from different points of view. The activities used in these programs require students' cooperation. If a student does not take the interaction seriously, the computer replies will not make sense. The watchwords are "garbage in, garbage out." It is important that you monitor student activity and be prepared to guide the student. Several of the activities in the preceding section were designed to increase student awareness of the limitations of computer understanding and to emphasize the need for reasonable expectations of the computer-student interaction. Those activities are a good foundation for establishing the need for "cooperation" on the part of the student.

**Activity 11—** 

Ray Rodrigues (1984) developed a successful prewriting activity using what he calls "synectic imagery." After students identify their topic, they are asked to look at a picture (selected by the teacher) and to identify several items noted in the picture. Each student is then asked how the topic is like each item. After the student has completed the visual analogy for each feature noted in the picture, the student is asked to explain what each analogy means. (See Figure 24-4 for a sample activity.) Although this activity uses the computer for convenience (self-pacing, printed copy of interaction), it can be done effectively without a computer.

## WRITING STAGE

Word processing programs can be used in several different ways to enhance the writing process: entering original text, learning about mood, combining sentences, and discerning the difference between writing and composing. In this section, we describe several such activities.

**FIGURE 24-4** A Sample Interaction Using Synectic Imagery

```
WHAT IS YOUR NAME: Sam

WHAT IS YOUR TOPIC: presidential candidates

DESCRIBE FOUR THINGS YOU SEE IN THE PICTURE?
   1. ?a sailboard
   2. ?a beach umbrella
   3. ?palm trees
   4. ?sea gulls

OKAY, SAM, NOW REMEMBER THAT YOU WANT TO WRITE ABOUT presidential candidates.

I WANT YOU TO THINK HOW YOUR TOPIC, presidential candidates, COMPARES TO a sailboard.

   ?They struggle to keep their balance amid turbulence
   and strong pressure.

HOW DOES YOUR TOPIC presidential candidates COMPARE TO a beach umbrella?

   ?They try to protect their constituency.

HOW DOES YOUR TOPIC presidential candidates COMPARE TO palm trees?

   ?Even though they go off in all directions, they try to
   maintain a firm root structure.

HOW DOES YOUR TOPIC presidential candidates COMPARE TO sea gulls?

   ?They try to promote lofty ideas.

EARLIER IN WRITING ABOUT presidential candidates, YOU SAID:
   they struggle to keep their balance amid turbulence and
   strong pressure.
PLEASE EXPLAIN WHAT YOU MEANT.
   ?
```

**Activity 12—** 

The most common uses of a word processing program are to enter and to edit text. The former was discussed in the previous chapter; the latter is discussed in the next section.

**Activity 13—**

Students can learn about *mood* by working with a short story that you have selected and entered into the word processor. Ask the students to read the short story to identify a mood, and then to delete those words or phrases that contribute to that mood. Ask them to make certain that complete sentences remain after the deletions. See Figure 24–5a for an example of a "horror" story; Figure 24–5b shows the same story without references to mood.

If you have computers for individuals or for several small groups, prepare a data diskette with a short story text from your anthology for each computer. The students can do deletions using the word processor. If you have only a demonstration computer, you can delete portions of text in front of the class using their suggestions. If you do not have a classroom computer, print a copy (double-spaced) for each student and have them cross out the "mood" words or phrases. In all cases, students can compare and contrast the revised stories.

**Activity 14—**

Using a mood-free or "flat" story from Activity 13, direct the students to add words or phrases that will result in a mood different from the original. If students are using paper and pencil, give them clean copies of the story,

**FIGURE 24-5a** Original Story with Descriptive Passages

**Avalanche**
by Anne Auten

They sat there, huddled around the fireplace, listening to the rain pelting hard on the roof. The warm, dancing light from the fire reflecting on their faces was subdued by the bright blue-white of lightning coming through the window. The blue-white, followed by the throb of thunder, highlighted the disappointment on their faces.

The door opened and Dan klumped in, water dripping from the front of his hood, muttering something about what a ridiculous way this was to spend a ski weekend. The door banged behind him as a gust of rain-drenched wind swirled into the cabin, blowing apart the card game in progress. He kicked the door shut and dropped into a disgusted heap at the end of the couch. Leaning forward, he unfastened his ski boots and slowly extracted his sodden, stockinged feet.

Minutes passed, with the only sounds the clicking of plastic-coated pasteboard against the hardwood floor, a murmured "I'll stay" or "Hit me," and the expulsion of air from a pop-tab can. Finally, Dan rose and took himself and his ski boots into the bunk room. When the rain sounded as though it were easing off, Dan reappeared in dry clothes and hiking boots and announced to the room in general that the rest of them could sit around and play cards all night, but *he* was going off on an adventure. As the door slammed behind him, the clock struck twelve midnight.

**FIGURE 24-5b** Story with Descriptive Passages Removed

They sat around the fireplace, listening to the rain. The light from the fire and lightning showed the disappointment on their faces.

The door opened and Dan came in, complaining about their ski weekend. As the door shut behind him, a gust of wind blew the cards around. He sat at the end of the couch and took off his wet ski boots.

Minutes passed, with only a few sounds in the cabin. Finally, Dan went into the bunk room. When the rain sounded as though it were easing off, Dan came out and announced that he was going off on an adventure. As the door shut behind him, the clock struck twelve.

which you have prepared ahead of time. Again, compare and discuss the new versions.

### Activity 15—

The word processor can be used to prepare sentence-combining activities for individual students or small groups. Begin with at least two factual main ideas related to a topic. For example, for the topic "dinosaurs" two main ideas might be "why the dinosaurs died out" and "compare/contrast the Tyrannosaurus Rex and the Brontosauraus." A dozen or so short, simple sentences should be written to support each main point. Using the word processor and tractor-feed mailing labels, prepare labels using all the sentences. Put each label on a 3″ × 5″ index card and prepare a set of cards for each small group of students.

The task for the students is to read the individual cards and choose those that are related to one of the main ideas you select for the activity. After the students have chosen their cards, they should arrange them so that they would make a good paragraph. If you have discussed transitions and sentence-combining strategies, the students can apply those skills as they develop their paragraph.

If the students are using a word processor, have them type the new paragraph. After all students are finished, compare and discuss the paragraphs.

## REVISION

### Ease of Use

A major strength of word processing programs in composition instruction is the ease of *revision*. Students have demonstrated that they feel freer about committing their thoughts to paper with the knowledge that the printed page is no longer a permanent record of their composing impotence.

Initial writing blocks are overcome when working with a screen display instead of a blank sheet of paper. The screen offers ease of erasure through simple backspacing, a capability that often stimulates a flow of words that paper inhibits. Mechanical difficulties with poor handwriting and spelling are overcome when composing on a computer. The copy looks professional, boosting a writer's self-confidence. Spelling is easily corrected after a first draft, causing writers to be more relaxed about putting words down. Because of the ease of revising without tedious recopying, writers are more open to suggestions for change and less inhibited about implementing suggestions.

Much student revision, however, is in areas of letter and word substitution rather than phrase, sentence, or paragraph replacement. Research suggests that beginning writers seldom revise discourse structures higher than the sentence. Programs such as text analysis checkers that focus on such mechanics as punctuation, capitalization, or vocabulary use have contributed to an emphasis on these discrete revisions. These programs, designed as automated style guides, can determine when a grammar rule is violated or when a writing style is turgid because of excessive use of passive voice verbs or prepositional phrases. Spelling checkers, spelling correctors, and readability indexes have all been automated to give a breakdown of what is wrong with an author's text. Students are often more open to making and taking suggestions because of the ease of revising.

### Early Warning

It is essential that before students are set loose with a spelling or style checker, they have an opportunity to develop a working relationship with how these programs operate. To ask students to concentrate on composing at the same time they are learning to work with an unfamiliar program dilutes the attention and energy available for either. Students often have difficulty working in a computer environment and will make errors owing to their unfamiliarity with the territory (the context) rather than to their inability to complete the task (the content). The current state of the art in spelling checkers provides opportunities for students to become comfortable with this new tool in a controlled environment.

### Activity 16—

Challenge the content of a spelling checker (they range from as few as 10,000 entries in MECC Speller to as many as 90,000-plus entries in ALPS' MacProof or IBM's Epistle) by asking students to enter in a text file lists of words that they think might be too esoteric for the program dictionary. They might earn points for every word that is not recognized by the spelling checker. Some spelling programs allow words to be added to the dictionary.

### Activity 17—

After a typical spelling dictation test, students might verify their spellings by running them through a spelling checker. This same verification could be run after a prose oral dictation, a technique many teachers use to increase students' mastery of sentence construction.

**Activity 18—** 

Choose a spelling checker, such as Bank Street Speller, that will allow students to choose specific character strings (such as-R—D) to search for words in the speller dictionary. Lists of words with certain patterns are then used to construct crossword puzzles, with appropriate definitions.

*Teacher's aide.* In addition to the application of utility programs such as spelling and style checkers as aids in text revision, the simple capabilities of the word processor to store and print text can contribute much to the revision process.

**Activity 19—** 

Teachers respond to first drafts of students' writing assignments by entering their remarks in a text file possibly titled with the name and due date of the assignment. After each student's name, the teacher would enter comments regarding that student's first draft, including suggestions for revision. To respond to the next draft, the teacher could use the search function of the word processor to locate each student's name, and enter responses to the second draft, noting whether or not the student heeded the suggestions regarding the earlier draft. The capability of inserting text at will in previously written copy can be an equally functional tool for the teacher-corrector and for the student-composer.

*Future directions.* What's needed for a computer to encourage large-scale rather than discrete revision is a text analysis program that can recognize faulty logic and organizational problems. Programs such as IBM's Epistle can detect a variety of grammatical errors, including subject–verb disagreement (He have a car); wrong pronoun case (It was written by Bill and I); noun–modifier disagreement (These report are wrong); and nonstandard verb forms (The book was wrote by him). Such programs can parse natural language based on the rules that already exist, however incompletely, for forming certain patterns in the English language, and thus have proven effective in guiding the language development of students of English as a second language. A computer program has yet to be developed, however, that can teach students the nuances of meaningful revision in the arenas of logic, audience, and purpose.

## SUMMARY

We have detailed a picture of the capabilities of the computer as a tool in composition. We have not recommended particular programs in the other areas of language arts, not because they are unavailable, but because they are still under development. Creative teachers have been using cloze and comprehension programs, animated primers and speed-reading programs, but they want programs that incorporate natural voice sounds for nonreaders and programs for the blind or visually impaired reader.

Creative teachers have been using prewriting and production (word processing) programs, but they would like programs that comment on student writing using artificial intelligence techniques that could produce responses such as "In your last paper . . . " to analyze writing progress.

Creative teachers would also like student text, in machine-readable format, that when laid on a mark-sensitive panel would be read and stored in text files for later analysis of diction, style, grammar, and syntax. After correcting their files, students could print and submit papers for personal readthroughs by a teacher for content. The original analyses would be stored in a database for comparison with future writing.

At the time of publication of this textbook, such programs may sound like pipe dreams. But perhaps they are currently on the design boards of software developers who recognize the needs of teachers of English who use computers in their classrooms.

## *REFERENCES*

*Bank Street Speller* (1984). San Rafael, CA: Broderbund Software (Sensible Software, Inc.).

BLAU, S. (1983, October). Invisible writing: Investigating cognitive processes in composition. *College Composition and Communication,* 297–312.

*CompuServe Information Service.* P.O. Box 20212, Columbus, OH.

DAIUTE, C. (1983, May). The computer as stylus and audience. *College Composition and Communication,* 134–145.

*DIALOG Information Services, Inc.,* 3460 Hillview Ave., Palo Alto, CA.

HILLOCKS, G., Jr. *Research on written composition: new directions for teaching.* Urbana, IL: NCRE and ERIC/RCS, 1986 (ERIC Document #265 552).

JOHANNESSEN, L., KAHN, E.A., & WALTER, C.C. (1982). *Designing and sequencing prewriting activities.* Urbana, IL: NCTE/ERIC.

KIEFER, K., & SELFE, C. *Computers and composition.* Quarterly Newsletter. Fort Collins, CO: Colorado State University English Department.

KRUTCH, J. (1981). *Experiments in artificial intelligence for small computers.* Indianapolis: Howard W. Sams.

*MECC Dataquest: The Presidents.* (1985). St. Paul, MN: Minnesota Education Computing Corporation.

*MECC Editor.* (1985). St. Paul, MN: Minnesota Education Computing Corporation.

*MECC Speller.* (1985). St. Paul, MN: Minnesota Education Computing Corporation.

*MECC Stuff and Fetch.* (1985). St. Paul, MN: Minnesota Education Computing Corporation.

RODRIGUES, R. & RODRIGUES, D.W. (1984, February). Computer-based invention: Its place and potential. *College Composition and Communication,* 78–87.

SCHWARTZ, M. (1984). *Prewrite.* Upper Montclair, NJ: Boynton/Cook.

SCHWARTZ, H., & BRIDWELL, L.S. (1984, February). A selected bibliography on computers and composition. *College Composition and Communication,* 27–29.

SHARPLES, M. (1983, Winter). The use of computers to aid the teaching of creative writing. *AEDS Journal,* 79–91.

STANDIFORD, S.N., JAYCOX, K., & AUTEN, A. (1983). *Computers in the English classroom: A primer for teachers.* Urbana, IL: National Council of Teachers of English.

WRESCH, W. (1984a). *Computers in composition instruction: A writer's tool.* Urbana, IL: National Council of Teachers of English.

——. *Writer's Helper* (1985b). Iowa City, IA: Conduit.

# TWENTY-FIVE
# INTEGRATING LANGUAGE ARTS INSTRUCTION IN THE PRIMARY GRADES

## INTEGRATING LANGUAGE ARTS INSTRUCTION IN THE PRIMARY GRADES

Studies over the last 20 years have shown the importance of the connection between language acquisition, cognitive development, and early reading progress (Anastasiow, 1979). Likewise, researchers are currently documenting the importance of writing at emerging preschool and beginning reading stages, showing the need for writing skills to develop naturally as *part* of learning to read (Wilson, 1981). Furthermore, many educators are advocating a holistic approach to language arts, where reading, writing, and thinking are taught with naturalistic language activities that build on children's experiences, prior knowledge, and need to communicate (Watson, 1984), at the same time incorporating specific teacher interactional strategies that have been shown to be effective in early language learning. (Applebee & Langer, 1983).

The purpose of this chapter is to present several language-based reading/writing activities that take advantage of children's experiential backgrounds in an integrative approach to oral language, reading, writing, and cognitive development. Collaborative writing strategies taught within a language experience model are considered. Secondly, individual composition strategies within a process writing model are presented. Major assumptions of these activities are that (1) teacher–pupil interaction is critical to skill development, (2) direct instruction of skills is vital, and (3) it is important that teachers model varied language patterns, that they scaffold, prompt, give relevant feedback, question skillfully, and listen attentively.

## PEER GROUP COMPOSITION: THE LANGUAGE EXPERIENCE MODEL

Probably one of the best strategies to help young children develop early writing and reading skills, and simultaneously to encourage thinking skills and oral language development, is the small-group language experience.

In the *language experience activity* (LEA), the teacher takes the children's speech, puts it into written form, and uses the product as the student's initial reading text. This is not only an instructional and diagnostic tool for reading and oral language but also a fine model for teaching independent writing skills within a small-group situation.

## INSTRUCTIONAL USES AND GUIDELINES FOR LEA'S

The language experience method provides the opportunity for the children to learn firsthand how the reading/writing process works. It is an excellent strategy to teach relationships among concepts, events, or objects and that of print. Besides the particular graphic forms and sounds of letters, the rules of convention of print are important reading/writing objectives and are easily taught in the joint-composition effort. At more advanced reading stages, the LEA is a credible vehicle for teaching structural analysis skills (compound words, syllables, possessives, contractions), comprehension skills (main ideas, drawing conclusions), and various story structures (narratives, expositions).

The following are suggested guidelines for a teacher in using the LEA as an instructional tool:

1. Use a stimulating topic, one that is in the children's experience, or build a joint experience to write about later. Use a book, toy, field trip, food, mutual problem, make-believe situation, or class incident.
2. Encourage lots of discussion and brainstorming before the actual writing occurs. Listen and record ideas on the board to help as the group composes together.
3. Determine the type and purpose of the LEA before the discussion and stimulus choice. Listed below are 10 different types of compositions with story title examples:
   a. Imaginative (Our Special Classroom Monster)
   b. Expository (The Work of a Dentist)
   c. Patterned (Father Said No) Use repetition of lines as in *Brown Bear, Brown Bear, What Do You See?* (Martin, 1970)
   d. Cloze (What We Like) Use repetition and a group theme as in "________ likes ___________."
   e. Comparative (How the Country and City Are Different)
   f. Group Descriptive (Our Friends)

   g. Summary (*Where the Wild Things Are,* Sendak, 1963) Retell a basal or trade book story.
   h. Recipes or Menus (How We Made a Peanut Butter Sandwich)
   i. Problematic (Ways to Solve Fights in the Playground)
   j. Cause-Effect (The Day It Was 70 Degrees Below Zero)
4. Use various scaffolding and prompting techniques to expand language and thinking. In this way you encourage students to talk without providing the answers. Listed below are examples of dialogue the teacher might use:
   a. Tell me more. Make a longer sentence about that idea. What else would you like to say about that?
   b. Say that another way. What is another word we could use?
   c. Does that idea make sense next in the story? Why? Why not?
   d. How could we combine John's thought with Jill's to make one big sentence?

## DIAGNOSTIC USES OF LEA

As a diagnostic measure, the language experience activity gives you a sense of the size of the children's spoken vocabulary and of how well a child orally commands the pragmatic, semantic, and syntactical aspects of the English language. In the reading and writing areas, the LEA provides a chance to evaluate continuously the children's knowledge about print (including its function, form, and convention), besides the extent of sight vocabulary, oral reading ability, word identification, and comprehension skills. In the cognitive area, the LEA prediscussion and joint construction of a product help the teacher assess different levels of thinking and the children's ability to make transitions from "thinking (what shall I say) to written expression, to reading, to thinking (what does that mean) in a concrete way" (Grabe & Grabe, 1985, p. 508). In assessing thinking and language skills the teacher needs to be aware of how well the children (1) use precise and complex thoughts, (2) sequence their thoughts, (3) tie thoughts together to form relationships, (4) identify and develop ideas, (5) use supporting details, (6) make comparisons, (7) problem-solve, (8) use creative and more divergent ideas, (9) use analogies, and (10) make relevant predictions.

## LEA AS A WRITING MODEL

Besides being a holistic instructional and diagnostic tool, the group language experience process provides an excellent model for transition to the independent writing process. As you and the children jointly produce a written product, whether narrative or expository, the students are given a model for their own future writings. They are engaged in giving verbal, then written, expression to their ideas as they create and share together. They learn to accept, reject, and edit their group's work. You can show them how to expand a thought and to combine others to make sense. Furthermore, LEA's are a chance for children to experiment together without a great amount of risk involved and to try various models of good writing and story structure found in stories that they have read or heard. The following is a list of skills that you can target during the LEA process and specifically teach for their importance in helping children write independently:

1. Developing a cohesive story line.
2. Choosing an appropriate title.
3. Developing main ideas with supporting details.
4. Developing paragraph sense.
5. Keeping a sequence of events in logical order.
6. Developing the characters and the setting.
7. Learning how to write quotations.
8. Developing surprise endings or unique conclusions.

In effect, with the LEA, the children are learning story structures and the process of writing and composition in cooperation with adults and peers *today,* so that they can do it on their own *tomorrow.*

## INDIVIDUAL COMPOSITION: THE WRITING PROCESS MODEL

The *writing process model* as described in previous chapters is an excellent approach for teaching individual composition. As with the language-experience approach, the key to successful writing is using the children's individual life experiences and capitalizing on their need to communicate those experiences to others. As with collaborative projects, the teacher can facilitate quality writing by supporting and guiding the students through the entire process of writing from the very beginning of the individual's topic selection to the finished product. Likewise, the teacher places the instructional emphasis on the process, not in analyzing the finished product.

The second section of this chapter describes strategies that work extremely well in helping primary-grade children learn to write narratives and content area expositories independently.

## PRIMARY WRITING STRATEGIES

During the writing process stages of prewriting, drafting, revising, and editing, the children can be given guides to assist them in organizing their compositions, whether they be narrative or expository. These writing frameworks can help the children systematically to order and group their ideas in some type of structure and can help them to write these ideas down in a cohesive and sequential manner.

### Strategies for Teaching Narrative Writing

*Five "wh" questions.* One strategy young children can easily learn for writing narrative stories is that of using "wh" questions as a guide to the content of their compositions. A good story will often answer the five questions: (1) Who are the characters? (2) Where does the story take place? (3) When does it happen? (4) What is happening? and (5) Why?

The following steps are suggested for using the five "wh" question approach:

1. Explain and discuss the five types of questions with the children. Write the five types on a large chart that everyone can see.
2. In a direct instructional setting, relate the questions to the students' own LEA stories or trade books that the children have read or heard. Do the stories have all five elements?
3. Analyze one favorite story or composition that a child wrote and make a detailed chart of how the story contents answered the questions—a visual display of the five questions with their answers.
4. Have the children write their own stories independently. In individual conferencing, encourage the children to compare their stories to the models you discussed and to test if their stories answer the "wh" questions.

*Three-part structure.* Another easy strategy is that of helping the students to learn a simple story structure with the three terms, *beginning, middle,* and *end.* The five "wh's" can be incorporated into the three parts.

1. A story needs a *beginning* where the characters and setting are generally developed.
2. The *middle* of the story generally is where the plot is developed—the "happenings."
3. The last part of the story, or the *ending,* usually gives the final conclusion or tells how the characters solved the problem.

The combining of the five "wh" approach and the concepts of beginning, middle, and end enable the children to grasp successfully and to use a simplistic concept of story structure and its components. As with the first strategy, that is, explanation of terms, the use of appropriate examples and analysis of other stories are components of instruction that will help the children use the frameworks independently. Both strategies are initially teacher-directed and may involve peer collaboration before the independent writing process begins.

### Strategies for Teaching Expository Writing

*Webbing/visual organizers.* For teaching expository writing or writing in the content area, the use of the *webbing technique* can be very effective. A visual display or graphic organizer can pictorially show how to organize ideas for a report and serve as a framework for cohesive content writing.

The strategy has three parts:

1. In a large group, have each child observe and write as many notes about a phenomenon as possible. No organization of ideas should occur at this time, just recording of observations.
2. When the individual notetaking is complete, develop a web with the whole group that visually displays how their observations might be organized into categories.
3. Instruct the children that each category (or circle) on the visual display should correspond to a paragraph in their written report. Each paragraph should be indented and contain all the child's observations included under that category. The final paragraph should be a summary statement or type of evaluation.

*Examples.* In science, the children were asked to observe and take notes on the tadpoles in their classroom aquarium. Reviewing the children's notes and being responsive to what they had written, the teacher organized the major concepts for the visual display on a chart for all to see. The majority of the observations fell into two categories: appearance and behavior. The teacher organized the webbing as shown in Figure 25–1.

Using this visual display as a guide to the structure of their report, the children first individually organized and clustered their own observations under the separate categories—under the numbers on the chart. Then as the students drafted their individual reports, they wrote the first paragraph on the general topic "tadpoles"; the second paragraph was on their appearance; the third, about their behavior; and the fourth, as a summary or conclusion.

As the children became more proficient at organizing and clustering their ideas, the teacher began using a more elaborate webbing with broader concepts and more categories. Instead of just the tadpoles, the teacher asked them to observe and take notes on the entire aquarium. Together with all the children in a large-group setting, the teacher built a visual display that organized the information they collected. See Figure 25–2.

Again, the children independently (and at times with the help of the

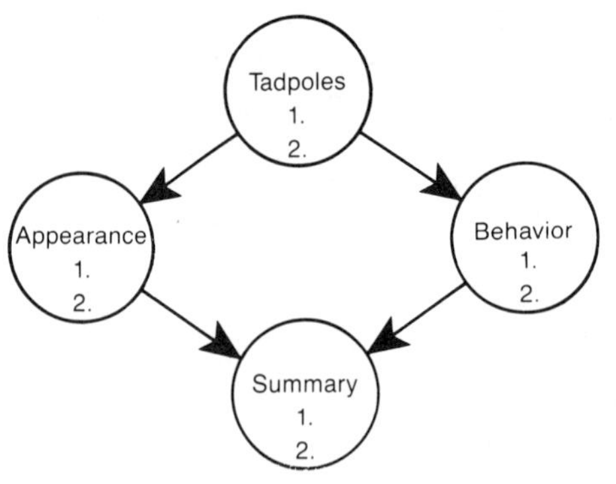


**FIGURE 25–1**
Example of Simple Webbing: Science Lesson on Tadpoles

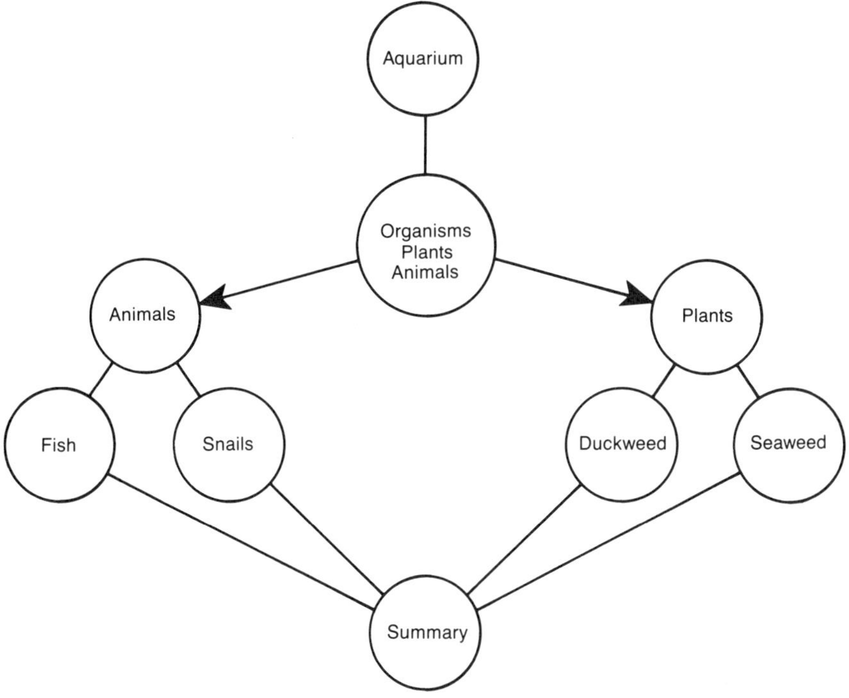


**FIGURE 25-2** Example of More Complex Webbing: Lesson on Aquarium Life

teacher) organized their individual notes under the categories in the webbing. They prepared a minimum of two or three sentences per paragraph on each circle. The first paragraph was a general one talking about the aquarium. The other paragraphs each contained the students' own ideas on the organisms, the animals, and the plants that they observed. The summary was a general conclusion or judgment about the activity. Although the final reports had the same structure, each was unique because each was based on the individual ideas of each child. Figure 25-3 is an example of one child's initial observations and the final report produced after the process of drafting, revising, and editing.

## CONCLUSION

In summary, this chapter outlined two different yet complementary models for the integrative teaching of writing, reading, oral language, and cognitive skills. The *language experience model* helps show children how to be readers/writers/thinkers together with the teacher and other peers. The *writing process model* helps children become independent readers/writers/thinkers in

What I observe

1 I see duck weed on the top.
2 I see snails.
3 I see fishes.
4 The fish is clear color.
5 The water is fresh.
6 There is pebles in the water.
7 The skin is shiny.
8. The duck weed is floating.
9 there diffrent color fishs.
10 Some are ~~orange~~ red fishes.
11 You can see the inside of the fish.
12 There are four diffrent kinds of seed weed.
13 Usual the snails stay still.
14 The snails stick to the glass.
15 We have seven fishes.
16 We have seren snails.
17 We see eggs in the container.
18 The eggs look very small.
19 The eggs are sticking too the glass.
20 there are lots of patches of eggs.
21 I see a baby fish.
22 Some of the snails are red.
23 The eggs are sticking to the container.
24 One of the fishes have dots on it.

**FIGURE 25-3a** Example of Observation Notes

Aquarium

the Aquarium has plants and animals. I'm going to tell you about a Aquarium.
In the Aquarium we have seven fishes and seaven snails and some times worms. The fish are cle-ar color. The fish are shinny. Some of the fish have a little of red in it. There was a baby fish in our Aquarium One of the fishes had dots on it.
Most of the time the snails

**FIGURE 25-3b** Example of Final Report

Stay one spot. Some of the snails stick to the glass. I saw snail eggs, sticking to the glass. The eggs are very small. There were alot of pa-thes of eggs. Some of the snails were brown or red.

There is duck weed and sea weed. There are for diffrent kinds of seaweed. The seaweed and duckweed are light green. The duckweed floates on the surface.

I like doing reports on Aquariums. And I like to learn about fishes and snails. I like fishes and snails.

**FIGURE 25-3b** Continued

an approach that emphasizes prewriting, drafting, revising, editing, and publishing. As emphasized in this chapter, there are a number of simple organizational strategies that can be incorporated and taught within the importance of (1) teacher–pupil and pupil–pupil interactions and oral communication, (2) experience and prior knowledge of the children in the reading and writing activities, and (3) the philosophy of modeling and direct instruction of specific strategies. Writing is seen as a natural part of learning to read, think, and talk. As children learn to be successful authors *jointly* (in a process with adult and peer support) they learn to be so *independently.*

## *REFERENCES*

ANASTASIOW, N. (1979). Oral language: Expression of thought. Newark, DE: International Reading Association.

APPLEBEE, A.N., & LANGER, J.A. (1983). Instructional scaffolding: Reading and writing as natural language activities. *Language Arts, 60,* 186–195.

GRABE, M., & GRABE, C. (1985). The microcomputer and the language experience approach. *The Reading Teacher, 38,* 508–511.

MARTIN, B., JR. (1970). *Brown bear, brown bear, what do you see?* New York: Holt, Rinehart & Winston.

SENDAK, M. (1963). *Where the wild things are.* New York: Harper & Row.

WATSON, D. (1984). *Two approaches to reading: Whole-language and skills.* Columbus, MO: University of Missouri. (ERIC Document Reproduction Service No. ED 247 546.)

WILSON, M.J. (1981). A review of recent research on the integration of reading and writing. *The Reading Teacher, 34,* 896–901.

## *SUGGESTED READINGS*

GRAVES, D. (1983). *Writing: Teachers and children at work.* Exeter, NH: Heinemann.

HILGERS, T. (1984). Toward a taxonomy of beginning writer's evaluation statements on written compositions. *Written Communication, 1,* 365–384.

LANCASTER, W., NELSON, L., & MORRIS, C. (1982). Inventive spelling in room 112: A writing program for low-reading second graders. *The Reading Teacher, 35,* 906–911.

NESSEL, D., & JONES, M. (1981). *The language experience approach to reading.* New York: Teachers College Press.

STAUFFER, R. (1980). *The language experience approach to teaching of reading* (2nd ed.) New York: Harper & Row.

# TWENTY-SIX
# TEACHING CHILDREN: AN INTEGRATED PLAN FOR LANGUAGE ARTS INSTRUCTION IN THE INTERMEDIATE GRADES

Hartland Public School's new teacher-orientation meeting was drawing to a close. Superintendent Kolve's address ended with this salient bit of advice:

> . . . and each day as you plan for instruction, ask yourself one basic question, "What am I going to teach today?" With all sincerity, I hope that you will answer in one word—*children.*"

Ms. Kolve's bit of wisdom needs to be carried to classrooms everywhere. Pressures to produce achievement scores have forced skilled, caring teachers to become so caught up in the demands of meeting curriculum goals that they have little time to consider the individual needs of children.

The major goal of this chapter is to convince you to hold the needs of children above all else as you plan instructional activities in language arts. The instructional activities you will find in the chapter promote integrated teaching of language arts skills.

## LEARNING LANGUAGE SKILLS: IMPLICATIONS FOR INSTRUCTION

A child gains proficiency in the English language by learning and expanding skills in listening, speaking, reading, and writing. As language skills are learned, children improve their ability to think. Acquiring these language/thinking skills encompasses an entire lifetime.

Let us examine some facts. Children *discover* oral language skills on their own. They learn to use oral language proficiently in order to communicate. Children learn at their own pace; all that seems to be necessary is an environment filled with natural language. On the other hand, children are *taught* literacy skills after they enter school. They learn literacy skills from teachers who decide *what* must be learned, *when* learning should take place, *how* and *when* practice should occur. The child-centered oral language paradigm is replaced by a teacher-centered written language paradigm. Few children have difficulty learning to speak, but untold numbers of children have problems learning to read and write.

What implications can be drawn for language arts instruction at the intermediate level? Two issues seem to stand out quite clearly. First, language skills seem to be learned with ease when children see a need for a skill and have a personal desire to learn it. You will be wise to plan lessons using materials and activities children perceive as meaningful and relevant. Second, because of past experiences, children exhibit diverse language knowledge and proficiency. Your language arts program must be designed to meet individual needs and ability levels.

## CONTENT-BASED INSTRUCTION

A visit to schools throughout the United States will reveal that teachers have tended to look at each area of the language arts curriculum as a separate entity. During the language arts block in many classrooms you are likely to find any of the following classes in progress: Creative Writing, Spelling, Penmanship, Grammar, Literature, Drama. In each case, the class objective is directed toward an isolated language skill (writing to write, spelling to spell, etc.) Apparently, teachers hope that as lessons are taught and learned, children will develop proficiency in usable communication skills.

## CHILD-CENTERED INSTRUCTION

An alternative to the content-based plan suggested above is to create a natural environment for learning; an environment where children are encouraged to use language skills to communicate with others. We might call this plan a *child-centered, integrated approach* to language arts education. To illustrate, an anecdotal account of a classroom will be presented.

### Self-Contained Classroom: An Integrated Curriculum

Room 402 is no ordinary classroom. LoRayne Schmidt, an enthusiastic, ambitious teacher, is guiding her sixth graders in a study of pioneer life in America. LoRayne has a dual goal for her unit of instruction: (1) she wants the history of our country to come alive for her students, and (2) she wants to encourage the development and use of language skills. A glance around the classroom leads an observer to note that many opportunities to explore and learn have already been exercised by the class. Reading and writing have traveled hand in hand. Samples of children's art and related stories have been bound into hardcover books and are featured in a glass cabinet near the front of the room. A script for an original radio play based on a chapter from *On the Banks of Plum Creek* (Wilder, 1937) lies next to a tape recorder in the listening center. Recipes for "maple-sugar candy," "trail soup," and "lye soap" have just been added to a recipe book the children are publishing in the writing center. In one corner of the room stands a replica of a log cabin surrounded by outstanding selections from children's literature: *A Gathering of Days* (Blos, 1979), *Caddie Woodlawn* (Brink, 1935, 1973), *The Courage of Sarah Noble* (Dalgliesch, 1954), *Bread and Butter Journey* (Colver, 1964). Empty slots on the book rack show that many selections are being read by the children. Mrs. Schmidt knows that wide reading will help her students vicariously experience historical events. Not only will the reading experiences increase their base of knowledge but they will also be filled with appreciation for the struggles faced by American pioneers.

The sixth-grade social studies curriculum has provided much of the base information for LoRayne's unit of study. Listening, speaking, reading, and writing activities grow naturally out of this learning environment. Let us take a look into LoRayne's planbook and find out how she encourages the natural growth of language skills. As you study her plans notice how she has acknowledged the varying levels of development.

*LANGUAGE ARTS ASSIGNMENTS MONDAY MORNING*

Group 1: (Leona, Cappy, Scott, Terry, Joan, Peggy)
LISTENING CENTER: (Note to Students)

Using headsets, listen to Chapter 4, parts 1 and 2, from your social studies textbook. Be certain to follow along in your book. Pay special attention to parts of the text underlined in yellow. Read the guide questions before you begin reading. After listening/reading along, work in pairs to create good answers to the questions—the underlined parts of the text will be helpful as you develop the answers. Be careful on question 6—you will have to use your own ideas to create an answer to this question. You won't find it in the book.

*Comments.* LoRayne wants all members of her sixth-grade class to become familiar with basic concepts from the social studies text. However, she realizes that the six students in this group are disabled readers who cannot possibly benefit from struggling through the text on their own. LoRayne knows that hearing the vocabulary in context and experiencing the organization of expository text will be an excellent language experience for these students. The questions she has developed to guide students' reading reflect both technical vocabulary and the sequence of events recorded in the exposition. LoRayne knows that these students need to be a part of whole-group discussions of basic concepts; by hearing the important information and reviewing it in the responses to questions, these poorer readers will have a better chance of contributing to the class discussions.

> Group 2: (Lillie, Steve, Alex, Wanda, Hiram, Angela)
> WRITING CENTER: (Note to Students)
>
> You have made good progress on the booklet on "maple-sugaring." Today you should begin reshaping the content you developed yesterday. Look at the set of questions I have attached to each of your papers. These questions will help you decide what information must be added to the themes. Remember, the audience you are writing for can only read third-grade level materials. Use the vocabulary list Mrs. Nelson gave you when you visited her third-grade class. Remember, too, that if you use "hard" words (words not on the list), you should try to plan pictures to help the children understand what you are trying to say.

> Group 3: (Pauline, Ryan, Fran, Ralph, Bev, Paul, Geneva)
> WRITING CENTER: (Note to Students)
>
> The reshaping you did yesterday really strengthened the introduction for your Recipe Book. I like the choice of words you decided upon. Today, your assignment is to work in pairs to check grammar, punctuation, and spelling. When you think the introduction is ready for my proofreading, put it into the basket. Tomorrow the entire book will be ready for you to bind. Don't forget to bring the materials for binding when you come to school in the morning.

*Comments.* Both of the above examples show that writing in this classroom is a process; ideas are recorded, drafts are reshaped (revised) and edited; occasionally products are bound. Earlier, instructional sessions based on samples of children's writing have provided an opportunity to explore the mechanics of writing. Although there are times when the whole class meets to review or reinforce some mechanical skill, most of the teaching occurs when a need is exhibited in children's work.

> Group 4: (Roxanne, Colette, Ron, Arnie, Ellie)
> READING CENTER: (Note to Students)
>
> Use this time to read the biographies you selected on Friday. As you read, remember to enter any facts/impressions on your American pioneer into the "character portrait" section of your reading journal. (If any of you have filled all the pages of your journal, new spiral notebooks are in the basket near the pencil sharpener.) Watch for your scheduled conference time; bring your book and reading journal to the conference.

*Comments.* LoRayne has come to realize that her good readers skim through their social studies textbook with few problems. They need the stimulation of more in-depth reading and will learn a great deal about pioneer life by studying on their own. Reading, thinking, and reacting in writing appeals to these able readers. As an end-of-unit activity, LoRayne will ask the students to develop cassette recordings (book talks) on their famous pioneer. LoRayne hopes that these tapes will motivate other children in the class to read the biographies.

Group 5: (Gene, Paul, Eric, Leon, Mary, Pat, Gordie)
MEDIA CENTER: (Note to students)

Continue to work on the slide/tape presentation of our trip to the Old World Settlement Museum. Check the script you have developed for slides 7, 9, and 13. Will viewers know what the cobbler is doing with the shoemaker's last? Will they understand how the crushed cardamon seeds will be used in baking? What is the threshing crew doing in this step of the process? Reread the brochures we gathered on our trip to the museum before you attempt to reshape the script for these slides.

*Comments.* Oral and written language skills combine forces as these children from different ability groups work to prepare a project that will be shared with visitors on Parent's Day. LoRayne is aware that the outlining of major topics, writing, reshaping, and editing process will be an invaluable project for these children. Rehearsing for the production of the tape will help the children work on oral language usage.

In LoRayne Schmidt's classroom, social studies concepts and language arts skills develop simultaneously. Immersed in interesting small-group activities structured to meet individual needs, children are given opportunities to observe, listen, speak, write, and read. Through a carefully designed environment, LoRayne has provided a child-centered program of instruction that invites children to learn. Careful observation will reveal that a focused, balanced, and purposeful language arts curriculum is in place. Language skills have become tools for learning, not skills learned as ends unto themselves.

### A Language Arts Classroom: Integrated Instruction

If your job description puts you into a departmentalized teaching position, LoRayne Schmidt's self-contained classroom plan will not meet your needs. This chapter will now turn to situations that exemplify activities you might use in this second type of organizational plan.

Steve Rubert's first teaching job has been no easy challenge. His seventh-grade language arts classes are all heterogeneously grouped. In individual conferences, Steve has learned that many of his students perceive themselves as poor readers and terrible writers. He feels that over several years of schooling, some of his students have been convinced of their inability to learn—they are no longer willing to put forth much effort academically. As Steve contemplated language arts instruction, he realized that he must find ways to convince these youngsters that reading, writing, speaking, and listening skills have value. If the students can be convinced to work toward meeting personal achievement goals in language arts, their self-image will likely improve. Successes can lead them to new heights of learning. Along with the affective domain, Steve must find instructional formats that will allow him to meet the needs of all students in his classes. The high- , middle- , and low-group students must all be challenged to learn.

As Steve began to organize ideas for instruction, he searched through his university course notebooks, skimmed articles in journals, visited other teachers and curriculum specialists, and, as the year progressed, attended a number of professional curriculum meetings. What follows are some thoughts and ideas Steve gleaned—some techniques he found worthwhile and some ideas for future instruction.

*Sharing literature.* One page in Steve Rubert's planbook is filling up with titles of books he wants to share with his students as the year moves along. He knows that if his students are going to develop a value for reading, they will have to be turned on to books. Steve's immediate plans for sharing good books include:

1. Calhoun, Mary. *White Witch of Kynance,* Harper, 1970
2. Fritz, Jean. *Homesick: My Own Story,* Putnam, 1982
3. Hinton, S. E. *The Outsiders,* Dell, 1967
4. Howe, James. *Howliday Inn,* Atheneum, 1982
5. Rawls, Wilson, *Where the Red Fern Grows,* Doubleday, 1961

Steve realizes that time will not permit the reading of entire books. As an alternative, he will introduce selections, highlight major characters, and read excerpts to whet students' appetites for reading. Steve feels that, if motivated, even the poorer readers in his class may be able to read several ability-leveled selections throughout the term.

*Responding to literature.* Mary Mueller, the district language arts consultant, gave Steve an excellent idea for interacting with students on books they were reading. In a recent issue of *Language Arts* (a professional journal of the National Council of Teachers of English), Mary had read an article describing a program developed by an eighth-grade teacher in Maine (Atwell, 1984). Mary shared the article with Steve and they worked together to adapt Atwell's ideas to Steve's seventh-grade classes. As a first step, students received a notebook that included the following instructions:

> This folder is a place for you and me to talk about books, reading, authors, and writing. You're to write letters to me, and I'll write letters back to you. In your

> letters to me, talk with me about what you've read. Tell me what you liked and didn't like and why. Tell me what these books meant to you and said to you. Ask me questions or for help. And write back to me about my ideas, feelings, and questions. (Atwell, 1984, p. 242)

Steve realizes that although the letter-writing task is time-consuming it is a good way for him to keep in touch with what students are reading. The correspondence will give him a chance to explore ideas with each child on a personal basis.

*Storytelling.* At a conference sponsored by the National Council of Teachers of English (NCTE), Steve was attracted to a session on storytelling. His notebook was full of new ideas by the end of the session. Notebook in hand, he hurried into the exhibits arena to track down a book-cassette package introduced in the storytelling session. The package was entitled "The Girl Who Cried Flowers and Other Tales" (Yolan, 1974). The set contained stories read by their author, Jane Yolan, and Steve thought these would provide an added boost for his reluctant readers/writers. Students would have an opportunity to immerse themselves in the beautiful language of these modern tales. The stories would offer many opportunities for class discussions, and Steve could picture how these talks would provide opportunities to introduce the students to classic folktales. During the session on storytelling, the speaker had suggested giving extra credit to students who read a new tale, learned it, and shared it with classmates; Steve planned to incorporate that idea into his grading scale. He also wanted to pick up on the speaker's suggestion of starting a "clipping file" of current events; this file could one day become the source of original tale-spinning in the classroom. On the whole, the storytelling activities provide Steve with many opportunities to interrelate the language arts.

*Composing.* In team meetings, Steve learned that students needed to be able to produce different forms of written material and to write for a variety of purposes. He knows that his "letter writing" responses to literature will offer a chance for practicing one form and style required by the district's curriculum guidelines. Prose-writing skills will develop as students work on the storytelling projects. Each teacher on the team spends time working with story grammar as a means of improving the development of narrative prose. Recognizing major story elements or categories (Setting, Theme, Plot, Resolution) and using these elements to guide the creation of good stories have proven to be sound techniques and have resulted in improved student compositions. Steve plans to find a way to use story grammar lessons based on books the students are reading in class; these lessons can form the basis for writing projects. Students will alter the settings of stories, change the plot, or create new endings for stories they have read. Report-writing skills will develop as the classes jointly publish the *Middle School Gazette,* a student newspaper. Students are totally responsible for this publication and must base articles on observations, interviews, and research reading. Groups of students are responsible for reporting on what's being learned in content area classes, music, art, and physical education. Reporting on these classes forces the students to adapt their writing to the expository style of the particular content.

In each of these writing experiences, Steve feels that his students will learn to apply the mechanics of writing. He will frequently remind them of the audience for whom they are writing. First-draft papers will be subjected to peer edits, and reshaping or revising will usually be the result. Papers will go to peer-editing teams for mechanical review and then be submitted to Steve for final proofreading and reactions. Direct instruction on all aspects of the writing curriculum will be offered as Steve sees various needs arise.

## PLANNING FOR DIRECT INSTRUCTION

Nowhere in this chapter have you found lists or sequences of language arts skills. The author's bias is that specific skill instruction should grow out of the careful, daily observation of children's work. Once again, examples of a teacher working with children will be used to illustrate the point:

1. Timothy, a seventh grader, is working on the school newspaper as music editor. His task is to write up interviews conducted each month with the school's vocal and instrumental music instructors. Vivian Shay, Tim's teacher, notices that Tim's articles often contain long, run-on sentences with little punctuation. Ms. Shay will allow the draft to go through peer-editing and on to the publication stage. However, she will add Tim's name to a list of five other students who have exhibited similar problems in their compositions. Ms. Shay will soon call the group together to work on the specific problem. Samples of each child's work will be examined and improved through small-group discussion/instruction. The "flexible group" will disband as soon as Ms. Shay feels progress has been made.
2. Rosario does fine on measures of literal comprehension during literature class but seems to miss many questions that require inferential reading/thinking. Although her teacher, Jerry Daniels, has offered whole-group instruction on connecting "in-the-head with on-the-page" ideas, Rosario needs more help. During an individual conference on reading, Mr. Daniels will work directly with Rosario on selections followed by questions that require that inferences be made. Together they will explore text clues and in-the-head clues that lead to the creation of an inference. Next, Mr. Daniels will send Rosario to work on passages—to respond to questions designed to probe her ability to form inferences. Rosario will always have to indicate to Mr. Daniels how she arrived at the inference. This will help her identify steps in the process of making inferences. Follow-up conferences will give Mr. Daniels opportunities to check Rosario's progress.
3. The book *Jacob Have I Loved* (Paterson, 1981) has been assigned to the top readers in Eric Matthew's sixth-grade class. Mr. Matthew's students are capable readers, but the vocabulary and some of the concepts in the book are beyond their realm of experience. Knowing that insufficient prior knowledge will interfere with comprehension, Eric chooses to spend a class period building bridges between what the students do know and what they need to know about concepts/vocabulary in the text. Eric intends to follow this plan prior to each section of the books that his groups read.

In each of these cases, teaching grew out of children's needs to learn either specific skills or language information. Direct instruction offered by each teacher was relevant to the immediate needs of the learners.

## CLOSING REMARKS

The intent of this chapter has been to help you serve children by offering a broad array of language experiences from the perspective of an integrated, interrelated language arts program. The chapter will have been worthwhile if, upon reading and reflecting, you decide that the following ideas make sense to you: (1) children learn the quantity and quality of language they perceive as being desirable and useful in order to function in the home, school, or world environment; (2) children learn language skills best when the skill work is embedded in meaningful, purposeful whole-language activities; and (3) children learn by experiencing and receiving appropriate feedback; they learn to read by reading; listen by listening; speak by speaking; and write by writing.

### *REFERENCES*

ATWELL, N. (1984). Writing and reading literature from the inside out. *Language Arts, 61,* 240–252.
BLOS, J.W. (1979). *A gathering of days.* New York: Scribner's.
BRINK, C.R. (1935, 1973). *Caddie Woodlawn.* New York: Macmillan.
CALHOUN, M. (1970). *White witch of Kynance.* New York: Harper & Row.
COLVER, A. (1964). *Bread and butter journey.* New York: Holt, Rinehart, & Winston.
DALGLIESCH, A. (1954). *The courage of Sarah Noble.* New York: Scribner's.
FRITZ, J. (1982). *Homesick: My own story.* New York: Putnam's.
HINTON, S.E. (1967). *The outsiders.* New York: Dell Publishing.
L'ENGLE, M. (1962). *A wrinkle in time.* New York: Dell Publishing.
HOWE, J. (1982). *Howliday Inn.* New York: Atheneum.
NANCE, J. (1982). *Lobo of the Tasaday: A stone age boy meets the modern world.* New York: Pantheon.
HORTON, M. (1982). *The borrowers avenged.* New York: Harcourt Brace Jovanovich.
PATERSON, C. (1977). *Bridge to Terabithia.* New York: Thomas Y. Crowell.
PATERSON, K. (1980). *Jacob have I loved.* New York: Avon.
RAWLS, W. (1961). *Where the red fern grows.* New York: Doubleday.
SLEATER, W. (1972). *Blackbriar.* New York: Dutton.
WILDER, L. I. (1937). *On the banks of Plum Creek.* Harper & Row.
YOLAN, J. (1974). *The girl who cried flowers.* New York: Thomas Y. Crowell.

### *SUGGESTED READINGS*

ATWELL, N. (1984). Writing and reading literature from the inside out. *Language Arts, 61,* 240–252. This article describes a classroom experiment that used a letter-writing paradigm to create a literature environment for junior high students.
EVANS, C.S. (1984). Writing to learn in math. *Language Arts, 61,* 828–835. Believing that writing can be a powerful learning tool, Evans conducted an experiment to see if writing would help her fifth graders learn math skills.
FREEMAN, J. (1984). *Books kids will sit still for: A guide to using children's literature for librar-*

*ians, teachers and parents.* MD: Alleyside Press. This book contains annotations of 1,200 read-aloud books for children. Interspersed within the book are short chapters filled with ideas for activities such as booktalks, creative dramatics, storytelling, and book-celebrating.

GRAVES, D., & HANSEN, J. (1983). The author's chair. *Language Arts, 60,* 176–183. This article is based on data the authors collected in a study of the relationship between reading and writing. Although based on a study of young children's writing, the article is valuable for teachers of older students.

# TWENTY-SEVEN
# WRITERS' LAB: A SCHOOLWIDE WRITING PROGRAM

The purpose of this chapter is to familiarize you with *Writers' Lab,* a successful writing program now in operation in a number of schools in central Pennsylvania. Writers' Lab clearly reflects various research findings in the area of writing instruction, particularly those emphasized in the 1984 National Assessment of Educational Progress report (NAEP, 1984).

Writers' Lab is probably best described as a time set aside daily for writing in a laboratory setting. Students do *all* of their writing under the direct supervision of the teacher. Students are not *told* to write; they are *taught* to write.

Students in the Writers' Lab program learn that any piece of writing begins with careful attention to the *prewriting* stage. *Composing* follows with the emphasis on getting all of one's prewriting ideas down on paper without pressure for perfection. Students then *conference* with a peer or the teacher, who offers ideas for *revision*. The *editing* stage is then addressed, again using peer and teacher assistance. Many but not all edited pieces are *published,* perhaps recopied for the teacher or other specified "audience" or typed as booklets for sharing with other students in the class during free reading time (Graves, 1983).

In the early primary years, children write most often in the narrative form, generally the most comfortable composing mode for young children. Such writings fall under the category of *self-selected topic* writings and are an important part of the writing program at all grade levels.

Because *assigned topic* writing activities such as reports and essays are the kinds of tasks students face more and more often as they move through the grades, teachers introduce this type of writing early in the curriculum. Assigned topic writing often demands a precision and discipline not necessary in the narrative form.

## THE PREWRITING STAGE

During Writers' Lab activities involving assigned topics, most teachers help students make three specific prewriting decisions. First, *audience* for the piece is clearly established. Second, a "*shopping list*" of possible writing ideas is generated. Third, an *effective beginning* or topic sentence for the piece is developed.

Writers' Lab teachers have found that the friendly letter format helps define audience for assigned writings. If, for example, first graders are going to write about their favorite cafeteria lunch, they might decide to write letters to the cafeteria staff.

One successful prewriting strategy many Writers' Lab teachers use lends itself best to assigned topic writings and is therefore introduced to children early in the writing curriculum. Teachers devise carefully worded questions related to science, social studies, literature, and other curricular topics. One question is selected and duplicated for the students on a "sloppy copy" work sheet.

Third graders studying the pioneers are well prepared to respond to the stimulus question, "Why did the pioneers go west?" Students decide that their parents are the most appropriate audience for this assigned writing topic. Together the class brainstorms ideas that might be included in a paragraph explaining the pioneers' decision, the teacher recording all the suggested ideas. Students make a "shopping list" of those ideas they wish to use in their paragraphs.

Let us look at one child's work sheet at this point in the Writers' Lab lesson. Note that Robbie has chosen three ideas for his "shopping list":

Question: Why did the pioneers go west?
Audience: Mom and Dad

### MY SHOPPING LIST OF WRITING IDEAS

1. adventure
2. get rich
3. curious

All Writers' Lab students receive direct instruction in using the "Six Magic Steps" for turning questions into clear beginning or topic sentences. Figure 27–1 presents these six steps in a form many teachers use as a classroom chart to remind students of the procedure to follow.

Recall that our third graders have each jotted down a few ideas they wish

STEP ONE: Read the question, consider possible answers, and make a shopping list of writing ideas.

STEP TWO: Cross out the question word(s), the question mark, and change *you* to *I* if necessary.

~~Why did~~ the pioneers go west~~?~~

STEP THREE: Find a possible starting word and circle it.

~~Why did~~ (the) pioneers go west~~?~~

STEP FOUR: Capitalize your starting word.

STEP FIVE: Underline words in the question you want to use in your answer; add and/or change words.

~~Why did~~ (The) pioneers ~~go~~ went west~~?~~ for several reasons.

STEP SIX: Read your sentence to be sure that it makes sense and is a good answer to the question.

**FIGURE 27-1** The Six Magic Steps!

to include in their individual paragraphs. They are now ready to use the "Six Magic Steps" to create several possible "good beginnings." At lower-grade levels the teacher is likely to work with the entire class using the board or the overhead projector. As the teacher demonstrates each of the six steps, the children work on their "sloppy copy" work sheets. Children may come to the board to cross out, circle, or underline the words in the example question (see Figure 27–1). Teachers encourage children to "experiment with language" by helping them create more than one possible good beginning sentence using the "Six Magic Steps."

Robbie has elected to use "The pioneers moved west for many reasons" as his beginning sentence. Because his teacher has invested adequate time in *prewriting,* it should be relatively easy for Robbie to complete an initial draft with several follow-up sentences, each one an expansion of one of the three ideas from his "shopping list."

Instruction in topic sentence development differs from classroom to classroom. For example, another teacher might present the example question and direct the children to spend a few minutes working on their own to construct possible topic sentences. Another teacher might provide a slightly different "sloppy copy" work sheet with the same question printed more than once, perhaps worded in two or three different ways. Students might spend part of the Writers' Lab lesson working together to construct one common topic sentence. The teacher might then ask the students to use one or more of the other questions on the work sheet for devising a *different* topic sentence independently.

Use of the Six Magic Steps strategy *should* encourage students to *experiment with language,* to risk trying out a variety of ways for creating effective beginnings for assigned writings based on teachers' questions. Although many students fall into the habit of beginning most of their writings in the same way, most will move toward sophistication in their writing style *if* teachers provide adequate guidance and encouragement.

## THE COMPOSING STAGE

Many teachers characterize the *composing* stage as similar to the daily *uninterrupted sustained silent reading* period (USSR). Children, as well as the teacher, concentrate on getting their ideas down on paper without pressure for perfection. During the *uninterrupted sustained silent writing* period (USSW), children are encouraged to create initial drafts that are truly "sloppy copies," subject to lots of revision. The "teacher as writer" serves as an important "model" of effective writing behavior.

In order to foster an environment conducive to composing initial drafts that really are "subject to revision," Writers' Lab teachers set up various ground rules. Students are expected to focus on getting their "shopping list" ideas down on paper without worrying about spelling, capitalization, and sentence construction. Students are encouraged to use pencil, to skip lines in order to allow space for revisions, and to use phonemic spellings for "hard words." Students who recognize that initial drafts are really just that are likely to create initial drafts with real promise.

Our third graders have been writing quietly for about 20 minutes. The teacher has spent the first few minutes of the composing period writing along with the children and has spent the remainder of the period circulating about the room in the role of "cheerleader." As a cheerleader, the teacher is available to give encouragement when words don't come easily, to listen to a student's experimental sentences, and to suggest ways of getting more information down on paper.

As children complete their "sloppy copy" initial drafts, many Writers' Lab teachers conclude the day's writing lesson with a brief sharing period. On a voluntary basis, several children read aloud what they have written thus far. Again the teacher acts as cheerleader, not "corrector." Every child's "sloppy copy" has *some* redeeming feature about which the teacher can make a positive comment.

Let us examine what Robbie has written during his quiet composing time:

Dear Mom and Dad,

The pioneers went west for many reasons. Sum whanted to have an adventure. Thay whanted get rich to. Sum of the pioneers where curios, thay whanted to see what was out ther in the west.

Love,
Robbie

Note that Robbie has used his "shopping list" to compose three follow-up sentences. He has done a good job of getting his ideas down on paper. Note that he has not had any trouble spelling the words *adventure* and *rich,* which appeared on the sample shopping list on the board. Note that Robbie has, however, misspelled curious, even though this word too was included in the sample shopping list.

If you are uncomfortable about the other words Robbie has misspelled, the *to* he has omitted, or the fact that he has a run-on sentence, you have missed the point of composing initial drafts that focus on content, not mechanics. Because Robbie is part of a writing program that emphasizes process, he feels free to get his ideas down on paper even if he isn't totally confident about his spelling and sentence structure. Robbie knows that it is a long, long way from sloppy copy to published product and that lots of help will be available along the way.

## THE REVISION STAGE

It has been suggested that hearing one's own initial draft read aloud is the single most effective way to ensure that revisions will be made. Early in the primary grades, Writers' Lab children are encouraged to read their sloppy copies aloud to each other, the first step in conducting a writing conference. Student writers understand that, during the initial conference, they are to *listen* to a partner's draft; this is not the time to *look* at the writing, for doing so is likely to change the emphasis from *content* to *mechanics*. Thus, most teachers suggest that conferencing partners sit opposite each other so that there is no temptation to *look* at the piece at this point in the process.

Teachers need to be patient as students learn to conference with each other. Students *will* get better at conferencing; they *will* begin to ask constructive questions that will help a partner add something significant during revision, and they *will* learn to listen more intently to their own work as they read it aloud.

Returning to our third-grade classroom, we find that the children are completing their conferences. As each conference ends, students return to their seats to work on the third stage of the five-stage model, namely, *revision*. By now it is hoped that each child has at least one idea for revision, perhaps a sentence to add, perhaps an idea to delete, possibly only a word to change. Because students have written in pencil and because they have skipped lines on their sloppy copies, they can make revisions easily.

Let us look again at Robbie's writing efforts. Robbie has now conferenced with Shawnee, who listened to his "sloppy copy" and commented that she liked what he said about the pioneers being "curious." Shawnee asked Robbie if he could "maybe say something more about adventure so the reader will know what you mean." She asked Robbie to reread his piece and then suggested that it might be even better if he would add an "ending." Thus, Robbie left the writing conference with some clear ideas of what to do next.

Here is Robbie's piece following some work in the *revision* stage. Note that he has made only two mechanical changes, correcting his spelling of *they* and inserting the missing word *to*. Note, however, the extent to which Robbie has revised the *content* of his piece:

> Dear Mom and Dad,
>
> The pioneers went west for many reasons. Sum whanted to have an adventure. They wear bord. They whanted to get rich to. They whanted gold. Sum of the

pioneers where curios, they whanted to see what was out ther in the west. This is why the pioneers went west.

Love,
Robbie

Robbie has clearly benefited from his writing conference. He has acted on his partner's suggestion to say something more about adventure and he has added a conclusion.

## THE EDITING STAGE

The fourth stage of the process model for teaching writing, *editing,* is generally the part of the model that worries teachers most. This is the "bottom line" item for teachers traditionally committed to obtaining "letter-perfect products" from all students.

Let us look again at our third-grade writers and see how skills instruction might be integrated into the editing stage. While students were finishing up their conferences and working on revisions, the teacher was circulating around the room, being a good listener and observing what her students had written up to this point. This involved stopping now and then to provide direct assistance to a child "stuck" on how to improve the sloppy copy, perhaps taking time to hold a small-group conference with several students appearing to be having similar composing problems.

Now let us look at what our third-grade teacher does during the next day's Writers' Lab period. While observing the revision process, the teacher had watched for one or two specific skills for direct instruction. Many students, like Robbie, were having difficulty spelling those troublesome "w" words, and some students neglected to write concluding sentences.

Before the children return to their sloppy copies the next day, our third-grade teacher conducts a directed lesson focusing on one *mechanical* skill, the correct spelling of high-frequency "w" words, and one *content* skill, writing concluding sentences. The children are asked to look at their sloppy copies, directing them to circle their "w" words. A chart might then be prepared, with the children spelling the words *went, want, wanted, where, who, what* for the teacher to record.

Next the teacher asks the children to explain why it is important for a paragraph to have a conclusion or "ending sentence," requesting that one or two children read aloud their sloppy copies to illustrate the point.

The children then begin to work on editing. They are directed to do their own editing first, paying particular attention to the two "focus areas" of the day's skills instruction lesson. The teacher also reminds the children that they are, of course, expected to edit for other areas such as end punctuation, capital letters, indenting, and other skills that have been previous focus areas.

Editing is a busy time in the writing process and needs to be carefully monitored in order to ensure high productivity. Most students are eager to get this part of the writing process over with in a hurry, often taking a hasty glance at their pieces and saying, "I've checked it and it's fine," long before their writings have in fact been taken to the point of "best possible effort."

Let us examine Robbie's piece following his self-editing. Keep in mind the two "focus areas" the teacher has asked the children to look at in their pieces. Compare this *edited* "sloppy copy" with Robbie's previously *revised* piece:

> Dear Mom and Dad,
>
> The pioneers went west for three reasons. Sum wanted to have an adventure. They were bord. They wanted to get rich to. They wanted gold. Sum of the pioneers were curios, they wanted to see what was out ther in the west. This is why the pioneers went out west.
>
> Love,
> Robbie

It is apparent that Robbie has in fact attended to his teacher's reminder to check on the spelling of the "w" words. Robbie had already written a concluding sentence, but note that he has also added the word *out* during his self-editing time.

The children in Robbie's room know that once they have completed their self-editing, they are to work with at least one other student to edit each other's pieces. Robbie now takes his writing to a classmate, they exchange papers, and, using a simple editing checklist, they look over each other's sloppy copies. Robbie's editing partner points out that the word *curious* is not copied correctly from the board and that the word *there* lacks an "e" on the end. Robbie makes these corrections and is satisfied that his piece is "finished."

No, Robbie's letter to his parents is not "letter perfect." He still has several misspelled words and he has a run-on sentence. The teacher, however, recognizes that Robbie has likely taken his piece as far as he can on his own. The writing reflects Robbie's current developmental writing stage. Further "corrections" would reflect the teacher's skill, not Robbie's!

The teacher may or may not get around to Robbie for a brief editing conference about his piece. No teacher can get to every child individually for each writing activity, and you should not try to do so. Manage to see several children during one or two small-group conferences during both the conferencing and editing stages while students are meeting with each other. And, of course, circulate about the room during each stage of the writing activity, holding mini-conferences with children as they are writing.

If the teacher *is* able to meet with Robbie once more, she will likely focus on his run-on sentence. She might, for example, stop at his desk and ask that he read aloud, beginning with "Sum of the pioneers." Robbie may or may not "hear" his mistake. If he does not, and if the teacher believes that further attention to this mechanical skill is appropriate for Robbie, he may be asked to read the same section of his paragraph to a partner to see if together the children can correct the error.

At this point the writing activity in Robbie's room may or may not be concluded. The children may be directed to copy their letters on good paper, perhaps during cursive writing practice later in the day. Finished letters will then go home in the children's weekly work folders, probably with a note explaining the "focus skill areas" so that parents will recognize that these are the only areas that the teacher *required* the students to "correct."

## THE PUBLISHING STAGE

In most process-writing programs the publishing stage is reserved for special pieces of writing, usually those selected by the writer as worthy of preparation for the "public." Writers' Lab teachers have found a variety of ways to publish student writings. Because many assigned topic-writing activities involve the use of the friendly letter form, teachers make a real effort to see that many of these writings are received by the designated "audiences." For example, first graders write a birthday letter to the President whereas a fourth-grade class writes letters on tooth care and sends them to the school's dental hygienist. Because students are aware that their finished copies may be published, they are likely to invest quality time and effort in their writings.

A weekly Spotlight Writing Award for each classroom provides another publishing opportunity in the Writers' Lab program. The names of all Spotlight Writers are announced over the loudspeaker, writings are displayed, and writers receive special certificates.

You have seen how the Writers' Lab program incorporates many of the implications from current research into the nature of the writing process. Although Writers' Lab is a schoolwide program, it should be clear that the program can be implemented successfully in individual classrooms as well.

Even the youngest primary children are surprisingly receptive to the instructional procedure described in this chapter for assigned writing topics. With teacher guidance they are able to compose "good beginnings" in response to carefully worded questions. Earlier than you would think possible, these children are able to write several follow-up sentences and conclusions.

In the upper grades, most teachers are able to use this same instructional procedure for moving students into multiparagraph writing assignments in the content areas. The procedure lends itself particularly well to early report writing; students are helped to develop a number of carefully constructed questions about their topics, each question forming the basis of a paragraph in their reports. Thus, Writers' Lab activities using the "Six Magic Steps" become the cornerstone of a writing program intended to help students develop the basic skill of clear, organized writing in response to assigned topics.

### *REFERENCES*

GRAVES, D.H. (1983). *Writing: Teachers and children at work.* Heinemann Educational Books, Portsmouth, NH.

*Writing Objectives, 1983–84 National Assessment.* National Assessment of Educational Progress (NAEP) No. 15–W–10.

# TWENTY-EIGHT
# DEVELOPING YOUNG AUTHORS AND POETS

The purpose of this chapter is to present ideas and activities that help to develop creative writing and that are implemented easily in the classroom. The overall objective for the young authors and poets is that they "write to read." This approach for developing young writers specifies the reading-writing connection and emphasizes communication. Specifically, this chapter will provide instructions for writing instant success selections, expanding and revising first drafts, editing compositions, illustrating content, binding completed manuscripts, and sharing bound books with other students, parents, and teachers.

## THREE PHASES OF THE WRITING PROCESS

In general, students are involved in three phases of the writing process: the *prewriting* phase, which occurs before the actual writing begins; the *composing* phase, which occurs during the actual process of writing; and the *postwriting,* or *editing* phase, which occurs after the writing has taken place (Squire, 1983). These phases of the writing process have been described in detail in previous chapters and will be evident in the activities suggested here.

## WRITING ACTIVITIES FOR INSTANT SUCCESS

Simply encouraging students to write without providing activities that are intrinsically motivating often produces discouragement and antagonism among writers. Children need to be turned on to writing, and the best way to accomplish such a task is to provide them with activities that have built-in success. Both open-ended writing activities and patterned writing activities can be structured to ensure writing success. Initially, *open-ended writing activities* tend to be more successful in the early elementary grades; *patterned writing activities* tend to be more successful in the upper-elementary-grade levels. Once writing has become a meaningful part of the regular class routine, however, both kinds of activities seem to work equally well for all age groups.

### Open-Ended Writing Activities

These divergent-thinking-types of writing activities use materials and methods that encourage discussion. Have your students *talk first* and then *write.* To initiate the classroom discussion, use activities such as magazine pictures, ink/color blots, sponge painting, collage, pantomime, and music. Discussion questions help to motivate students to explore their feelings and attitudes as they prepare for their writing. The ideas that the children develop from these discussions become the framework for their writing.

*Magazine pictures.* Have students find a picture that shows how they see themselves (physical characteristics, interests, family). Other classmates look at the magazine pictures and tell why they think each student selected that particular picture. Individuals may respond with their own reasons for their picture selections. Biographies and autobiographies are written from these discussions. Another way to use magazine pictures is to have students select one picture and develop three-part stories by telling what happened before the picture, what is happening now in the picture, and what happened after the picture.

*Ink/color blots.* These activities can be done either in groups or as individual projects. For group work, place a Pyrex dish with a little water in it on an overhead projector; put one drop of food coloring in the water and then have the students describe what happens. How do the colors make them feel? What do they see? What can they smell?

For an individual activity, instruct students to take a piece of construction paper, fold it in half, and then open it up. Place blobs of different colored tempera paint on the right side. Then fold the left side over the right and blot the paper together pushing and patting the paint toward the center and sides. Black printer's ink may be substituted for the tempera paint for black-and-white compositions. Students describe what the color or inkblots look like. Students use these descriptions as the basis for a story. Several students could work together to produce a group story.

*Sponge painting.* Cut dry sponges into various shapes, soak them in different colored paint (one sponge per paint dish), and then use the sponges like printing blocks to make designs on art paper. Vegetables, fruits, and cardboard may be used, too. Name poetry, cinquains, and limericks are good writing activities to accompany these printed designs.

*Collage.* Encourage children to use all kinds of materials—paper (tissue, construction, poster), cloth remnants, items from nature (leaves, bark, weeds, seeds, pressed flowers), objects (match sticks, confetti, cord, fish net) and magazine pictures to create an assemblage. No words are allowed—only pictures and objects. Encourage the children to move items around on the page, putting them together until they begin to look like something—an animal, a space creature, a machine. Encourage students to identify what the thing is that they have created. Give it a name. What is it doing? What has happened to it in the past? What will happen in its future? Continue to develop more collages as the story develops.

*Pantomime.* Choose a topic that students can dramatize. For example, if sports are selected, students can act out being a pitcher (baseball), a punter (football), a golfer, or a swimmer. If careers are selected, students can act out being a teacher, a doctor, a firefighter, a waiter, or a car mechanic. Students describe what they see. Emphasis may be placed on listing as many powerful verbs as possible to explain the action. The pitcher is "throwing," "hurling," or "firing" the ball toward home plate. Three-part stories could be developed by telling what happened before, during, and after the pantomime.

*Music.* Listen to records or tapes that set a mood. Some examples of classical music that stir the imagination are the third movement (scherzo) of Ludwig von Beethoven's *Symphony No. 7,* Peter Tchaikovsky's *The Nutcracker Suite* (one movement per session), Frédéric Chopin's *Les Sylphides,* or Wolfgang Amadeus Mozart's *Overture of the Magic Flute.* Selections from popular music such as *Bridge Over Troubled Water,* by Paul Simon and Art Garfunkel; *Everything is Beautiful,* by Ray Stephens; *Beat It,* by Michael Jackson, and *I'm Dreaming of a White Christmas,* by Irving Berlin provide students with ideas for creative writing. When the music is over, the students describe their feelings. Discussions may focus on listing as many descriptive adjectives as possible. Have the students use these adjectives in their creative writing.

### Patterned Writing Activities

Patterned writing activities either follow definite rules and procedures or consist of content substitutions (paraphrasing) of published works. Poetic forms such as name poetry, cinquain, diamante, haiku, tanka, catalog poems, and limericks have specific rules. Transmographies,* story adaptations, and

*"Transmographies" is a coined word for a type of poetry based on the process of transmografication. As far as we know, it has not yet appeared in the literature but has appeared in practice. One known reference occurred in a "Write to Read" workshop in a presentation. We suspect that, like "diamante" which was also a coined word for an invented poetry form, it will soon appear in print. In fact, it has, hasn't it!

pattern-book substitutions utilize patterns and structures that are well-known in the published form. The students replace some of the published content with their own words and experiences. To ensure success in these writing activities *provide lots of examples and proceed step by step.* Except for the "Old King Cole" transmography, which was developed by a group of teachers at a workshop conducted by the author, the author's family contributed the examples presented in this chapter.

*Name poetry.* Students write their own names or the name of some object in a vertical line with each letter below the other. Next to each letter, the student writes an adjective, adjective and noun, or adjective phrase that describes the person or object.

S tewart
N ice
O ld
W inter
M an
A mbling
N orth

N atural athlete
A ctive
T houghtful
H appy
A nimal lover
N ot easily bored

*Cinquain.* This is a useful form for summarizing subject matter topics. Students follow a specific form whereby the first line names the subject, second line describes the subject, third line shows action with "-ing" words, fourth line expresses a feeling, and fifth line gives a synonym for the subject.

Cat
Soft, black
Scratching, running, purring
Likes to catch mice
Midnight

*Diamante.* Use this poetry form only if students really know their parts of speech. Originated by Iris M. Tiedt (Tiedt & Tiedt, 1978), it is a contrast poem and an extension of the cinquain.

1st Line—one noun (opposite of line 7)
2nd Line—two adjectives describing line 1
3rd Line—three "-ing" or "-ed" verbs describing line 1
4th Line—four related nouns
5th Line—three "-ing" or "-ed" verbs describing line 7
6th Line—two adjectives describing line 7
7th Line—one noun (opposite of line 1)

cold
white, clear
freezing, snowing, slipping
ice, slush, water, puddles
raining, steaming, shining
gold, red
hot

*Haiku.* In this poetry form some aspect of nature is usually described. It contains only three lines and must have exactly 17 syllables. The first line has five syllables, the second line has seven syllables, and the third line has five syllables.

Sunny summer day
The barnyard is all quiet
Gone to take a nap.

*Tanka.* This poetic form is very similar to haiku except that it contains 31 syllables and uses the following structure: five syllables, seven syllables, five syllables, seven syllables, seven syllables.

*Catalog poems.* Using a single topic, have students list as many characteristics as they can to describe an object. Each line adds new information. No specific form is used, but a discernible pattern is repeated and each phase of the pattern has closure.

Dogs, dogs, dogs
Big dogs
Little dogs
Black spotted Dalmatian dogs
Long skinny wiener dogs
These are just a few
Playful dogs
Working dogs
He'll save your life
A Saint Bernard dog

*Limerick.* This poetic form is more difficult to write than the previously mentioned forms because it uses rhyme and a metered rhythm. It is a nonsense poem of five lines in which line one rhymes with lines two and five, and line three rhymes with line four.

There once was a salmon named Swish
Who desired to be a main dish
He bit on some worms
That were full of germs
Thus, Swish didn't get his wish

*Transmographies.* Familiar proverbs, nursery rhymes, or commercials form the structure for this writing activity. These familiar phrases are paraphrased or rewritten using synonyms for the original words. If the words rhyme and the rhythm from the original work is maintained, transmographies sound better. These writing activities are useful assignments for editing committees. A thesaurus for beginners such as *In Other Words* (Schiller & Jenkins, 1978) is a useful tool.

The aging Monarch was a jovial senior citizen
And a jovial senior citizen was he, so
He summoned his corncob
And, he beckoned his basin
And, he bid for his royal string trio.

*Story adaptations.* These written selections are created from published works. Children retell the stories using their own words. Short stories with a specific line of action are recommended. The following excerpt from a story adaptation follows the story line of *The Boy Who Called Wolf* (Evans, 1960), but the form imitates *The Giving Tree* (Silverstein, 1964).

***Boy Who Called Wolf***

Once upon a time there was a sheep boy.
He wanted some company. So, he called, "Wolf, Wolf!"
And all the farmers
and all the people came running to help the boy. . . .
He laughed, "Ha! Ha! It was just a joke."
The next day he called, "Wolf, Wolf!" again.
But, all the farmers
and all the people just laughed. . . .
The boy tried to keep the wolf away.
But, the wolf bit him.
And the boy was scared
and he ran away. . . .

*Pattern book substitutions.* These writing activities are a combination of transmographies and story adaptations. Many of the words from the published book are left the same in order to maintain the patterned writing found in the book, but the content is altered by the writer. A particularly good book for this activity is *The Important Book,* by Margaret Wise Brown (1949).

The most important thing about a cup is that you drink from it.
    You mix paint in it
    You build towers with it
    You store spare change in it.
But, the most important thing about a cup is that you drink from it.

Some other good books to use for pattern book adaptations are *Alexander and the Terrible, Horrible, No Good, Very Bad Day* (Viorst, 1972), *Hailstones and Halibut Bones* (O'Neill, 1961), and *Someday* (Zolotow, 1978).

## REVISING AND EDITING WRITTEN COMPOSITIONS

All of the instant success writing activities can be used for revising and editing practice, but manuscripts that are an adaptation of other published materials seem to work best. The student-author has already changed some parts of an existing publication; when another person suggests further changes, the concept of writing as rewriting is being established, and students are more motivated to revise their original manuscripts.

### Incorporating Mechanics and Grammar Through Revision

"Instruction in the grammar and mechanics of English, albeit unimportant in helping children compose, is essential to helping them revise. But, to do so it must be taught as a part of the revision process, not independently or as part of actual writing" (Squire, 1983, p. 7). One strategy to help students in the revising phase is to provide classroom instruction in sentence-combining, decombining, and recombining. This procedure for teaching grammar does not use sentence and paragraph building, which was described in Chapter 11.

### Using Students As Editors

As many students as possible should serve as editors. Whether editing should be done on anonymous compositions is subject to your discretion but is preferred by some teachers. You may want to work with a few children at a time on a specific aspect of the revision process. As the students become efficient editors, they will internalize their editing skills and improve their own compositions.

### Using Questions to Communicate Editorial Concerns

Based on Carl Rogers' nondirective procedures, reflective questions rather than critical comments provide the best means of communicating an editor's concerns. Using these procedures, editors ask open-ended questions about the writing/communication process or work-in-progress. Then they pause until the student makes a response. Based on this response, the editor asks a question that helps the writer further develop the manuscript.

## ILLUSTRATING, PUBLISHING, AND BINDING COMPLETED WORKS

The art activities (magazine pictures, ink/color blots, sponge painting, collage) described earlier in this chapter make extremely effective illustrations for completed works. When children understand that they do not need to strive for realistic illustrations, they become more creative in the artwork they include in their books. Allow children to work in teams so that their best talents are utilized. Also, enlist the help of art teachers, parents, and/or older students who have an interest in illustrating.

Publishing students' work is very important because it enables students to see their written compositions in finished form. Children in grades one and two publish their written works more quickly than older children, but all children should have a book published within the first month of a creative writing program. As creative writing becomes an ongoing process in the classroom, first and second graders tend to publish once every two to three weeks; third graders and above tend to publish about one book a quarter (Graves, 1983).

The published book should not contain errors that would be a source of embarrassment to the young author. Children should be responsible only for editing and revising content, which is within their potential as writers. When a book goes "to press" the teacher corrects and amends the writing to suit the expected audience. Once the final editing has been completed, the manuscripts are ready for binding.

Many different procedures have been devised to bind books. Some of the common procedures used by teachers include staple books, ring books, shape books, and plank books. *Staple books* use construction paper, poster board, or cardboard for the outer cover. The text of the book is placed inside the cover and the entire book is stapled along the spine. *Ring books, shape books,* and *plank books* are based on the same procedure. Holes are punched through the cover and all the pages. Notebook rings or shower curtain rings are used to bind the book together. A plank book uses thin plywood (3/16″) for the cover and the holes are drilled through the wood. Shape books have the pages and the front and back cover cut in a shape that fits the content of the book. Usually these books are in the shape of an object or animal.

## SHOWCASE THE BOUND BOOKS

Finally, the books that the young authors and poets have worked so hard to create are available to be read for enjoyment. Place the books in convenient places to be read such as the school library or classroom reading corner, and exchange them with other teachers who have published their students' books.

A "Young Authors' Conference," "Hug a Book Week," or some other activity that displays the student authors' bound books in a public place and celebrates the culmination of the finished product is highly recommended. If an entire school, county, or district works together displaying the young authors' books, greater public attention will be focused on writing in the schools. Parents, other teachers, and classmates can be invited to the display. If a program is planned, children can tell the audience about the book and how they developed their ideas; some books may be dramatized, and others could be shared through choral reading (patterned books lend themselves especially well using this format). The overall goal of these activities is to celebrate the accomplishments of the student authors and to share their works with others.

## SUMMARY

The goal of this chapter has been to provide ideas for increasing creative writing activities in the classroom. Emphasis was placed on writing activities that can produce an immediate sense of accomplishment and on revision activities that are embedded in the composing phase of the writing process. Suggestions for illustrating, publishing, and showcasing students' manuscripts have also been included.

### *REFERENCES*

BROWN, M.W. (1949). *The important book.* New York: Harper & Row.
EVANS, K. (1960). *The boy who called wolf.* Chicago: Whitman.
FRANK, M. (1979). *If you're trying to teach kids to write you've gotta have this book.* Nashville: Incentive Publications.
GRAVES, D. (1982). *Writing: Teachers and children at work.* Exeter, NH: Heinemann.
O'NEILL, M. (1961). *Hailstones and halibut bones.* Garden City, NY: Doubleday.
SCHILLER, A., & JENKINS, W. (1978). *In other words: A beginning thesaurus.* Wooster, OH: Lathrop.
SILVERSTEIN, S. (1964). *The giving tree.* New York: Harper & Row.
SOBOL, D.J. (1978). *Encyclopedia Brown: Boy detective.* New York: Bantam.
SQUIRE, J.R. (1983). *Instructional focus and the teaching of writing.* (Ginn Occasional Paper No. 1.) Columbus, OH: Ginn.
TIEDT, S.W., & TIEDT, I.M. (1978). *Language arts activities for the classroom.* Boston: Allyn & Bacon.
VIORST, J. (1972). *Alexander and the terrible, horrible, no good, very bad day.* New York: Atheneum.
ZOLOTOW, C. (1978). *Someday.* New York: Harper & Row.

### *SUGGESTED READINGS*

CRAMER, R. (1979). *Children's writing and language growth.* Columbus, OH: Chas. E. Merrill. This textbook contains many suggestions for helping teachers motivate and maintain creative writing activities in the classroom. The extensive list of pattern books in the appendix is particularly helpful in developing patterned writing activities.

FRANK, M. (1979). *If you're trying to teach kids to write you've gotta have this book.* Nashville: Incentive Publications. This text provides numerous creative writing ideas that teachers can use in the classroom. The format for presenting these ideas is especially appealing.

GRAVES, D. (1982). *Writing: Teachers and children at work.* Exeter, NH: Heinemann. Provides extensive information and many examples for using the conference/interview procedure in developing creative writing. Extremely helpful in guiding students in the revision process through the use of reflective questioning.

PLUM, L. (1980). *Flights of fantasy activity book.* Carthage, IL: Good Apple. Provides directions for activities that stir the imaginations of children. Through relaxation exercises and imaginary journeys, children are taken to unknown lands, hidden forests, and the center of the earth. Facilitates the use of open-ended creative writing activities.

# TWENTY-NINE
# HAVING FUN WITH LANGUAGE

## INTRODUCTION

The mule, the farmer, and the plow stood motionless in the field. Taking a large stick, the farmer gave the mule a sharp rap on the nose, then said "giddap." The mule giddapped and the field was plowed. Later, the farmer was asked why he hit the mule before issuing his orders. His answer is instructive: "Before you can get him to do anything, you got to get his attention."

So is it with much that occurs in schools. Before students will learn and, even more important, before they will like what they learn, teachers must get their attention. Sharp raps on students' noses are not only unwise and inhumane but lead to shortened teaching careers. Language games will work just as well and have the added advantage of bringing an element of fun into the classroom.

What we propose in this chapter is the use of as many different kinds of language activities as possible that have, at bottom, the purpose of making students aware of language, fascinated by its potential, eager to play with it, shape it, run with it. Once students come to love language, once it has "got their attention," then instruction on formal elements of language—grammar rules, spelling codes, writing strategies—are more likely to take. The fun and games are legitimate first steps. Our goal here, then, is to acquaint you with language activities to try with your students. Our illustrative examples may need modification, usually in terms of altering them to fit different age or ability groups, but all of them are amenable to such modification and all of them are likely to appeal to many of your students. A number of the activities can be varied to permit a different focus.

## ODD PERSON OUT

Which person does not belong in each group?

(a) Richard Hoggs
James Katz
Michael Jones
Timothy Lyons

(b) Irene Ford
Mary Carter
Becky Lincoln
Ruth Clarke

(c) Barbara C. Dixon
Susan J. Andrews
Rachael S. Todd
Joann K. Lawson

(d) Bruce Peters
Pamela A. Malone
Theodore E. Daniels
Dorothy O. Taylor

Possibly the best answers (but just possibly) are *Jones* in (a) because the others have names that sound like animals, *Clarke* in (b) because the others have presidents' last names, *Andrews* in (c) because the others have alphabetical initials, and *Peters* in (d) because the others have initials that spell their own nicknames. But different thoughtful responses should be encouraged. For example, one of your students might choose *Katz* in (a) as the only person with a one-syllable first name or *Malone* in (d) as the only person whose name ends in a vowel. Such divergent thinking is both to be encouraged and to be rewarded.

An additional note: Where do these exercises come from? You make them up *and so do your students.*

## ANAGRAMS

*hatW liwl htye kinht fo exnt?* Use anagrams with your students. Their puzzling for the right configuration of letters will stimulate their interest in language. And, of course, they can create their own anagrams and share them with their classmates.

## ALLITERATION

*All apples at Aunt Abigail's are awful. Black bears beg bread.* Students like alliteration, like playing with it. Even kindergarteners can come up with *crazy cats* or *lazy lions,* and older students can try their hands at creating fairly extended discourse units, even including sentences.

It's but a slight variation from alliterative sentences or phrases to ask students to alphabetize their contributions: *All boys can do each figure grandly.*

## MY GRAMMA'S GAME

*My Gramma likes apples, not oranges; books, not magazines; spoons, not forks; eggs, not bacon; yellow, not red; pepper, not salt.* By now, you've gathered that Gramma likes things that have double letters in their names. It's easier, by the way, when you see the words in print, as in this paragraph, than when you hear them. Your best strategy with this exercise, then, is to do it orally. Give your students as many clues as they need, but don't let them blurt out the explanation for Gramma's likes and dislikes. Instead, make responders contribute in kind. For example, if a student says that her Gramma likes *jelly, not jam,* you can be reasonably certain she has caught on.

And Gramma can change daily—liking things today that begin with vowels, tomorrow those names with two-syllable words, next week those with an "r" in them. Indeed, she has virtually endless possibilities for entertaining and instructing your students and heightening their interest in language.

Students can create their own preference lists for Gramma. Ask those who want to try their hand to come up with at least 10 pairs, 10 items that Gramma likes, and 10 somewhat related items she does not like. For example, a student might have on a list something like the following: *coffee, not tea; trees, not firs; sleep, not rest; creeks, not rivers; green, not red; bookkeepers, not accountants.* Did you catch the variation here? Gramma likes words with a double "e" in them.

It may be useful to pause here and explain another virtue of these kinds of activities: They encourage thinking from your students. Most statements of school purpose, books and articles on school reform, and teachers' conventions include a call for improving the thinking students do in school. Sometimes, there's even a charge that most students do almost no thinking about school subjects during the entire day. The kinds of activities we are suggesting will cause them to think, to make deductions and generalizations, to infer, to take calculated guesses. The activities are fun, the children will like them and learn from them, but they additionally are valuable thinking aids.

## WHO STOLE THE COOKIE?

Choral activities appeal to students, challenge them to listen, facilitate their thinking and their responding, and often provide a good way for students to get to know each other. The following activity achieves all these goals. You begin by singling out a child and conducting the following dialogue:

YOU: Bill stole the cookie from the cookie jar.
BILL: Who? Me?
CLASS: Yes. You.
BILL: Couldn't be.
CLASS: Then who?
BILL: Mary stole the cookie from the cookie jar.

The playlet continues then between Mary and the class and, after the class asks "Then who?" Mary identifies another student.

With older students you can use positive descriptions of the selected cookie snatcher: "A girl with brown hair and blue eyes who plays the piano stole the cookies." The play continues then only if the accused recognizes herself. At the end of the scene she must identify, by characteristics, the next suspect: "A boy in the second row who is on a Little League team stole the cookies."

## REMOTE CONTROL ART

*Listening* is the often overlooked language art, the one we seem to take for granted. Yet some students listen better than others and all can improve. A good way to capture their attention and hold it for an extended time is to give them directions, like the following:

> Take out a sheet of paper. In the center, one inch down from the top, draw a square with sides of about four inches. At the lower-left corner of that square draw three vertical strips about one-inch high. Next, draw a horizontal line from the middle of the left side of your square to the upper-right-hand corner. In the center of the square place four dots. About three inches below the square place four dots. About three inches below the square draw a circle about two inches in diameter. Using diameters, divide the circle into four roughly equal parts. Shade in the upper-left part. Attach the circle to the large square with two wavy lines.

## DIALECT STUDY

How do your students (how do you) say *route, eggs, greasy, idea, oil, either?*

Help your students become "dialect detectives." They can check with friends and relatives to see how different words are pronounced and can keep track of their discoveries. In areas where tourism is common and many visitors are available for students to query, the results gleaned from students' surveys can be exciting to study. (An important learning should come out of this kind of teaching: A person's dialect does not say anything about his or her character. The student who says EE-ther is different from, but not better or worse than, the student who says I-ther. The fact that fried foods in the north may be greaSy and in the south greaZy tells more about geography than character or conduct.)

## CATEGORIES

A language activity that can be fun and instructive is *categories,* in which students devise different categories and fill in the blanks they have created. Two different paradigms are presented:

| Names of: | W | O | R | D | S |
|---|---|---|---|---|---|
| musical instruments | | | | | |
| TV stars | | | | | |
| breeds of dogs | | | | | |
| state capitals | | | | | |
| rivers | | | | | |

| Names of: | B | R | O | W | N |
|---|---|---|---|---|---|
| animals | | | | | |
| colors | | | | | |
| vegetables | | | | | |
| birds | | | | | |

The students' task is to fill in the grid, a job that requires a bit of thinking.

This activity can be modified to show students the importance of collaboration. After your students have worked individually for a few minutes, ask them to cluster in groups and share their answers. Then, a few minutes later, put the grid on the chalkboard and ask the entire class to give answers. What you and your students will likely find is that no individual or small group was able to complete the grid, but the entire class could, suggesting, of course, that cooperative teamwork is a good way to solve problems.

## HINK PINK

Provide your pupils with a definition and ask them to create the rhyming adjective and noun that fit it. A short poem is a *terse verse.* The chief of police is a *top cop.* A cooked specter is a *roast ghost.* The name of the game expands according to the number of syllables required in the adjective and noun. One-syllable phrases are called *hink pinks.* Two-syllable phrases are *hinky pinkies,* as in a dieting gambler who is lucky (a *thinner winner*) or an insane flower (a *crazy daisy*). A hinkety pinkety for a high-class theft is a *snobbery robbery.* Finally, three hinketeties pinketeties: What is a middle European farmer? (A *Bavarian agrarian*). What is a middle Eastern fruit stall? (An *Afghanistan banana stand*). What is a New Yorker's whiskey cabinet? (A *Knickerbocker liquor locker*). Your pupils will get that last one if you ask them to think of New York's professional basketball team (the Knicks).

## GOING ON TRIPS AND PICNICS

CHILD ONE: I'm going on a trip and I'm taking a bear.
CHILD TWO: I'm going on a trip and I'm taking a bear and a doll.
CHILD THREE: I'm going on a trip and I'm taking a bear, a doll, and a basket of fruit.

And so forth. By the time you get to student 16, he or she has a pretty long list of things to take along, a list he or she may forget but you may be surprised at how much students can remember.

### VARIATION 1:

CHILD ONE: My name is Dick, I'm going on a trip, and I'm taking a radio.
CHILD TWO: My name is Lynn, I'm going on a trip, and I'm taking a book. Dick is also going and he is taking a radio.
CHILD THREE: My name is Susan, I'm going on a trip, and I'm taking some bubble gum. Lynn is also going and she is taking a book. Dick is also going and he is taking a radio.

### VARIATION 2:

CHILD ONE: My name is Donna, I'm going on a picnic, and taking a doughnut.
YOU: You can go, Donna, and bring your doughnut.
CHILD TWO: My name is Tom, I'm going on a picnic, and taking some candy.
YOU: You can't go, Tom.
CHILD THREE: My name is Bill, I'm going on a picnic, and taking a banana.
YOU: You can go, Bill, and bring your banana.
CHILD FOUR: My name is Ruth, I'm going on a picnic, and taking a camera.
YOU: You can't go, Ruth.

It will take your students some hard thinking before they realize that their picnic attendance depends on their taking something that begins with the same letter as their names.

## TRIVIA-MANIA

The whole country seems caught up in the pursuit of trivia, with games, cards, stationery, and media events asking who the vice-president was in 1865 (Johnson), who played Mr. Grant in the "Mary Tyler Moore Show" (Ed Asner), and where the Prado Museum is (Madrid). Why not your students? Vary the difficulty of your questions to fit their age and ability, but don't make them too easy. A good question is one some students, but not all, know.

It is but a short duration from your creating the questions—no easy task, by the way—to asking your students to create them. This can be a good team activity and can be followed by a competition among the teams.

## COMMERCIALS

Chances are your students know commercials better than you do, as they probably watch a lot more television and are not yet sufficiently mature to tune out the commercials. So, use their knowledge to ask them to create their own products and the commercial messages that would go with them. For example, what would they call a new toothpaste? a new car? a new soft drink? How would they go about advertising it? If you want to go first class, get the school's media equipment and make a sound recording or even a videotape of the students' efforts.

A useful variation on the making of commercials is to give each student a piece of paper and ask him or her to create a billboard. Students can learn the use of white space, the need for but a few words, the value of central images. Moreover, this activity provides a chance for those who draw well to display their talents.

Most commercial advertising is done by groups of Madison Avenue–types sitting around a big table and bouncing ideas off each other. Ultimately, one idea gets consensus and a new commercial is born. Let your students work in groups on some of their advertising activities. Their results will probably be better than any they would create individually.

## JABBERWOCKY

Read "Jabberwocky," the Lewis Carroll poem in *Through the Looking Glass* that contains nonsense words, then ask your students to provide several sentences of their own that contain nonsense words that seem to make sense. For example, "The students perliverated through several library books." Or, "The weather during the ice storm was slippy." Sharing their entries will teach your students much about the way language operates. "Perliverate," they will discover, is a verb; "slippy," an adjective.

## SHORT-STORY INTRODUCTIONS

The common assignment to write a short story is difficult for many students, but virtually all of them can write a short-story introduction. Here students are simply asked to begin a short story, give its opening few sentences or, with older children, its opening few paragraphs. Kindergarteners can tell theirs orally: "The big bear came to the edge of our campsite. It looked hungry." Students in the middle grades can write effective and grabbing introductions: "It was clearly going to be one of those days. I knew I would flunk the history test, as I hadn't even read Chapters Four and Five. My math wasn't done. And Mrs. Ellis would never believe that I had lost my English assignment. But I never guessed that Kathy's walking into my life would change all of this, make all of it all right."

## INTERVIEWING

*Interviewing* is as common as the corner television set, a daily feature on the morning news, on *Sixty Minutes,* on *Entertainment Today.* Ask your students to identify a major figure they would like to interview (they all agree on one), then create 10 questions they would like to ask the interviewee. Their sharing of the questions they would ask will provide them some interesting insights on how different students view the same character.

Variation: Let each student select his or her own famous figure and then do the questions.

## TOM SWIFTIES

Think of a quotation for Tom, followed by an adverb that describes how he says it that relates to the content of the quotation in a malapropian manner.

> "That's a gem," said Tom preciously.
> "I quit!" said Tom resignedly.
> "I'll have to bend down," said Tom stupidly.
> "He should not receive an award," said Tom implacably.
> "I think I'll clip that coupon," said Tom cuttingly.
> "He flirts with all the girls," said Tom wolfishly.
> "This fog is thick," said Tom densely.

"Tom Swifties" appeal to children of *all ages.* For example, heard in a nursing home, "'I'm taking a multiple vitamin and mineral pill,' said Tom ironically."

The key word is *malapropian.* A Tom Swiftie can't be funny if it makes sense.

## DAFFY DEFINITIONS

One way to get students to use a dictionary, and have fun doing it, is to have them write their own definitions for interesting words. Some examples are:

> Potable: a movable object in Alabama
> Spirit: an action similar to "stab it"
> Carpel: a contest held at Fairs where they don't have tractors
> Bisects: stand in the girls' line or the boys' line
> Propaganda: seen only with the propah goose in Bahston
> Defeat: attachments at de bottom of de legs.

Can you add a Daffy Definition of your own?

## COLLECTIVE NOUNS

This activity is especially appropriate as a "warm-up" for a creative writing session when imagery and figurative language are appropriate.

Start by making a list of true collective nouns used with groups of animals. A partial list is:

a pride of lions
a pod of whales
a gaggle of geese
a flock of geese
a murder of crows
a leap of leopards
a rotter of turkeys
a patch of seals
a skulk of foxes
a paddling of ducks
a knot of toads
a parliament of owls
a muster of peacocks
a troop of kangaroos
a school of fish

Go beyond this by encouraging children to make their own collective nouns for groups of abstract nouns. Notice that these must be plurals, not collective abstract nouns (*happies* is O.K.; *happiness* is not). Some examples might be:

a doing of joys
an embrace of loves
a volcano of angers
a leap of hopes
a haunt of hates
a spray of pleasures

From these, collect a student-made list of original collective nouns for nouns other than animals. Some of these might be:

a shadow of mists
a rainbow of butterflies
a drop of tears
a march of ants
a pillow of clouds
a flagon of fools

## SUMMARY

What we are proposing in our descriptions of these language activities is that you explore language with your students from as many different perspectives as you can—listening, speaking, writing, reading—and that you regularly try to help your students become as fascinated with language as you are. Using *Jumbles* or *Word Finds* from the newspaper, playing *Boggle* or *Scrabble*, creating headlines for actual or made-up events, assigning new names to newly discovered planets or anticipated or imagined baby siblings, studying the lyrics of popular music, looking at the language advertisers use—the possibility of classroom uses of language is virtually endless. It is important for us to point out that not all of these activities are popular with all students, but most of them are popular with most students. Most of the activities will cause students to think. Most of them will help students to become excited about language. And most of them will get students' attention.

# THIRTY
# CARING FOR THE LOW-ABILITY READER

The purpose of this chapter is to identify the special problems of low-ability readers in language arts classrooms and to present practical guidelines for activities that will help them develop language arts skills.

Low-ability readers in language arts classrooms present a challenge to the teacher. However, an integrated language arts program makes it possible to address the special problems of these students while still meeting the needs of the at-level and above-level readers. By integrating the language arts—speaking, writing, listening, and reading—you create an instructional environment that makes the interrelationships of the language arts apparent. Students, particularly low-ability readers, benefit in both cognitive and affective development from learning how these skills of language are related and interdependent.

In order to understand how low-ability readers function or fail to function in language arts classrooms it is necessary to understand that reading is not the only language art that requires students to construct meaning. Students construct meaning also while speaking, listening, and writing as they interact with the language being used. Language learning, therefore, is an interactive process by which students as active participants learn language and learn about language use by sharing language through speaking, listening, reading, and writing and, through this interaction, are able to construct meaning.

If students are to be successful in constructing meaning in any given situation, they need to know how to be actively involved in seeking meaning; they must also have background knowledge appropriate to the situation, experience with language, and the ability to monitor their understanding. Without these skills any student may fail to construct meaning; for the low-ability reader the magnititude of the problem is expanded.

## SPECIAL PROBLEMS OF LOW-ABILITY READERS

Typical problems for low-ability readers include: inability to follow oral and written directions because of poor memory for sequence, inability to remember what is read or heard, inability to monitor understanding, inability to answer questions on something they have just read or participated in, lack of appropriate oral expression, low verbal fluency, lack of confidence, lack of appropriate study habits, low tolerance for abstractions, poor attention span, inability to apply learned skills to new tasks, limited range of topics of interest, and lack of interest in reading and writing.

Given this range of possible problems for low-ability readers, language arts instruction within the regular classroom may seem impossible. However, it is important to keep in mind that not all low-ability readers will have all of these problems and most will have varying degrees of difficulty with different aspects. You may find that you have a student, for example, who has beautiful oral expression and is interested in reading, but who can't answer questions on material just read.

The following guidelines, when incorporated into an integrated language arts classroom, should make your instruction more successful with low-ability readers. These guidelines are intended to be taken as a whole, for alone none is sufficient to make language and its use meaningful enough to compensate for the many possible problems of low-ability readers. However, taken together they can provide the type of instructional environment that makes it possible for low-ability readers to make the connections among the language arts of speaking, writing, listening, and reading.

## GUIDELINES FOR ACTIVITIES FOR LOW-ABILITY READERS

### Teach Students to Monitor Their Understanding

Vygotsky (1978) describes what he calls self-speech, which young children use to help them sequence actions, solve problems, and control their own behavior. He maintains that this self-speech takes on a planning function and later becomes internalized as part of thinking. Brown (1980) identifies this self-speech as *metacomprehension*—thinking about understanding. She proposes that there are four basic types of metacomprehension: knowing when you know, knowing what you know, knowing what you need to know, and knowing the utility of active intervention. Teaching students how to think about their understanding can help them become active participants in their learning. Typical students will develop these self-monitoring skills without direct instruction. Low-ability readers, on the other hand, will need to be taught how to identify what they don't understand so that they can seek clarification from the text, a peer, or you—the teacher. This requires that you encourage students to admit when they don't understand without fear of being scolded or embarrassed by their lack of understanding.

Likewise, it is important for students to be aware of what they know and what they don't know. Low-ability readers will frequently answer "I don't know" to questions for which they have partial answers. When this occurs it is best to use a *shaping technique* and reinforce any attempt at a response as you help the students realize that they do know at least part of the answer. The following example of a shaping episode may clarify the technique for you:

TEACHER: Why did Sara pop her balloon?
STUDENT: I don't know.
TEACHER: Did Sara pop her balloon on purpose?
STUDENT: Yes.
TEACHER: Very good, Sara popped her balloon for a special reason to play a trick. What trick was Sara playing on Toby?
STUDENT: She wanted to scare him?
TEACHER: That's right! Very good! See, you do know!

By pinpointing what students don't know, you then make it easier on both of you to concentrate on particular areas of weakness—what they need to know.

The fourth type of metacomprehension identified by Brown (1980), namely, knowing the utility of active intervention, is the most difficult to develop in students. Brown cites evidence of students being able to identify appropriate intervention strategies, such as *lookbacks* (Alessi, Anderson, & Goetz, 1979), for a particular task, but then not applying those strategies themselves. Brown suggests that being able to follow up on the prediction of a best strategy with the performance of that strategy is developmental. That is, fifth graders do better than third graders, who in turn, do better than first graders.

It is clear that metacomprehension skills will need to be taught and reinforced repeatedly throughout the grade school years, especially for low-ability readers. In an integrated language arts classroom, metacomprehension strategies can be reinforced every day. You can begin by modeling self-questioning as you perform an activity (reading a story, writing a letter, listening to a tape). Students can then work in pairs and help one another by asking the questions you had modeled as you performed the same activity. You can also make a wall chart with questions listed for the children to ask themselves as they listen and read, and to ask one another as they speak and share written work. Questions should include: (1) "Do I know (understand) what is being said?" If so, continue; if not, ask next questions; (2) "What do I know?" (3) "What do I need to know in order to understand fully?" and (4) "What should I do to help me understand?"

### Be More Concerned with the Process than the Product

If you emphasize the *process* of communicating through language in listening, reading, writing, and speaking, then low-ability readers will more readily engage in these language activities than if they are forced to be concerned with the correctness of the product. Given the lack of confidence typical of low-ability readers and their lack of interest in reading and writing, you will not want to weaken their motivation further by insisting on "perfect" products for all activities.

Being more concerned with the process than the product means waiting to correct oral miscues in reading, as well as spelling and usage errors in writing, and usage errors in speaking. Because communication, that is, constructing meaning, is the goal of language arts activities, then students, particularly low-ability readers, can be taught to adapt the form of their message until it conforms to the audience's needs for consistency of presentation. You need not see errors and miscues as permanent—oral miscues can be self-corrected by students after their initial oral reading; written messages can be revised and edited in pairs or small groups until the message is clear. Students should be taught to ask themselves the comprehension-monitoring questions suggested above as they work on language arts activities. If constructing meaning either for themselves, when listening and reading, or for others, when speaking and writing, is understood by the students to be what you think is important, then low-ability readers will be less reluctant to participate in class activities.

### Don't Isolate Low-Ability Readers from the Rest of the Class for Skills Work

Language learning is an interactive process, and children need to interact with other children in situations where language can be shared in order to continue learning. Isolating low-ability readers only serves to limit further their experiences in language, which in turn makes it difficult to construct meaning in ever-expanding situations. Pinnell (1975) found that when children are using language functionally it is because they encountered real problems to which they want to find solutions and because two or more children are working and talking together about the problem.

One way to ensure that low-ability readers will have interaction with other children is to use a "buddy" system. You pair students for activities that you believe may prove difficult and frustrating for low-ability readers. Buddies can provide clarifying information, examples, and feedback for low-ability readers. They do not serve as "little teachers"; rather, they experience the activity with the low-ability reader and share information as they complete the assignment. It is important to remember to use this system only when the complexity of the activity demands it. Otherwise, the at-level and above-level readers may feel they are being cheated of their own individual study time.

You should also develop other activities that promote sharing of language, both expressive and receptive. Experience stories, both group and individual, can serve as an excellent way to provide interaction. During these activities students should be reminded to ask themselves and/or their buddies the comprehension-monitoring questions suggested above. Low-ability readers who are reluctant to share their stories (because of low self-confidence, low verbal fluency) may benefit from having a puppet "read" their stories for them. The puppet may even "answer" questions the child "didn't know." By listening to and responding to other children's stories, low-ability readers are expanding their general knowledge and their experience with language and its usage.

### Provide Useful Contexts for Language

Without context, language has no apparent purpose, and children will learn it reluctantly or not at all (Smith, 1979). Typical students who can see the long-range purposes for learning language will learn when given the opportunity. Low-ability readers, however, may need to have the context made explicit.

It is possible to provide varied contexts for language learning by helping students see the connections between the language arts. That is, they need to be aware of the writer when they are reading, to be aware of the listener when speaking, of the reader when writing, and of the speaker when listening. This sense of author and audience is crucial in helping students interact with language and construct meaning, and when they can't construct meaning, knowing what to do so that they can. Awareness of author and audience also helps the low-ability reader see that the purpose of language is to communicate with someone. This understanding is important in providing a purpose for language activities.

If you, for example, tell low-ability readers that the purpose of creating an experience story is to communicate what happened on their class trip to the zoo so that their parents, or grandparents, or favorite uncle, or friend down the block can share that experience with them, then the language has context and you can help them make the connections among the language arts—a speaker has a listener and a writer has a reader, and vice versa. As a more explicit reminder, you can have low-ability readers write the name(s) of their intended audience at the top of their story. If their only audience is you, the teacher, the story has no apparent purpose—you were on the trip with them and know what happened so they have no need to communicate.

Students must be aware of the reader when they compose their story so that it communicates what they intend. They can ask themselves the comprehension-monitoring questions suggested above, but substitute the reader for themselves—"Will the reader understand?" "What does the reader know?" "What does the reader need to know to understand fully?" "What should I do to help the reader understand?" For different audiences (readers) these questions will be answered in different ways, and the language of the communication will be changed to fit those needs. At-level and above-level readers will normally have developed the capacity to define their audience and adapt their messages. Low-ability readers will not have done so, and they may not be able to complete the exercise successfully without a great deal of help from you and/or their buddies.

### Adapt the Amount and Type of Assignment and Material Given

It is important to keep in mind that you are requiring more effort, concentration, and, therefore, motivation from the low-ability readers when you ask them to engage in the same activity with the same material as at-level or above-level readers. If they lack the background knowledge and language necessary to construct meaning, they are unlikely to be successful.

Given that you don't want to isolate low-ability readers from the rest of the class, activities need to be developed that allow the low-ability readers to interact with the rest of the class, yet work with materials and on assignments that are more appropriate to their instructional needs. Learning centers and learning-activity packets allow you to group students for instruction without physically isolating them.

Learning centers typically contain a variety of packets of materials and work that may be numbered, lettered, named, or even printed in different colors. Each student may be given an assignment sheet telling what to do at the learning center. One student may be told to do any three of the four assignments in packet C. Another student, a low-ability reader, may be told to complete activities 1 and 2 from packet A and any two activities from packet B. This arrangement allows you to adapt assignments easily. You can develop learning-activity packets, which children work on individually, in much the same way.

### Plan for a Great Deal of Practice of Language Skills

Low-ability readers will need more practice in applying skills than will be required of at-level and above-level readers. Low-ability readers have difficulty applying learned skills to new situations and will need prompting from you to help them decide that a previously learned skill is appropriate for solving a new problem or to complete a new task. If appropriate repetition of skills in new situations is not provided, low-ability readers will not succeed in mastering them. If at-level or above-level readers can master a skill after two or three repetitions, it may require 10 or more repetitions for low-ability readers. Careful planning for small-group activities (or learning centers or learning-activity packets) for short periods of time will help you provide the needed repetition for low-ability readers without isolating them from the class and without boring the at-level and above-level readers.

It is important that practice doesn't just become meaningless repetition. Three or four times as many work sheets on a particular skill will not ensure that a skill has been learned and can be applied when required. However, review and reinforcement of previously taught skills in new situations and with new materials as new skills are introduced can provide the distributed practice essential for learning and can help low-ability readers develop a solid foundation of language skills on which to build.

For example, if you have taught students how to find the main idea in a story and have reinforced the process of self-questioning that leads students to identifying main ideas, then, as you introduce the concept of supporting details, it is essential that you connect the new concept (supporting details) to the known concept (main idea). Making the connection between these two concepts helps the low-ability reader understand the new concept while at the same time reinforcing and reviewing the known concept.

### Adapt the Amount and Type of Instructions Given for Assignments

Low-ability readers have poor memory for sequence, which makes it difficult for them to follow oral and written directions. They need simple, clear, and consistent directions. If a task requires several steps in order to complete it, it may lessen the confusion to give only one step of directions at a time. Written directions on the chalkboard or a handout, accompanied by oral directions and examples explained by you, will help to clarify for low-ability readers what they are to do. However, be prepared to repeat the directions as you go through each step in the sequence and provide additional clarification and examples as the activity progresses.

It may be very frustrating for you to have to give instructions over and over again, but it is very important that you do so without showing exasperation and that you not allow other students to make fun of or show annoyance with low-ability readers who request that the directions be repeated. Low-ability readers have little confidence as it is; they do not need the added problem of being ridiculed for their lack of understanding. Using the buddy system suggested above will allow low-ability readers to seek guidance without interrupting the entire class. Good preplanning on your part for activities will also lessen the amount of confusion as one activity is completed and put away and another is begun.

### Read Aloud to Students

Hearing stories and articles read aloud helps low-ability readers to expand their world knowledge, vocabulary, language knowledge, listening comprehension, and schemata, or story structures. Numerous studies have supported reading to children as a way to help them develop and understand language and its use (Applebee, 1979; Holdaway, 1979; Cohn, 1981). This is an activity that you should plan to do every day. You can keep the activity fun and rewarding by varying the type of material read to include stories, poems, plays, newspaper articles, short content pieces, recipes, and other types of materials. Varied writing, speaking, and reading activities can then be planned to help students make the connections among the language arts skills.

Books with predictable plots help low-ability readers gain control over the language and structure of stories (Rhodes, 1981). Students can then read in pairs the material that they listened to. They can also read aloud to one another and then write summaries of the story they heard, or they can read a story into a tape recorder and then listen to their own tape as they follow along in the book, correcting their own miscues. Repeated tapings can be done until the child has "perfected" the story. This "perfect" rendition can then be shared with a small group of students, you, the whole class, a group of students from a lower grade, or be taken home to share with the child's family.

While students are being read to they must maintain their attention on the speaker. They need to be reminded to monitor their understanding of what they hear by asking themselves the questions suggested above. Because low-ability readers have short attention spans, you should try to keep the selections read to them short.

A variation of this activity is to select sentences or short paragraphs from a story or article and dictate it to the students. This gives them further practice in writing well-formed language and in attending to detail while listening.

## SUMMARY

This chapter has proposed that an integrated language arts classroom provides the best language environment for low-ability readers. Language use becomes more meaningful when students can see how speaking, listening, reading, and writing are interrelated. Seeing these relationships helps them to construct meaning as they interact with language.

Eight guidelines for planning language arts activities for low-ability readers were presented to help ensure cognitive and affective development. The task, although not easy, is easier within an integrated language arts classroom. It takes careful planning and patience, but the rewards in terms of language development for your low-ability readers are worth the effort.

### *REFERENCES*

ALESSI, S.M., ANDERSON, T.H., & GOETZ, E.T. (1979). An investigation of lookback during studying. *Discourse Processes, 2,* 197–212.

APPLEBEE, A.N. (1979). Children and stories: Learning the rules of the game. *Language Arts, 56,* 641–646.

BROWN, A.L. (1980). Metacognitive development and reading. In R.J. Spiro, B.C. Bruce, & W.F. Brewer (Eds.), *Theoretical issues in reading comprehension: Perspectives from cognitive psychology, linguistics, artificial intelligence, and education.* Hillsdale, NJ: Erlbaum.

COHN, M. (1981). Observations of learning to read. *Language Arts, 58,* 549–556.

HOLDAWAY, D. (1979). *The foundations of literacy.* Sydney, Australia: Ashton Scholastic.

PINNELL, G.S. (1975). Language in primary classrooms. *Theory Into Practice, 14,* 318–332.

RHODES, L.K. (1981). I can read! Predictable books as resources for reading and writing instruction. *Reading Teacher, 34,* 511–518.

SMITH, F. (1979). *Reading without nonsense.* New York: Teachers College Press.

VYGOTSKY, L.S. (1978). *Mind in society: The development of higher psychological processes.* In

M. Cole, V. John-Steiner, S. Scribner and E. Souberstein (Eds.). Cambridge, MA: Harvard University Press.

## *SUGGESTED READINGS*

BURNS, P.C., & BASSETT, R. (1982). *Language arts activities for elementary schools.* Boston: Houghton Mifflin. This book of activities is arranged developmentally around 11 topic areas. Detailed instructions are given for each activity, including objectives, intended grade level, list of materials, and variations. Many of these activities are appropriate for low-ability readers.

JOHNSON, D.D., & PEARSON, P.D. (1984). *Teaching reading vocabulary* (2nd ed.). New York: Holt, Rinehart & Winston. This book contains dozens of activities for vocabulary development that are appropriate for low-ability readers.

SMITH, C.B., & DAHL, K.L. (1984). *Teaching reading and writing together: The classroom connection.* New York: Teachers College Press. This text contains many suggestions for activities to integrate reading, writing, listening, and speaking, which can easily be adapted to low-ability readers.

SMITH, R.J. (1985). *Using poetry to teach reading and language arts: A handbook for elementary school teachers.* New York: Teachers College Press. This book contains poems and lesson plans to teach the poems. The author suggests most suitable grade level for instruction with each plan. Many of the lesson plans are easily adapted for low-ability readers.

# THIRTY-ONE
# EVALUATING PROGRESS IN THE LANGUAGE ARTS

With the growing emphasis on accountability in education, the use of standardized tests to assess performance in all areas of the curriculum is proliferating. Such formal measures are appropriate for making comparisons to a national norm-referenced group; however, they fall short when knowledge about placement in materials or performance on school-related activities is desired. What is needed are informal methods for assessing students' abilities that have relevance to the tasks and materials common to the classroom. It is the purpose of this chapter to meet those needs by presenting a variety of teacher-developed informal assessment techniques appropriate for reading and writing.

## READING

### Principles of Effective Assessment

*Assessment is an ongoing process of hypothesis testing.* Assessment is a process that can take place while students are in the reading circle, doing seat work, or discussing a story. Frequent mental or written notations can be made of changes in student performance, to retest hypotheses, and to adjust instruction accordingly.

*A score on a reading test should not stand alone.* Many factors must be taken into consideration in addition to the quantitative score yielded from standardized tests or other commercially prepared inventories. Some of these factors include data from teacher-made assessment devices, historical information, teacher observation, and judgment about student performance on similar tasks.

*Each measure of assessment is context-specific.* It is inappropriate to use data from one source to predict performance in another setting. For example, a score of second-grade level on a commercially prepared inventory does not tell the teacher if a student can read the second-grade basal reading book. The best way to determine if a student can handle a textbook is to observe the student reading from that textbook.

*Observation-based assessment is a viable and necessary measure of reading ability.* The value of observing students in natural surroundings cannot be underestimated. It is through this continuous observation in varied situations and under varied conditions that a keen perception or "intuition" about students' abilities begins to develop. Effective, intuitive teachers value their own judgments and view quantitive data with a critical eye and a flexible mind.

*All oral reading errors (miscues) are not alike.* It is important to note the quality of miscue as well as the quantity. A miscue such as the substitution of "woods" for "forest" in the sentence "He walked in the forest" does not interfere with the meaning. However, when a substitution occurs such as "frest" for "forest," the sentence loses its intended meaning. Similarly, dialect miscues that preserve meaning such as "ask" for "asked" or "don't" for "does not" should not be weighted as heavily as other miscues that disrupt the meaning.

*Assessment is a dynamic, not a static, process.* Effective diagnosis means locating students' strengths as well as their weaknesses, determining their potential for further progress, and finding out the conditions under which that progress can be made (Cioffi & Carney, 1983). Thus, rather than blindly accepting the results of a test as static and unchangeable, the teacher may allow the student to read more passages beyond frustration level or may preteach a few key terms to determine if such teacher intervention will increase performance. In this way, the teacher is continually looking for the instructional conditions under which the student can achieve maximum potential.

### Assessing Reading Ability

Your primary concern as a classroom teacher is determining if students are placed in materials appropriate to their reading level. It is not uncommon to find a span of six to eight grade levels within a given heterogeneously grouped class. Therefore, you will want to know at the onset who can and cannot benefit from instruction in the textbook intended for the subject and which topics or areas of need should be emphasized for this particular group of students. Two assessment techniques that accomplish these tasks are the *cloze procedure* and the *directed reading activity* used diagnostically.

*The cloze test.* The *cloze test* (Taylor, 1953) is a method of assessment and instruction wherein every nth word of a passage is deleted or "clozed" (for example, The little ________rode his three-wheeled ________). Used as an assessment device, it is an expedient way to determine which students can handle the textbook intended for the subject. The cloze test requires that students make predictions based on their background experiences and their knowledge of how language operates. You can use it with the basal reading book and content area textbooks such as science, social studies, and health. The example shown in Figure 31-1 uses narrative material similar to selections common to basal readers.

#### DEVELOPING THE CLOZE TEST

1. Select a passage of approximately 300 words that the students have not seen before.
2. Beginning with the last word in the passage, count backward circling every fifth word. Do this until you have 50 words. (Avoid deleting proper nouns, because they are hard to predict.) Type the passage on a duplicator master, replacing each word with a blank 10 spaces long. Number the blanks as you go along (for example, (1)________).

#### ADMINISTERING THE CLOZE TEST

1. Model the cloze test for the class by presenting a brief passage on the board or on an overhead projector. In this way students will be familiar with the demands of the task before the actual testing situation.
2. Explain to the class that only one word fits in the blank and that students will not be expected to replace every word correctly. Explain, too, that a score of 50 percent is considered good. Give them ample time to complete the test.

**FIGURE 31-1** Sample Cloze Test Passage

Not long ago, a mean old ugly (1) ________ cast a spell on (2) ________ beautiful little village close (3) ________ the sea simply because (4) ________ didn't have her favorite (5) ________ of tea.

"I'll show (6) ________," she screamed. Then she (7) ________ on the door-step (8) ________ little bespectacled grocer. She (9) ________ an awful sort of (10) ________, whirled around three times (11) ________ mumbled some funny words.

**SCORING THE CLOZE TEST**

1. Accept only exact replacements. When using the test for instructional purposes, synonyms may be used and encouraged.
2. Add two points for each correct replacement and adhere to the following scoring criteria.
   *60 percent or above—independent level:* minimal teacher assistance needed.
   *40 to 60 percent—instructional level:* teacher instruction and assistance are provided.
   *50 percent or below—frustration level:* alternative materials and methods needed.
3. Use a class profile such as the one shown in Figure 31-2 to depict the relationships between the students' reading abilities and the textbook.

*The directed reading activity as an assessment device.* The *directed reading lesson,* as used in conjunction with the basal reader, is an ideal time for informal assessment because it provides a natural environment and yields some valuable insights into students' strengths and weaknesses. You can develop a matrix such as the one shown in Figure 31-3 (adapted from Gillet & Temple, 1982), which details specific tasks required during a typical directed reading activity. Such a device is not intended for daily or even weekly use but can be implemented periodically to reevaluate current placement.

Looking horizontally at the matrix, you can determine that this group of students will need additional instruction in "determining word meanings through context" and "answering questions on all levels." Looking vertically at the matrix, one can see that both Sarah and Jenny appear to be having difficulty and may need extra attention.

**FIGURE 31-2** Cloze Test Profile

Teacher Mrs. Griffin Subject Science
Date November 24 Textbook The Earth Around Us

| Independent | Instructional | Frustration |
|---|---|---|
| Billy | Marcus | Todd |
| Eric | Jeny | Allison |
| Theresa | Lynne | Bryan |
| Jennifer | Katie | |
| Meredith | | |

Story "Freckle Juice" Date November 24

Genre: Narrative (realistic fantasy) Grade Third
Poetry
Plays
Exposition

| | Sarah | Billy | Jenny | Katie | Meredith | Gary | Eric |
|---|---|---|---|---|---|---|---|
| Makes predictions about story | – | + | – | S | + | S | + |
| Participates in the discussion | – | + | – | S | + | S | + |
| Answers questions on all levels | – | + | S | S | S | – | S |
| Determines word meanings through context | – | S | – | – | – | – | + |
| Reads smoothly and fluently | – | + | – | S | + | S | + |
| Can retell selection using own words | S | + | + | S | + | + | + |
| Comprehends after silent reading | N | N | N | N | N | N | N |
| Can read "between the lines" | S | + | S | S | + | S | + |
| Possesses broad background knowledge | S | + | S | + | + | + | + |

Comments: The students read the story with much enthusiasm. Sarah continues to remain quiet unless I call on her. (Will need to talk with her about possible discomfort. Jenny does not participate in discussion but can retell the story when asked.)

Often +
Sometimes S
Seldom –
Not Observed N

**FIGURE 31–3** Directed Reading Activity Matrix

## WRITING

### Principles of Effective Assessment

*Allow students to invent their own spellings.* Research shows that simply allowing students freely to invent their own spellings while they composed resulted in observable gains in both writing and spelling ability (Lancaster, Nelson, & Morris, 1982). Realizing that this suggestion may not be accepted by administration and parents, teachers may choose to allow invented spellings on rough drafts only, requiring the final copy to be carefully edited for misspellings. Chapter 7, "Spelling as a Language Art," offers a means of teaching children to proofread for spelling.

*Avoid the urge to grade every written product.* Knowing that everything they write may be returned with a scarlet mass of marginal corrections does little to foster students' interest in and desire to continue writing. However, described in this chapter are alternatives to traditional assessment procedures that will free the student to write and the teacher to teach.

*Follow the tenets of holistic assessment and select specific criteria for evaluation.* In *holistic assessment,* it is assumed that tallying errors alone does not adequately reflect writing competence and performance (Myers, 1980). Instead of drawing attention to the errors contained in the paper, the teacher reads to get an overall impression and then rates the product on a numerical scale. Additionally, the teacher has the option of choosing specific criteria such as elaboration, run-on sentences, or organization as focal points in determining the overall impression.

*Encourage buddy-system grading procedures.* In traditional grading techniques, the teacher grades the papers and returns them to the student where they are perused and promptly forgotten. Peer-editing groups can be set up with students of varied ability levels to assist in the composing and editing processes of their peers.

*Avoid excessive criticism and look for something to appreciate in every paper.* Try to make criticism constructive and nonjudgmental. Remember that elementary students are mere neophytes with written language and that with practice and with a supportive learning environment they can enhance their writing ability greatly.

### Assessing Writing Ability

You have read in previous chapters that the writing process is generally conceived of as having three stages: the prewriting, or brainstorming, stage in which the ideas are developed and outlined; the writing stage—the time for putting the ideas in print; and the postwriting, or editing stage, in which proofreading and recopying is undertaken. It is the postwriting stage that will receive the emphasis in this portion of the chapter because it involves the evaluation of the final product.

*Focused holistic scoring.* As mentioned previously, recent developments in the assessment of writing take into consideration the overall impression of how effectively the student has communicated with the reader. *Focused holistic scoring* is one type of general impression scoring that can be readily adapted for classroom use. The criteria are outlined and defined prior to the assignment and evaluation of the writing. You (or a peer editor) then determine the degree to which the paper matches with a set of criteria on the scoring guide and assign the corresponding number from 0 to 4. Figure 31–4 is a sample scoring guide that can be easily modified to reflect criteria specific to various writing tasks.

*Scan scoring.* *Scan scoring* is a time-saving method for grading writing assignments in which you can actively involve students in the grading process. The steps of scan scoring, beginning with the preparation of the grading forms, are outlined below along with sample sheets from a hypothetical fifth-grade student.

1. In preparation for the peer- and teacher-grading process, select both the content (composing) and proofing (mechanics) criteria to fit the writing assignment. Tell the students ahead of time on what criteria they will be graded.
2. Design a peer-editing sheet with spaces for the criteria such as the one shown in Figure 31–5, and a teacher-scoring sheet such as the one shown in Figure 31–6.
3. Allow the students to work in writing groups of four to five students. After the first draft is completed, have the students in the group scan each other's papers for the predetermined criteria.
4. You may choose to have students read several papers for one element of the criteria. Or, the students in the writing groups may take turns reading one person's paper for different criteria, as is demonstrated in Figure 31–5.
5. Revisions for the second draft can begin in class with the peer-editing sheets used as guides. The students must be certain that their papers are in final form before turning them in to you.
6. Collect the second drafts with the peer-editing sheets, scan-score them for content and mechanics, and assign a grade. The papers and a copy of the teacher-grading sheet are then returned for student sharing and review. Figure 31–6 shows a completed scoring sheet for the same fifth-grade student after the peer-editing process.

### Checkpoint Scales

Developed by Kirby and Liner (1981), the *checkpoint scales* are useful because teachers devise them to coordinate with their specific curricular objectives. The checkpoint scale focuses on specific aspects of writing and pro-

0 — Papers in this category cannot be scored because they are not relevant to the assigned topic. Examples include papers that:

are illegible
are written in a language other than English
are on a different topic
have been copied
merely restate the assignment

1 — Papers in this category do not deal directly with the topic. Examples include papers that:

merely list information
ramble extensively and are incoherent
deviate from the stated topic
have numerous sentence fragments

2 — Papers in this category are sketchy or inconsistent. Examples include papers that:

use very general terms
begin to stay on the topic but later digress
lose the reader in extraneous information
have major gaps in the sequence of events
give no elaboration or detail

3 — Papers in this category generally fulfill the assignment with a minimal amount of confusion. Examples include papers that:

give sequential presentation of ideas with few gaps
use detailed explanations with only minimal distractions
give elaborations, but more exact words are needed
would be a 4 but include numerous mechanical errors that interfere with the content

4 — Papers in this category are coherent, unified, and well-developed. Examples include papers that:

are appropriate to the audience
present no difficulty in following the sequence of ideas
give elaboration and detail that is relevant and helps the reader visualize the information
possess a solid beginning, middle, and ending.

**FIGURE 31-4** Holistic Scoring Guide

vides for an overall impression of the writing as does holistic scoring. As the scale shown in Figure 31–7 indicates, a score is circled for each criteria and then multiplied by a specified number at the end of the row, depending on how much weight is alloted to each element. Then an overall numerical grade and comments are given for each paper. The student in this example can readily see that his weakest area is the organization of ideas. Teacher comments at the bottom further explain the places in need of repair.

*Student self-evaluation.* Yet another alternative assessment technique involves *student self-evaluation* of their writings. This technique helps focus students' attention on individual errors and encourages careful proofreading of written assignments. Figure 31–8 presents a sample self-evaluation form in which the student used circles to indicate that the corrections were made.

Peer-Editing Sheet for

Creative Writing
(assignment name)

Name Meredith
Date October 14
Class Mrs. Whitley
Grade 5

---

Author Meredith Editor Scott
Criteria Beginning

The beginning really makes me want to read more!

---

Author Meredith Editor Fletcher
Criteria Middle/End

The middle is okay but the ending is weak. It just drops off.

---

Author Meredith Editor Eric
Criteria Run-on sentences/ fragments. Check the first sentence in the second paragraph. It doesn't make sense. The rest is great.

---

Author Meredith Editor Jennifer
Criteria Spelling

You've got a lot of spelling errors. I circled the ones I noticed

---

**FIGURE 31-5** Peer-Editing Sheet

Teacher-Scoring Sheet

Score Results for

Creative Writing - Scary story
(name of assignment)

Name Meredith Mason

Date October 14

Class Language Arts

Grade 5

Teacher Mrs. Whitley

---

| Content Criteria | Proofing Criteria |
|---|---|
| good beginning | run-on sentences |
| good middle | spelling |
| good ending | sentence fragments |

---

Grade Scale

A = all 3 content criteria and no proofing errors
B = all 3 content criteria with proofing errors
C = two of the three content criteria, no proofing errors
D = two of the three content criteria with proofing errors
E = not enough content for assignment credit

---

Final Grade B

Comments: Watch those spelling errors, Meredith. You almost had an A paper.

**FIGURE 31-6** Teacher-Scoring Sheet

## SUMMARY

Presented in this chapter were a few of the many informal assessment techniques available to teachers. These techniques were chosen because they are easily developed and administered and are adaptable to all grade levels and subject areas. For additional information regarding informal assessment, consult the References and Suggested Readings that follow.

Name Gray

Date March 10

Your revised draft received the following rating:

1) Organization (Beginning, middle and end)

| 1 | 2 | (3) | 4 | 5 | × 4 = 12 |
|---|---|---|---|---|---|
| I couldn't follow your plan at all. Rethink your outline and try to tighten this up. | | You're on the right track, but it's still hard to follow your plan. | | Great organization. I was right with you. | |

2) Details (Reasons, elaboration)

| 1 | 2 | 3 | (4) | 5 | × 4 = 16 |
|---|---|---|---|---|---|
| You didn't give enough information. Be more specific and stay away from lists. | | There are some good ideas here. You need to tell your reader a little more. | | Good, vivid details. I get the picture. | |

3) Mechanics (proofing)

| 1 | 2 | 3 | 4 | (5) | × 3 = 15 |
|---|---|---|---|---|---|
| Can't tell what you're trying to say with all the errors. Try again. | | A few errors got by you this time. See if you can find them. | | What a proofreader! You really have an eye for that job. | |

4) Overall impression

| 1 | 2 | 3 | (4) | 5 | × 6 = 24 |
|---|---|---|---|---|---|
| You could do much more with this assignment. Return to the prewriting outline and start again. | | The potential is there. With a little more effort, you'll have it. | | What a pleasure to read. You composed a fine piece of writing. | |

Total..............67

Comments: Gray, your paper is almost there although you started to lose me around the third paragraph. Rework that and I think you'll have a paper to be proud of.

**FIGURE 31-7** Checkpoint Scale

Name Eric Assignment Description

Date April 1 Teacher Mrs. Ashley

A. Content

✓ Does it make sense?

✓ Did I use interesting words to help the reader "picture" what I wrote?

✓ Did I keep to the topic?

B. Sentence and Paragraph Structure

(−) Did I use capital letters at the beginning of each sentence and for proper nouns?

✓ Did I end each sentence with the correct punctuation?

(−) Did I write complete sentences?

(−) Did I have any run-on sentences?

✓ Did I use commas, apostrophes, quotation marks, and other punctuation correctly?

(−) Did I spell each word correctly?

✓ Did I indent the first word of each paragraph?

C. Handwriting

✓ Did I write this in my best handwriting?

**FIGURE 31-8** Student Self-Evaluation

## REFERENCES

CIOFFI, G., & CARNEY, J. (1983). Dynamic assessment of reading disabilities. *The Reading Teacher, 36,* 764–768.

GILLET, J.W., & TEMPLE, C. (1982). *Understanding reading problems: Assessment and instruction.* Boston, MA: Little, Brown.

KIRBY, D., & LINER, T. (1981). *Inside out: Developmental strategies for teaching writing.* Montclair, NJ: Boynton/Cook Publishers.

LANCASTER, W., NELSON, L., & MORRIS, D. (1982). Invented spellings for low-reading second graders. *The Reading Teacher, 35,* 906–911.

MYERS, M. (1980). *A procedure for writing assessment and holistic scoring.* Urbana, IL: National Council of Teachers of English.

TAYLOR, W. (1953). Cloze procedures: A new tool for measuring readability. *Journalism Quarterly, 30,* 415–433.

## *SUGGESTED READINGS*

GILLET, J.W., & TEMPLE, C. (1982). *Understanding reading problems: Assessment and instruction.* Boston, MA: Little, Brown. This text contains numerous informal techniques based on current theories of reading comprehension and assessment.

JENSEN, J.M. (Ed.). (1981). *Language Arts, 58,* 722–839. This entire issue of *Language Arts* is devoted to writing instruction. One article focuses solely on holistic assessment and provides examples of student writing.

KIRBY, D., & LINER, T. (1981). *Inside out: Developmental strategies for teaching writing.* Montclair, NJ: Boynton/Cook Publishers. Chapters 8, 12, and 14 of this text deal with the editing process by presenting a number of useful and expedient strategies adaptable for all grade levels.

PIKULSKI, J.J., & SHANAHAN T. (Eds.). (1982). *Approaches to the informal education of reading.* Newark, DE: International Reading Association. This volume contains a number of articles devoted to the issue of informal assessment of reading, writing, and content-area materials.

RINGLER, K.K., & WEBER, C.K. (1984). *A language-thinking approach to reading: Diagnosis and teaching.* New York: Harcourt Brace Jovanovich. Unique to this text are chapters on using the language-experience approach diagnostically, and assessing students' understanding of stories using free recall. Other notable features include content-area and writing assessment, and teaching students with special needs.

# INDEX